THE PRICE OF INDEPENDENCE

THE PRICE OF INDEPENDENCE

The Economics of Early Adulthood

SHELDON DANZIGER AND
CECILIA ELENA ROUSE

EDITORS

A Volume of the Research Network on Transitions
to Adulthood of The John D. and Catherine T.
MacArthur Foundation

Russell Sage Foundation • New York

The Russell Sage Foundation

The Russell Sage Foundation, one of the oldest of America's general purpose foundations, was established in 1907 by Mrs. Margaret Olivia Sage for "the improvement of social and living conditions in the United States." The Foundation seeks to fulfill this mandate by fostering the development and dissemination of knowledge about the country's political, social, and economic problems. While the Foundation endeavors to assure the accuracy and objectivity of each book it publishes, the conclusions and interpretations in Russell Sage Foundation publications are those of the authors and not of the Foundation, its Trustees, or its staff. Publication by Russell Sage, therefore, does not imply Foundation endorsement.

Library of Congress Cataloging-in-Publication Data

The price of independence : the economics of early adulthood / Sheldon Danziger and Cecilia E. Rouse, editors.
   p. cm.
  ISBN 978-0-87154-316-5
  1. Adulthood—Economic aspects—United States. 2. Young adults—United States—Economic conditions. 3. Labor market—United States. 4. Cost and standard of living—United States. 5. Family—Economic aspects—United States. I. Danziger, Sheldon. II. Rouse, Cecilia Elena. III. Title: Economics of early adulthood.
  HQ799.97.U5P75 2007
  305.2420973—dc22   2007018408

Text design by Suzanne Nichols.

RUSSELL SAGE FOUNDATION
112 East 64th Street, New York, New York 10021
10   9   8   7   6   5   4   3   2   1

Contents

About the Authors

Sheldon Danziger is Henry J. Meyer Distinguished University Professor of Public Policy and codirector of the National Poverty Center at the Gerald R. Ford School of Public Policy at the University of Michigan, and a member of the MacArthur Foundation Research Network on Transitions to Adulthood.

Cecilia Elena Rouse is Theodore A. Wells '29 Professor of Economics and Public Affairs at Princeton University, Director of the Princeton Education Research Section and a member of the MacArthur Foundation Research Network on Transitions to Adulthood.

Sofya Aptekar is a graduate student in the department of sociology and Office of Population Research at Princeton University.

Lisa Bell is a graduate student in the public policy department at the Goldman School of Public Policy, University of California, Berkeley.

Gary Burtless holds the John C. and Nancy D. Whitehead Chair in Economic Studies at the Brookings Institution.

Ngina S. Chiteji is an associate professor in the department of economics at Skidmore College.

Henry S. Farber is the Hughes-Rogers Professor of Economics at Princeton University.

Maria D. Fitzpatrick is a Spencer Foundation Dissertation Fellow and an Institute for Education Sciences Pre-Doctoral Fellow in the economics department at the University of Virginia.

Janet Gornick is professor of political science and sociology at The Graduate Center, City University of New York (CUNY), professor of political science at Baruch College, CUNY, and director of the Luxembourg Income Study.

Melanie Guldi is an assistant professor at Mount Holyoke College.

Carolyn J. Hill is an assistant professor in the Georgetown Public Policy Institute at Georgetown University.

Harry Holzer is professor of public policy at Georgetown University, visiting fellow at the Urban Institute, and a former chief economist at the U. S. Department of Labor.

Helen Levy is a Research Assistant Professor at the Institute for Social Research at the University of Michigan.

Katherine Newman is the Forbes Class of 1941 Professor of Sociology and Public Affairs at Princeton University and director of the Princeton Institute for International and Regional Studies.

Marianne E. Page is an associate professor of economics at the University of California, Davis, and a member of the National Bureau of Economic Research.

Steven Raphael is professor of public policy at the University of California, Berkeley, and a Research Affiliate of the National Poverty Center.

Timothy M. Smeeding is Distinguished Professor of Economics and Public Administration at the Maxwell School of Syracuse University, and will be a visiting scholar at the Russell Sage Foundation in 2007–2008.

Ann Huff Stevens is an associate professor of economics at the University of California, Davis, and a member of the National Bureau of Economic Research.

Sarah E. Turner is associate professor of education and economics at the University of Virginia, and a member of the National Bureau of Economic Research.

Aaron S. Yelowitz is an associate professor in the department of economics at University of Kentucky.

Chapter 1

Introduction: The Price of Independence: The Economics of Early Adulthood

SHELDON DANZIGER AND CECILIA ELENA ROUSE

Who is an "adult"? Many would identify having completed schooling, working steadily, living independently of one's parents, marrying, and having children as the markers of adulthood, traditionally achieved between the late teens and the early thirties (Furstenberg, Rumbaut, and Settersten 2005).[1] However, compared with their parents' generation, young people today are taking longer to complete their schooling and to settle into steady employment, are establishing their own households at later ages, and are delaying marriage and childbearing. The ordering of the markers of adulthood has also changed and become more varied (Fussell and Furstenberg 2005). For example, a greater percentage of young women are having children before marrying, and a greater percentage of young people are combining work and schooling or family responsibility and schooling. Although most young adults have completed several markers of adulthood by age thirty, a substantial fraction have not.

The psychologist Jeffrey Arnett (2000, 269) describes the period of life for those now between the ages of eighteen and twenty-five as distinguished by "relative independence from social roles and from normative expectations." As such, emerging adulthood provides some young people, especially those who have access to parental resources and supports into their twenties, with new opportunities for exploring their identity, particularly in the areas of work, love, and worldviews. For others, particularly those who have completed no more than a high school degree, who have developed few labor market skills, or who have little access to parental resources and support, the delay, especially in securing stable employment, may be detrimental to their future economic well-being. From a societal perspective, young adults who experience delay in obtaining "good" jobs may also increase their reliance on social safety nets and increase their risk of not having health insurance, and delayed marriage and childbearing may lower national fertility rates, which in turn will mean fewer young people to care for the next generation of the elderly.

Many observers have speculated about the factors that have made the transition to adulthood more complex and variable. Some hypothesize that industrialization, improved health, and increased life expectancies have changed the traditional life sequences of the early twentieth century (Côté 2000; Hareven 1994). Others speculate that the rising cost of housing in some parts of the country explains why young people are increasingly likely to live with their parents (see, for example, Draut 2006). Still others suggest that because this generation's parents had fewer children, they are able to make larger investments in each child, allowing their children to prolong their dependence and lengthening the time it takes them to complete their education and find stable employment and independent living arrangements (see Newman and Aptekar, this volume).

Few authors have provided empirical evidence on how economic conditions might have affected the transition to adulthood, even though many cite economic changes as a causal factor. The chapters in this volume begin to fill this void by examining the extent to which changes in economic factors—wage rates, job opportunities, access to health insurance, housing costs, and debt—can explain the lengthening and increasingly varied transition. We emphasize from the outset that it is difficult to determine the extent to which economic factors have had a causal impact on the lengthening transition because many factors are likely to have affected both the economic environment and the decisions young people make that delay "adulthood." For example, if changes in social norms both open up new occupations to women and reduce the stigma of divorce and single parenthood, more young women are likely to pursue a college degree, enter the labor force, and delay marriage and childbearing. In this case, the causal factor leading to both increased work and delayed marriage and childbearing among women is the change in social norms, not changes in the economy at large (see Goldin 2006). The authors in this volume attempt to establish causal relationships to the extent possible given the data. However, because it is an extremely difficult task to quantify such factors as "social norms," some findings may reflect factors other than economic changes.

In the next section, we present descriptive evidence on trends in marriage and living arrangements. We then describe the key findings of the eleven chapters that compose this volume, emphasizing what we know and what we do not know about the interplay between economic changes and changes in the transition to adulthood.

Trends in Marriage and Living Arrangements Among Young Adults

Marriage has always been a key marker of adulthood. In recent years, young women, who are now more likely to attend college and almost as likely as young men to enter the labor force, are postponing marriage and childbearing to complete their schooling and establish their careers (Furstenberg, Rumbaut, and Settersten 2005). Figure 1.1 documents long-run trends in the median age at first marriage for men and women from 1890 to 2004. The median age at first marriage for both women and men followed a U-shaped pattern over the twentieth century. At the turn of the twentieth century, the median age at first marriage for women was about twenty-two. It fell to about twenty-one in 1920, rose slightly during the Great Depression, and then fell to about age twenty between 1950 and 1960. By 2004, the median age at first marriage had risen to an unprecedented twenty-six.

Figure 1.1   Estimated Median Age at First Marriage for U.S. Males and Females, 1890 to 2004

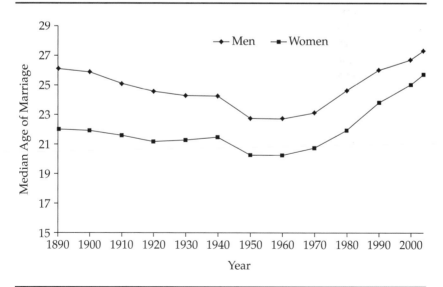

Source: U.S. Bureau of the Census (2005).

Men have always married later than women. In 1890 and 1900, the median age at first marriage for men was about twenty-six, decreasing to about twenty-three in 1950 and 1960, then increasing to over twenty-seven in 2004. Because the delay for women has been much greater since the 1960s, the gender age gap in first marriage has never been smaller. The gap was about four years at the turn of the twentieth century, but it fell to less than two years at the turn of the twenty-first century.

Delayed marriage has been accompanied by both a delay in childbirth and an increase in the percentage of all births outside of marriage. Lawrence Wu and Jui-Chung Allen Li (2005) calculate that among a cohort of white women born between 1914 and 1924, only 17 percent were childless at age thirty-five, compared with 50 percent of those born between 1965 and 1970 (see figure 1.2). There has been a similar, but less dramatic, delay among Hispanic women: the percentage who were childless at age thirty-five among those born between 1914 and 1924 was 17 percent, compared to 28.2 percent among those born between 1965 and 1970. Among African American women, the magnitude of the change depends on when we begin documenting the trend. Nearly 29 percent of those born between 1914 and 1924 were childless at age thirty-five, a much higher share than among whites and Hispanics. This share decreased to only 17 percent among those born between 1925 and 1934. Nearly 30 percent of thirty-five-year-old black women today are childless—a rate about the same as among Hispanics but lower than among whites.

The changing nature of the transition to adulthood is even more evident when we consider the number of women who are not only childless but have never married by age thirty-five. Wu and Li (2005) estimate that only 5.6 percent of white women, 7.1 percent of black women, and 5.7 percent of Hispanic women born between 1914 and 1924 were both childless and never-married by age thirty-five. Today, among thirty-five-year-old women, these percentages have increased to 27.3 percent of whites, 23.9 percent of blacks, and 16.6 percent of Hispanics. Elizabeth Fussell and Frank Furstenberg (2005) document similar changes in marriage and fatherhood for men and by race and ethnicity.

Although women on average are delaying marriage and childbearing, some women are delaying marriage but not childbearing. As a result, the proportion of all births to unmarried women increased from 5 percent to 37 percent between 1960 and 2005. In 2004, 28 percent of births to twenty-five- to twenty-nine-year-old women and 55 percent of births to twenty- to twenty-four-year-olds were to unmarried mothers (Child Trends 2007). Some researchers attribute this increase to a variety of economic and social factors, such as changes in social norms, women's increasing economic independence, and declines in the economic status of less-educated men (Edin and Kefalas 2005; Wilson 1987).

Figure 1.2   Women Who Are Childless at Age Thirty-five, by Race and Birth Cohort

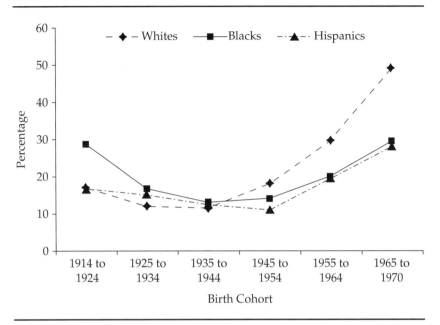

Source: Wu and Li (2005, 122).

One aspect of the delayed transition to adulthood that has captured the attention of the media and many parents is the increased likelihood that young adults are living with their parents. This trend is evident in the United States and in other countries. However, its importance in the United States has been exaggerated. The most striking trend in living arrangements among unmarried young adults is the greater percentage that live on their own or with persons other than a spouse, not the increased percentage who are living with parents. For example, over the last four decades the percentage of women age nineteen to twenty-four living with a spouse declined from 57 to 22.5 percent (34.5 percentage points). Those living on their own or with other (unrelated) persons increased by 25.5 percentage points, from 17 to 42.5 percent, while those living with parents increased by 9 percentage points, from 26 to 35 percent. Among those between the ages of twenty-five and twenty-nine, the percentage living with parents increased by only 3 percentage points for men between 1960 and 2000 (to 18 percent) and by 3.5 points for women (to 14 percent) (Matsudaira 2006). Overall, living arrangements have indeed changed for young adults, but the increase in the percentage of those living with their parents has been modest; the greatest shift among young people has been toward living on their own or with others who are not their spouse.

Overview of the Chapters

The key economic outcome in the transition to adulthood is the achievement of stable employment. The first three chapters in part I of this volume document that it has taken young adults longer in recent decades to find stable, well-compensated employment, both in the United States and abroad. In chapter 2, Lisa Bell, Gary Burtless, Janet Gornick, and Timothy Smeeding describe changes from the mid-1980s to the end of the century in the labor market outcomes and living arrangements of young adults between the ages of eighteen and thirty-four in the United States and five other industrialized countries. In chapter 3, Henry Farber asks whether U.S. employment became more "unstable" between 1973 and 2005. In chapter 4, Helen Levy documents the increased likelihood that young people will have no health insurance as they age out of public and parental coverage, probably as a consequence of the lengthening time it takes them to find stable employment.

The chapters in part 1 suggest not only that young people are likely to change employers more often than their parents did, but that it is taking them longer to complete their college education. As Maria Fitzpatrick and Sarah Turner document in chapter 5, an important reason for the lengthening time to degree is the increased flexibility offered to students by colleges to mix schooling and work or schooling and child-rearing. This flexibility has allowed more students from low-income families and more older students to continue their education.

The four chapters in part II investigate the extent to which labor market changes, housing market changes, and other factors have affected various aspects of the transition to adulthood. In chapter 6, Carolyn Hill and Harry Holzer find that labor market changes can explain only a small part of the recent trends in living arrangements and marriage rates. In chapter 7, Aaron Yelowitz finds that, before 2001, housing costs had not increased dramatically in most areas of the country and therefore, except in certain locales, were not a compelling reason for the delay in independent living. Introducing a comparative perspective, in chapter 8 Katherine Newman and Sofya Aptekar show that U.S. youth are not alone in this lengthening transition. Taking an international perspective, they reveal the link between economic conditions and social policies and differences in the living arrangements of young adults in Canada and various European countries.

Some have argued that high levels of debt might impede the transition to adulthood. In chapter 9, Ngina Chiteji examines whether rates of college, credit card, and other forms of debt today are as high for young adults as they were in the past. She finds few differences over time and concludes that debt has only a minor influence on the transition to adulthood.

Part III focuses on other factors that might affect the transition to adulthood. In chapter 10, Melanie Guldi, Marianne Page, and Ann Huff Stevens investigate how parents' socioeconomic status influences early adult income levels, educational attainment, and the probability of starting a family. Despite recent increases in wage and income inequality, the authors find that there has been little change in the effect of family background on adult transitions. Stephen Raphael, in chapter 11, focuses on the powerful negative impact that incarceration has on marriage, living arrangements, and employment among young men.

We now turn to a more detailed review of the relationship between economic changes and changes in the transition to adulthood. We highlight key empirical findings reported in this volume and, where applicable, supplement these findings with additional information.

Part I: Securing Employment and Completing Schooling

The labor market today is different in many ways from that of the 1950s and 1960s, the benchmark for the "traditional" ages at which the young transition to adulthood. The economy grew very rapidly from the end of World War II to the early 1970s, and wages increased rapidly for most workers. In contrast, the last few decades have been characterized by falling, or stagnant, real wages and employment for men with a high school degree or less. This period has also seen increased employment and real wages for women, as well as increased wage and income inequality.

Figure 1.3 documents trends in hourly wages by education for U.S. workers age twenty-five to sixty-five for each year relative to the 1980 value. High school dropouts in 2004 earned about the same hourly wage in 2004 as they did a quarter-century earlier, and high school graduates earned only about 7 percent more. However, college graduates earned 30 percent more. Less-educated men have fared particularly poorly, while young women's economic status has increased both absolutely and relative to that of young men.

In addition, it is taking young men longer to earn a sufficient amount on their own to support a family. Figures 1.4 and 1.5 show the percentage of young adults who earned less than the poverty line for a family of four, using data from the Current Population Survey (CPS) in 1969 and 2004. The earnings data in each year are adjusted for inflation and expressed in 2004 constant dollars. We consider these young adults to be "low earners" who could not support a family of four.[2] For young men,

Figure 1.3   Hourly Wages of Twenty-five- to Sixty-five-Year-Olds, by Education Group, Relative to 1980 Hourly Wages

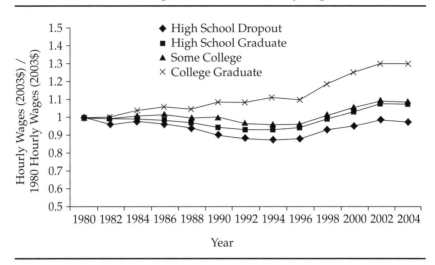

Source: Barrow and Rouse (2005), based on data from the 1980 to 2004 (even years only) Current Population Survey Outgoing Rotation Group (ORG) files available from Unicon. The sample is limited to individuals between twenty-five and sixty-five years of age, and drops observations with wages less than half of the minimum wage or above the ninety-ninth percentile of the distribution.

the percentage of low earners tends to fall as they age into their mid-thirties. For women, this pattern holds in the later cohort, but not in the earlier one. These patterns and additional analyses (not shown) suggest that as individuals age they are better able to support a family regardless of educational attainment. However, the figures also suggest that it is taking longer for young men to achieve self-sufficiency.

Consider males between the ages of twenty-one and thirty-five (figure 1.4). In 1969, 23.1 percent of twenty-five-year-olds earned less than the poverty line. In 2004, it was not until age thirty that this age group's poverty rate fell to 23.2 percent. In 1969, between the ages of thirty and thirty-five, only about 10 percent of men were low earners; in 2004 more than twice as many in this age range, about 23 percent, remained low earners.

In contrast, over these thirty-five years a decreasing percentage of women earned too little to support a family, and an age gradient developed (figure 1.5). In 1969 there was virtually no age gradient for young women. At any age between twenty-one and thirty-five, about 75 to 80 percent were low earners. In 2004, 75 to 80 percent of twenty-one- to twenty-two-year-olds still had low earnings, but at age twenty-six, that had declined to about 50 percent. These numbers remain high, however,

Figure 1.4   Males with Earnings Less Than the Poverty Line for a Family of Four in 1969 and 2004, by Age

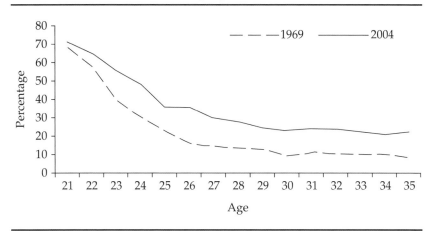

Source: Authors' calculations from March Current Population Survey files provided by Unicon.

Figure 1.5   Females with Earnings Less Than the Poverty Line for a Family of Four in 1969 and 2004, by Age

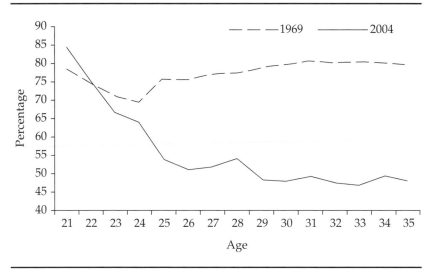

Source: Authors' calculations from March Current Population Survey files provided by Unicon.

in part because women are less likely to work owing to child-rearing responsibilities and in part because women still earn lower wages than men.

The most recent cohort of males, especially high school graduates, is taking much longer to earn enough to support a family, and at every age young men are now less likely to do so than their counterparts were a quarter-century ago. It is taking young men longer to reach self-sufficiency regardless of educational attainment. The most recent cohort of women, in contrast, is doing much better than young women did in 1969.

In most industrialized countries, there has been a similar worsening of economic conditions for young adults since the early 1970s. Bell and her colleagues (chapter 2) analyze data from Belgium, Canada, Germany, Italy, the United Kingdom, and the United States and conclude that the transition of young adults from parental dependence to economic self-sufficiency is generally taking longer in all these countries. They document that the relative earnings of young workers in these countries have declined in comparison with earnings at older ages and in relation to the income needed to support an independent household.

In all of the industrialized countries they examine, younger adults (below age twenty-five) have suffered employment and earnings declines, while after age twenty-five, women have achieved some economic gains. For example, between the mid-1980s and the late 1990s, the employment-to-population ratio fell in all six countries for men between the ages of twenty and twenty-four, but rose in all countries for women between the ages of twenty-five and thirty-four. The percentage of young males whose wages and salaries were above 50 percent of the national median income declined between the mid-1980s and the end of the 1990s for some or all age groups in every country; for women in this age group, the percentage earning more than this standard increased in four of the six countries (and increased for women age twenty-six to thirty-four in all but one country). Thus, although young women have generally increased their labor market activities and are earning higher real wages, young men are less likely to be self-sufficient than they were twenty years ago. Bell and her colleagues also find that the income declines were smaller for young adults who lived with their parents and hypothesize that the delayed departure of young adults from their parents' household might well be a response to declining economic prospects.

Employment instability provides another dimension of the economic difficulties facing young workers. In the quarter-century following World War II, much attention focused on "the company man," the worker who spent most of his career with a single employer. In recent years, however, much attention has been paid to the fact that workers are more likely to move from firm to firm over the course of their career, in part because they choose to take advantage of new opportunities and in part because of involuntary lay-offs and plant closings.

Annette Bernhardt and her colleagues (2001) found declines over time in job stability for two cohorts of young males with a high school degree or less: those who turned twenty-six between 1970 and 1978 and those who did so between 1983 and 1991. A young man is considered to have a stable job if he held it for at least forty-eight weeks during the year. At age twenty-six, 77 percent of the men in the first cohort had a stable job compared with only 64 percent in the most recent cohort. Bernhardt and her co-authors (1999) analyzed changes in the likelihood that young men would change employers over a two-year period. They found that the job change rate was 46 percent for men age twenty-six to thirty-four between 1970 and 1981 and 53 percent for men in this age group between 1983 and 1994.

Henry Farber (chapter 3) documents these changes over a longer period of time. He analyzes data from more than thirty years of the Current Population Survey and finds that, at any age, the amount of time male workers have spent with their current employer has fallen. In 1973 about 50 percent of employed men between ages thirty-five and sixty-four had been with their current employer for at least ten years; by 2006 fewer than 40 percent had such a tenure. For women, the incidence of ten-year employment increased from about 30 percent to 34 percent over these three decades. This increase stems in part from the fact that more women, especially those with young children, have entered and stayed in the labor force in recent decades.

Farber also documents that today's young adults are more likely to have very short job tenures. The percentage of men and women in their thirties who had been in their current job for less than one year was three to four percentage points higher at the end of the study period compared to the beginning. Thus, young men today are taking longer to establish themselves in good jobs, and they are less likely than their fathers to have a career characterized by a lifetime job with a single employer. Again, in contrast, young women are more likely than their mothers to be working, less likely to have short job tenures (less than one year) and more likely to have long job tenures (at least ten years).

Additional, indirect evidence on the difficulty for young men of finding stable, quality jobs comes from rates of health insurance coverage, which is often viewed as one marker of a "good" job. Helen Levy (chapter 4) shows that young adults are the most likely to be uninsured, in part because public coverage ends when a child turns age eighteen and parents' employer-provided policies also terminate coverage for young adults who are no longer students. In recent years, the probability of being uninsured has been about 15 percent for teenagers, rising to more than one-quarter of those in their early twenties, and then falling back to about 15 percent for those in their early thirties. Between 1988 and 2005, the portion of uninsured young adults (age eighteen to thirty-four) rose from 21 to 28 percent. In 1988, 42 percent of those in this age group had employer-subsidized health insurance coverage; that proportion had fallen to 34 percent in 2005.[3]

Young men are more likely than young women to be uninsured, in part because some young women have coverage through a spouse and others, particularly single mothers, through public coverage such as Medicaid. Just as the employment situation for young men has deteriorated over the last few decades, so too has the probability of their being uninsured. About 35 percent of men born in the 1960s were uninsured at age twenty-three (the peak age of uninsurance); 44 percent of those born in the 1980s were uninsured at that age. These results provide additional evidence that young people are taking longer to secure stable jobs that both pay well and provide overall good compensation with benefits such as health insurance.

Another traditional precursor to reaching adulthood is completing one's education. Traditionally, young individuals, particularly men, chose to marry and have children only after achieving economic independence, often after finishing their education. For example, Ted Mouw (2005) traced the trajectories of a cohort of individuals age fifteen to twenty-two in 1979 until they were thirty-five. At least 37 percent of men and 24 percent of women completed their schooling or found full-time employment before marrying or starting a family. (The numbers increase to 71 percent of men and 69 percent of women when we count either completing school or finding full-time employment in the same year with either marriage or child-rearing.)[4]

A natural explanation for why young people are taking longer to find stable employment is that record numbers of them, especially women, are attending college and taking longer to complete their degrees. Table 1.1 shows the increase in college attendance and completion for high school graduates born between 1950 (who were fifty-six years old in 2006) and 1975 (age thirty-one in 2006). On average, male high school graduates born in 1950 had spent 2.10 years in college by age thirty-five, and women 1.36 years. Fifteen percent of these male and female high school graduates had received a bachelor's degree by age twenty-two. In contrast, male and female high school graduates born in 1970 had completed an average of 2.21 and 2.38 years, respectively, by age thirty-five, yet only 12 percent had received a bachelor's degree by age twenty-two. Nonetheless, more of the 1970 cohort than the 1950 cohort had completed a BA by age twenty-eight: 28 versus 25 percent. Thus, increasing numbers of young people are attending college, and yet they are taking longer to complete their degree. Maria Fitzpatrick and Sarah Turner (chapter 5) also find protracted college careers among today's young

Table 1.1 Years of College Attended and Bachelor's Degree Receipt by High School Graduates, by Year of Birth

Year of Birth	Average Number of Years Enrolled in College by Age Thirty-five, Males	Average Number of Years Enrolled in College by Age Thirty-five, Females	Proportion with a BA by Age Twenty-two	Proportion with a BA by Age Twenty-five	Proportion with a BA by Age Twenty-eight	Proportion Who Have Attended College by Age Twenty-two	Proportion Who Have Attended College by Age Twenty-five	Proportion Who Have Attended College by Age Twenty-eight
1950	2.10	1.36	0.15	0.22	0.25	0.44	0.48	0.50
1955	1.70	1.46	0.14	0.19	0.23	0.44	0.43	0.48
1960	1.68	1.63	0.12	0.19	0.23	0.45	0.45	0.47
1965	1.81	1.83	0.12	0.20	0.25	0.47	0.49	0.52
1970	2.21	2.38	0.12	0.27	0.28	0.54	0.57	0.56
1975	2.25	2.43	0.12	0.26	0.29	0.56	0.58	0.57

Source: Computations by Maria Fitzpatrick from the October Current Population Surveys

adults. Over the last three decades, the median time it takes to complete an undergraduate degree has increased from four to five years, and about one-quarter now take more than six years. The lengthening time to degree is concentrated among students attending public colleges and universities. Data analyzed in chapter 2 show that young people are accumulating more education in five other industrialized countries as well.

One reason for the increasing educational attainment is that education has become increasingly important to succeed in the labor market. In 1980 individuals with a bachelor's degree or higher earned roughly 39 percent more per year than high school graduates; by 2004 they earned about 2.3 times more (Barrow and Rouse 2005).

Federal financing programs, such as Pell grants and Stafford student loans, and programmatic changes made by colleges regarding part-time enrollment have allowed students more flexibility in attendance, which can facilitate increased enrollment. For example, Fitzpatrick and Turner in chapter 5 note that the share of Pell grant recipients who are financially independent (generally those age twenty-four and older) almost doubled over the past three decades, from 30 to 58 percent. Some students take advantage of the increased flexibility by combining work and schooling to better meet their long-run employment goals. Others, particularly those from low-income families, find their college years extended by the need to work to pay college costs, particularly to cover the forgone income and the living expenses associated with college. The result has been a decline in the share of undergraduates of traditional age (eighteen through twenty-one), from 74 to 56 percent. Combined, these changes have allowed more students to complete some postsecondary education and afforded them more time to do so.

Changes in economic conditions also play a role in explaining increases in educational attainment and time to degree. Fitzpatrick and Turner document that students over the age of twenty-four are more likely to enroll in college during economic downturns than are traditional-aged college students, given that the opportunity costs of college attendance are lower when jobs are harder to find.

Part II: Living with Parents Longer and Starting Families Later

Perhaps the most visible evidence that young people are taking longer to transition to adulthood is that many are marrying later and some are living with their parents longer. Carolyn Hill and Harry Holzer (chapter 6) analyze the effects of labor market experiences on the living arrangements of two cohorts of young adults between the ages of twenty and twenty-two. Among the first group, who were age twenty to twenty-two in 1985, 46 percent lived with their parents. In the second cohort, who were twenty to twenty-two in 2003, 57 percent lived with their parents.[5] Men were slightly more likely to live with their parents than women, blacks and Hispanics were more likely than whites, and those from higher-income families were more likely than those from lower-income families.

To what extent can changes over time in living arrangements be explained by changes in economic opportunities? Hill and Holzer find that young adults with better employment and wage outcomes are indeed less likely to live with their parents and more likely to marry. For example, being in one of the lower wage quintiles (the bottom 80 percent) increases the probability of living with one's parents by four to nine percentage points for young men compared with top-quintile earners. Nonetheless, these estimated economic effects are too small to account for much of the substantial changes in living arrangements that have taken place over recent decades.

With growing wage and income inequality, if changing labor market prospects were an important contributor to living arrangements, we would expect to see a greater increase among those with the fewest skills. However, Hill and Holzer find little difference in the trends in living with one's parents by education, race-ethnicity, or gender. For example, those with some college or a college degree were seven percentage points more likely to live with their parents in 2003 than this education group in 1985; high school graduates were nearly ten percentage points more likely to live with their parents, but high school dropouts (including those with the general equivalency diploma [GED]) were only about two percentage points more likely to do so. And yet these individuals experienced dramatically different labor market outcomes over these decades.

If labor market opportunities are not a primary factor for the lengthening time that children are living with their parents, perhaps unaffordable housing has become a significant factor. Aaron Yelowitz (chapter 8), analyzing extensive data on the costs of homeownership and rents, and after accounting for credit market conditions, tax deductibility, and changes in house quality, finds that the median real cost of housing actually fell between 1980 and 2000. Often overlooked in discussions of the rapid rise in housing costs is the emergence of historically low interest rates. Inflation-adjusted median monthly housing payments fell from $1,476 to $1,092 from 1980 to 2000. Over the same period, the inflation-adjusted median monthly rent—often the first stop for young adults—increased from only $726 to $741.

Yelowitz does find that when home prices increase, the percentage of young adults who live independently declines, and that the influence of housing costs on living arrangements appears to be stronger for nonwhites than for whites, possibly because of differing access to credit markets. Yelowitz concludes that housing cost increases can explain only a small portion of the total decline in independent living between 1980 and 2000. He does point out that in the years after his analysis ended, housing prices increased dramatically in a few states, such as California and Florida.

Katherine Newman and Sofya Aptekar (chapter 8) show that the age of departure from the parental home has been increasing in all developed countries, especially in southern Europe. They find that housing market conditions, such as the prevalence of owner-occupied housing versus affordable rentals, are related to the proportion of young people who live independently at any point in time. For example, Scandinavian countries—where the age of departure from the parental home is about twenty and only 10 percent of eighteen- to thirty-four-year-olds live with their parents—have substantial amounts of affordable public housing. In contrast, in Italy—where the median age of departure for men is around age thirty and about 60 percent of eighteen to thirty-four year olds live with their parents—there are limited affordable rental units. Labor market conditions, such as rates of idleness, unemployment, and temporary employment, also influence the living arrangements of young people, as do variations in the design of social welfare programs. Although highly suggestive, these are correlations that might also be explained by other factors that differ across countries. It is also unclear the extent to which they explain recent *changes* in living arrangements.

Some writers have suggested that one reason young people today are having a more difficult time establishing independent households is that they are more burdened with college and credit card debt (Draut 2006; Draut and Silva 2004; Kamenetz 2006). Ngina Chiteji (chapter 9) examines the extent and composition of the debt of young adults over the last four decades. In contrast to recent popular accounts, today's young adult household heads (age twenty-five to thirty-four) do not appear overly burdened with debt. Mean total debt increased from $26,562 to $55,616 (in constant 2001 dollars) between 1963 and 2001. However, mean net worth rose as well, leaving the debt-to–net worth ratio at 0.57 in both years. Annual income did not grow as rapidly as either wealth or debt, so the young adult debt-to-income ratio rose from 0.73 to 1.11 over these four decades. However, despite the attention often devoted to student loan and credit card debt, these two types of debt are not the most widely held types of debt. For example, although the extent of education loans has received much attention, mean education debt in 2001 was less than $3,500 per household.

Chiteji concludes that the total debt loads borne by young adults pose problems for only a few—about 9 percent of young adult households and 11 percent of all households have monthly debt payments that exceed 40 percent of their monthly income. On the other hand, 16 percent of young adult households do have monthly debt obligations so large that they would be unable to finance more than three months of debt payments from savings if they lost their regular monthly income sources.

Although many decry a large increase in indebtedness among today's youth, it seems that the concern is unwarranted for most of them. Further, if debt levels have not increased dramatically, they cannot have been responsible for the large changes in living arrangements. Chiteji also finds no consistent support for the assumption that increases in non-collateralized debt have lowered a young person's ability to buy a home.

Taken together, the chapters in part 2 suggest that changes in the factors analyzed—labor market outcomes, housing costs, debt—can explain, at most, only a modest portion of the trends toward declining marriage and childbearing and increased rates of living with parents.

Although this volume focuses on the possible effects of changing economic conditions on adult transitions, some of the chapters also offer insights about some non-economic factors that might be important. For example, according to Hill and Holzer, at any point in time performance, work experience, and higher wages in high school, as well as personal attitudes and behaviors that indicate independence and maturity, are all better predictors of living independently of one's parents than are labor market conditions. That said, there is little evidence that changes in high school performance and personal attitudes can explain the *change* in living arrangements.

Part III: Family Background, Incarceration, and the Transition to Adulthood

There are many other factors that might have contributed to the lengthening transition to adulthood. The chapters in part III focus on two factors that would seem likely to have had large effects—differences in family background and the increased incarceration rates of the last several decades.

Reaching adulthood is nearly synonymous with breaking economic ties with one's natal family. Melanie Guldi, Marianne Page, and Ann Huff Stevens (chapter 10) compare various markers of adulthood for two cohorts of young adults. The first came of age in the mid-1970s, the second in the early 1990s. Analyzing the extent to which family background affects early adult income, educational attainment, and the probability of starting one's own family, they find large differences between those whose parents had higher income and education and those whose parents had lower income and education. For example, consider young adults who were twenty-nine or thirty between 1999 and 2003. Among those whose parents had completed college, approximately two-thirds had also completed college, and about 37 percent were parents themselves. In contrast, among those whose parents had completed only high school, only about one-fifth had completed college, and about 60 percent had become parents.

Nonetheless, Guldi and her colleagues find little evidence that the influence of the family background factors associated with family income has changed much when we compare young adults (age twenty-five to thirty) who came of age in the 1970s with those who came of age almost two decades later. They do find that relative to those who grew up in low-income families, those who grew up in high-income families seem to be delaying childbearing more than they did in the past.

Thus, increased inequality in the economic status of parents over these years cannot account for the lengthening in the transition to early adulthood. Differences may emerge at later ages, however, if it turns out that the impact of family background is more important for outcomes reached after age thirty. For example, given that individuals from more advantaged families are more likely to attend college and that college attendance is associated with higher earnings (which generally increase with age), the change in the association between family background and income may be more pronounced when measured among older individuals.

The number of people imprisoned in the United States more than quadrupled, from 500,000 to 2.1 million, between 1977 and 2004. Between 1974 and 2001, the proportion of men who were either currently in prison or had a record roughly doubled, from 2.3 to 4.9 percent; for black men, the percentage increased from 8.7 to 16.6 percent. Having served time early in one's life is likely to delay the achievement of conventional markers of the transition into adulthood. Newly released offenders have little savings and are barred from receiving federal housing assistance, both factors that are likely to drive new releases into the homes of their parents or other relatives. In addition, many employers are averse to hiring former inmates, and in many states and localities convicted felons are legally barred from certain occupations; both of these factors reduce the likelihood that former inmates will achieve stable employment and economic self-sufficiency. They also have less to offer to potential spouses, with obvious consequences for their marriage prospects.

Steven Raphael's chapter paints a clear portrait of this subpopulation of largely young men whose development has been stunted. He shows that men who have been incarcerated are less likely to marry and more likely to live with their parents, work fewer weeks per year, and earn less when they do work than similar men who have not been incarcerated. After accounting for the fact that men who become incarcerated differ from those who do not, there is probably a causal impact of incarceration on marriage and employment stability. Young men who have been incarcerated are roughly six percentage points more likely to have never been married, and they work about six fewer weeks per year. These arguably causal impacts of incarceration suggest a role for attempts to improve the ability of former prisoners to care for themselves and their families, either while in prison or upon release (see Altschuler 2005; Chung, Little, and Steinberg 2005; Travis and Visher 2005; Uggen and Wakefield 2005).

Summary

The chapters in this volume document that it is taking young men longer to secure well-paying, stable employment that will allow them to support a family—the critical economic outcome in the transition to adulthood. In contrast, women are better able to support a family on their own than ever before, even though their economic status continues to lag that of men. Many commentators have argued that decreased employment prospects, lower wages, higher housing prices, and increased debt have made it more difficult for young people, especially men, to assume the responsibilities that have traditionally characterized adulthood. Taken together, the chapters in this volume suggest a limited role for such economic factors in explaining recent trends in other young adult outcomes. These new studies confirm that changes in the economy over the last several decades have affected individual decisions to establish an independent household, marry, have children, and complete education. However, the delay in these markers of the transition to adulthood that has occurred in the United States and in most industrialized countries over the past several decades does not appear to have been primarily driven by changing economic conditions. The delay is more likely to have been caused by changes in the social norms of young people, their parents, and society in general; changes in young adults' expectations regarding female labor force participation, marriage, and childbearing; and changes in opportunities for combining schooling with work or family roles.

It is possible that some of the factors analyzed here will have a greater overall impact on the outcome of recent cohorts of young adults at later ages in the life course. Consider the growing prison population. The evidence suggests that former inmates are significantly less likely to find stable employment, to marry, and to reach the other markers of adulthood. Thus, as rates of incarceration continue to increase (particularly in some subpopulations), fewer young people may ever achieve all of the traditional markers of adulthood. If these future generations are less able to care for themselves and their children, this responsibility will increasingly fall on the rest of society. As such, there may well be an ever more important role for workforce development programs and basic education programs in prisons and for substance abuse and reentry programs for soon-to-be released prisoners.

Further, while the current media attention regarding the debt of young adults appears to have neglected the distinction between debt to finance schooling and housing, which helps build long-run human capital and wealth, and debt to finance current consumption, the increasing availability of easy credit may become a problem for future generations. Finally, although earlier generations were more likely to stay with a single employer for periods lasting at least ten years, today's youth are likely to hold multiple "long" jobs. Whether this change will result in substantially less lifetime income and wealth and lower the ability of today's young adults to pay down their debts remains to be seen.

There are many uncertainties regarding the long-term impact of the delayed attainment of the markers of adulthood. However, evidence from Europe suggests that as these changes become the norm, at a minimum the life satisfaction of young people will increase. As discussed by Newman and Aptekar (chapter 8), European youth who live with their parents have lower life satisfaction than youth who live independently, holding other factors constant. However, in countries where higher proportions of young adults live at home, this negative effect is attenuated. These data suggest that social anxiety declines when living with one's parents becomes widespread enough to be considered socially acceptable rather than an indicator of personal failure. Thus, while at the moment many express concern about the changing life course, ultimately it may become accepted as the norm.

There are many questions that could not be addressed in a single volume. Our hope is that the new research presented here will stimulate a long and careful examination of the impact of economic conditions on the transition to adulthood.

We thank Frank Furstenberg and Rukmalie Jayakody for helpful conversations; Maria Cancian, Barbara Ray, Kristin Seefeldt, and two anonymous reviewers for helpful comments on a previous draft; and Ngina Chiteji, Maria Fitzpatrick, Jordan Matsudaira, David Ratner, and Sarah Turner for providing background statistics.

Notes

1. Some readers will question our use of the "traditional" markers of marriage and childbearing, given recent increases in cohabitation, same-sex partnerships, and the voluntary choice not to bear children. This volume focuses on how all of the traditional markers to adulthood have changed over time. We are not undertaking a normative discussion of any of them.
2. Specifically we compute the percentage of young adults who earned less than $16,566 in 2004 (and adjusted for inflation for earlier years). This

amount is equivalent to what the official poverty line for a family of four would have been in 2004 if the Census Bureau had adjusted its poverty lines each year since 1967 by the most recent price index used by the Bureau of Labor Statistics (BLS), the CPI-U-RS. The official poverty line in 2004 was higher, $19,307, because the price indices used for the official line showed more inflation than the CPI-U-RS.

3. If we include coverage through a spouse's employer, 54 percent of individuals age eighteen to thirty-four had such health insurance in 1998 compared to 43 percent in 2005.

4. Authors' calculations from Mouw (2005, table 8.4).

5. The percentage of twenty to twenty-two year olds living with parents in any year is higher than the percentage of nineteen to twenty-four year olds living with parents cited above from Matsudaira (2006) because living with parents declines as young adults age. Both studies show an increase over time in living with parents—an increase of 11 percentage points for men and women in Hill and Holzer and an increase in 9 points for women in Matsudaira.

References

Altschuler, David M. 2005. "Policy and Program Perspectives on the Transition to Adulthood for Adolescents in the Juvenile Justice System." In *On Your Own Without a Net: The Transition to Adulthood for Vulnerable Populations*, edited by D. Wayne Osgood, E. Michael Foster, Constance Flanagan, and Gretchen R. Ruth. Chicago, Ill.: University of Chicago Press.

Arnett, Jeffrey Jensen. 2000. "Emerging Adulthood: A Theory of Development from the Late Teens Through the Twenties." *American Psychologist* 55(5): 469–80.

Barrow, Lisa, and Cecilia Elena Rouse. 2005. "Does College Still Pay?" *The Economists' Voice* 2(4, article 3, September). Accessed at http://www.bepress.com/ev/vol2/iss4/art3.

Bernhardt, Annette, Martina Morris, Mark Handcock, and Marc A. Scott. 1999. "Changes in Job Stability and Job Security." *Journal of Labor Economics* 17(4, pt. 2, October): S65–90.

———. 2001. *Divergent Paths: Economic Mobility in the New American Labor Market*. New York: Russell Sage Foundation.

Child Trends. 2007. "Percentage of Births to Unmarried Women." Accessed at http://www.childtrendsdatabank.org/pdf/75_PDF.pdf.

Chung, He Len, Michelle Little, and Laurence Steinberg. 2005. "The Transition to Adulthood for Adolescents in the Juvenile Justice System: A Developmental Perspective." In *On Your Own Without a Net: The Transition to Adulthood for Vulnerable Populations*, edited by D. Wayne Osgood, E. Michael Foster, Constance Flanagan, and Gretchen R. Ruth. Chicago, Ill.: University of Chicago Press.

Côté, James. 2000. *Arrested Adulthood: The Changing Nature of Maturity and Identity*. New York: New York University Press.

Draut, Tamara. 2006. *Strapped: Why America's 20- and 30-Somethings Can't Get Ahead*. New York: Doubleday.

Draut, Tamara, and Javier Silva. 2004. "Generation Broke: The Growth of Debt

Among Young Americans." Borrowing to Make Ends Meet Briefing Paper 2 (October 13). Accessed at http://www.demos.org/pubs/Generation_Broke .pdf.

Edin, Kathryn, and Maria Kefalas. 2005. *Promises I Can Keep: Why Poor Women Put Motherhood Before Marriage.* Berkeley, Calif.: University of California Press.

Furstenberg, Frank F., Jr., Rubén G. Rumbaut, and Richard A. Settersten Jr. 2005. "On the Frontier of Adulthood: Emerging Themes and New Directions." In *On the Frontier of Adulthood: Theory, Research, and Public Policy* edited by Richard A. Settersten Jr., Frank F. Furstenberg Jr., and Rubén G. Rumbaut. Chicago, Ill.: University of Chicago Press.

Fussell, Elizabeth, and Frank F. Furstenberg. 2005. "The Transition to Adulthood During the Twentieth Century: Differences by Race, Nativity, and Gender." In *On the Frontier of Adulthood: Theory, Research, and Public Policy*, edited by Richard A. Settersten Jr., Frank F. Furstenberg Jr., and Rubén G. Rumbaut. Chicago, Ill.: University of Chicago Press.

Goldin, Claudia. 2006. "The Quiet Revolution That Transformed Women's Employment, Education, and Family." *American Economic Review* 96(2): 1–21.

Hareven, Tamara K. 1994. "Aging and Generational Relations: A Historical and Life Course Perspective." *Annual Review of Sociology* 20: 437–61.

Kamenetz, Anya. 2006. *Debt Generation: Why Now Is a Terrible Time to Be Young.* New York: Riverhead Books.

Matsudaira, Jordan D. 2006. "Economic Conditions and the Living Arrangements of Young Adults." Network on Transitions to Adulthood working paper (May). Accessed at http://www.transad.pop.upenn.edu/downloads/matsu daira.pdf.

Modell, John, Frank F. Furstenberg Jr., and Theodore Hershberg. 1976. "Social Change and Transitions to Adulthood in Historical Perspective." *Journal of Family History* 1(1): 7–32.

Mouw, Ted. 2005. "Sequences of Early Adult Transitions." In *On the Frontier of Adulthood: Theory, Research, and Public Policy*, edited by Richard A. Settersten Jr., Frank F. Furstenberg Jr., and Rubén G. Rumbaut. Chicago, Ill.: University of Chicago Press.

Shanahan, Michael J., Erik J. Porfeli, Jeylan T. Mortimer, and Lance D. Erickson. 2005. "Subjective Age Identity and the Transition to Adulthood." In *On the Frontier of Adulthood: Theory, Research, and Public Policy*, edited by Richard A. Settersten Jr., Frank F. Furstenberg Jr., and Rubén G. Rumbaut. Chicago, Ill.: University of Chicago Press.

Travis, Jeremy, and Christy A. Visher. 2005. "Prisoner Reentry and the Pathways to Adulthood: Policy Perspectives." In *On Your Own Without a Net: The Transition to Adulthood for Vulnerable Populations*, edited by D. Wayne Osgood, E. Michael Foster, Constance Flanagan, and Gretchen R. Ruth. Chicago, Ill.: University of Chicago Press.

Uggen, Christopher, and Sara Wakefield. 2005. "Young Adults Reentering the Community from the Criminal Justice System: The Challenge of Becoming an Adult." In *On Your Own Without a Net: The Transition to Adulthood for Vulnerable Populations*, edited by D. Wayne Osgood, E. Michael Foster, Constance Flanagan, and Gretchen R. Ruth. Chicago, Ill.: University of Chicago Press.

U.S. Bureau of the Census. 2005. *Current Population Survey: Historical Time Series,*

Marital Status, March and Annual Social and Economic Supplements, 2004 and earlier, table MS-2. Accessed at http://www.census.gov/population/www/socdemo/hh-fam.html.

Wilson, William Julius. 1987. *The Truly Disadvantaged: The Inner City, the Underclass, and Public Policy*. Chicago, Ill.: University of Chicago Press.

Wu, Lawrence L., and Jui-Chung Allen Li. 2005. "Historical Roots of Family Diversity: Marital and Childbearing Trajectories of American Women." In *On the Frontier of Adulthood: Theory, Research, and Public Policy*, edited by Richard A. Settersten Jr., Frank F. Furstenberg Jr., and Rubén G. Rumbaut. Chicago, Ill.: University of Chicago Press.

PART I

Securing Employment and Completing Schooling

Chapter 2

Failure to Launch: Cross-National Trends in the Transition to Economic Independence

LISA BELL, GARY BURTLESS, JANET GORNICK, AND
TIMOTHY M. SMEEDING

I n contrast to retirement, which is happening earlier for many, the transition to adulthood, especially economic self-sufficiency, is taking longer in most industrialized countries. One possible reason for this "failure to launch" is that well-compensated jobs now require more schooling. That is not the only answer, however, at least not in the United States, where educational attainment among twenty-five- to thirty-four-year-olds has increased relatively little since the early 1980s (Haveman and Smeeding 2006). Another reason for delayed economic independence may be labor market changes that have made well-paid employment more elusive for young people. If so, the relative earnings of young workers may have declined compared with earnings at older ages, or earnings may fall short of the income needed to support an independent household.

This chapter examines these and other possible reasons for the lengthening transition to adulthood in six industrialized countries: the United States, Belgium, Canada, Germany, Italy, and the United Kingdom. We compare the employment rates, earnings levels, and net incomes of cross-sections of young adults in the mid-1980s and young adults in the late 1990s. In Belgium, our income data cover 1985 and 1997; in Canada, 1987 and 1997; in Germany, 1984 and 2000; in Italy, 1987 and 2000; in the

United Kingdom, 1986 and 1995; and in the United States, 1986 and 2000. Although the data do not cover the same years or even the same number of years in all countries, in each nation the data span at least nine years. To make the data for Germany comparable in both periods, we confine our analysis of income data to young adults in the former West Germany. Our income and household composition data are primarily drawn from the Luxembourg Income Study (LIS).[1] The LIS database contains comparable household income measures for several nations, and it also contains sufficiently comparable time-series information on individual wages, which allows us to analyze earnings by age at several points in time for the six nations we study here. We supplement the LIS data with information on employment drawn from national labor market surveys.

Specifically, we examine trends in household headship, employment, earnings relative to median national income levels, and income adequacy among young adults who live with their parents and those who live independently. Young adults in this study are age eighteen to thirty-four, and we group the population into overlapping five-year age groups. The youngest age group is eighteen to twenty-two and the oldest is thirty to thirty-four. By using these overlapping age groupings, we reduce the sampling variability of our estimates. A longer discussion of many of the statistical issues we confront here is found in Timothy Smeeding and Katherin Ross Phillips (2002).

In short, we find that young adults are increasingly less likely to form independent households. The decline in headship is most striking among young adults age twenty-two and older, and it is more noticeable in continental Europe than in either the United Kingdom or North America (the United States and Canada). Compared with other countries in the sample, the United States experienced relatively small changes in headship patterns between 1986 and 2000. Our findings on employment and trends in wage and salary income provide one partial explanation for this broad pattern. Young adult men in continental Europe typically experienced larger employment losses and a bigger drop in wage income than did their counterparts in the United Kingdom or North America. This pattern most likely reflects continental Europe's persistently weak employment growth, especially for workers with limited skills who are struggling to enter the labor force. Whatever the cause of the earnings losses, they are likely to have made it harder for young men to establish independent households.

In contrast to men, women between ages twenty-five and thirty-four in all six countries experienced gains in employment, and in the United Kingdom and North America these gains were accompanied by notable improvements in wage income. Even though fewer women than men earn wages high enough to support a household, the combination of female earnings gains and male earnings losses substantially reduced the gender wage gap.

Household income trends show, not surprisingly, a decline in income adequacy among households headed by eighteen- to thirty-four-year-old adults. Further, the losses are larger in Europe than in North America, and the income gap between young Americans and Europeans narrowed during the time span. We also find that income inadequacy was much more of an issue among young adults who lived independently of their parents. Young adults who remained in their parents' households were therefore partially protected against the drop in living standards that presumably accompanies a decline in job opportunities and wage losses, a finding consistent with Katherine Newman and Sofya Aptekar's chapter in this volume.

Taken as a whole, these results imply that reduced employment rates and wages among young adults took a toll on living standards, especially for young adults living independently of their parents. Interestingly, the decline in "independent" young adults' income adequacy was smaller in the United States than in the other countries, perhaps because male employment prospects declined less than in most other countries.

Data

Most of our analysis relies on LIS data files. The LIS data provide accurate information on household net income, which can be disaggregated into identical components for households in each of the LIS-member countries.[2] The source of the LIS information for the United States is the Current Population Survey (CPS). This household survey provides high-quality and comprehensive data on household composition, income, and labor force status for all adults for at least a twenty-five-year period. Although other countries provide LIS with equal or even superior information on household income, few countries provide datasets with such high-quality records on respondents' recent work experience and labor force attachment. This shortcoming represents a challenge for analyzing the path to economic independence, and so the LIS data are supplemented with information on employment status drawn from official labor force surveys in these same nations. The labor force surveys include detailed employment data, but the data available to us from those surveys include no information on family structure, living arrangements, wages, or other components of income.[3]

Household Headship

One indicator of economic self-sufficiency is living independently from one's parents. By continuing to live with their parents, young adults can enjoy a more comfortable (and stable) standard of living with a small cash income. The household head is usually defined as the person most knowledgeable about "household matters," the person who owns the dwelling occupied by the household or in whose name the dwelling is rented, or the person with the highest income. Under any of these definitions, a young person who lives with his or her parents would rarely be classified as the household head. In the exceptional cases where young adults are classified as heads and their parents are identified as secondary household members, it is likely that the child is supporting the parent rather than vice versa. We also classify the spouse of the LIS-identified head as a household head.

Figures 2.1 and 2.2 show the percentages of young people at successive ages who were heads of households or the spouses of household heads between 1995 and 2000 for men and for women.[4] For both groups, the older the young adults are, the more likely they are to live independently. At any given age, men are less likely to be a head of household (or the spouse of a head) than are women. This is because women typically marry at younger ages and thus are classified as household heads at a younger age. As Newman and Aptekar (this volume) also found, young Italians have exceptionally low rates of household headship, a pattern that is apparent for both genders and in both periods. In 2000, for example, just 30 percent of twenty-four- to twenty-eight-year-old Italian women were household heads or spouses of a head. This compares with 65 percent in Belgium and 85 percent in the United Kingdom. Young people in the United Kingdom form their own households at somewhat younger ages than is the case in the other countries, perhaps owing to the availability of subsidized council housing and low-cost market rentals. In part, the very late formation of Italian households may be due to the relatively high cost of home owning and renting in Italy (Bucks and Pence 2005; Giannelli and Monfardini 2003; Ruiz-Castillo and Martinez-Granado 2002). It may also be due to cultural factors (Giuliano 2006) or parental income gains that make it possible for parents to live in houses large enough to house their adult children (Manacorda and Moretti 2002).

In all six countries, household headship rates declined between the 1980s and the late 1990s (see table 2A.1). The only notable exception was among British women, who were somewhat more likely to head households or to be married to a household head in the later period. There were only small changes in household headship in the youngest age groups, but the decline in headship was progressively larger among adults in their mid-twenties. The falloff in headship was particularly large in Belgium and Italy and among German women in their late twenties and early thirties. Headship declined twenty percentage points among Italian men ages twenty-six to thirty-four, and among Italian

Figure 2.1   Young Males Who Are Household Heads, by Age, 1995 to 2000

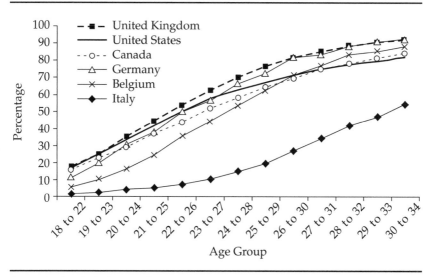

Source: Authors' tabulations of LIS database.

Figure 2.2   Young Females Who Are Household Heads, by Age, 1995 to 2000

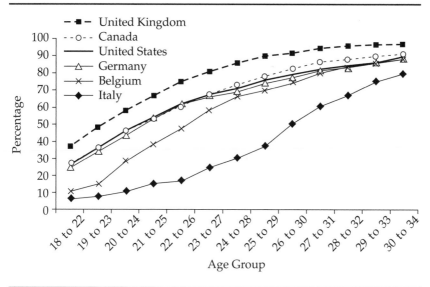

Source: Authors' tabulations of LIS database.

women between twenty-two and twenty-six. The changes in household headship were smaller in the United Kingdom, Canada, and the United States. As we shall see, this may be explained in part by the more favorable labor market conditions in those countries.

Employment Patterns: Levels, Trends, and the Impacts of Fertility and Higher Education

Because the LIS is not ideal for determining employment patterns, we turned to official labor force surveys in the six countries for a more dependable and consistent way to measure employment trends.[5] We obtained annual estimates of the employment-to-population ratio for four age groups from Eurostat, Statistics Canada, and the U.S. Bureau of Labor Statistics (BLS). Table 2.1 shows employment rates from 1985 to 2005.[6] We have included the 2005 data because in several countries, including Belgium, Germany, the United Kingdom, and the United States, there was a sharp deterioration in young adults' employment rates after 2000.

In all six countries and in each year, male employment rates increased sharply with age while women's rates were more varied. In 1985 teenage (age fifteen to nineteen) employment rates were much lower in Belgium and Italy than in the other four countries, but male employment rates in all six countries converged at older ages. Belgian and Italian women were less likely than women in other countries to be employed in their early years. By age thirty to thirty-four, North American women were more likely to be employed than their European counterparts. After age twenty, young women's employment rates were notably lower than those of men the same age. In both the earlier and later periods, the male-female employment gap typically grew with age.

Employment and Birthrates

In the 1980s, the employment rates of women in all six countries dipped slightly in their mid-twenties (see table 2.1), probably owing to child-rearing responsibilities. However, the dip had disappeared by 2005. On first glance, this might suggest that women were postponing first births until after age thirty. However, birthrates did not decline in all countries (United Nations Economic Commission for Europe 2005). The more likely explanation is that European mothers had become less willing to withdraw from market work after the birth of a child. Even if they temporarily left the labor force, the interruption in a new mother's career typically did not last as long in 2000 or 2005 as it had lasted in earlier decades. Although these patterns may differ across countries, owing in

Table 2.1   Employment-to-Population Ratio, in Six Countries, by Gender and Age,
1985 to 2005

Year	Males				Females			
	15 to 19	20 to 24	25 to 29	30 to 34	15 to 19	20 to 24	25 to 29	30 to 34
Belgium								
1985	11%	59%	88%	91%	9%	48%	62%	58%
1995	6	49	85	89	3	43	70	69
2000	10	55	85	91	6	44	76	74
2005	9	50	83	87	5	43	75	75
1985 to 2005	−2	−9	−5	−4	−4	−4	13	17
Germany[a]								
1985	41	70	82	90	35	65	59	54
1995	32	68	80	89	26	64	67	66
2000	33	67	81	89	26	63	70	71
2005	28	60	74	85	22	58	65	67
1985 to 2005	−13	−11	−7	−5	−13	−7	6	13
Italy								
1985	21	59	83	94	14	38	47	49
1995	15	45	71	86	8	31	47	50
2000	13	46	69	86	8	34	49	55
2005	11	49	73	86	5	35	54	62
1985 to 2005	−11	−10	−10	−8	−9	−3	7	13
United Kingdom								
1985	46	74	84	87	45	61	54	53
1995	39	70	83	86	39	62	67	65
2000	43	75	88	89	43	66	72	71
2005	38	74	87	89	40	65	73	73
1985 to 2005	−8	−1	3	3	−5	4	19	19
Canada								
1985	44	71	82	85	44	66	65	62
1995	41	68	80	83	41	65	69	69
2000	43	71	84	87	44	68	75	75
2005	43	70	84	88	47	70	76	77
1985 to 2005	−1	−1	2	2	3	4	11	15
United States [b]								
1985	46	75	87	90	43	64	66	65
1995	45	75	87	89	44	64	70	71
2000	45	77	89	91	45	68	73	73
2005	35	71	86	89	38	65	69	70
1985 to 2005	−11	−4	−1	−1	−5	0	4	5

Sources: For EU member countries, Eurostat Labor Force Survey; for Canada, Statistics Canada; for the United States, U.S. BLS.
a. Data are for western Germany in 1985 and for unified Germany in 1995 to 2005.
b. The youngest age group in the United States is sixteen to nineteen years old.

part to variation in institutional factors such as child care and family leave (Gornick and Meyers 2003), the basic pattern is evident in all nations (on Germany and France, for example, see Köppen 2006).

Employment Trends

Trends in employment after 1985 differed across the six countries, and stark gender differences were evident as well. Unlike in the United Kingdom and North America, men age twenty-five and older in continental Europe experienced a slump in employment. In Belgium, Germany, and Italy, the employment rate of men age twenty-five to thirty-four fell between four and ten percentage points, a substantial drop for a population that is expected to be largely self-supporting (table 2.1). In contrast, women age twenty-five to thirty-four experienced rising employment rates in all six countries. The increase was smallest in the United States, where female employment was already common in the mid-1980s. Owing to their large gains, women age twenty-five to thirty-four in Belgium, Canada, and the United Kingdom are now more likely than U.S. women to be employed.

The contrasting employment trends of men and women significantly narrowed the gender employment gap between 1985 and 2005. Among thirty- to thirty-four-year-olds, the gap shrank twenty-one percentage points in Belgium and Italy, eighteen points in Germany, sixteen points in the United Kingdom, thirteen points in Canada, and six points in the United States (table 2.1). It may be tempting to conclude that the job gains of young women were achieved at the expense of young men. In the United Kingdom and North America, however, the employment gains of twenty-five- to thirty-four-year-old women were not accompanied by any employment losses among their male counterparts.

Employment and Education

Employment rates among younger men (under age twenty-five) and women (under twenty) have been declining since 1985, and this decline is undoubtedly linked to rising school attendance and increased educational attainment among this age group. However, education is not the only reason, given that job-holding has declined among teenagers and adults in their early twenties, both those who are out of school and those attending school. Among men older than age twenty-six, the drop in employment has been much larger in continental Europe than in either Great Britain or North America. In the United Kingdom and North America, the employment rates of twenty- to twenty-four-year-old males ranged from 70 to 74 percent in 2005. In Belgium, Germany, and Italy, they ranged from 49 to 60 percent (table 2.1).

Clearly, statistics on educational attainment do not provide a simple

Table 2.2   Educational Attainment Expressed in Average Number of Years in Formal Education for Persons Age Twenty-five to Thirty-four in 2002 to 2003

Country	Males	Females
Belgium	12.4	12.7
Germany	13.5	13.4
Italy	11.2	11.6
United Kingdom	13.1	13.0
Canada	13.6	14.1
United States	13.7	14.0

Source: OECD (2005).

explanation for the employment gap between the different countries. Table 2.2 presents Organization for Economic Cooperation and Development (OECD) estimates of the number of years of formal schooling in our sample countries for the population age twenty-five to thirty-four in 2002. On average, North American men and women in this age group have more years of schooling than their counterparts in Belgium, Germany, and Italy. Assuming that few young people work when they are full-time students, this evidence suggests that careers begin later in Canada and the United States than they do in Belgium, Germany, and Italy, but in fact paid employment begins at a considerably younger age in North America than it does in Belgium or Italy.

Summary

The employment statistics reveal many consistent trends across the six countries. Employment rates have generally fallen among teenagers, both male and female. Women's employment rates after age twenty-five have increased, with particularly large gains in countries that had low female employment rates in the mid-1980s. In contrast, employment rates among men age twenty-five and older have remained unchanged or declined (see Ghidoni 2002). The combination of these two trends has meant that the working careers of men and women under age thirty-five are now much more similar.

However, major differences across the countries still remain. Employment begins earlier in the three English-speaking countries than it does in the three continental European countries, especially in Belgium and Italy, even if the cross-national age employment gap largely disappears among men by the time they reach their early thirties. And important cross-national differences among twenty-five- to thirty-four-year-old women remain. Moreover, explanations for the different levels and trends in employment are varied, with no single dominant explanation for either men or women.

Earnings and Self-Sufficiency

Holding a job, even a full-time, year-round job, does not assure workers of an income high enough to live independently or to support a family (for an analysis of U.S. data, see Duncan, Boisjoly, and Smeeding 1996). To examine income self-sufficiency, we have developed two measures of earnings adequacy among young adults.

Our first indicator compares young adults' average earnings with the median adjusted disposable (net) household income in their country. If every person lived in a single-person household, this concept would be easy to measure as the median after-tax and after-transfer income in the country. However, household sizes differ, and household spending needs vary as a result. One way to address these differences is to estimate the change in income required to maintain living standards when a household gets larger or smaller. In principle, such an adjustment allows us to calculate "equivalent" incomes for households of different sizes. A common adjustment, which we use here, is to assume that a household's income requirements increase in proportion to the square root of the number of household members.[7] For each country and time period included in our analysis, we computed the national median adjusted disposable personal income (ADPI). Table 2.3 shows estimates of the average earnings of young adults measured in relation to the national ADPI.

Another approach to measuring economic self-sufficiency is to calculate the percentage of young people who have sufficient wage and salary income to live on their own at or above the national poverty threshold in a given year. We define the poverty threshold as equal to one-half the national median ADPI. If a worker earns or has access to enough independent income to exceed this threshold, we classify him or her as self-sufficient.

Average Earnings

Table 2.3 shows average annual earnings by age group for young adults who earn wage and salary incomes. We may understate this capacity by excluding self-employment income. We address this issue by examining young adults' total net incomes in a later section.[8] In this section, we are mainly interested in determining whether adults can support themselves comfortably with the wages they earn in the labor market. Even though the calculations exclude self-employment income and thus understate some people's total earnings, the trend in wage and salary income offers a clear indicator of the main income source that young adults must depend on to support themselves.

The six countries in our sample are not uniform in how they report person-level earnings in the LIS data files. Belgium and Italy report after-tax wages, while Germany, the United Kingdom, Canada, and the United States report pretax wages. Most workers pay taxes on their earn-

Table 2.3   Mean Wage and Salary Earnings of Young Adults in Six Countries, as a Percentage of Median National ADPI, 1984 to 2000

Country	Year	Males				Females			
		18 to 22	22 to 26	26 to 30	30 to 34	18 to 22	22 to 26	26 to 30	30 to 34
Earlier period (1984 to 1987)									
Belgium[a]	1985	28%	67%	103%	117%	20%	50%	57%	58%
West Germany	1984	47	92	147	191	34	68	71	67
Italy[a]	1987	18	51	83	91	17	32	39	45
United Kingdom	1986	67	113	132	149	51	66	51	51
Canada	1987	43	83	108	132	31	60	65	64
United States	1986	40	87	124	144	28	56	69	69
Later period (1997 to 2000)									
Belgium[a]	1997	13	50	71	84	9	40	55	54
West Germany	2000	32	70	108	148	26	54	69	72
Italy[a]	2000	17	39	49	69	11	30	40	41
United Kingdom	1995	47	88	123	146	39	65	72	71
Canada	1997	34	74	101	121	24	52	69	72
United States	2000	35	81	122	146	28	59	80	83
Percentage change between periods[b]									
Belgium[a]	1985 to 1997	-52	-26	-31	-28	-54	-20	-3	-7
West Germany	1984 to 2000	-33	-24	-26	-22	-22	-21	-2	7
Italy[a]	1987 to 2000	-6	-23	-40	-24	-38	-7	2	-9
United Kingdom	1986 to 1995	-30	-22	-7	-2	-23	-2	41	39
Canada	1987 to 1997	-21	-10	-6	-8	-22	-14	7	12
United States	1986 to 2000	-13	-7	-2	1	-2	6	16	19
Percentage change between periods in average earnings of young adults who had wage and salary earnings only									
Belgium[a]	1985 to 1997	-25	-14	-18	-22	-23	-11	-15	-17
West Germany	1984 to 2000	-33	-30	-26	-24	-24	-18	-10	-11
Italy[a]	1987 to 2000	-20	-28	-26	-18	-29	-19	-22	-16
United Kingdom	1986 to 1995	-19	-14	1	-1	-15	-7	4	11
Canada	1987 to 1997	-11	-6	-2	-3	-13	-11	5	9
United States	1986 to 2000	-8	-5	-2	-2	2	4	10	9

Source: Authors' tabulations of LIS files.

a. Wage and salary income is measured net of income and payroll tax payments.

b. Change in earnings between earlier and later periods divided by the level of earnings in the earlier period.

ings, including both payroll taxes and income taxes. These taxes are already subtracted for Belgian and Italian workers, but they are included in the earnings estimates for the other four countries. Ignoring tax payments would *understate* the net earned incomes of many low- and moderate-income Americans who have child dependents given that the United States pays the refundable Earned Income Tax Credit (EITC) to low-income working families. For low-wage earners, the EITC can easily exceed their other payroll and income tax liabilities. When the credit was significantly liberalized between 1986 and 2000, the after-tax incomes of low-income wage earners were boosted much faster than is indicated by the change in their pretax wages. Because of the difference between the earnings measures for Belgium and Italy, on the one hand, and Germany, Britain, Canada, and the United States, on the other, readers should interpret the results showing average earnings levels with caution.

Men have a steeper earnings trajectory than women, and this is true in both the earlier and later survey years. One reason may be that men are more steadily employed than women. The more important reason, however, is that our data reflect the mean earnings across all persons, regardless of whether they have any wage earnings. Because the employment gap between men and women rises with age, this produces a larger rise in measured earnings gains among men than among women, since they remain more likely to be employed than women.

Table 2.3 shows sizable differences among the six countries in both average level of young people's earnings and earnings gains with age. Among men, the age-earnings growth pattern is highest in Germany, where a steep rise in earnings with age produced the highest wage levels in the mid-1980s. However, the subsequent drop in Germany's young male employment rates depressed earnings levels among men in all age groups between 1984 and 2000. By the mid- to late 1990s, twenty-six- to thirty-four-year-old men in the United Kingdom, Canada, and the United States earned relative wages that rivaled or exceeded those earned by German men. Among women in their late twenties and early thirties, average wages were higher in the United States than they were in the other countries.

Earnings Differences and Trends

The more interesting statistics in table 2.3 are the sizable reductions in average earnings for both men and women between the two time periods (third panel). The average losses were typically much bigger in continental Europe than they were in the United States. Women who were in their mid-twenties or older saw their (mean) earnings rise in Britain, Canada, and the United States, and those age eighteen to twenty-two experienced smaller earnings losses than younger women in continental

Europe. Women overall also experienced much smaller losses than those suffered by men.

The bottom panel in table 2.3 shows the even more striking trends when we limit the sample to those who had actual earnings.[9] Employed men experienced a decline in average wages in all countries and in virtually all age groups. The declines were smaller in the United States than in other countries, and among men older than age twenty-five they were notably smaller in the United Kingdom, Canada, and the United States than in the three countries in continental Europe.

The average earnings changes experienced by employed women show a somewhat more hopeful pattern, especially among women older than twenty-two. Women in these groups experienced relative earnings improvement, at least in the English-speaking countries, and women in those groups that experienced earnings reductions saw their earnings decline much less than men in the same age group.

The combined results for men and women suggest that men in these countries saw a much steeper decline in their ability to maintain independent households. In contrast, women in their mid-twenties and older experienced real improvement in their capacity to support a family in several of the countries, notably the United Kingdom, Canada, and the United States (Gornick and Meyers 2003; Neyer 2003).

Self-Sufficiency

Table 2.4 shows the percentage of young adults who can support themselves on their wages in a one-person household. As noted, a person is considered self-sufficient if he or she earns at least one-half the national median ADPI.[10]

The fraction of young men who can support themselves with wage and salary income is modest at ages eighteen to twenty-two but climbs with age. By age thirty to thirty-four, a large majority of men in all countries earn enough to surpass the poverty line. However, the percentage of self-sufficient young men has declined over time for some or all age groups in every country (table 2.4, bottom panel). Only one group of males saw improvement: American men age twenty-six and older. The self-sufficiency losses were negligible for younger Italian men, who already had an exceptionally low rate of self-sufficiency in the mid-1980s. The drop in earnings self-sufficiency was also more modest among men age thirty and older. In some of the younger age groups, the fraction of men who could support themselves fell ten percentage points or more between the mid-1980s and the period 1995 to 2000.

Women had lower rates of earnings self-sufficiency than men in all countries and in both time periods. The gender gap was small in the youngest group, but it rose with age. Between the mid-1980s and the

Table 2.4 Adults with Wage and Salary Earnings Above 50 Percent of the National Median ADPI in Six Countries, 1984 to 2000

Country	Year	Males 18 to 22	22 to 26	26 to 30	30 to 34	Females 18 to 22	22 to 26	26 to 30	30 to 34
Earlier period									
Belgium[a]	1985	29%	64%	86%	88%	23%	53%	57%	55%
West Germany	1984	30	67	79	84	25	57	51	48
Italy[a]	1987	16	41	61	64	16	27	32	37
United Kingdom	1986	56	70	71	69	50	52	35	33
Canada	1987	34	63	74	78	23	52	51	49
United States	1986	29	66	77	79	22	46	53	52
Later period									
Belgium[a]	1997	16	55	73	81	11	46	62	57
West Germany	2000	21	50	70	80	19	44	48	49
Italy[a]	2000	16	40	47	59	12	33	42	38
United Kingdom	1995	42	62	65	69	38	50	48	43
Canada	1997	22	55	69	73	15	41	54	54
United States	2000	27	63	79	81	20	49	59	58
Percentage change between periods									
Belgium	1985 to 1997	-13	-9	-13	-8	-12	-6	5	2
West Germany	1984 to 2000	-9	-17	-10	-4	-6	-13	-3	1
Italy	1987 to 2000	0	-1	-15	-5	-4	6	9	1
United Kingdom	1986 to 1995	-14	-8	-6	-1	-13	-2	13	10
Canada	1987 to 1997	-12	-8	-5	-6	-9	-11	3	4
United States	1986 to 2000	-2	-4	1	2	-2	3	6	5

Source: Authors' tabulations of LIS files.
a. Wage and salary income is measured net of income and payroll tax payments.

period 1995 to 2000, however, women were more likely than men to see an improvement in their earnings self-sufficiency. The improvement was much more pronounced among women who were at least twenty-six (table 2.4, bottom panel). Women in the youngest age groups saw a drop in earnings self-sufficiency in all five countries, with sizable declines occurring in every country except Italy and the United States.

Summary

Declines in employment and in earned income have typically favored young women over young men, reducing the gender gap in self-sufficiency, especially at relatively older ages. Proportional losses in employment and earnings have been larger among people in the youngest age groups. Finally, wage gains among twenty-six- to thirty-four-year-old women have been larger and wage losses among twenty-six- to thirty-four-year-old men have been smaller in the United Kingdom, Canada, and the United States than in Belgium, Germany, and Italy. The losses in self-sufficiency among the youngest men and women, primarily as a result of lower employment rates and wages, certainly contribute to the decision of some young people to postpone establishing an independent household. Past age twenty-six, however, the gains in employment and self-sufficiency among women are likely to have acted as partial offsets to the employment and earnings losses of men the same age.

Household Income Adequacy

The results we have presented so far focus on trends in household headship, employment, and wage income, but they ignore the potential contributions of other sources of income, such as income from self-employment, savings, or property. Nor do these results account for the public transfers that might be available to an independent household that receives little private income. Finally, the calculations ignore the potential income contribution of a spouse, housemate, or unmarried partner. Even though earnings self-sufficiency has fallen among men age twenty-six to thirty-four, it has risen among women the same age. As a result, men alone may have less capacity to support themselves independently, but when their earnings are combined with those of a working spouse or partner, the independent household's combined resources may be enough to support the couple in relative comfort.

To fill out this picture of income adequacy, we divided eighteen- to thirty-four-year-old adults into two groups: "parental dependents" and "independents." People who are dependents in a household headed by their parent or stepparent are classified as parental dependents. Young adults classified as independents include household heads or those nonhousehold heads who are living independently (such as with a spouse or partner).[11] For young adults in each of the two groups we then calculate the ADPI of the adult's household. This calculation takes into account all net income received by the household regardless of whether it was earned by the young adult.

Dependents' Self-Sufficiency

Table 2.5 displays estimates of the income adequacy of young adults who remain members of a household headed by their parent. As with the individual measure, we classify a household as having adequate income if its ADPI is at least 50 percent of the national median ADPI (income).[12] Using this threshold, the percentage of households deemed to have an adequate income is very high except in Italy and the United States. This result is consistent with the finding that relative poverty rates in Italy and the United States are higher than those found elsewhere in the OECD (Smeeding 2006). In some age groups, the number of young adults tabulated is very small, mainly because the percentage of all adults who remain parental dependents declines with age (see figure 2.1). Thus, the sample sizes used to estimate income adequacy in some of the older age groups may be too small to yield precise estimates.

The striking result in table 2.5 is the very small change in income adequacy for parental dependents in the LIS samples (see bottom panel). Income adequacy rates typically declined between the mid-1980s and the period 1995 to 2000, but the decline was proportionately much smaller than the fall in young adults' employment rates or wage income might suggest.

The reasons why parental dependents fared so well probably differ across countries. Some countries may have strengthened public income protection, partly or fully offsetting the decline in young adults' earnings. In other countries, the earnings or property income of older adults in the households may have risen, compensating the household for some of the loss in young adults' wages. Young adults with poor employment prospects may have been more tempted to remain in their parents' household when the parents were relatively well off. If a child with meager earnings remains in the parental household, the household's size-adjusted income declines, but the *average* income across households containing a dependent adult child is not necessarily reduced. On the contrary, if adult children are disproportionately likely to remain in the households of increasingly *affluent* parents, the average income of households containing adult children might actually rise over time, even as the earnings prospects of young adults and their actual earnings deteriorate.

Table 2.5   Parental Dependents Who Have Adjusted Disposable Incomes Above 50 Percent of the National Median ADPI, 1984 to 2000

		Males				Females			
Country	Year	18 to 22	22 to 26	26 to 30	30 to 34	18 to 22	22 to 26	26 to 30	30 to 34
Earlier Period									
Belgium	1985	99%	97%	98%	100%	97%	98%	97%	94%
West Germany	1984	96	99	99	100	96	97	91	85
Italy	1987	86	87	90	81	87	89	92	88
United Kingdom	1986	98	96	95	98	95	98	94	88
Canada	1987	94	96	95	95	92	94	94	99
United States	1986	87	90	88	83	85	91	88	84
Later Period									
Belgium	1997	95	95	97	97	94	96	99	87
West Germany	2000	96	99	90	98	97	96	92	97
Italy	2000	87	93	90	92	87	89	92	87
United Kingdom	1995	92	95	96	92	94	97	96	100
Canada	1997	90	93	95	97	91	95	94	96
United States	2000	88	91	90	89	88	91	90	87
Percentage change between periods									
Belgium	1985 to 1997	-4	-2	-2	-3	-3	-2	2	-7
West Germany	1984 to 2000	0	0	-9	-2	1	-1	1	12
Italy	1987 to 2000	1	6	0	11	0	-1	-1	-1
United Kingdom	1986 to 1995	-5	-1	1	-5	-1	-1	2	12
Canada	1987 to 1997	-4	-2	0	1	-1	1	0	-4
United States	1986 to 2000	1	1	2	6	3	-1	2	2

Source: Authors' tabulations of LIS files.

Nondependents' Self-Sufficiency

Table 2.6 shows an identical set of tabulations for all young adults who were not dependents in a parent's household. These households typically have lower rates of income adequacy, although the difference is considerably smaller in the older age groups. An interesting exception to this pattern is Italy, where income adequacy among independent young adults is higher or only slightly worse than it is among parental dependents. Of course, living with one's parents is much more common in Italy than it is in the other five countries, and it remains common until later in life; thus, it is harder to compare Italy to other nations where most young adults leave the parental household much earlier (Giuliano 2006). Another interesting finding is that self-sufficiency among independent women in the United States is below average. Many independent young American women head single-parent families, and these families have exceptionally high relative poverty rates, compared with both other American families and similar households in other OECD countries (Smeeding 2006).

In contrast to their dependent peers, independent young adults show a pervasive and sizable decline in self-sufficiency, especially the youngest age groups (table 2.6, bottom panel). These results imply that reduced employment rates and wages among young adults impose the largest penalty on living standards for young adults who have moved out of their parents' home. The decline in independent young adults' income adequacy was typically smaller in the United States than in the other countries, and among independent American women age twenty-six to thirty-four, income adequacy improved slightly. As in the other countries, income adequacy fell most among independent U.S. adults in the youngest age category.

Income Adequacy Among Young Adults Irrespective of Dependency Status

We combine the results from tables 2.5 and 2.6 in table 2.7 to show levels and changes in income adequacy for the entire population of young adults, regardless of their living arrangements. The weighted results reflect the relative proportion in each age group of those who live with their parents and those who live independently of their parents. Taken broadly, the results in table 2.7 show that income adequacy among young adults is lower in the United States than it is in Europe, but the U.S.-European gap declined between the mid-1980s and the period 1995 to 2000. U.S. income adequacy comes closest to matching that in other countries for men in their late twenties and early thirties. The gap between the United States and Europe is larger for younger men and for

Table 2.6 Household Heads, Spouses, and Other Independent Young Adults Who Have Adjusted Disposable Incomes Above 50 Percent of the National Median ADPI, 1984 to 2000

Country	Year	Males				Females			
		18 to 22	22 to 26	26 to 30	30 to 34	18 to 22	22 to 26	26 to 30	30 to 34
Earlier period									
Belgium	1985	82%	92%	96%	97%	86%	93%	96%	96%
West Germany	1984	84	86	90	96	67	82	92	93
Italy	1987	84	85	91	89	91	86	88	91
United Kingdom	1986	84	90	90	91	83	86	87	89
Canada	1987	79	85	89	93	72	83	85	89
United States	1986	71	85	87	88	68	76	80	81
Later period									
Belgium	1997	80	77	86	93	78	87	90	90
West Germany	2000	71	70	87	91	55	71	85	90
Italy	2000	77	81	83	88	80	71	84	87
United Kingdom	1995	76	84	88	88	72	78	82	84
Canada	1997	66	87	85	89	61	78	85	87
United States	2000	71	80	87	87	67	75	80	82
Percentage change between periods									
Belgium	1985 to 1997	-1	-16	-10	-4	-9	-6	-6	-5
West Germany	1984 to 2000	-13	-16	-3	-4	-12	-11	-7	-3
Italy	1987 to 2000	-7	-4	-8	-1	-11	-15	-4	-4
United Kingdom	1986 to 1995	-8	-6	-2	-3	-11	-8	-4	-4
Canada	1987 to 1997	-13	2	-4	-4	-11	-5	0	-2
United States	1986 to 2000	0	-5	-1	-1	-1	0	0	1

Source: Authors' tabulations of LIS files.

Table 2.7   Young Adults Who Have Adjusted Disposable Incomes Above 50 Percent of the National Median ADPI, 1984 to 2000

Country	Year	Males				Females			
		18 to 22	22 to 26	26 to 30	30 to 34	18 to 22	22 to 26	26 to 30	30 to 34
Earlier period									
Belgium	1985	97%	95%	97%	97%	94%	95%	96%	95%
West Germany	1984	94	92	92	96	88	86	92	93
Italy	1987	86	86	91	87	87	88	90	91
United Kingdom	1986	94	92	91	92	90	89	88	89
Canada	1987	91	89	90	93	85	86	86	90
United States	1986	83	87	87	87	78	79	81	81
Later period									
Belgium	1997	94	88	89	93	91	91	92	90
West Germany	2000	91	83	88	92	83	78	86	90
Italy	2000	86	91	88	90	86	85	88	87
United Kingdom	1995	87	88	89	88	83	82	83	85
Canada	1997	85	90	88	89	81	84	86	87
United States	2000	82	83	87	87	79	79	81	82
Percentage change between periods									
Belgium	1985 to 1997	−3	−7	−8	−4	−4	−4	−4	−5
West Germany	1984 to 2000	−3	−8	−4	−4	−4	−8	−6	−3
Italy	1987 to 2000	0	5	−2	3	−1	−3	−2	−4
United Kingdom	1986 to 1995	−7	−4	−1	−4	−7	−7	−5	−4
Canada	1987 to 1997	−5	1	−3	−4	−4	−2	0	−2
United States	1986 to 2000	0	−4	0	0	1	−1	0	1

Source: Authors' tabulations of LIS files.

women. This suggests that between 1986 and 2000 there was little deterioration in the labor market position of young American adults, at least in comparison to the deterioration experienced by young men and eighteen- to twenty-six-year-old women in continental Europe. The results in the bottom panel of table 2.7 show there was also little deterioration in the income adequacy of U.S. households containing young adults. In contrast, young adults in all of the European countries experienced a decline in income adequacy. In Belgium, Germany, and the United Kingdom, the deterioration occurred for both genders and in every age group. Young adults in Canada experienced declines in income adequacy that fell approximately in between those that occurred in the United States and Europe.

Summary

These calculations reveal losses in income adequacy across most of the age groups in nearly all of the countries in our sample. It is worth repeating, however, that the losses were much bigger among young adults who lived independently of their parents. Young adults who remained in their parents' households were partially protected against the drop in living standards that might be expected to accompany a decline in job opportunities or a loss of wages. In results not shown, we found that the declines in income adequacy were typically much larger among independent adults who lived in single-person households. Young adults who lived as heads or spouses in households containing two or more people saw larger drops in income adequacy than adults who remained in their parents' households, but the drop in income adequacy was typically smaller than the drop experienced by independent young adults living alone. The proportion of young adults who live in one-person households is so small, however, that we cannot be confident of this result in most countries. We are much more confident of the finding that the young adults who lived more independently of their parents sustained bigger losses in income adequacy than the adults who continued to live with their parents.

Conclusion

Our results point to a decline in the ability of young adults to form independent households over the fifteen-year period leading up to 2000. At the same time, more young adults are "failing to launch" and establish independent households. Our calculations offer a generally consistent picture of declining economic self-sufficiency among young men and very young women in the countries in our study. In contrast, women in their late twenties and early thirties have seen improved prospects for economic independence, although from a starting level well below that of men of the same age. North America and to some extent the United Kingdom offer partial exceptions to this general pattern. Between the mid-1980s and 2000, employment rates improved among young Americans in their late twenties and early thirties, and earnings levels either remained stable or increased modestly. The stability of U.S. employment levels helped to offset an apparent reduction in male hourly wages, giving twenty-six- to thirty-four-year-old American men larger gains or smaller losses in economic self-sufficiency than those experienced by their counterparts in continental Europe. In addition, young American women who were twenty-six and older saw larger improvements in wage self-sufficiency than most of their counterparts in continental Europe.

A striking finding of this study is that although income adequacy among young adults typically declined over the analysis period, the declines were largest among those who did not live with their parents. These losses were especially large among the youngest adults in independent households. Young adults who lived with their parents suffered smaller losses in relative incomes, possibly because their earnings losses represented a small percentage of net household income or were offset by the income gains of their parents. These findings suggest that the extended family as well as the state is a source of income protection that buffers young adults against the full effects of an economic reverse (for Italian evidence on this issue, see Manacorda and Moretti 2002). Delayed departure from the parents' household is a plausible response to deterioration in a child's economic prospects.

Several issues are beyond the scope of this chapter but should be considered when interpreting our findings. The cross-national pattern of employment, earnings, and income gains and losses is almost certainly affected by the entry of immigrants as well as young adults into the workforce. The highest immigrant countries we studied are the United States and Canada, followed in order by the United Kingdom, Germany, Italy, and Belgium. There are not enough immigrant youth in some of these countries to analyze them separately in this chapter. However, we know that the United States has had much more low-skill than high-skill immigration than Canada and the United Kingdom, where a larger percentage of immigrants bring average or above-average skills upon entry into the country (Parsons and Smeeding 2006). We suspect that high rates of unskilled immigration into the United States have had a modestly depressing effect on wages for low-skilled native U.S. workers, including many of the young adults we study here (Borjas and Katz 2005). The cross-national effects of immigration on the

Figure 2.3   Population in Six Countries That Has Attained at Least Upper Secondary Education, 2002 to 2003

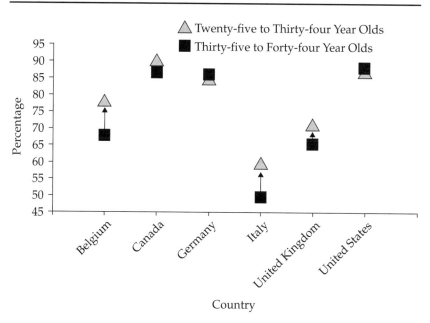

transition to independence must, however, be the topic of separate analysis (for more on recent issues related to EU immigration, see Parsons and Smeeding 2006).

An optimistic interpretation of our findings is that young adults have postponed the formation of independent households because they are accumulating more education than earlier generations did. By spending more time in school, they are delaying financial independence and temporarily giving up labor income, but they are improving their capacity to earn good wages in the future. Figures 2.3 and 2.4 compare school completion rates in the six countries among twenty-five- to thirty-four-year-olds (triangles) and thirty-five- to forty-four-year-olds (squares). As the figures reveal, in all countries except Germany and the United States, younger adults (the twenty-five- to thirty-four-year-old cohort) are indeed accumulating more education than their older peers.[13] However, additional education is not driving the earnings losses in either Germany or the United States, given that education levels have not been rising and may even be falling in Ger-

Figure 2.4   Population in Six Countries That Has Attained Tertiary Education, 2002 to 2003

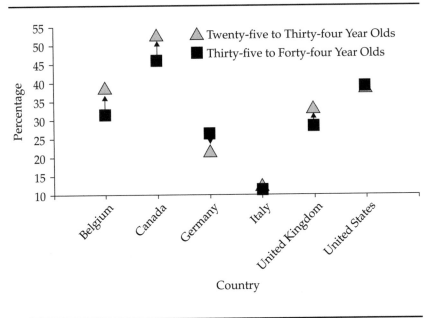

Source: OECD (2005).

many. Although an education-based interpretation of the trends in employment, earnings, and the age of financial independence may be valid for youth in Belgium, Canada, the United Kingdom, and (marginally) Italy, it does not appear to explain the "failure to launch" in Germany or the United States.

Appendix

Young adults are divided into four overlapping age groups in table 2A.1. The top panel of the table shows the percentage of men and women in each age group who were household heads or spouses in the 1980s wave of the LIS surveys, while the middle panel shows identical tabulations of headship status in the later LIS survey. The bottom panel shows the difference between headship rates in the 1995 to 2000 period and the mid-1980s.

Table 2A.1 Persons in Six Countries Who Are Household Heads or Spouses of Household Heads, 1984 to 2000

Country	Year	Males				Females			
		18 to 22	22 to 26	26 to 30	30 to 34	18 to 22	22 to 26	26 to 30	30 to 34
Earlier period									
Belgium	1985	9%	43%	82%	92%	17%	61%	84%	90%
West Germany	1984	11	53	81	92	21	66	87	94
Italy	1987	1	8	47	74	6	37	67	80
United Kingdom	1986	19	57	84	92	35	72	88	94
Canada	1987	17	50	73	87	30	65	84	91
United States	1986	15	51	75	85	28	64	82	90
Later period									
Belgium	1997	6	36	71	88	10	47	73	88
West Germany	2000	12	50	82	92	24	60	77	88
Italy	2000	2	7	27	54	6	17	49	79
United Kingdom	1995	18	53	81	92	37	74	91	95
Canada	1997	16	44	69	84	27	59	81	90
United States	2000	17	50	71	81	26	61	79	86
Percentage change between periods									
Belgium	1985 to 1997	-3	-8	-10	-4	-6	-15	-11	-3
West Germany	1984 to 2000	0	-3	0	0	3	-5	-10	-6
Italy	1987 to 2000	1	-1	-20	-20	0	-20	-17	-1
United Kingdom	1986 to 1995	-1	-4	-3	0	1	2	2	2
Canada	1987 to 1997	-1	-6	-4	-3	-3	-6	-3	2
United States	1986 to 2000	1	-1	-3	-2	-4	-4	-4	-1

Source: Authors' tabulations of LIS files.

Notes

1. For a description and documentation, see www.lisproject.org/techdoc.htm.
2. The database does not always include information on each household member's labor earnings, employment status, or usual paid hours of work. This is one reason our analysis focuses on just six out of the thirty LIS countries. To be included in our sample of countries, a nation's LIS survey information had to meet minimum requirements. First, information from an identical or very similar survey instrument was needed for two points in time, one around the middle of the 1980s and a second after the mid-1990s. Second, the LIS database had to contain information about the individual labor earnings of adults who headed households as well as those adult household members who were not heads. For instance, the LIS labor force data do not necessarily cover a consistent reference period across all of the countries in our sample.
3. In the six countries examined here, we measure a person's capacity for economic independence by his or her labor income. The early LIS data on labor earnings are subject, however, to an important limitation. The LIS datasets from the mid-1980s contain information on individuals' wage and salary earnings, but data on self-employment income are available only at the household level. In the later LIS datasets, self-employment income as well as wage and salary earnings are available for individuals. To create comparable measures of labor earnings for both periods, we confined our analysis to wage and salary income. We also present information showing how this limitation may affect our findings. Although it would be desirable to find or create datasets that include reliable information on both income and work hours, we were unable to identify comparable data files that cover a broad cross-section of countries. Thus, at this point the LIS surveys are the best microscope available for examining these differences in cross-national perspective.
4. In Italy spouses cannot be distinguished from partners of the household head in one of the two surveys. Therefore, our classification of Italian spouses should be understood to include both spouses and partners of the household head.
5. The survey used in the four EU member countries was Eurostat's quarterly Labor Force Survey; in Canada, it was the monthly Labor Force Survey; and in the United States it was the monthly Current Population Survey. Eurostat, Statistics Canada, and the U.S. Bureau of Labor Statistics define the employment-to-population ratio in very similar but not identical ways. All employment statistics were obtained from the Internet sites of the Eurostat, Statistics Canada, and BLS.
6. Unfortunately, Eurostat has not published employment data by age group for western Germany since the early 1990s. Therefore, the German data in table 2.2 refer to West Germany in 1985 and to unified Germany in the period 1995 to 2005. We show employment rates for a single year, 1985, in the mid-1980s, but for three separate years between 1995 and 2005. For some countries, the 1995 data cover a reference period that is close to the second LIS survey we analyze. For other countries, the 2000 data are more comparable.

7. Formally, adjusted disposable personal income (ADPI) is equal to unadjusted household income (DPI) divided by household size (S) raised to an exponential value (e), that is, $ADPI = DPI/S^e$. Our assumption implies that the value of e is one-half. We chose one-half, a common value used in research on household income, because it represents the halfway point between two extreme assumptions about the economies of scale that individuals achieve when they live in larger households.

8. Although it would be preferable to measure each worker's total labor income, including self-employment as well as wage and salary earnings, self-employment income was not separately recorded in the LIS data files in the mid-1980s. Because the calculations do not include self-employment income, they understate young adults' total labor income in all the countries. The exclusion of self-employment earnings is more important in Italy than it is in other countries because a relatively large percentage of young Italians are self-employed, and the income they derive from such employment is significant. To calculate the potential importance of self-employment earnings, we tabulate labor earnings in 2000 in Germany, Italy, and the United States using two definitions, one that includes and a second that excludes a person's self-employment income. Self-employment income does not contribute materially to the earned incomes of very young people in any of the countries or to the incomes of U.S. men and German and U.S. women, regardless of their age. However, including self-employment income in the earnings definition boosts the earnings of twenty-six- to thirty-four-year-old German men by about 10 percent. The effect on the earnings of Italian men and women is much greater. Between ages thirty and thirty-four, the measure of net earnings that includes net self-employment income is about 40 percent larger than a definition that includes only net wage and salary income. For this reason, any analysis that excludes self-employment earnings seriously understates the relative incomes of Italians age twenty-five or older.

9. Because employment rates changed between the two surveys, this calculation does not compare the earnings levels of two identically selected populations. If the employment rate fell between the first and second surveys, the population included in the calculation for the second year may differ in many ways from the population included in the first-year sample. For example, if the percentage of young adults at work declined because of higher enrollments in postsecondary education, the sample of wage earners in the later year may exclude some of the most able adults who would have held jobs in the absence of an enrollment rise. The fall in average wage levels in the bottom panel of table 2.3 cannot be interpreted as unambiguous evidence that the wages available to young people declined. Instead, it may partly reflect the change in the composition of the employed population.

10. As noted, this calculation is based on reported after-tax earnings in Belgium and Italy and on pretax earnings in western Germany, Canada, the United Kingdom, and the United States. The calculations may therefore overstate the percentage of Germans, Britons, and Americans who are self-sufficient based on their *net* wage income. The tabulations are biased against Italy for another reason as well. Self-employment income is more important for

young people in that country than it is in the other four. Since data limitations prevent us from including self-employment earnings in the calculations, the results seriously underestimate the labor incomes of Italians.

11. Although the living arrangements of adults who are neither heads nor
     parental dependents vary widely, we assume that on balance the people in
     this group are more independent of their parents than young adults who
     live in their parents' homes.

12. Note that since our calculations are based on households' after-tax and af-
     ter-transfer incomes, the results are comparable across all six countries, in-
     cluding both Belgium and Italy. We also performed the calculations using a
     higher income threshold to measure income adequacy, but the pattern of re-
     sults was similar to the patterns displayed in tables 2.6 to 2.7.

13. The German findings are undoubtedly affected by German unification. Our
     income and earnings analysis has focused on residents of western Germany,
     but the education statistics show attainment levels for all of Germany. It is
     conceivable that young western Germans have accumulated more school-
     ing than older cohorts, even though the national-level statistics do not re-
     flect these gains.

References

Borjas, George J., and Lawrence F. Katz. 2005. "The Evolution of the Mexican-
Born Workforce in the United States." Working paper 11281. Cambridge,
Mass.: National Bureau of Economic Research (April).

Bucks, Brian, and Karen Pence. 2005. "Measuring Housing Wealth." Paper presented to the working conference of the Luxembourg Wealth Study. Perugia, Italy
(January 29). Accessed at http://www.lisproject.org/lws/files/buckspence
_rev.pdf.

Duncan, Greg J., Johanne Boisjoly, and Timothy M. Smeeding. 1996. "Economic
Mobility of Young Workers in the 1970s and 1980s." *Demography* 33(4):
497–509.

Ghidoni, Michele. 2002. "Determinants of Young Europeans' Decision to Leave
the Parental Household." Unpublished paper. University College London
(February).

Giannelli, Gianna Claudia, and Chiara Monfardini. 2003. "Joint Decisions on
Household Membership and Human Capital Accumulation of Youths: The
Role of Expected Earnings and Labor Market Rationing." *Journal of Population
Economics* 16: 265–85.

Giuliano, Paola. 2006. "Living Arrangements in Western Europe: Does Cultural
Origin Matter?" IZA DP 2042. Bonn, Germany: Institute for Study of Labor
(March).

Gornick, Janet C., and Marcia K. Meyers. 2003. *Families That Work: Policies for Reconciling Parenthood and Employment*. New York: Russell Sage Foundation.

Haveman, Robert, and Timothy M. Smeeding. 2006. "The Role of Higher Education in Social Mobility." *Future of Children* 16(2): 125–50.

Köppen, Katja. 2006. "Second Births in Western Germany and France." *Demographic
Research* 14(14): 295–330. Accessed at http://www.demographic-research.org/
volumes/vol14/14/.

Manacorda, Marco, and Enrico Moretti. 2002. "Why Do Most Italian Youths Live with Their Parents? Intergenerational Transfers and Household Structure." Unpublished paper. London: London School of Economics (January).

Neyer, Gerda Ruth. 2003. "Family Policies and Low Fertility in Western Europe." MPIDR WP 2003-021. Rostock, Germany: Max Planck Institute for Demographic Research.

Organization for Economic Cooperation and Development. 2005. *Education at a Glance: 2005.* Paris: OECD. Accessed at www.oecd.org/edu/eag2005.

Parsons, Craig A., and Timothy M. Smeeding, editors. 2006. *Immigration and the Transformation of Europe.* Cambridge: Cambridge University Press.

Ruiz-Castillo, Javier, and Maite Martinez-Granado. 2002. "The Decisions of Spanish Youth: A Cross-Section Study." *Journal of Population Economics* 15(2): 305–30.

Smeeding, Timothy M. 2006. "Poor People in Rich Nations: The United States in Comparative Perspective." *Journal of Economic Perspectives* 20(1): 69–90.

Smeeding, Timothy M., and Katherin Ross Phillips. 2002. "Cross-Nantional Differences in Employment and Economic Sufficiency." *Annals of the American Academy of Political and Social Science* 580(1): 103–33.

United Nations Economic Commission for Europe. 2005. *Trends in Europe and North America 2005.* New York and Geneva: United Nations.

Chapter 3

Is the Company Man an Anachronism? Trends in Long-Term Employment in the United States, 1973 to 2006

HENRY S. FARBER

The typical characterization of a work career is that after some turnover early on, most workers find a more or less lifetime job. However, this trajectory has been challenged in the last twenty years as large corporations have engaged in highly publicized layoffs and the industrial structure of the U.S. economy has shifted in the face of global competition. To the extent that there has been a substantial change in career employment dynamics, young workers who entered the labor force in recent years and those who enter in the future will face a very different type of career path than their parents.

In this study, I examine evidence on job durations from 1973 through 2006 to determine the extent to which the structure of careers and the likelihood of long-term employment have changed. I use Current Population Survey (CPS) data from 1973 to 2006 that contain information on how long workers have been employed by their current firm. Specifically, I examine the length of employment relationships for different birth cohorts from 1914 through 1981.

The evolution of careers in the United States has played out in the context of dramatic growth in employment over the last forty years. Civilian employment rose from 85.1 million in 1973 to 144.4 million in 2006.[1] Thus, almost 60 million jobs have been created on net in the past thirty-three years, for an average rate of employment growth of 1.6 percent per year. Despite this record of sustained employment growth, there is long-standing concern that the quality of jobs is deteriorating. This concern arises in part from the declining share of manufacturing employment.[2] As high-quality jobs, both in manufacturing and in the service sector, are lost, the concern is that they are being replaced by low-quality, service-sector jobs (so-called hamburger-flipping jobs). The high-quality jobs are characterized by relatively high wages, full-time employment, substantial fringe benefits, and, perhaps most important, substantial job security (low rates of turnover). The low-quality jobs are characterized disproportionately by relatively low wages, part-time employment, an absence of fringe benefits, and low job security (high rates of turnover).

The perceived low quality of many newly created jobs fuels the concern that the nature of the employment relationship in the United States is changing from one based on long-term, full-time employment to one based on short-term and casual employment as employers move toward greater reliance on temporary workers, subcontractors, and part-time workers. This shift may be occurring because employers need to remain flexible in the face of greater uncertainty about product demand and to avoid increasingly expensive fringe benefits and long-term obligations to workers.

The results of the analysis in this chapter show that by virtually any measure more recent cohorts of male workers have been with their current employer for less time at specific ages. Interestingly, while mean tenure has fallen sharply for men and men are less likely to be in long-term jobs, the pattern is different for women. There has been some increase in job tenure and long-term employment for women, reflecting their increased commitment to the labor market. In more recent years, however, this trend has been offset by the overall decline in the availability of long-term jobs.

Background on American Job Stability

In an early influential analysis of job stability, Robert Hall (1982) found that, although any particular new job is unlikely to last a long time, a job that has already lasted five years has a substantial probability of lasting twenty years. He also found that a substantial fraction of workers work in a "lifetime" job (defined as lasting at least twenty years) at some point in their life.

More recently, Kenneth Swinnerton and Howard Wial (1995) documented a secular decline in job stability in the 1980s. In contrast, Francis Diebold, David Neumark, and Daniel Polsky (1994) found that aggregate retention rates were fairly stable over the 1980s, but that retention rates declined for high school dropouts and for high school graduates relative to college graduates over this period. Later studies by both

Diebold, Neumark, and Polsky (1996) and Swinnerton and Wial (1996) support the view that the period from 1979 to 1991 saw fairly steady job stability. In my own study (Farber 1998) on job tenure from 1973 through 1993, I found that the prevalence of long-term employment had not declined over time, but that the distribution of long-term jobs had shifted. I found that less-educated men had become less likely to hold long-term jobs, but that this was offset by a substantial increase in the rate at which women held long-term jobs. In a later study (Farber 2000), I found that the prevalence of long-term employment relationships among men had declined by 1996 to its lowest level since 1979. In contrast, long-term employment relationships were somewhat more common among women. Also arguing for increasing instability has been Stephen Rose (1995), who found that the fraction of workers who reported no job changes in a given length of time was higher in the 1970s than in the 1980s.

Evidence presented at a Russell Sage Foundation conference on the topic in 1998 was mixed.[3] David Jaeger and Ann Huff Stevens (1999) found no change in the share of males in short-term jobs and some decline between the late 1980s and mid-1990s in the share of males with at least ten years of tenure. David Neumark, Daniel Polsky, and Daniel Hansen (1999) found a similar decline in long-term employment, but concluded that this was not a secular trend. Peter Gottschalk and Robert Moffitt (1999) found no evidence of increasing job insecurity in the 1980s and 1990s. Finally, Robert Valletta (1999) found some decline in long-term employment relationships from 1976 to 1993.

In more recent work, Jay Stewart (2002) investigated two aspects of job security. The first, the likelihood of leaving a job, shows no particular trend from 1975 through 2000. The second, the likelihood of making an employment-to-employment transition, increased over this period, while the likelihood of making an employment-to-unemployment transition decreased. Stewart concludes that the cost of changing jobs has decreased.

Ann Huff Stevens (2005) examined data from several longitudinal histories of older male workers (late fifties and early sixties) and found no change in the length of the longest job held during their careers between the late 1960s and the early 2000s. Her results showed an increase and then a reduction in average longest tenure, from 22 years among older workers in 1969 to 24 years in 1980 to 21.4 years in 2002. A reasonable interpretation of this pattern is that the earliest cohorts had jobs interrupted by military service during World War II, resulting in lower average longest tenure than subsequent cohorts. The decline since 1980 may then reflect a real decline in job durations. In addition, the most recent cohort examined by Stevens was born in the 1940s, and thus she misses the experience of more recent birth cohorts.

A careful reading of this earlier research yields no clear answer on changes in long-term employment relationships. The study reported here covers a long time span in a consistent way and sheds more definitive light on what in fact has happened to long-term employment in the United States.

Measuring the Change in Tenure over Time

My analysis relies on a sample consisting of workers age twenty to sixty-four (excluding the self-employed) from the twenty-one CPS supplements from 1973 to 2006. To have data for each birth cohort over a five-year period, I further restrict my analysis to the 1914 to 1981 birth cohorts. The sample contains 876,063 workers, and the data are described in more detail in the appendix. No one statistic can completely characterize a distribution; therefore, to examine the changes over time in the distribution of job durations I focus on several measures:

1. *Mean job tenure (years with the current employer)*. This is not mean completed job duration, because the jobs sampled are still in progress.

2. *The age-specific probability that a worker reports being on his or her job at least ten years*. Because younger workers cannot have accumulated substantial job tenure, I restrict this analysis to workers at least age thirty-five, and I examine how these probabilities have evolved from early to more recent birth cohorts. From the statistics in table 3A.1, there are workers age thirty-five and older in my sample born in the six decades from the 1910s to the 1960s. This allows me to investigate changes in the transition from the early "job-shopping" phase of a career to more stable, longer-term employment relationships in mid-career.

3. *The age-specific probability that a worker reports being in his or her job at least twenty years*. Because younger workers cannot have accumulated substantial job tenure, I restrict this analysis to workers age forty-five and older, and I examine how these probabilities have evolved from early- to mid-twentieth-century birth cohorts. From the statistics in table 3A.1, there are workers age forty-five and older in my sample born in the five decades from the 1910s to the 1950s. This allows me to investigate changes in the incidence of longer-term employment relationships later in careers.

4. *The age-specific probability that a worker reports being in his or her job for less than one year*. This provides another approach to investigating changes in the transition from the early job-shopping phase of a career to more stable, longer-term employment relationships.

It is clear that workers with little seniority are more likely than high-tenure workers to lose their jobs in downturns (Abraham and Medoff

1984). Thus, we would expect that the incidence of long-term employment, as measured by the fraction of workers with tenure exceeding some threshold, to be countercyclical. Tight labor markets will lead the distribution of job durations to lie to the left of the distribution in slack labor markets. Since secular rather than cyclical changes are of interest here, an alternative measure of the distribution that is relatively free of cyclical movements would be useful.

One alternative would be to use the entire population in the relevant category (for example, individuals in a given age range) regardless of employment status, assuming that those not employed have zero tenure (Farber 1994). One could compute mean tenure and population fractions in different tenure categories using these population-based data. While these population-based measures do not suffer to the same degree from the cyclical fluctuations that affect the employment-based measures, they have their own problems of interpretation. Secular changes in labor supply directly affect the population-based measures. If a group has increased its labor supply over time (as, for example, women have done), the population-based measures of the incidence of long-term employment for that group are likely to be affected in hard-to-predict ways. For example, if women are less likely to leave the labor force after some initial period of working, then there is likely to be an increase in the fraction of women in long-term employment relationships. Similarly, if a group has decreased its labor supply over time (as, for example, older men have done), the population-based measures for that group are likely to show a decrease in the incidence of long-term employment. Changes in population-based measures due to shifts in labor supply do not reflect changes in the underlying structure of jobs.

I choose to present employment-based measures in this study to avoid confusing secular changes in labor supply with changes in the structure of jobs. But cyclical influences should be kept in mind when interpreting the results.

The Evolution of Job Tenure

Mean Tenure

Figure 3.1 plots mean tenure by age and gender for the five decade-of-birth cohorts from the 1920s through the 1960s.[4] The figure shows clearly that (1) mean tenure rises with age and (2) women have lower mean tenure than men after about age thirty. With regard to shifts over time, age-specific mean tenure for males has declined substantially, particularly for later cohorts. For example, mean tenure for males at age fifty declined from 13.4 years for the 1930s birth cohort to 9.7 years for the 1950s birth cohort. There appears to be little systematic change for women.

Figure 3.1   Mean Tenure, by Sex, Age, and Birth Cohort

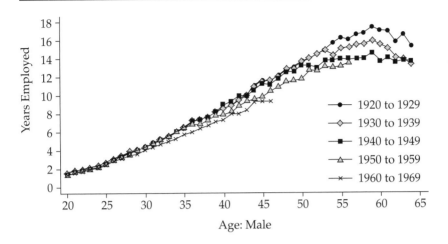

Age: Male

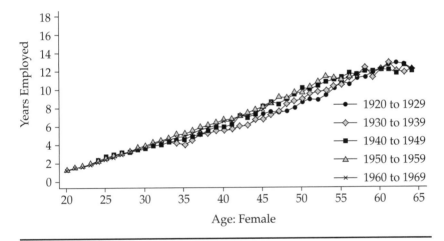

Age: Female

Source: Current Population Survey.

Classifying individuals by birth decade is not necessarily appropriate. There may be important differences within a decade, particularly with regard to the age distribution. An approach to summarizing the data that allows each birth year to be independent is to estimate a linear model of the natural logarithm of tenure of the form

$$ln(T_{ijk}) = C_j + A_k + e_{ijk}, \tag{3.1}$$

where T_{ijk} is tenure in years for individual i in birth cohort j aged k, C_j is a birth-year indicator, and A_k is a years-of-age indicator. This logarithmic specification embodies the plausible assumption that proportional cohort effects on mean tenure are constant across ages and, equivalently, that the proportional age effects on mean tenure are constant across birth cohorts.[5] A more detailed investigation would allow for cohort effects that vary by age, since changes in job security could express themselves differentially at various ages. However, the model in equation 3.1 fits the data quite well, and it serves as a good summary of the data.[6]

I estimate the model separately for men and women using ordinary least squares (OLS), weighted by the CPS final sample weights. The estimated cohort effects summarize changes across birth cohorts that are age-specific in mean tenure. I convert the estimated cohort effects to proportional differences in mean tenure relative to the 1914 birth cohort. These proportional differences are plotted in figure 3.2, and they show a sharp decline of about 50 percent in mean tenure for male workers between the 1914 and the mid-1970s birth cohorts.

The pattern is quite different for female workers. Mean tenure for female workers did not change between the 1914 and 1940 birth cohorts,

Figure 3.2   Proportional Difference from 1914 Birth Cohort in Mean and Mean Tenure, Controlling for Age

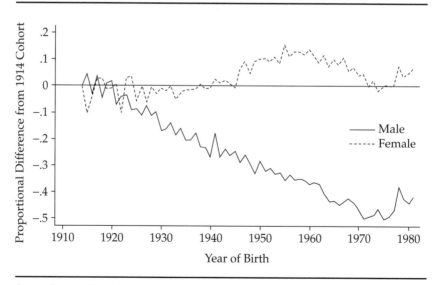

Source: Current Population Survey.

but it increased by about 15 percent between the 1940 and 1960 birth co-horts before declining to its original level among the mid-1970s birth co-horts. The increase in mean tenure for women born between 1940 and 1969 reflects the increased commitment of women to the labor force, tem-pered by (1) high rates of withdrawal from the labor force, even if only for a short time, during childbearing years and (2) the general decline in long-term employment opportunities, which is apparent in the data for males. The subsequent decline in tenure for females born in the 1970s may reflect a continued general decline in long-term employment op-portunities that is not offset by a further increase in female commitment to the labor force.

Education and the Decline in Mean Tenure   In addition to the increased presence of women in the labor force, other important changes could be associated with declining tenure. The first is the large increase in educa-tion among workers during the twentieth century, summarized in table 3.1. While there is no clear relationship between educational attainment and tenure, I investigate how the decline in mean job tenure is related to the general increase in educational attainment.[7] The top graph of figure 3.3 contains plots for each of four education categories (less than twelve years of school, twelve years of school, thirteen to fifteen years of school, and sixteen or more years of school) for males. Mean tenure has fallen for all education categories, with the largest decline since 1914 for college graduates. For women (bottom graph), there is no consistent pattern.

To provide a summary across educational categories of the propor-tional change in mean tenure over time accounting for changes in the

Table 3.1   Distribution of Education, by Birth Cohort

Birth Decade	Less Than Twelve Years	Twelve Years	Thirteen to Fifteen Years	Sixteen or More Years
1914 to 1919	39.53%	37.54%	10.92%	12.02%
1920 to 1929	31.18	39.30	12.83	16.69
1930 to 1939	21.28	40.57	16.57	21.58
1940 to 1949	11.82	35.58	23.09	29.50
1950 to 1959	8.75	34.88	27.28	29.08
1960 to 1969	9.10	34.78	28.00	28.12
1970 to 1981	9.40	30.46	33.82	26.32
All	11.96	35.04	25.88	27.12

Source: Current Population Survey.
Note: Based on data for not self-employed workers age twenty to sixty-four from twenty-one CPSs covering the period from 1973 to 2006. Weighted by CPS final sample weights.

Figure 3.3   Proportional Difference from 1914 Birth Cohort in Mean Tenure, Controlling for Age, by Education

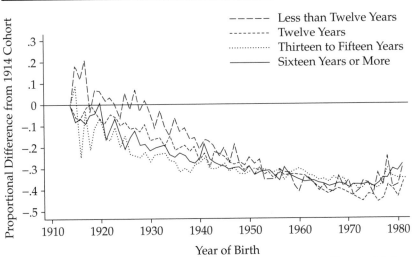

Proportional Difference from 1914 Birth Cohort, Mean Tenure: Males

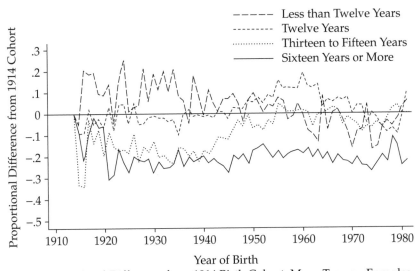

Proportional Difference from 1914 Birth Cohort, Mean Tenure: Females

Source: Current Population Survey.

Figure 3.4   Proportional Difference from 1914 Birth Cohort in Mean Tenure, Controlling for Age and Education

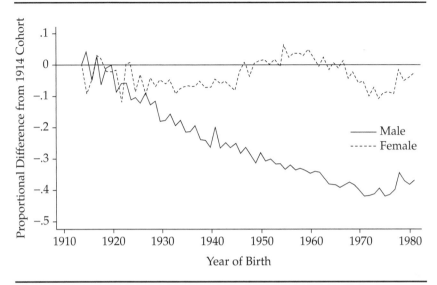

Source: Current Population Survey.

educational distribution, I estimate an augmented version of the regression model for mean tenure in equation 3.1 as

$$ln(T_{ijk}) = ED_{j\gamma} + C_j + A_k + e_{ijk},$$ (3.2)

where ED_i is a vector of dummy variables indicating educational attainment and γ is a vector of associated coefficients. The estimated proportional changes in mean tenure relative to the 1914 birth cohort are plotted in figure 3.4, and while the time-series patterns are very similar in shape to those derived without controlling for education (figure 3.2), there are some differences. Accounting for changes in the distribution of education, the estimated decline in mean tenure for males was approximately 40 percent between the 1914 and 1975 cohorts, compared with a 50 percent decline without controlling for education. Therefore, about 20 percent of the decline in tenure for males born between 1914 and 1975 is accounted for by changes in educational attainment. When education is controlled for, women show an initial decline in mean tenure for those born between 1914 and the mid-1940s, followed by an increase for those born in the mid-1950s. The increase, however, is followed by a decline of 10 to 15 percent between the 1960 and 1975 cohorts.

Increased Immigration and the Decline in Mean Tenure   A second and potentially more important factor that could account for the decline in
tenure is the increased presence of immigrants in the U.S. labor force. By
definition, newly arrived immigrants cannot have substantial tenure.
Data on immigration are unavailable in the CPS prior to 1995. Therefore,
I use data from the eleven CPS supplements with tenure and immigration data between 1995 and 2006. To have data for each birth cohort over
a five-year period, I further restrict my analysis to the 1935 to 1981 birth
cohorts. The weighted immigrant fraction of the labor force in my sample increased steadily from 9.5 percent in 1995 to 15.0 percent in 2006. In
every year, immigrants had about 2.2 years' fewer tenure than natives on
average (the overall average difference was 2.19 years [standard error =
0.035]). Immigrants were only slightly younger than natives (the overall
average difference = 0.99 years [standard error = 0.049]).

How much of the decline in tenure is due to the increased immigrant
presence in the labor force? Figure 3.5 contains separate plots for natives
and immigrants of the proportional difference in mean tenure relative to
the 1935 birth cohort, accounting for differences in age and education.
The plot for natives in the top graph shows a substantial decline in age-
specific average tenure for men between the 1940 and mid-1970s birth
cohorts of the same magnitude as the decline for all males (figure 3.4).
There is not much change in age-specific average tenure across birth cohorts for native females.

The bottom graph of figure 3.5 contains the proportional changes in
mean tenure for immigrants. These show no systematic change in age-
specific average tenure for immigrant males between the 1940 and early-
1970s birth cohorts, although tenure does increase for later cohorts. Immigrant females show steady increases in average tenure from the 1940
birth cohort forward.

To summarize the effect of increased immigration on overall changes
over time in job tenure, I reestimated the basic model to include an indicator for immigrant status. This model is:

$$ln(T_{ijk}) = \alpha IMM_i + ED_{i\gamma} + C_j + A_k + e_{ijk'}$$ (3.3)

where IMM_i is an indicator variable if worker i is an immigrant.[8] The proportional differences relative to the 1935 birth cohort from a base model
without the immigrant variable (equation 3.2) are plotted in the top
graph of figure 3.6. The bottom graph contains the proportional differences in mean tenure from the model with the immigrant variable (equation 3.3).

The base model shows a 20 percent decline in age-specific tenure for
male workers between the 1935 and early-1970s birth cohorts. When I
control for immigrant status, the decline in tenure for males between

Figure 3.5   Proportional Difference from 1935 Birth Cohort in Mean Tenure, Controlling for Age and Education: Native-Born and Immigrants

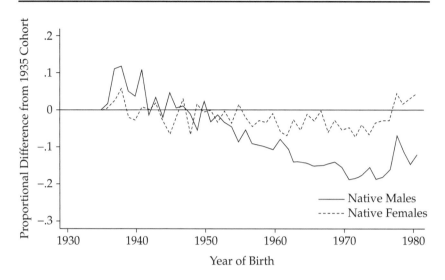

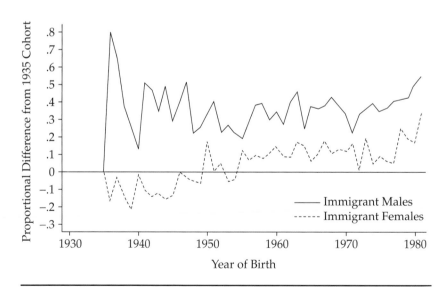

Source: Current Population Survey.

Figure 3.6   Proportional Difference from 1935 Birth Cohort in Mean Tenure, Controlling for Age and Education

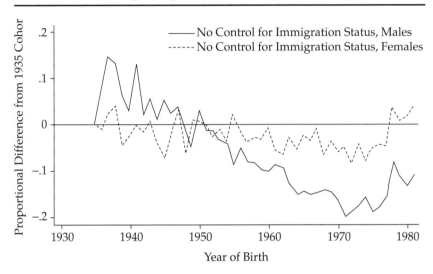

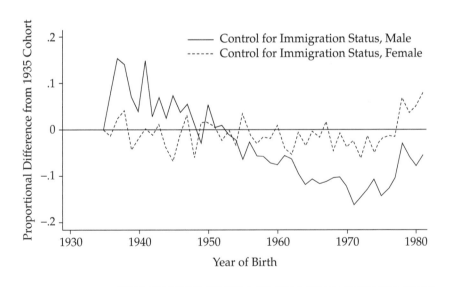

Source: Current Population Survey.

these birth cohorts is 16 percent. A similar pattern emerges for females, with a decline of 8 percent without a control for immigrant status and a decline of 6 percent with a control for immigrant status. Overall, about 20 to 25 percent of the decline in tenure between the 1935 and early-1970s birth cohorts is due to an increase in immigration.

A remaining problem is that immigration status is not known prior to 1995, so that this analysis does not use information on the birth cohorts between 1914 and 1934. However, immigrant status is strongly correlated with race and Hispanic ethnicity, which are observed in all years.[9]

To account, at least partly, for the role of increased immigration in the decline in tenure, I estimate age-specific proportional differences in mean tenure relative to the 1914 birth cohort using the 1973 to 2006 sample for the 1914 to 1981 birth cohorts, controlling for race and ethnicity as well as age and education. I derive the birth-cohort effects by estimating

$$ln(T_{ijk}) = \alpha_1 NW_i + \alpha_2 H_i + ED_{i\gamma} + C_j + A_k + e_{ijk'} \tag{3.4}$$

where NW_i is an indicator for nonwhite and H_i is an indicator for Hispanic ethnicity.

Figure 3.7 contains plots of the proportional differences from the 1914 birth cohort in mean tenure based on equation 3.4. These show a decline for men in age-specific tenure of about 38 percent between the 1914 and 1975 birth cohorts. This contrasts with an estimated decline over the same period of about 42 percent when there are no controls for race and Hispanic ethnicity (figure 3.4). Thus, about 10 percent of the decline in age-specific average tenure is related to changes in racial and ethnic composition. Age-specific average tenure for females, estimated when race and ethnicity are accounted for in figure 3.7, peaks for cohorts born in the late 1950s and declines from this point by about 15 percent by the mid-1970s. This is similar to the decline over the same period of about 14 percent when there are no controls for race and ethnicity (figure 3.4).

In short, mean tenure has declined dramatically over time, and only a small fraction of this decline can be accounted for by the sharp growth in immigrants in the labor market. This decline is concentrated among men and is less apparent among women, for whom labor supply considerations are more important.

Long-Term Employment

I consider next two measures of long-term employment: the fraction of workers age thirty-five to sixty-four who have been with their employer at least ten years (the "ten-year rate") and the fraction of workers age forty-five to sixty-four who have been with their employer at least twenty years (the "twenty-year rate").

Figure 3.7   Proportional Difference from 1914 Birth Cohort in Mean Tenure, Controlling for Age, Education, Race, and Hispanic Ethnicity

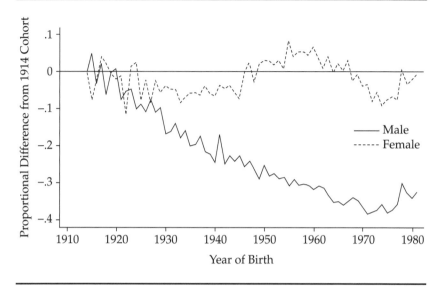

Source: Current Population Survey.

Figure 3.8 shows clearly that the incidence of long-term employment has declined dramatically for men, with the ten-year rate falling from about 50 percent to less than 40 percent and the twenty-year rate falling from about 35 percent to less than 25 percent between 1973 and 2006. In contrast, the incidence of long-term employment increased among women: their ten-year rate increased from 30 to 34 percent, and their twenty-year rate increased from 13 to 17 percent between 1973 and 2006.

Because these measures are sensitive to the age distribution and other observable characteristics, I estimate birth-cohort effects using the same approach I used for means. I estimate linear probability models using the same specification of explanatory variables (birth cohort, age, education, race, Hispanic ethnicity) as in equation 3.4, and I report the estimated birth-cohort effects from the analysis in figure 3.9.

The top graph of figure 3.9 contains separate plots for males and females of the birth-cohort effects (1914 = 0) for the ten-year rate. The age-specific probability that a male worker had been with his employer for at least ten years fell dramatically by twenty percentage points between the 1914 and 1966 birth cohorts.[10] The age-specific probability that a female worker had been with her employer for at least ten years was constant between the 1914 and the mid-1940s birth cohorts and then increased slightly between the mid-1940s and late-1950s cohorts before declining to its original level.

Figure 3.8   Fraction of Workers in a Long-Term Job, by Year

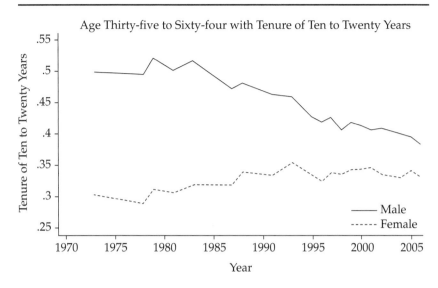

Age Thirty-five to Sixty-four with Tenure of Ten to Twenty Years

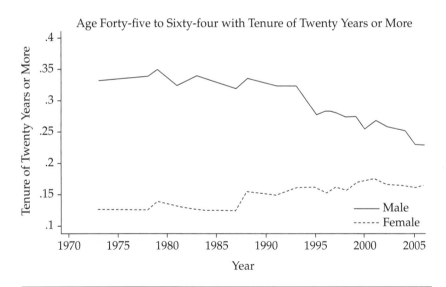

Age Forty-five to Sixty-four with Tenure of Twenty Years or More

Source: Current Population Survey.

The bottom graph of figure 3.9 shows the change in twenty-year tenure rates. Again, the age-specific probability that a male worker had been with his employer for at least twenty years fell sharply, by about twelve percentage points, between the 1914 and 1955 birth cohorts.[11] The

Figure 3.9   Proportional Difference from 1914 Birth Cohort, by Birth Year, Controlling for Age, Education, Race, and Hispanic Ethnicity

Difference from 1914 Birth Cohort, Linear Probability
Model (Tenure of Ten to Twenty Years)

Difference from 1914 Birth Cohort, Linear Probability
Model (Tenure of Twenty Years or More)

Source: Current Population Survey.

age-specific probability that a female worker had been with her employer for at least twenty years was fairly steady between the 1920 and mid-1930s birth cohorts, before rising through the 1950 cohort.

Taken together, the analysis of the change in both mean tenure and the likelihood of long-term employment shows clearly that average tenure has declined and long-term employment has become much less common for males. Among females, average tenure increased slightly from those born in the 1920s to the 1950s before declining among later cohorts. The likelihood of long-term employment for females grew slowly between those born in the 1920s through the 1950s cohorts as well.

This difference in patterns between males and females reflects the common factors reducing tenure for all workers offset for females by their dramatically increased commitment to the labor force over the past half-century. As that increase in commitment among women has slowed, average tenure and the incidence of long-term employment among women have begun to decline. A key conclusion is that the structure of employment in the United States appears to have become less oriented toward long-term jobs. It appears that young workers today will be less likely than their parents to have a "lifetime" job.

Churning: Are There More Very Short-Term Jobs?

The opposite but related pole of the job tenure distribution is short-term jobs. In other research (Farber 1994, 1999), I have shown that one-half of all new jobs (worker-employer matches) end within the first year. As I show in this section, a substantial fraction (around 20 percent) of all jobs have current tenure of less than one year ("new jobs"). Not surprisingly, young workers are more likely than older workers to be in new jobs. High rates of job change among young workers are a natural result of search for a good job or a good match.[12]

Table 3.2 shows the sharp decline in the new-job rate as workers age through their twenties and into their thirties. The new-job rate is slightly higher for females in all age groups, but the general pattern is the same as that for males. This contrast by age raises two interesting questions regarding the decline in mean tenure and long-term employment and how this decline is related to the rate of "churning" in the labor market:

1. Are young workers taking longer to find good (long-lasting) matches or jobs? This would imply an increase in the new-job rate among younger workers.

2. Are older workers having more difficulty finding good matches

Table 3.2   New Job Rate, by Gender, 1973 to 2005

Age	All	Male	Female
Twenty to twenty-nine	0.349	0.335	0.365
Thirty to thirty-nine	0.181	0.162	0.205
Forty to forty-nine	0.124	0.111	0.139
Fifty to fifty-nine	0.090	0.084	0.097
Sixty to sixty-four	0.077	0.075	0.079
All	0.191	0.176	0.206

Source: Current Population Survey.
Note: Based on data for non-self-employed workers age twenty to sixty-four from nineteen CPSs covering the period from 1973 to 2006. Weighted by CPS final sample weights. N = 876,063.

when they lose jobs that may formerly have been lifetime jobs? This would imply an increase in the new-job rate among older workers.

To investigate how the overall new-job rate has changed over time, I estimate age-specific birth-cohort effects using the same approaches used earlier for long-term employment. Figure 3.10 shows that, relative to the 1914 birth cohort, the probability that a male worker has been with his employer for less than one year increased by about six percentage points between the 1914 and 1970 birth cohorts. Women, in contrast, saw no change between the 1914 and 1940 birth cohorts, but the probability then fell by about two and a half percentage points by the 1960 birth cohort before returning to its original level. These patterns mirror those found for mean tenure and for long-term employment.

An implicit constraint in my model is that cohort effects are constant across age groups. Given the role that job change plays in matching and job search early in careers, I estimated separate birth-cohort effects for different age groups. The top graph of figure 3.11 contains differences by birth cohort in the new-job rate relative to the 1949 birth cohort. I estimated this using a sample of workers age twenty to twenty-nine. (The sample includes birth cohorts between 1949 and 1980.) These estimates, which are very similar for males and females, show a sharp *decline* in the new-job rate between the 1949 and 1960 cohorts, followed by an increase through the early 1970s cohorts, with a subsequent decline.

The bottom graph of figure 3.11 contains differences by birth cohort in the new-job rate relative to the 1939 birth cohort, estimated using a sample of workers age thirty to thirty-nine. (This sample includes birth cohorts between 1939 and 1970.) These effects differ substantially from those of workers in their twenties. We see an increase of about 3 percent in the new-job rate for males in their thirties and a decrease of more than 4 percent for females in this age group. The pattern for males suggests that men are job-shopping in their twenties and over time have become less likely to settle into longer-term jobs in their thirties. The pattern for

Figure 3.10   Cohort Effects on the Linear Probability Model (Tenure Less than One Year), by Birth Year, Controlling for Age, Education, Race, and Hispanic Ethnicity

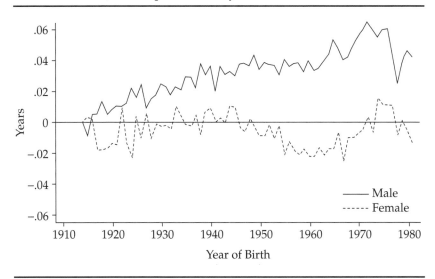

Source: Current Population Survey.

females probably reflects an increase in attachment to the labor force by women as they enter their thirties.

Given that older workers have become less likely to be in long-term jobs, I next investigate how the new-job rate has changed for workers age forty and older (top graph of figure 3.12) and for workers age fifty to sixty-four (bottom graph). Males in both age groups have seen an increased probability of being on a new job. The magnitude of the increase (about two percentage points) is substantial when compared with the overall mean new-job rates for older men in table 3.2. The new-job rate for women in their forties or older shows no consistent pattern.

In general, we see an increase over time for men age thirty and older in the percentage holding new jobs. Part of this increase reflects an extension of the period of job-shopping early in their careers, and part of it reflects the increased probabilities of jobs ending later in careers. Women, in contrast, see little change over time, aside from the substantial decline for women in their thirties, which probably reflects the fact that women have been more likely in recent years to remain in the labor force at that age.

Conclusion

Long-term employment relationships in the United States, while not a thing of the past, are not as dominant as they once were. Males age

Figure 3.11   Cohort Effects on the Linear Probability Model (Tenure Less than One Year), by Birth Year, Controlling for Age, Education, Race, and Hispanic Ethnicity

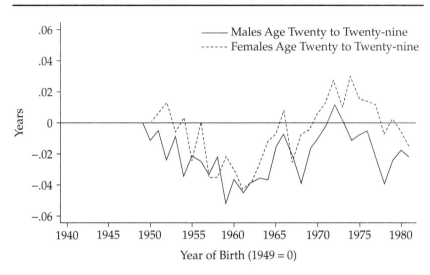

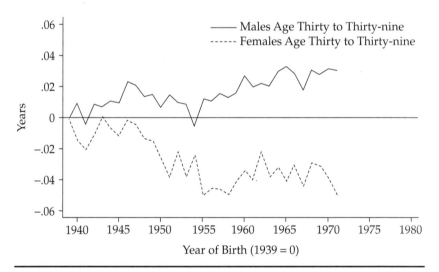

Source: Current Population Survey.

thirty-five to sixty-four in recent birth cohorts (around 1965) are almost twenty percentage points less likely to be in ten-year jobs as males in the same age range born around 1920. Similarly, forty-five- to sixty-four-year-old males in recent birth cohorts (around 1955) are about twelve

Figure 3.12   Cohort Effects on the Linear Probability Model (Tenure Less than One Year), by Birth Year, Controlling for Age, Education, Race, and Hispanic Ethnicity

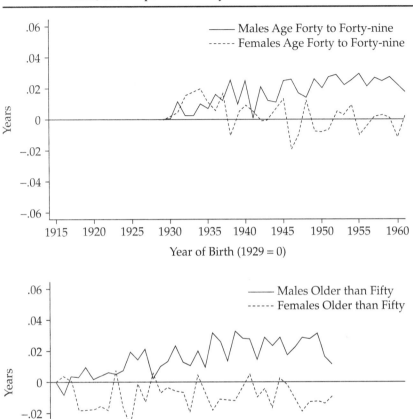

Source: Current Population Survey.

percentage points less likely to be in twenty-year jobs as males in the same age range born around 1920.

There has always been a high level of turnover for young workers (under age thirty), as reflected in the new-job rate (the fraction of jobs with tenure of less than one year), both male and female. However, even as male workers age into their thirties, they have become less likely to settle into longer-term jobs. In contrast, females in their thirties have become more likely to stay in their jobs.

The decline in all measures of tenure and long-term employment for males more accurately reflects the changing nature of the employment relationship than does the less obvious pattern for females. This is because changes in the distribution of tenure for women are a mix of common (across genders) changes in the structure of employment relationships and changes in labor supply decisions over time that are specific to females. On this basis, I conclude that the nature of the employment relationship in the United States has changed substantially in ways that make jobs less secure and workers more mobile.

The reasons for these changes are unclear and beg further research. One possibility is that the move away from long-term employment reflects less demand by employers for a stable labor force, perhaps owing to increased competitive pressure. What is clear is that young workers today should not look forward to the same type of "company man" career experienced by their parents.

Appendix: The CPS Data on Employer Tenure

At irregular intervals, the Census Bureau has appended mobility supplements to the January or February Current Population Surveys. The years in which they did so include 1951, 1963, 1966, 1968, 1973, 1978, 1981, 1983, 1987, 1991, and the even years from 1996 to 2006. These supplements contain information on how long workers have been continuously employed by their current employer, and the supplement questions are asked of all eight CPS rotation groups. However, only the supplements since 1973 are available in machine-readable form. Information on job durations is also available in pension and benefit supplements to the CPS in May 1979, May 1981, May 1983, May 1988, and April 1993. These supplements contain information on how long workers have been working for their current employer, and their questions are asked of four of the eight CPS rotation groups. Finally, information on job durations is available in the Continuous and Alternative Employment Arrangement Supplements (CAEAS) to the CPS in February 1995, 1997, 1999, 2001, and 2005. In total, there are twenty-one CPS supplements with information on employer tenure available in machine-readable form over the period from 1973 to 2006, and my analysis relies on these data.

A question of data comparability over time arises because of a significant change in the wording of the central question about job duration.

The early mobility supplements (1951 to 1981) asked workers what year they started working for their current employer. In later mobility supplements (1983 to 2006), in all of the pension and benefit supplements (1979 to 1993), and in all of the CAEASs (1995 to 2005), workers were asked how many years they had worked for their current employer. If the respondents were perfectly literal and accurate in their responses (a strong and unreasonable assumption), then these two questions would yield identical information (up to the error due to the fact that calendar years may not be perfectly aligned with the count of years since the worker started with his or her current employer). But responses are not completely accurate, and this is best illustrated by the heaping of responses at round numbers. The empirical distribution function has spikes at five-year intervals, and there are even larger spikes at ten-year intervals. In the early question, the spikes occur at round calendar years (1960, 1965, and so on). Later the spikes occur at round counts of years (five, ten, fifteen, and so on).

There are also subtle but potentially important changes in the wording of the key questions even within these surveys. All of the mobility supplements since 1983 ask individuals how long they have worked *continuously* for their current employer. However, neither the pension and benefit supplements nor the CAEASs include the word "continuously." The May 1979 and 1983 pension and benefit supplements ask individuals how long they have worked for their current employer and specify that if there was an interruption greater than one year, to count only the time since the interruption. The May 1988 and April 1993 supplements and the CAEAS ask individuals how long they have worked for their current employer without any reference to interruptions or continuity. Thus, the mobility supplements may yield shorter tenures than the pension and benefit supplements and the CAEAS owing to the requirement of continuity in the former. And the early two pension and benefit supplements may yield shorter durations than the later two pension and benefit supplements owing to the consideration given in the early supplements to long interruptions. I make no explicit allowance for these differences in my analysis, but they should be kept in mind when interpreting the results.

With the exception of jobs of less than one year, all of the supplements before the February 1996 mobility supplement collect data in integer form on the number of years employed. For jobs of less than one year, the mobility supplements report the number of months employed, while the pension and benefit supplements report only the fact that the job was less than one year old. The February 1996 and later mobility supplements ask workers how long they have worked continuously for their current employer and accept a numerical response where the worker

Table 3A.1   Distribution of Age by Birth Cohort

Birth Decade	Number of Cases	Mean	Standard Deviation	Minimum	Maximum
1914 to 1919	12,016	59.32	3.18	54	64
1920 to 1929	50,797	54.74	4.90	44	64
1930 to 1939	85,342	50.51	7.85	34	64
1940 to 1949	177,966	44.86	9.89	24	64
1950 to 1959	246,830	37.85	9.43	20	56
1960 to 1969	181,172	32.91	6.53	20	46
1970 to 1980	108,593	26.44	4.05	20	36
All	862,716	39.28	11.42	20	64

Source: Current Population Survey.
Note: Based on data for all workers age twenty to sixty-four (excluding self-employed workers) from twenty CPS supplements spanning 1973 to 2005. Weighted by CPS final

specifies the time units. The 1995 to 2005 CAEASs ask workers how long they have worked for their current employer and accept a numerical response where the worker specifies the time units. Virtually all workers in jobs even five years old and all workers in jobs ten years old or older report job durations in years.

One reasonable interpretation of the integer report of the number of years is that workers round to the nearest integer when they report jobs of durations of at least one year. This ignores the heaping of the tenure distribution at multiples of five and ten years. For example, a response of ten years would imply tenure greater than or equal to nine and a half years and less than ten and a half years. To create a smooth tenure variable, I assume that the distribution of job tenure is uniform in these one-year intervals. Given a reported tenure of T years, I replace T by T $0.5 + u$ where u is a random variable distributed uniformly on the unit interval. Where reported tenure is zero years, I assume that tenure is uniformly distributed between zero and one and define tenure as u. Given that jobs are more likely to end earlier in the first year than later in the first year, this is not completely accurate (Farber 1994). However, the measures I use in my analysis are not affected by this representation. Where reported tenure is exactly one year, I assume that true tenure is uniformly distributed between 1 and 1.5 and define tenure as $1 + u/2$.

My sample consists of 876,063 persons age twenty to sixty-four (excluding self-employed workers) from the twenty-one CPS supplements spanning 1973 to 2006. The self-employed are not included because the concept of employer tenure is less clear for the self-employed, and in any case, the CPS supplements do not contain consistent information on tenure for the self-employed.

I classify workers by year of birth, and I limit my analysis to birth cohorts for which the earliest and latest observations are at least five calendar years apart. As a result, my sample includes workers born between 1914 and 1981. Workers born between 1909 and 1913 were sampled in 1973 but in no other years. Workers born between 1982 and 1986 were sampled in different CPS supplements between 2002 and 2006, but none five years apart. Elimination of workers in these birth cohorts results in the elimination of 2,894 individuals born between 1909 and 1913 (0.33 percent of the overall sample) and 10,453 individuals born between 1981 and 1985 (1.19 percent of the overall sample). Individuals from the early cohorts who were eliminated were age sixty to sixty-four at the time of sampling. Individuals from the late cohorts who were eliminated were age twenty to twenty-four at the time of sampling.

The resulting sample contains 862,716 workers (excluding self-employed workers) age twenty to sixty-four born between 1941 and 1981 from the twenty-one CPS supplements from 1973 to 2006.

To summarize these data, I classify workers by decade of birth; workers born in 1980 and 1981 (age twenty-six and twenty-five, respectively, in 2006, the last sampled year) are classified as belonging to the 1970s birth cohort. My analysis sample includes workers born in the seven decades from the 1910s through the 1970s. Table 3A.1 contains summary statistics on age by decade of birth. The earliest birth cohorts have predominantly older workers, and the more recent birth cohorts have predominantly younger workers. No single birth cohort covers the entire age spectrum.

Notes

1. These statistics are taken from U.S. Bureau of Labor Statistics (BLS), series ID LNU02000000. This is the civilian employment level derived from the CPS for workers age sixteen and older.

2. The manufacturing share of nonfarm employment has been falling for over fifty years. Manufacturing's share was 30.9 percent in 1950 and fell to 10.4 percent in 2006. These statistics are taken from U.S. BLS series ID CEU00000001 and CEU30000001, derived from the Current Employment Statistics (CES) payroll data.

3. The proceedings of this conference were published in David Neumark (2000), and a number of the papers were published in the *Journal of Labor Economics* 17(4, pt. 2, October 1999).

4. Means are calculated weighted by CPS final sample weights. The 1914 to 1919 birth cohort and the 1970s birth cohort are omitted for clarity of presentation and because of the narrow range of ages covered by these cohorts.

5. I do not estimate this model using absolute tenure because the implicit as-

sumption in that case would be that absolute cohort effects on mean tenure are constant across ages and, equivalently, that absolute age effects on mean tenure are constant across birth cohorts. This is clearly not plausible on inspection of figure 3.1, given the fact that younger workers have very low levels of tenure.

6. I computed (separately for men and women) weighted mean tenure for each age/birth-year combination and regressed these measures on a complete set of age and birth-year fixed effects. This is essentially the main-effects model in equation 3.1 aggregated to the cell level. The R-squared from the mean regression is 0.98 for both men and women.

7. Mean tenures in my analysis sample for the four educational categories are 7.3 years (less than twelve years), 7.4 years (twelve years), 6.5 years (thirteen to fifteen years), and 7.3 years (sixteen or more years).

8. The estimates of the immigrant effect on mean log tenure (a) is -0.211 (standard error = 0.008) for males and -0.185 (standard error = 0.009) for females.

9. Only 3.6 percent of white non-Hispanics are immigrants, while more than 50 percent of Hispanics (white and nonwhite) are immigrants. In addition, the fraction of nonwhite non-Hispanics who are immigrants rose from 18.7 percent in 1995 to 28.2 percent in 2006. The rising overall immigrant share over this period is reflected in the growing share of Hispanics and nonwhites in the labor force. The Hispanic share of employment in my sample increased from 9.0 percent in 1995 to 13.4 percent in 2006, and the nonwhite share of employment increased from 15.2 to 17.2 percent over the same period.

10. I do not include workers born after 1966 because they have not been observed in my sample over a five-year period at the age of at least thirty-five.

11. I do not include workers born after 1956 because they have not been observed in my sample over a five-year period at the age of at least forty-five.

12. Kenneth Burdett (1978) presents a model of job search with this implication. Boyan Jovanovic (1979) presents a model of matching in the labor market with the same implication.

References

Abraham, Katharine G., and James L. Medoff. 1984. "Length of Service and Layoffs in Union and Nonunion Work Groups." *Industrial and Labor Relations Review* 38(1): 87–97.

Burdett, Kenneth. 1978. "A Theory of Employee Job Search and Quit Rates." *American Economic Review* 68(1): 212–20.

Diebold, Francis X., David Neumark, and Daniel Polsky. 1994. "Job Stability in the United States." Working paper 4859. Cambridge, Mass.: National Bureau of Economic Research.

———. 1996. "Comment of Kenneth A. Swinnerton and Howard Wial: Is Job Stability Declining in the U.S. Economy?" *Industrial and Labor Relations Review* 49(2): 348–52.

Farber, Henry S. 1994. "The Analysis of Interfirm Worker Mobility." *Journal of Labor Economics* 12(4): 554–93.

———. 1998. "Are Lifetime Jobs Disappearing? Job Duration in the United

States, 1973." In *Labor Statistics Measurement Issues*, edited by John Halti-
wanger, Marilyn Manser, and Robert Topel. Chicago, Ill.: University of
Chicago Press.

———. 1999. "Mobility and Stability: The Dynamics of Job Change in Labor Markets." In *The Handbook of Labor Economics*, vol. 3B, edited by Orley Ashenfelter
and David Card. Amsterdam: North-Holland Publishing.

———. 2000. "Trends in Long-Term Employment in the United States:
1979–1996." In *Global Competition and the American Employment Landscape as We
Enter the Twenty-first Century: Proceedings of New York University Fifty-second
Annual Conference on Labor*, edited by Samuel Estreicher. Frederick, Md.:
Kluwer Law International.

Gottschalk, Peter, and Robert Moffitt. 1999. "Changes in Job Instability and Insecurity Using Monthly Survey Data: Has Job Stability Declined Yet? New Evidence for the 1990s." *Journal of Labor Economics* 17(4, pt. 2): S91–126.

Hall, Robert E. 1982. "The Importance of Lifetime Jobs in the U.S. Economy."
American Economic Review 72: 716–24.

Jaeger, David A., and Ann Huff Stevens. 1999. "Is Job Stability in the United
States Falling? Reconciling Trends in the Current Population Survey and Panel
Study of Income Dynamics." *Journal of Labor Economics* 17(4, pt. 2): S1–28.

Jovanovic, Boyan. 1979. "Job Matching and the Theory of Turnover." *Journal of
Political Economy* 87(5, pt. 2): 972–90.

Neumark, David, editor. 2000. *On the Job: Is Long-Term Employment a Thing of the
Past?* New York: Russell Sage Foundation.

Neumark, David, Daniel Polsky, and Daniel Hansen. 1999. "Has Job Stability Declined Yet? New Evidence for the 1990s." *Journal of Labor Economics* 17(4, pt. 2):
S29–64.

Rose, Stephen J. 1995. "Declining Job Security and the Professionalization of Opportunity." Research report 95-04. Washington: National Commission for Employment Policy.

Stevens, Ann Huff. 2005. "The More Things Change the More They Stay the
Same: Trends in Long-Term Employment in the United States, 1969–2002."
Working paper 11878. Cambridge, Mass.: National Bureau of Economic Re-
search.

Stewart, Jay. 2002. "Recent Trends in Job Stability and Job Security: Evidence
from the March CPS." Working paper 356. Washington: U.S. Bureau of Labor
Statistics.

Swinnerton, Kenneth, and Howard Wial. 1995. "Is Job Stability Declining in the
U.S. Economy?" *Industrial and Labor Relations Review* 48(2): 293–304.

———. 1996. "Is Job Stability Declining in the U.S. Economy? Reply to Diebold,
Neumark, and Polsky." *Industrial and Labor Relations Review* 49(2): 352–55.

Valletta, Robert. 1999. "Declining Job Security." *Journal of Labor Economics* 17(4, pt.
2): S170–97.

Chapter 4

Health Insurance and the Transition to Adulthood

HELEN LEVY

About one in six Americans had no health insurance in 2005 (De-Navas-Walt, Proctor, and Lee 2006). Not surprisingly, the unin-sured tend to be poorer than the insured (Institute of Medicine 2001). They are also younger. In fact, one-half of all uninsured adults are between the ages of eighteen and thirty-four (author's calculations based on DeNavas-Walt et al. 2006, table 8). Even though young adults have the highest rates of uninsurance of any age group, very little research has focused on their health insurance coverage.[1] Nor has any of the research on the transition to adulthood examined health insurance coverage. This is surprising because health insurance seems like an excellent marker of adulthood, given that it is closely tied to other frequently studied out-comes, such as employment stability. Most teenagers are covered as de-pendents on a parent's private insurance policy; Medicaid covers a sub-stantial fraction as well. But at some point eligibility for this coverage runs out, and young adults must find health insurance on their own. This passage may be rocky, either because of problems with insurance markets or because of conditions that characterize the transition to adulthood, such as weak attachment to the labor force.

Health insurance coverage in the United States is closely linked to em-ployment, with health insurance more likely to be provided as a fringe benefit of a long-term, full-time job (Farber and Levy 2000). Of course, these are exactly the jobs that young adults may take some time to find (for details, see Yates 2005). We also know that the transition from school to sta-ble employment can take a surprisingly long time. For example, Julie Yates (2005) documents that the median worker takes nearly a year after first leaving school to start a job that will last for at least one year. For the median high school dropout, it takes more than three years. The consequences of high job mobility for health insurance coverage are clear: nonworkers are much more likely than workers to be uninsured. Even among workers, low-tenure jobs are much less likely to provide health insurance (Farber and Levy 2000). It may be, then, that this period of financial instability is the reason for higher rates of uninsurance among young adults.

On the other hand, markets for health insurance may suffer from imperfections that lead young adults, who are relatively healthy, to face prices for insurance that are actuarially unfair, resulting in lower demand for coverage. This could occur either because of information asymmetries in the insurance market or because of regulation-induced distortions in the market. In the first scenario, a classic case of "adverse selection," insurance companies may have less information than consumers about risk, and therefore the low-risk individuals (in this case, young adults) are not fully insured (or in this case, they are uninsured) (Rothschild and Stiglitz 1976). In the second scenario, community rating requirements may limit insurers' ability to vary premiums by individual, which results in the same problem as information asymmetries: young adults face actuarially unfair prices and therefore do not buy insurance. This could also be caused by the de facto community rating that employers appear to practice (Pauly and Herring 1999). However, James Cardon and Igal Hendel (2001), in the only study that tests directly for adverse selection in health insurance markets, find no evidence of adverse selection.[2]

This chapter analyzes the trajectories of young adults' health insurance coverage and offers some insight into the reasons why so many young adults experience gaps in coverage. Understanding how much "financial immaturity" (lack of job stability, for example) can explain high rates of uninsurance among young adults has important implications for public policy. If financial immaturity explains young adults' failure to obtain coverage, then policies aimed at making coverage available to them, such as increasing the maximum age of eligibility for dependent coverage, may be met with a blank stare reminiscent of adolescence. Mandates or further expansions of public coverage, both of which take the decision about coverage out of the hands of the young adults, may be necessary to cover them in this case.

The chapter begins by describing the life-cycle profiles of health insurance coverage for men and women from childhood through age thirty-five. I also estimate the flows between different types of coverage (private, public, none) to shed light on the dynamics of gaps in coverage: where do all those uninsured young adults come from? The overall picture that emerges is one in which lack of health insurance is part of a more general lack of financial maturity. This is not the whole picture, however, given that coverage rates among young adults remain significantly lower than for individuals at other ages, even after controlling for employment and other markers of financial maturity. The residual effect of young adulthood on coverage may therefore be due to differences by age in other characteristics that I have not measured, such as risk preferences, or it may be due to adverse selection in health insurance markets.

I also investigate whether the transition to adult health insurance has changed over time. Given the close link between employment and health insurance, the changing nature of the labor market facing young adults—for example, the increased job churning documented by Henry Farber in this volume—may be causing young adults in more recent years to take longer to get their own insurance. Indeed, I find that young adults born in the 1980s are more likely to be uninsured than those born in the 1960s and 1970s. Moreover, these changes are the result of a delay in obtaining "adult" insurance coverage (in one's own name or through a spouse) rather than any decline in public coverage or coverage by a parent's policy. In other words, the "changing timetable for adulthood" discussed by Frank Furstenberg, Rubén Rumbaut, and Richard Settersten (2005) appears to apply to health insurance too.

Data

The data for the analysis come from two different sources: the Survey of Income and Program Participation (SIPP) (1996 and 2001 panels) and the Annual Social and Economic Supplement (ASEC) to the March Current Population Survey (CPS). After restricting the sample to account for nonresponse, as detailed in the appendix, my sample includes 33,443 individuals age fifteen to thirty-five. Health insurance coverage includes whether the individual has any and, if so, whether it is from a parent's private policy, a spouse's private policy, the individual's own private policy, or a public program (Medicaid or the State Children's Health Insurance Program [SCHIP]). An individual with none of these is uninsured.

My analysis of changes over time relies on the ASEC supplement to the March CPS from 1989 through 2006. In any one year, the March CPS includes 40,000 to 60,000 respondents age fifteen to thirty-five. Although the structure of the survey and the wording of the questions differ from the SIPP (see appendix for details), the CPS also collects information that allows me to construct a measure of health insurance coverage similar to the one based on the SIPP: parental coverage, own coverage, spouse's coverage, public coverage, uninsured.

Life-Cycle Profiles of Health Insurance Coverage Through Age Thirty-five

How does health insurance coverage evolve as youth mature into adults? Figures 4.1 (males) and 4.2 (females) show that coverage through

Figure 4.1   Sources of Health Insurance Coverage by Age: Mean Age Birth to Thirty-five

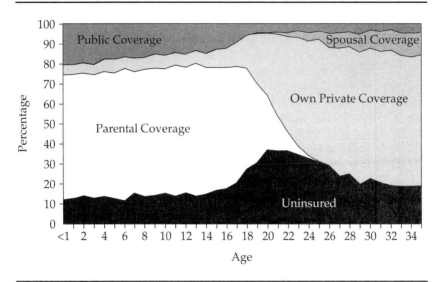

Source: SIPP, 1996 and 2001 panels.

a parent's policy begins to decline after age seventeen, and that by age twenty-four only a negligible fraction of adults are still covered by their parent's policy. Figure 4.3 presents trends in parental coverage separately for those who are still in school full-time and for those who are not. The decline in parental coverage starts about four years later for those who remain enrolled in school full-time than for nonstudents—at age twenty-one rather than age seventeen. Interestingly, the declines in parental coverage for nonstudents begin before the typical maximum age of eligibility for nonstudents (eighteen or nineteen), suggesting that the maximum age cutoff may affect fewer young adults than we might think. At about the same age that parental coverage drops off, young adults begin to obtain their own private health insurance policies. Rates of their own private coverage for both men and women increase sharply between the ages of seventeen and twenty-three (figures 4.1 and 4.2), at which point women's coverage levels off while men's continues to increase, until it levels off around age twenty-eight. Spouses are an important source of coverage for women starting in their early twenties and throughout the rest of their adult lives. Men rely on spousal coverage as well, but it is a less important source of coverage, never covering more than 15 percent of men and covering fewer than 10 percent of men under the age of thirty. The male-female differentials in their own private coverage and spousal coverage offset one another so that overall, rates of private insurance coverage are nearly identical for men and women.

Figure 4.2   Sources of Health Insurance Coverage by Age: Women Age Birth to Thirty-five

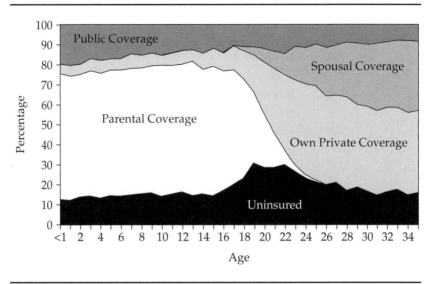

Source: SIPP, 1996 and 2001 panels.

Figure 4.3   Probability of Parental Health Insurance, by Age, Sex, and School Enrollment

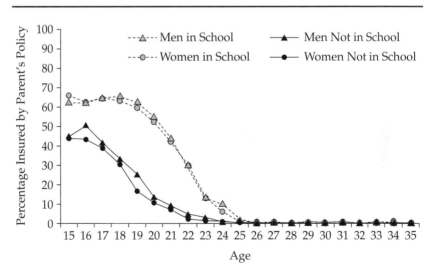

Source: SIPP, 1996 and 2001 panels.

Looking at private coverage from any source—whether the policy is held by oneself, a spouse, or a parent—shows that there is a gap between when parental coverage declines and one's own or spousal coverage increases. This results in a pronounced dip in the probability of private health insurance coverage for both men and women between the ages of eighteen and twenty-seven. For men, this dip is exacerbated by a drop in the probability of public coverage that also occurs around age eighteen, presumably as a result of Medicaid program rules. Thirteen percent of eighteen-year-old young men have public insurance; by the time they are twenty-one, only 4 percent do. The decline in public coverage for women is much more gradual and does not really begin until age twenty-two, probably because women with children have greater access to public insurance.

The net effect is that the probability of being uninsured peaks between the ages of eighteen and thirty for both men and women, as shown in figure 4.4. At age seventeen, about 20 percent of men and women are uninsured. By age twenty-two, 36 percent of men and 30 percent of women are uninsured. By age thirty, the fraction of women who are uninsured has dropped to 16 percent and remains relatively flat through the remainder of their working lives. For men, the fraction uninsured drops to about 18 percent by age thirty-three and remains reasonably flat thereafter.

Figure 4.4   Probability of Having No Health Insurance at a Point in Time, by Age and Sex

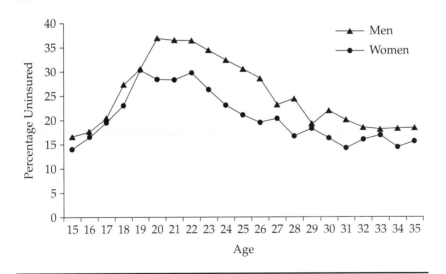

Source: SIPP, 1996 and 2001 panels.

Figure 4.5   Probability of Being Uninsured at One or More Waves in the Next Two Years, by Age at Wave 1

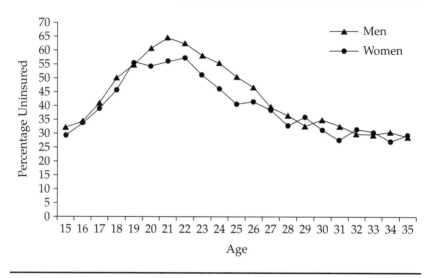

Source: SIPP, 1996 and 2001 panels.

The risk of being uninsured is even higher if, instead of looking at a point in time, we look across a period of time. Figure 4.5 shows that more than half of all young men age eighteen to twenty-five will be uninsured at some point over a two-year span, and that two-thirds of young men will be uninsured at some time between ages twenty-one and twenty-three. For women, the risk is slightly lower. The maximum risk of being uninsured at some point in a two-year window is 58 percent at age twenty-two, as opposed to 65 percent at age twenty-one for men. The median uninsured young adult lacks coverage for about sixteen months, according to the SIPP data (figure 4.6).

Flows Into and Out of Insurance

Figures 4.1 and 4.2 suggest that coverage rates among young adults are so low because they lose parental coverage or lose public coverage and fail to pick up the slack for themselves. Examining year-to-year transitions confirms that this is in fact what is happening. Figures 4.7 and 4.8 present a summary of flows into and out of insurance for men and women, respectively. The line running over the bars is the increase in the fraction uninsured that will occur in the upcoming year. For example, the peak of

Figure 4.6   How the Median Remaining Length of an Uninsured Spell Changes with Age

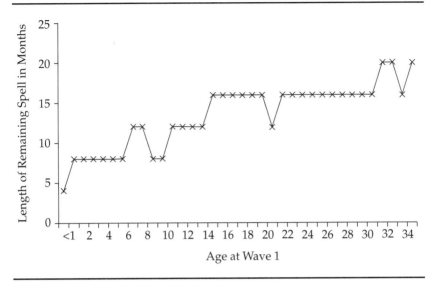

Source: SIPP, 1996 and 2001 panels.

0.125 at age nineteen in the line in figure 4.7 reflects the fact that the fraction of men who are uninsured will increase by twelve and a half percentage points between ages nineteen and twenty. The bars show where that increase will come from, and the white and gray bars above the horizontal axis represent the flow out of different types of insurance. For example, the chart shows that between ages nineteen and twenty, 10 percent of men in the sample will lose parental coverage and become uninsured; 4 percent will lose public coverage and become uninsured; and 2.6 percent will lose their own private coverage and become uninsured. At the same time, a few—about 4 percent—will gain insurance. This is shown in the black bar below the horizontal axis. The sum of these flows into and out of insurance is the net change in insurance coverage.

The analysis in figures 4.7 and 4.8 is pretty much what we would expect given how the distribution of coverage evolves with age. Young adults lose parental and private coverage in large numbers in their late teens; several years later they begin to get their own insurance coverage (primarily private coverage, though this is not shown in the figure). The spike in the fraction without any coverage that is evident in figure 4.4 occurs because of the lag between these two sets of events.

Figure 4.7   Flows Into and Out of Uninsurance, by Age: Men

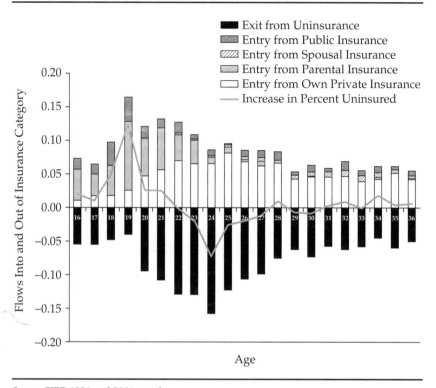

Source: SIPP, 1996 and 2001 panels.

Which Characteristics Explain Lack of Insurance?

To determine the extent to which characteristics of young adults explain their low rates of coverage, I estimate multivariate regression models where the dependent variable is equal to one if an individual is uninsured and zero if he or she is not as a function of age and other characteristics.[3] The models are estimated separately for men and women. I begin by estimating average rates of no insurance at each age without controls for any of the factors that might influence coverage, such as employment (the no-covariates model). Then for each group I estimate the model eleven times using the following sets of control variables:

1.   Whether the individual works full-time or part-time, is in school full-time, or none of the above (the omitted category)

Figure 4.8   Flows Into and Out of Uninsurance, by Age: Women

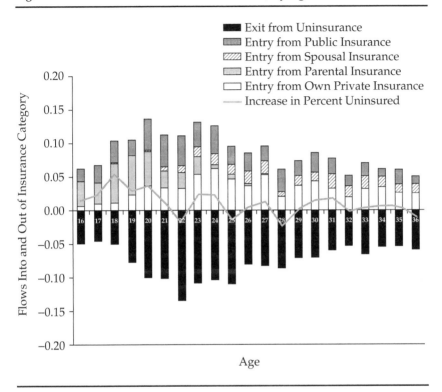

Source: SIPP, 1996 and 2001 panels.

2. The individual's family income relative to the poverty threshold

3. Marital status

4. Marital status and separate indicators for being a single or married parent

5. A set of variables reflecting the activity of the individual's spouse (full-time work, part-time work, full-time school, none of the above [omitted])

6. Race (black, other nonwhite) and Hispanic ethnicity

7. For workers, the size of the establishment where they work

8. Homeownership

9. Living with parents and the interaction between that living arrangement and being a full-time student

10. Whether the individual works full-time, works part-time, is in school full-time, or none of the above (the omitted category), plus an indicator for whether the person has more than one job and variables reflecting job tenure on the main job

11. A "kitchen sink" regression including all of the covariates listed here

I also determine what effect, if any, different controls have on the age profile of coverage by comparing the average rate of uninsurance at each age with the "adjusted" rate at each age based on the regression models.[4]

For men, some of the covariates—most notably, income and establishment size—explain very little of the spike in uninsurance. (Complete results for men from the no-covariates and all-covariates models are reported in table 4A.2.) Other covariates, however, explain quite a bit of the age profile of coverage, and all of the covariates taken together account for one-half of the peak in the probability of being uninsured among young men. For example, without adding controls, the peak of uninsurance (at age twenty-three) is 19.4 percentage points higher than at age sixteen, but only 9.3 percentage points higher when all the controls are added. The variables that are most important are full-time school, full-time work, part-time work, plus job tenure for full-time workers. Figure 4.9 illustrates the importance of these characteristics by comparing the fraction of men who are uninsured at each age (the solid line) with the fraction who would be uninsured if their other characteristics (income, employment, and so on) were the same at each age, based on the regression models.[5] It is clear from figure 4.9 that while some of the peak in lack of coverage among young men is due to their other characteristics, even after we control for these other characteristics, young men are more likely than either teenage boys or older men to be uninsured.

The analysis for women is similar, although the spike is smaller and the amount of it that can be explained by covariates is larger (see figure 4.10). There are also some differences, compared with men, in which covariates matter. Family income, marital status, and spouse's employment explain as much of the spike for young women as their own employment information. The general pattern, however, is similar to that for men: covariates reduce the spike, but the probability of being uninsured remains significantly elevated in young adulthood for women even when we have controlled for these other attributes.

To summarize: other characteristics such as employment and job tenure can explain half of the spike in uninsurance in young adulthood for men and slightly more than half of the spike for women. This means that financial immaturity as measured by income, employment, and other characteristics explains about half of why young adults have unusually low rates of health insurance coverage. Although there is still room for insurance market problems like adverse selection to explain low rates of

Figure 4.9   Can Observable Characteristics Explain the Spike in Uninsurance for Men?

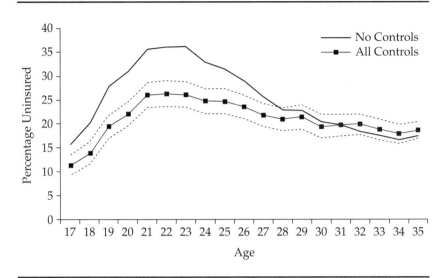

Source: SIPP, 1996 and 2001 panels.

Figure 4.10   Can Observable Characteristics Explain the Spike in Uninsurance for Women?

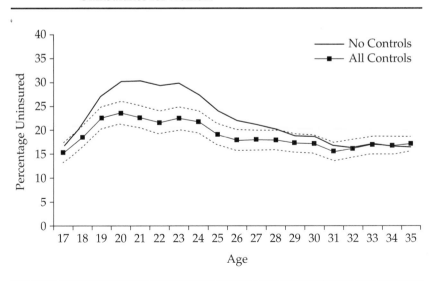

Source: SIPP, 1996 and 2001 panels.

coverage among young adults, a more general lack of financial maturity is clearly a very important part of why young adults are uninsured.

Analysis of Changes in Insurance Coverage Across Time

Next I turn to the CPS for an analysis of whether the transition to adult health insurance has changed over time. Figure 4.11 shows that each successive birth cohort (those born in the 1960s, 1970s, and 1980s) has a higher probability of being uninsured. Moreover, the peak of uninsurance occurs a year later for the young adults born in the 1970s and 1980s than for those born in the 1960s—at age twenty-two instead of twenty-one.[6] Figure 4.12 shows that there has been essentially no change in when young adults lose coverage from their parents' policy. If anything, the two more recent cohorts are slightly more likely to be covered in their early twenties than are those born in the 1960s. Results for public coverage (not shown) show very little change across cohorts in the fraction of young adults with public coverage, so this is not an important factor in the change in coverage across cohorts. Rather, it appears that changes in gaining one's own coverage as an adult drive the shift in the probability of being uninsured (figure 4.13). On average, each successive cohort acquires

Figure 4.11   Probability of Having No Health Insurance, by Age and Birth Cohort

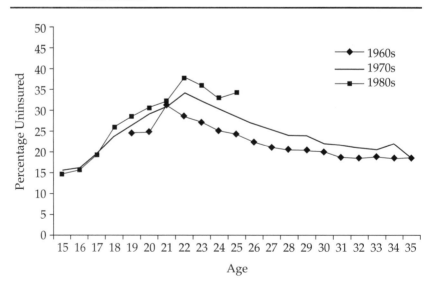

Figure 4.12   Probability of Having Parental Health Insurance Coverage, by Age and Birth Cohort

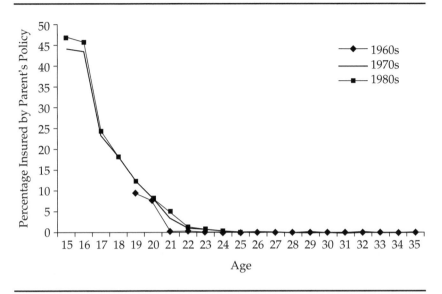

Source: March CPS, 1989 to 2006.

Figure 4.13   Probability of Having Own or Spouse's Health Insurance, by Age and Birth Cohort

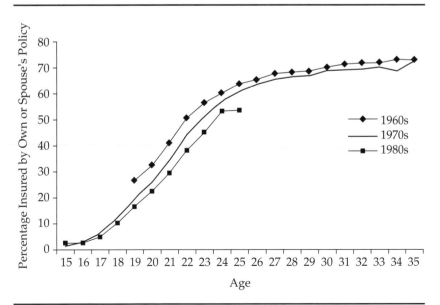

Source: March CPS, 1989 to 2006.

adult health insurance (private coverage in one's own name or through a spouse) one year later than the last cohort.[7] It appears that twenty-three is the new twenty-two, which was itself the new twenty-one. This is consistent with the increased job instability in more recent cohorts documented by Henry Farber in this volume. These shifts in timing may not be as large as some of those associated with other markers of the transition to adulthood, such as establishing one's own home or having children. But the "changing timetable for adulthood" discussed by Furstenberg and his colleagues (2005) appears to apply to health insurance too.

Conclusion and Policy Implications

To recap the results of this analysis:

1. There is a sharp peak in the probability of being uninsured in young adulthood, when individuals lose parental or public coverage but have not yet obtained their own adult coverage.

2. About half of this peak can be explained by controlling for employment and other characteristics such as job tenure, marital status, and family income.

3. The peak is slightly larger and occurs slightly later for more recent cohorts of young adults.

4. The change across time is driven by more recent cohorts taking longer to get their own insurance rather than by any change in patterns of losing public or parental coverage.

These results leave unanswered a number of questions that should be a high priority for future research. The first issue is finding a definitive answer to the question of how important health insurance market failure is in explaining lack of coverage. My results suggest that one-half of the lack of coverage among young adults is due to employment instability and other characteristics rather than market imperfections. This suggests that public policy toward the uninsured should not focus exclusively on correcting problems in insurance markets, since this would miss a lot of what is causing young adults to be uninsured. Whether adverse selection plays any role in explaining young adults' unusually low rates of insurance coverage remains to be determined. Another important question that remains unanswered is how much of a threat lack of coverage poses to young adults' health and financial security. How likely are catastrophic health events among uninsured young adults, and what consequences do they have? Understanding the consequences of lack of coverage among young adults will help determine how urgent the search for remedies should be.

Even without answering these larger questions, the results presented in this chapter have implications for public policy. The importance of stable employment to young adults' health insurance coverage suggests that one way to expand coverage for this group would be to facilitate a smoother transition to the labor force and reduce employment instability. However, high rates of job mobility for young workers are not necessarily undesirable per se and may even be desirable if they result in higher-quality job matches. Any gains in coverage in young adulthood associated with reduced job mobility would have to be weighed against the possibility of poorer job matches in the long run.

The results also speak to a number of other policies that have been proposed to increase rates of health insurance coverage among young adults, such as (1) requiring students to obtain coverage through their colleges or universities, (2) extending eligibility for Medicaid and SCHIP beyond age eighteen; and (3) extending the age of eligibility for dependent coverage on parental policies (see Collins et al. 2006). Each of these policies would reach some, but not all, uninsured young adults. For example, 17 percent of uninsured twentysomethings in the SIPP are enrolled in school full-time; an additional 6 percent are enrolled part-time. A mandate that students obtain insurance would reach these young adults, but not the majority of the uninsured in this age group. Extending eligibility for public coverage to later ages would probably reach a different subset of young adults.

Several states have recently extended the maximum age at which children are eligible for dependent coverage. For example, in 2006 Colorado and New York extended this age to twenty-five and New Jersey extended it to thirty (for details, see Collins et al. 2006). Although these policies may help an important subgroup of uninsured young adults, the impact of this policy may be smaller than the policy's supporters predict. The age profiles of parental coverage by school enrollment (figure 4.3) show that coverage begins to drop off well before the current common maximum ages of eighteen for nonstudents and twenty-five for students. That is, if parents already do not want to cover their twenty-three-year-old adult children, they are unlikely to cover their twenty-eight-year-old children just because they are now allowed to do so by law. Of course, evaluating what happens in states that change their laws will be the acid test of the effectiveness of these policies.

It is interesting that two of these three policies involve raising the age at which children are considered adults for purposes of health insurance coverage. An increasing body of research supports the notion that the transition to adulthood is occurring later than it did in the past, and also that expectations about adulthood are changing, as discussed by Richard Settersten, Frank Furstenberg, and Rubén Rumbaut (2005). The results presented in this chapter suggest that health insurance is affected by this trend as well. Viewed in this light, policies that extend the age of eligibility for Medicaid or parental coverage reflect these changing norms. Current policies and insurance market rules may be predicated on an outdated set of expectations that lag behind the new reality of adulthood in the twenty-first century.

Appendix

Survey of Income and Program Participation

The data for the main analysis come from the 1996 and 2001 panels of the Survey of Income and Program Participation (SIPP). The 1996 SIPP panel first interviewed 36,730 households containing 95,315 individuals in March, April, May, or June 1996 and then attempted to reinterview each household every four months for the next four years. The 2001 SIPP panel began with 35,106 households containing 90,408 individuals who were followed for up to three years. The SIPP collects four months' worth of retrospective monthly information at each interview. Because of the well-documented problem of "seam bias," I use data for the fourth reference month only (the month in which the interview actually occurred). "Seam bias" refers to respondents' tendency to report any changes as occurring in the month when a reference period began. For instance, a respondent's status may have changed in the second month of a four-month reference period, but respondents tend to report that they had the same status for the entire period. Thus, transitions in health insurance, employment, and so on, are more likely at the "seams" of the survey.

I restrict my sample for analysis to individuals who provided at least two years of data beginning with wave 1, and I further restrict the sample to data from the first two years for which these individuals were observed. The first restriction reduces the sample of individuals by about one-third, to 185,723 (counting both the 1996 and 2001 panels). The second restriction requires that I throw away additional information on these individuals—up to two years' worth, depending on the panel. Preliminary analyses using the additional observations suggest that the same substantive story emerges if I look at a longer time period. The resulting sample consists of 122,776 individuals in 42,212 households. By construction, I have exactly six observations on each individual. My analysis focuses on children and young adults through age thirty-five. Table 4A.1 shows the distribution of the sample by age at wave 1, sex, and panel.

The SIPP asks about public and private health insurance coverage—whether private insurance is in the respondent's own name, and who the policyholder is if it is not. This enables me to construct a variable reflect-

Table 4A.1   Sample Size by Age and SIPP Panel

Age at Wave 1	1996 Panel		2001 Panel		Total
	Men	Women	Men	Women	
Under one	438	462	382	342	1,624
One	515	491	406	447	1,859
Two	530	500	466	414	1,910
Three	591	563	445	391	1,990
Four	604	584	424	421	2,033
Five	589	558	427	415	1,989
Six	561	596	397	409	1,963
Seven	598	578	421	436	2,033
Eight	582	564	415	461	2,022
Nine	536	552	439	427	1,954
Ten	600	546	466	482	2,094
Eleven	560	506	468	446	1,980
Twelve	552	554	423	433	1,962
Thirteen	552	495	455	417	1,919
Fourteen	506	556	459	384	1,905
Fifteen	578	550	423	387	1,938
Sixteen	507	482	458	384	1,831
Seventeen	424	428	385	348	1,585
Eighteen	403	410	347	341	1,501
Nineteen	404	373	313	319	1,409
Twenty	324	368	283	326	1,301
Twenty-one	338	351	263	304	1,256
Twenty-two	309	349	258	295	1,211
Twenty-three	308	419	292	334	1,353
Twenty-four	329	425	257	317	1,328
Twenty-five	410	516	255	301	1,482
Twenty-six	424	442	299	310	1,475
Twenty-seven	407	435	291	367	1,500
Twenty-eight	420	509	325	361	1,615
Twenty-nine	420	465	348	377	1,610
Thirty	422	555	334	384	1,695
Thirty-one	483	585	317	419	1,804
Thirty-two	530	537	387	369	1,823
Thirty-three	516	580	349	385	1,830
Thirty-four	542	604	388	411	1,945
Thirty-five	547	617	360	427	1,951
Total ages fifteen to thirty-five	9,045	10,000	6,932	7,466	33,443
Total ages birth to thirty-five	17,359	18,105	13,425	13,791	62,680

Source: SIPP, 1996 and 2001 panels.

Table 4A.2   **Regression Results: Effect of Covariates on Age Profile of Uninsurance for Men, Linear Probability Model with Dependent Variable = 1 if Uninsured**

Independent Variables	No-Covariates Model		All-Covariates Model	
	Coefficient	Standard Error	Coefficient	Standard Error
Age (omitted: sixteen)				
Seventeen	−0.011	0.010	−0.052**	0.011
Eighteen	0.035**	0.012	−0.027*	0.012
Nineteen	0.111**	0.013	0.027*	0.013
Twenty	0.143**	0.014	0.054**	0.013
Twenty-one	0.188**	0.014	0.093**	0.014
Twenty-two	0.193**	0.015	0.095**	0.014
Twenty-three	0.194**	0.015	0.093**	0.014
Twenty-four	0.162**	0.015	0.079**	0.013
Twenty-five	0.147**	0.015	0.078**	0.013
Twenty-six	0.123**	0.014	0.067**	0.013
Twenty-seven	0.090**	0.014	0.048**	0.012
Twenty-eight	0.062**	0.013	0.038**	0.012
Twenty-nine	0.061**	0.017	0.045**	0.013
Thirty	0.037*	0.015	0.026*	0.012
Thirty-one	0.030*	0.013	0.027*	0.011
Thirty-two	0.017	0.012	0.028**	0.011
Thirty-three	0.008	0.012	0.014	0.010
Thirty-four	−0.001	0.011	0.006	0.010
Thirty-five	0.007	0.009	0.017*	0.008
Family income relative to poverty threshold (omitted: less than 50 percent)				
50 to 100 percent			−0.030**	0.014
100 to 150 percent			−0.065**	0.014
150 to 200 percent			−0.122**	0.013
200 to 250 percent			−0.197**	0.013
250 to 300 percent			−0.240**	0.013
300 to 350 percent			−0.286**	0.013
350 to 400 percent			−0.297**	0.013
400 percent or more			−0.340**	0.013
Lives with own children			−0.021**	0.008
Single parent			0.020	0.015
Spouse does not work			−0.067**	0.012
Spouse in school full-time			−0.075**	0.020

Table 4A.2   *(Continued)*

Independent Variables	No-Covariates Model		All-Covariates Model	
	Coefficient	Standard Error	Coefficient	Standard Error
Spouse working full-time			−0.084**	0.009
Spouse working part-time			−0.093**	0.010
Establishment size (omitted: nonworker)				
Unknown			0.229**	0.020
Fewer than 25 workers			0.082**	0.013
25 to 99 workers			−0.013	0.013
100 workers or more			−0.066**	0.013
Homeowner			−0.050**	0.006
Lives with parents			0.071**	0.014
Lives with parents and is full-time student			−0.086**	0.019
In school full-time			−0.069**	0.020
Works part-time			0.035**	0.012
Has more than one job			0.066**	0.008
Job tenure if full-time worker			0.000**	0.000
Full-time worker, tenure less than one year			−0.084**	0.007
Hispanic			0.145**	0.010
Black			0.033**	0.009
Other nonwhite race			0.019	0.012
Intercept	0.178**	0.009	0.517**	0.017
Number of observations	89,855		89,855	
Number of individuals	14,999		14,999	
R-squared	0.0252		0.2012	

Source: SIPP, 1996 and 2001 panels.
* significantly different from zero with $p < 0.05$
** significantly different from zero with $p < 0.01$

ing whether the respondent has his or her own private coverage, coverage from a parent, or coverage from a spouse. Individuals with both public and private coverage are counted as having private coverage. The SIPP asks about paid employment during the reference period, whether it was part-time or full-time, and whether the respondent was enrolled in school part-time or full-time during the reference period. My analysis of health insurance coverage by parental education uses the highest education ever reported by either parent of a child in any wave of the survey.

All estimates from the SIPP are weighted using the wave 1 sampling weights.

The Current Population Survey and Annual Social and Economic Supplement

For an analysis of changes in health insurance coverage across cohorts, I use data from the Annual Social and Economic Supplements (ASEC) to the Current Population Survey (CPS) for 1989 through 2006 (the "March supplements"). These supplements contain information on health insurance in the calendar year prior to the survey. Unlike the SIPP, which asks about coverage at a point in time, the CPS asks about coverage at any point during the prior year. Despite the differences between the surveys, a comparison of figure 4.4 and figure 4.12 reveals remarkable similarity in the age profile of the probability of being uninsured across the two surveys. One complication of using the CPS is that a considerable fraction of children and young adults (about 30 percent of respondents age fifteen to nineteen and 10 percent of those in their twenties) have "other private" coverage, the source of which (own employer, parent, or spouse) cannot be determined. The patterns of change across cohorts in figures 4.13 and 4.14 are robust to recategorizing these individuals as covered by parental insurance or covered by their own private insurance.

All estimates from the CPS are weighted using the March supplement sampling weights.

I am grateful to colleagues at the Economic Research Initiative on the Uninsured (ERIU) at the University of Michigan and to members of the MacArthur Foundation Research Network on Transitions to Adulthood for helpful comments and discussions. Financial support for this project from the Robert Wood Johnson Foundation through ERIU is gratefully acknowledged.

Notes

1. Sherry Glied and Mark Stabile (2000, 2001) analyze the health insurance coverage of young men, but the youngest men in their analyses are already

twenty-five. Sara Collins and her colleagues (2006) document the high rates of uninsurance among young adults, especially those who are low-income or do not go on to college after leaving high school. The Institute of Medicine (2001) attributes lack of coverage among young adults to "social, economic and demographic factors" such as family income, employment in small firms, and low-wage jobs, although they do not test the extent to which these factors do in fact explain higher rates of uninsurance among young adults.

2. Tests for adverse selection generally have low power to distinguish between adverse selection and moral hazard. See Pierre-André Chiappori and Bernard Salanié (2000) on empirical tests for adverse selection in general and Jaap Abbring and others (2003) on the difficulty of distinguishing between the two phenomena.

3. Specifically, I estimate the following linear probability model:

$$Unins_{it} = X_{it} \bullet b + \{(\text{age} = 17) \bullet a_{17} + \ldots + (\text{age} = 35) \bullet a_{35}\} + e_{it}$$

where i indexes individuals, t indexes survey waves (six for each individual), and X is the vector of control variables. Standard errors are robust to the presence of multiple observations from each person.

4. That is, I compare the vector of age dummies from the no-covariates model to the age dummies from the models that include covariates.

5. Specifically, the solid line in figure 4.9 represents that vector of age dummies from the no-covariates model, and the line with squares represents the vector of age dummies from the model with all covariates, plus the mean fraction uninsured at age sixteen (the omitted age category). The dashed line represents the 95 percent confidence interval around the age dummies from the model with all covariates. A Hausman test for the equality of the two sets of dummies rejects that they are equal with $p < 0.001$, but the age dummies in the early twenties remain significantly different from zero even in the model with all covariates.

6. Results are not shown separately for men and women because the trends across cohorts for the two groups are similar. The probability of being uninsured is higher for young men than for young women in each cohort.

7. Again, the patterns for men and women are similar across cohorts, so I do not show the results separately.

References

Abbring, Jaap H., Pierre-André Chiappori, James J. Heckman, and Jean Pinquet. 2003. "Adverse Selection and Moral Hazard in Insurance: Can Dynamic Data Help to Distinguish?" *Journal of the European Economic Association* 1(2–3): 512–21.

Cardon, James, and Igal Hendel. 2001. "Asymmetric Information in Health Insurance: Evidence from the National Medical Expenditure Service." *Rand Journal of Economics* 32(3): 408–27.

Chiappori, Pierre-André, and Bernard Salanié. 2000. "Testing for Asymmetric Information in Insurance Markets." *Journal of Political Economy* 108(1): 56–78.

Collins, Sara R., Cathy Schoen, Jennifer L. Kriss, Michelle M. Doty, and Bisundev Mahato. 2006. "Rite of Passage? Why Young Adults Become Uninsured and How New Policies Can Help." Commonwealth Fund issue brief. Originally released May 2003; updated May 24, 2006. Accessed at www.cmwf.org.

DeNavas-Walt, Carmen, Bernadette D. Proctor, and Cheryl Hill Lee. 2006. "Income, Poverty, and Health Insurance Coverage in the United States: 2005." *Current Population Reports* P60-230. Washington: U.S. Government Printing Office for the U.S. Bureau of the Census.

Farber, Henry, and Helen Levy. 2000. "Recent Trends in Employer-Sponsored Health Insurance: Are Bad Jobs Getting Worse?" *Journal of Health Economics* 19(1): 93–119.

Furstenberg, Frank F., Jr., Rubén G. Rumbaut, and Richard A. Settersten Jr. 2005. "On the Frontier of Adulthood: Emerging Themes and New Directions." In *On the Frontier of Adulthood: Theory, Research, and Public Policy*, edited by Richard A. Settersten Jr., Frank F. Furstenberg Jr., and Rubén G. Rumbaut. Chicago, Ill.: University of Chicago Press.

Glied, Sherry, and Mark Stabile. 2000. "Explaining the Decline in Health Insurance Coverage Among Young Men." *Inquiry* 37(3): 295–303.

———. 2001. "Age-Cohort Differences in Employer-Sponsored Health Insurance Coverage." *Health Affairs* 20(1): 184–91.

Institute of Medicine. 2001. *Coverage Matters: Insurance and Health Care*. Washington: National Academies Press.

Pauly, Mark, and Bradley Herring. 1999. *Pooling Health Insurance Risks*. Washington: American Enterprise Institute Press.

Rothschild, Michael, and Joseph E. Stiglitz. 1976. "Equilibrium in Competitive Insurance Markets: An Essay on the Economics of Imperfect Information." *Quarterly Journal of Economics* 90(4): 629–49.

Settersten, Richard A., Jr., Frank F. Furstenberg Jr., and Rubén G. Rumbaut, editors. 2005. *On the Frontier of Adulthood: Theory, Research, and Public Policy*. Chicago, Ill.: University of Chicago Press.

Yates, Julie A. 2005. "The Transition from School to Work: Education and Work Experiences." *Monthly Labor Review* 128(2) 21-32.

Chapter 5

Blurring the Boundary: Changes in Collegiate Participation and the Transition to Adulthood

MARIA D. FITZPATRICK AND SARAH E. TURNER

Today college enrollment and activities like working and raising a family are not mutually exclusive. During the early 1970s, nearly three-fourths of undergraduate students fell into the eighteen-to-twenty-one age bracket, but today only about 56 percent fit that description (U.S. Bureau of the Census n.d.).

It is not just the age of college participants that has changed but the boundaries between college-going and other adult activities such as employment, marriage, and child-rearing. Among those enrolled in college over the age of twenty-four, nearly 70 percent are also employed, while the share of college students under the age of twenty-four also employed has increased markedly as well. At the start of the 1970s, it was uncommon for a woman in her mid-twenties to be enrolled in college, and even rarer for married women or women with children to be college students. By the year 2000 the enrollment rate of women in their twenties had surpassed that of men, while the barriers to college enrollment for married women and women with children had fallen appreciably.

In effect, the boundary between collegiate enrollment and adulthood has become blurred. This chapter traces these changes in the timing and duration of college participation over the course of the last three decades and explores various reasons for the change. One possible explanation involves market failures or barriers that prevent or delay students from earning degrees through a full-time, direct course of study.[1] Such barriers include credit constraints (the inability to borrow against future earnings to finance full-time collegiate enrollment), poor information about college choices, and deficits in college preparation. A quite different type of explanation is that the increase in adult collegiate enrollment reflects an adaptation to changes in the labor market and more college offerings, including continuing education, retraining, and skill development for displaced workers.

The expansion of collegiate opportunities to allow students the flexibility to return to study after a time in the labor force or to combine school and work may be one of the great success stories of higher education. And in fact, significant growth over the last three decades has occurred on the extensive margin, drawing into higher education older, nontraditional students. Yet there is also cause for concern that some of the growth in nontraditional students represents the consequences of barriers to attainment, including credit constraints that may limit the capacity of students to withdraw from the labor force to complete collegiate programs. The growing presence of nontraditional students is probably the result of *both* beneficial changes in the market and instances of market failure, though much of the evidence points to the former as the more influential factor driving the changes of the last three decades.

College Enrollment by Age and Gender

College enrollment rates (defined as the share of high school graduates with less than a bachelor's degree enrolled in college) have generally increased for all ages over the last quarter-century. Figure 5.1 shows the broad trend in undergraduate enrollment rates from 1968 to 2003, with younger students in the top graph and older students in the bottom graph. Despite the overall increase, there are differences in the timing and relative rates of growth by age group. For the youngest groups (age eighteen to nineteen and age twenty to twenty-one), which are most likely to represent recent high school graduates and the "traditional" college student, enrollment fell between 1968 and 1973 (from 52.3 percent to 45 percent for the eighteen- to nineteen-year-old group) before starting a relatively steady climb through the late 1990s, when enrollment rates reached 64 percent in 1998 (and again in 2003). In contrast, after relatively flat enrollment rates through 1986, older students saw substantial enrollment increases, particularly for twenty-five- to twenty-six-year-olds, for whom enrollment rose from 10 percent in 1986 to over 19 percent in 2002.

Changing Enrollment and Attainment

Enrollment—time spent participating in college—should be understood in the context of collegiate attainment. Increases in enrollment rates by

Figure 5.1   College Enrollment by Age, 1968 to 2003

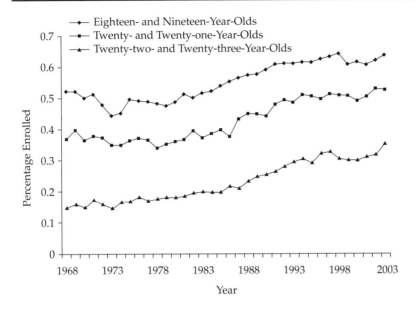

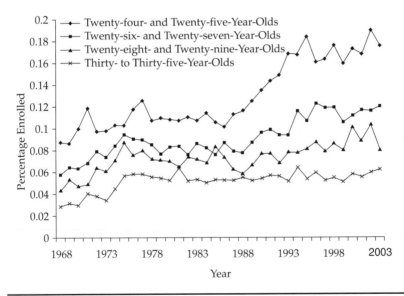

Source: Authors' calculations based on data from the October CPS: CPS weights are used.
Note: The measures of years are calculated by counting the total number of years of reported enrollment at the collegiate level for a birth cohort over the period in which they are
eighteen to twenty-eight and dividing by the size of the cohort. The percent with "some
college" is calculated as the percent of the sample with a high school degree who have attended at least some college by the specified date. Similarly, the percent with a BA degree
is calculated as the percent with a BA degree (or sixteen years of schooling) by the specified
age relative to all high school degree recipients.

age imply that the number of years spent enrolled in college has increased markedly over the last three decades. Indeed, the average years of undergraduate college enrollment between the ages of eighteen and twenty-eight has increased from about 1.7 years for those born in 1950 to over 2.5 years for those born in 1975 (top graph, figure 5.2).[2]

One question is how this increase in college enrollment is divided between additional students entering the college pipeline and added years of college enrollment. As the second graph in figure 5.2 shows, college participation has risen over the interval, moving up steadily from 50 percent to 60 percent between the 1960 birth cohort and the 1975 birth cohort. What is also apparent is that there is little change in college participation after age twenty-two. Most students who go to college will still start college in their early twenties, although there is some increase in the "new" participation of women age twenty-five to twenty-eight in the most recent birth cohorts. Therefore, the growth in enrollment among those in their mid- to late twenties visible in figure 5.1 is not "new entry" into the collegiate pipeline in the main but the return to college among those with some prior college experience.

The third graph of figure 5.2 presents BA degree completion by age and birth cohort. Here we see substantial differences by age of observation: the rate of college degree attainment by age twenty-two has been largely flat over the last quarter-century, while the measurement at older ages shows gains in college completion. There has been a substantial increase in the share of college graduates receiving degrees between ages twenty-two and twenty-eight. These students have gone through an attainment process that is quite different from four years of continuous enrollment after high school graduation (see Turner 2004).

Comparing outcomes eight years after high school graduation for the cohorts of 1972 and 1992, John Bound, Michael Lovenheim, and Sarah Turner (2007) find that the median time to degree rose from four years to five, while the proportion of graduates taking five or more years increased from 16.2 percent to 23.8 percent.[3] Understanding the cause of increased time to degree at the undergraduate level—as distinct from the consideration of changes in the overall age structure of undergraduate enrollment pursued here—is the subject of the research by Bound, Lovenheim, and Turner, which examines the extent to which the shift is attributable to factors such as potential increases in the need for remediation, additional financial constraints, or reductions in the resources of colleges and universities. Comparing outcomes for the cohort of BA recipients graduating from high school in 1972 (National Longitudinal Study, or NLS-72) and students graduating from high school in 1992 (National Education Longitudinal Study, or NELS-88), preliminary estimates show little evidence that student achievement or the financial characteristics of parents explain the changes.[4] However, the change in

Figure 5.2   Enrollment and Attainment by Birth Cohort

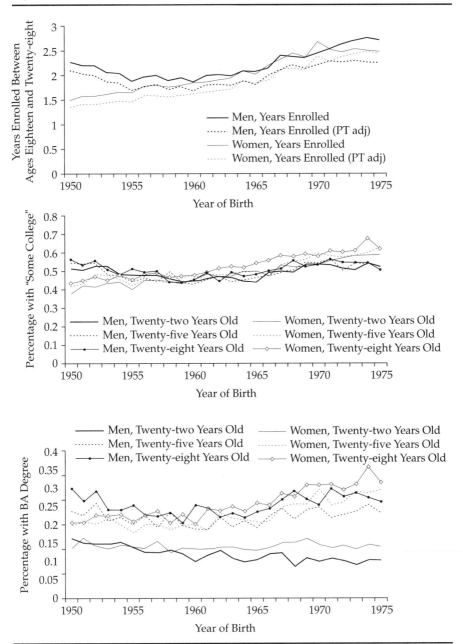

Source: Authors' calculations based on data from the October CPS; CPS weights are used.
Note: The sample includes those who have a high school diploma but who have not received a BA degree or completed sixteen years of education. Enrollment is defined as being enrolled in college (or enrolled in "grades" 13 to 16). Employment is defined as working in the month of the survey. Figures depict the employment rates of enrolled students.

time-to-degree is nearly entirely concentrated among students who attend public colleges and universities outside the most highly ranked research universities; further work is necessary to understand the mechanism tied to this dynamic.

We want to be clear that the effects of this shift are ambiguous at the theoretical level. Students may be taking longer to graduate because they cannot borrow against future earnings to finance full-time collegiate enrollment (what economists call "credit constrained"). In such cases, the need to work to finance college displaces time spent in collegiate study, and the resulting increase in time-to-degree is inefficient. However, the increased time to degree could also represent a change in behavior that is optimal for students. One example might be the student who takes a semester internship to better prepare for employment after graduation. In addition, with increased financial aid available to nontraditional students, it may be that students completing college in recent years might be those who had not been afforded the opportunity to complete a degree in earlier periods.

The Effects of Changing Norms on College Enrollment

The rise in college participation beyond the immediate post–high school years is a substantial transformation over the last three decades. Central to understanding this development is the rise in the participation of women in postsecondary education. Overall, one of the most dramatic changes in recent decades is the rise in the participation of women, including older women, in college. Figure 5.3 shows that, in the late 1960s, the enrollment rates of men exceeded those of women, sometimes by as much as three-to-one. However, by 2003, in each age group the fraction of women enrolled as undergraduates is larger than the fraction of men enrolled.

For women, the last three decades have brought substantial changes in labor force participation and, with the expectation of increases in labor force attachment, growth in collegiate investments (Goldin, Katz, and Kuziemko 2006).[5] It appears that changing labor force opportunities and expectations for women are a significant piece of the explanation for the convergence of enrollment rates in the 1970s. Martha Bailey (2006a, 2006b) also finds that variation in whether women had access to contraception at age eighteen, when they were likely to begin making collegiate investments and family commitments, had substantial effects on both fertility and labor force participation.[6] States reduced the age at majority (or the age of adulthood in the legal sense) from twenty-one to eighteen in different years in the late 1960s and early 1970s, while states also differed in the timing of offering access to family planning services

Figure 5.3   Undergraduate College Enrollment, by Age and Sex, 1968 to 2003

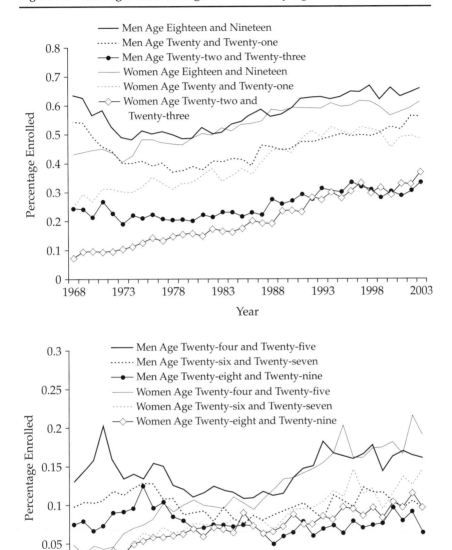

Source: Authors' calculations based on data from the October CPS. Enrollment rates are percentages of the population who have a high school diploma but have not received the BA degree or completed sixteen years of education. CPS weights were used.

to minors. These changes are used by Bailey (2006b), who finds a 14 percent reduction in births before age twenty-two and an approximately 8 percent increase in labor force participation for women age twenty-six to thirty. Bailey (2006a) also finds that early access to the pill and other contraception is tied to an increase in college enrollment rates of four to five percentage points for those age nineteen to twenty-two.

Building on Bailey's work, we are particularly interested in exploring whether the availability of contraception at early ages might also contribute to the substantial relative increase in enrollment for women in their mid- to late twenties observed in the 1970s. At the start of the 1970s, the relative gap between men and women enrolled in their mid-twenties was appreciably larger than the gap observed for traditional college-age students, with the undergraduate enrollment rate for twenty-four- and twenty-five-year-old men about 16 percent relative to an enrollment rate for women of about 4.5 percent. (To put this in perspective, men were only about 25 percent more likely to enroll as eighteen- or nineteen-year-olds in 1970, rather than the factor of 3.5 observed for the older group.) We might think of this gap as a result of two related forces. First, at the start of the 1970s women in their mid-twenties were much more likely to have young children, which would have increased the opportunity cost of attending college. Second, women in this group may have had lower labor force attachment and, in turn, lower returns to collegiate investments.

Using data from the October Current Population Survey (CPS), we find that early access to contraception (at age eighteen) increased undergraduate enrollment by nearly one percentage point among women age twenty-four to twenty-nine from 1977 to 1986.[7] This increase is substantial given the relatively low baseline level of enrollment for this group (table 5.1).[8]

The rise in collegiate participation beyond the immediate post–high school years is a substantial transformation over the last three decades. Central to understanding this development is the rise in the participation of women in postsecondary education among college students in all age groups, as it was in the enrollment outcomes for older students where the largest relative gaps between men and women existed in the early 1970s. Still, by the early 1980s women had largely "caught up" to men in enrollment, and the explanation of the overall expansion in the collegiate participation of those in their mid-twenties in the last fifteen years must rely on other changes in the labor market and collegiate sectors.

Although the enrollment rates of minorities have not quite caught up to those of whites, there have been large gains for these groups. In 1968 African Americans trailed their white counterparts in college enrollment at all ages.[9] For example, 41 percent of blacks were enrolled at age eighteen or nineteen in 1968, while 53 percent of their white peers were en-

Table 5.1   Parameter Estimates from Regressions of Undergraduate
Enrollment of Twenty-four- to Twenty-nine-Year-Olds, by Type of
Institution, on Early Legal Access (Bailey Measure) and Covariates
(Linear Probability Model)

	Women	Men
All institutions	0.008	–0.009
	(0.004)	(0.008)
By type of institution		
Public two-year	0.003	–0.001
	(0.002)	(0.003)
Public four-year	0.003	–0.006
	(0.003)	(0.004)
Private	0.001	0.001
	(0.002)	(0.004)

Source: October CPS, 1977 to 1986.
Notes: Each coefficient and standard error is from a separate regression with undergraduate enrollment as the dependent variable, limiting observations to those with at least a high
school degree and less than a college degree. Each regression includes a full set of state
fixed effects, time effects (CPS year), birth-cohort effects, and age effects. Regressions also
include the state-level unemployment rate and an indicator for race. Standard errors are
corrected for heteroskedasticity and clustered at the state level.

rolled. The enrollment rates of blacks age twenty-six or twenty-seven
were about half those for whites (about 3 and 6 percent, respectively).
The narrowing of the black-white gap in college enrollment has been de-
cidedly uneven by age. By 2003 younger African Americans (those age
eighteen or nineteen) still trailed their white peers, but African Americans age twenty-four and older were now somewhat more likely (13 percent) than whites to be enrolled as undergraduates (11 percent). To be
clear, what such data show is that the timing of college enrollment profiles differs by race, with whites more likely to enroll in the immediate
post–high school years.

The Circuitous Transition to Adulthood

Not only have enrollment rates changed by age and gender over the last
thirty years, but the characteristics of those enrolled have changed. The
transition to adulthood is traditionally defined in terms of both employment and formation of independent families.[10] College enrollment today
does not necessarily conflict with many indicators of adulthood: employment, marriage, and child-rearing are now less determinant of enrollment status than in the decade of the 1970s.

The age at first marriage has risen over the last two decades. Concur-
rently, the proportion of those age twenty-two or twenty-three who were

married declined from about 65 percent in 1968 to less than 30 percent in 2003. Despite these general changes, the last thirty years have seen a marked increase in the enrollment of married women. With similar changes for other age groups in their twenties, descriptive evidence suggests that, although marriage may make college enrollment less likely, it does not preclude it. Likewise, childbearing does not appear to hinder enrollment as it once did.

It is well known that fertility has declined somewhat among those in their twenties over the last three decades. The mean age of first births rose from 21.4 to 24.9 between 1970 and 2000, while the number of births per 1,000 women declined from about 150 to 115.[11] The data since 1980, and particularly since 1990, show that the college enrollment rates of parents with children have risen steadily. In 1980 the enrollment rates of individuals of all ages with children were 3.86 percent. In 2003 those rates had risen by almost 50 percent, to 5.75 percent.

Employment is another potential line of demarcation in the transition to adulthood. However, in a broad sense, we find no evidence of a persistent separation between work and school. At least since the 1970s, a sizable portion of students have combined work and undergraduate enrollment. As can be seen in the top two graphs of figure 5.4, the employment rates of male students older than twenty-two have remained fairly constant over the period, while the employment rates of younger male students have increased moderately. (For example, the share of those age eighteen or nineteen working while in school rose by about five percentage points.)[12] Meanwhile, the increase in the number of women working while in school is much more dramatic. For younger women age eighteen to twenty-three, the share of those working while enrolled in college rose by an average of about eighteen percentage points from 1970 to 2003. For women age twenty-four to thirty-five, the rise over the same period was slightly more moderate, averaging fifteen percentage points.[13]

These findings confirm those in Marigee Bacolod and Joseph Hotz's (2006) analysis of youth in the late 1960s, 1970s, and 1980s. Among young adults age eighteen to twenty-eight, the authors find, the fraction of men who worked at some point while in college increased only slightly (0.6 percent) between the 1970s and 1980s, but the fraction of women who worked while in college increased by 30 percent. What remains unanswered is why students choose to work while in school, especially since the evidence suggests that doing so does not lead to an increase in future earnings and may well increase time to degree attainment.[14]

One explanation is that students face credit constraints that prevent them from borrowing enough to support themselves while enrolled, although it is unlikely that credit constraints affect the entire population of working students. Another possibility is that students balance uncer-

Figure 5.4   Share of Those Enrolled in College and also Employed, by Age and Gender

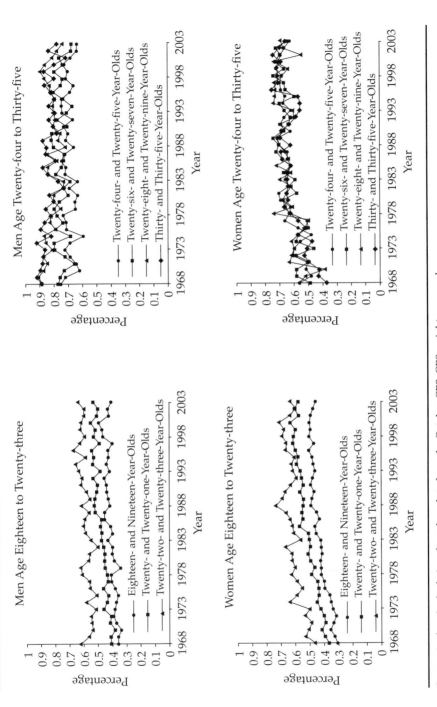

Source: Authors' calculations based on data from the October CPS; CPS weights are used.
Notes: The sample includes those who have a high school diploma but have not received the BA degree or completed sixteen years of education. Enrollment is defined as being enrolled in college (or enrolled in "grades" 13 to 16). Employment is defined as working in the month of the survey. Figures depict the employment rates of enrolled students.

tainty about the risks of enrolling in school, or the "opportunity cost" of attending (in wages lost, for example), by both working and attending school.[15] It may also be that colleges are increasingly responding to the preferences of students by offering courses of study that allow them to attend school while working. Alternatively, younger students may be working while in school to gain on-the-job skills and experience valued by employers. Understanding the nexus between employment and college attainment is of significant importance and represents an open area for future research.

Policy Changes and College Enrollment

Public policy designed to influence decisions to enroll in higher education is decentralized, with initiatives at the state, federal, and institutional levels affecting the financing of colleges and universities and the supply of college opportunities. Even within federal policy, there is no single "student aid policy" but rather a loosely aligned set of loan and grant programs administered on the basis of need, as well as some categorical programs such as veterans' benefits. Variation in funding for higher education at the state level and changes in tuition levels at state institutions also have a substantial effect on college decisions, namely through costs. What is more, a whole set of other social welfare programs and regulations that are not explicitly part of higher education policy, including welfare reform, unemployment insurance, and trade policy, may also affect college participation.

In this section, we focus first on how federal student aid policies have quite dramatically changed the financing of college for students outside the model of traditional high school graduates. We then turn to the question of how state policies and economic circumstances affect the enrollment of students of all ages, with particular attention to whether the current price and student aid structure leaves students from low-income families unable to afford full-time attendance.

Federal Aid Policy: The Transformation in "Access" for Older Students

At the federal level, higher education policies include grants, loans, tax credits, and savings incentives. Although broad-based federal funding for college outside of categorical programs (such as the GI Bill) dates to the Higher Education Act of 1965, it was the changes to that act in 1972 and the introduction of Pell grants (at that time known as the Basic Educational Opportunity Grant) and Stafford loans that dramatically changed funding options for many potential college students.[16] Tax credits (including Lifetime Learning Credits), adopted in 1997, are a much more recent addition.

Pell Grants   The Title IV financial aid programs are often described as the cornerstone of federal higher education policy; in the academic year 2003–2004, Pell grant aid totaled $12.6 billion, while loan programs provided over $55.4 billion in funding, about $25 billion of which was provided through the subsidized Stafford loan program (College Board 2005b). For federal means-tested programs, eligibility is determined through the evaluation of available assets and incomes through the FAFSA (Free Application for Federal Student Aid) form. A separate needs evaluation determines both loan and Pell grant eligibility for "independent" students who are no longer dependent on their parents for financial support.[17]

Today the maximum Pell grant is set at $4,050, which is higher in real terms than the award level in the mid-1990s, although well below its value in the mid-1970s (about $4,800). Given that college costs have risen over the last quarter-century, the Pell grant now covers a lower share of the burden of paying for college than it did originally.

Yet it is not clear that the erosion of the purchasing power of federal financial aid with respect to college costs is a primary factor explaining enrollment.[18] Empirical evidence on the behavioral effects of these programs is mixed. Focusing first on the enrollment effects for traditional college-age students (defined as students who are recent high school graduates and still depend on their parents for financial support), evaluations consistently yield no evidence that the program changed enrollment (Hansen 1983; Kane 1994).[19] One explanation for why the Pell grant program has had such modest effects on traditional students is its complexity. Coupled with the difficulty in determining benefit eligibility, this complexity may inhibit many potential students from applying. Another explanation is that factors beyond financial constraints, including academic achievement, are what limit college enrollment and college attainment for the marginal low-income student.

While the Pell grant program has not had a discernible effect on the collegiate attainment of recent high school graduates, the effects on college participation for nontraditional students have been marked, perhaps because the institutions attended by these students are unlikely to have provided much financial aid and also because few students in their early or mid-twenties would have accumulated assets for financing college. When Neil Seftor and Sarah Turner (2002) examined the effect of the program introduction on nontraditional students—following a difference-in-differences setup similar to that used by Thomas Kane (1994)—they found strong evidence of a substantial enrollment effect for nontraditional students. More generally, the share of Pell grant recipients who are independent has risen steadily over the last three decades, from about 30 percent in 1975 to more than 60 percent in the early 1990s, before dipping to about 58 percent in 2003–2004. Expansion of the availability of federal financial aid for undergraduates to older students appears to be one mechanism that is opening enrollment to many individuals who would not have been able to enroll in higher education in earlier decades.

Student Loans   Beyond grant funding, low-income students may turn to the federal government for loan assistance. Students can borrow (a limited amount) from the federal government; the government pays interest while the student is enrolled and then allows the student to repay the loan at a subsidized rate after college. Loan limits vary by year of study and student status (dependent, independent); dependent undergraduates are limited to borrowing $3,500 in the first year, with this amount rising to $4,500 in the second year and then $5,500 in subsequent undergraduate years.

Unfortunately, there is little evidence on student loans and even less evidence on their effect on college enrollment and attainment. What little evidence there is suggests that their impact on enrollment decisions is small (Ionescu 2006), perhaps because when all students are considered together, distinctions in behavior between student groups are missed.[20] For example, the increase in loans in the last decade has been driven mostly by the introduction of the unsubsidized Stafford loan program, which allows students to borrow regardless of demonstrated need (Baum 2003). It is likely that students who would attend college even without these loans are substituting them for other sources of funds (for example, borrowing from home equity) that they (or their families) would otherwise use.

Another possible reason why loans have had a small impact on enrollment decisions, pointed out by Christopher Avery and Caroline Hoxby (2004), could be that students are not responding "rationally" to loan packages. The authors show that students misevaluated the value of loans compared with grants and were misled by the name of a funding opportunity (for example, "scholarship" instead of "grant"). These misperceptions may be exacerbated among lower-income students, who are likely to have less information or lower-quality information. There is also some evidence that low-income families are more reluctant to borrow (Orfield 1992).

Although it is common to bemoan the potentially high loan burdens assumed by students, it is far from clear that student loan debt is causing a delay in the transition to adulthood (see Chiteji, this volume; for a brief discussion of both sides of the loan argument, see Briggs 2001). By one line of argument, greater access to credit would allow students an opportunity to attend full-time and complete degree programs in a shorter period of time.

The distribution of aid eligibility under the federal needs analysis formula does not, however, guarantee that a student will have all needs met, as it is quite possible that the sum of the Pell grant, the Stafford loan, and whatever aid is available from the institution may be less than total need in many circumstances. When low-income students are limited to federal sources of support to finance college, it is surely possible that they are credit-constrained—perhaps to the extent that they must combine school and work or turn down a residential collegiate program to live at home while attending college.[21] Even if low-income students are able to take advantage of private sources of financing, many are probably still credit-constrained in some sense of the term.[22]

Tuition Tax Credits and Lifetime Learning   Tuition tax credits are the final form of federal aid discussed in this chapter. Most notably, this aid is nonrefundable, implying that eligible students are unlikely to be among the most economically disadvantaged. Bridget Long (2004) notes that about two-thirds of the population is potentially eligible for these credits aimed at the middle class; those with limited tax liability are ineligible, as are those with incomes above a ceiling.[23] The extent to which advocates for need-based student aid viewed these policies as in opposition to established programs such as Pell may well have undermined the alternative of helping low-income students through a refundable tax credit (Strach 2005).

The evolution of federal student aid policy embodied in the title of the Lifetime Learning Tax Credit is that access and participation in postsecondary education can be expected to continue through one's working life. As such, these benefits do not follow the model of "once and for all" school completion or full-time attendance.[24] In principle, these benefits provide for either continuing education or "retooling" for adults through the postsecondary system and some opportunity for financial aid in the wake of job displacement. Yet, because these benefits are nonrefundable, it is unlikely that they serve the needs of those who have been displaced from permanent jobs.[25]

Taken as a whole, federal financial aid policy in the form of grants, loans, and tax benefits is probably insufficient to fund full-time college enrollment for students (of any age), and the share of total college-related expenses covered by federal sources has probably declined for many potential college students from low-income families since the early 1970s, since neither federal loan limits nor Pell grants have kept pace with inflation. Nevertheless, changes in federal student aid policy since the early 1970s—from the availability of aid for "independent" students through Title IV programs to the introduction of programs such as Lifetime Learning Tax Credits for adults participating in postsecondary education—have clearly opened some ways for nontraditional students to finance a college education.

Tuition Increases and College Enrollment

In the last three decades, the tuition (in constant dollars) charged at public four-year and public two-year institutions has doubled. It is common in the press and in policy circles to proclaim that such price changes reduce students' opportunities for enrolling in and completing college.[26] Many popular discussions focus on the changes in sticker price at the most selective private institutions, even though such changes are unlikely to affect the choices of students at the margin of college enrollment. Most college students are enrolled at schools where annual tuition is less than $6,000, not at schools where tuition exceeds $30,000.[27]

The Effect of Increasing Tuition Charges   We open a discussion about the impact of tuition and college costs on enrollment and attainment with two basic propositions. First, the demand for college education is decreasing in price or tuition—in other words, increasing tuition works in the direction of reducing the number of students enrolled. Second, credit constraints plausibly limit college attainment for students from economically disadvantaged households, and these effects are probably exacerbated by increases in tuition or other dimensions of college costs. However, for increases in tuition to be an important dimension in the growth in undergraduate enrollment beyond traditional college years, they must have led to either delays in college enrollment or increases in the share of students enrolled part-time.

Measuring this possible effect is not altogether straightforward: comparisons across states are likely to confound differences in public college pricing with other systematic differences across states, such as income. At the same time, within-state approaches are not immune from critique, since changes in tuition at state-supported institutions are likely to be tied to a host of other changes in local economic conditions that also affect enrollment. The same factors affecting the determination of tuition on the supply side of the market (for example, recessionary periods within a state) may also affect the demand for college. In such circumstances, the counterfactual to raising tuition at public institutions may be lower resources per student as states essentially raise tuition to compensate for declines in appropriations. When we observe a change in tuition within a local market, it may reflect changes in demand, changes in supply, or, as is most often the case, changes in demand and supply. Complicating the problem further, measurement of "price response" will vary with the scope of the market as well as individual characteristics.[28]

We take the approach of evaluating the effect of changes in price on changes in enrollment within states, essentially treating the state as the relevant definition of a market. There are two empirical approaches in this type of analysis. One approach is to use CPS data at the level of the individual (or aggregated to the level of the state). CPS microdata have the advantage of providing information on age and current economic circumstances, but relatively small sample sizes limit estimation.[29] The results in table 5.2 show the effect of tuition on enrollment rates (distinguishing total enrollment from enrollment at public institutions and enrollment at two-year schools). Overall, we find no effect of tuition on public college enrollment, indicating that total enrollment for all ages and for seventeen- to nineteen-year-olds is essentially inelastic. We would expect to see the larger price response or enrollment elasticities at two-year schools, since these institutions are most likely to reach students who are at the margin of enrollment. A $1,000 increase in tuition yields a predicted change in the two-year enrollment rate of between 8

Table 5.2   Effects of Tuition on Enrollment Rates (in Logs) Within States, Estimates from the CPS

Tuition Variables	All Seventeen- to Nineteen-Year-Olds			All Eighteen- to Thirty-five-Year-Olds		
	(1)	(2)	(3)	(4)	(5)	(6)
Four-year college	0.014	0.014	–0.165	–0.009	–0.033	–0.006
	(0.035)	(0.036)	(0.081)	(0.024)	(0.031)	(0.024)
Flagship university	0.005	0.006	-0.080	–0.008	–0.019	–0.002
	(0.016)	(0.019)	(0.044)	(0.014)	(0.015)	(0.016)
Community college	0.043	0.025	–0.115	0.029	0.027	0.040
	(0.032)	(0.054)	(0.103)	(0.040)	(0.048)	(0.041)
Type of enrollment	Overall	Public	Two-year	Overall	Public	Two-year

Notes: Data on enrollment are from the October CPS from the years 1977 to 2000. Data on tuition from the same years are from the Washington State Higher Education Coordinating Board. Only those with at least a high school diploma who have not yet received a BA degree or completed sixteen years of education are used in the calculation of enrollment rates. Tuition is in thousands of constant 2003 dollars. The dependent variable is the natural log of a state's enrollment rate of the reported type, where reported enrollment in October is assumed to be indicative of enrollment for the year and population is calculated using the CPS. Standard errors are clustered at the state level, and when enrollment is aggregated to the state level, the CPS weights are used. The regressions use the square root of a state's population age eighteen to twenty-four as weights. Population information can be found in the 2000 census summary file 3. Regressions include year and state fixed effects, the annual state unemployment rate, the natural log of the population age eighteen to twenty-four (from the census), and the indicated tuition variable. Overall enrollment is defined as enrollment at any type of institution, public enrollment is enrollment at any public institution, and two-year enrollment is enrollment at any two-year public institution. It should be noted that the authors ran specifications without weights, with levels of enrollment rates and logs of tuition, and the results were not qualitatively different from those presented.

and 16 percent for students in the 17 to 19 age range. This effect is only significantly different from zero when four-year college tuition is the price measure.

The average level of community college tuition for all states in our sample is $1,297 (in 2003 dollars); thus, an increase in community college tuition of $1,000 is almost so large as to be "out of sample" in that no changes of this magnitude are ever observed.[30] Although the largest change (in absolute terms) in the price of community college tuition from one year to the next in a given state was an increase of 80 percent, the average change from year to year within a state was less than 4 percent.[31] Using the 4 percent increase as a measure, our preferred estimates (column 3, table 5.2) indicate that enrollment rates at two-year institutions would decrease by about one-half of 1 percent (0.59 percent). Since the average enrollment rate across states for the period discussed is 15 percent, the predicted decrease is tiny—0.09 percentage points.

A different approach is to use institutional data or the responses from college and university surveys on the number of students enrolled at each level in the fall. In this setup, it is also then common to focus on the tuition charged by public universities and community colleges as the key explanatory variable, while also including state and year fixed effects so that the full identification of the coefficient on tuition is based on within-state changes over time. One problem in relating this type of enrollment measure to the enrollment rates generated from a microsurvey like the CPS is that it is necessary to turn to another source (such as age by state population counts) to generate a denominator; as such, we refer to these measures as "enrollment ratio" rather than "enrollment rates."[32]

At first glance, it is clear that estimates using state-level enrollment to population ratios yield a substantial negative effect on tuition at public colleges and universities and the two-year community colleges. Table 5.3 shows this basic comparison with the dependent variable specified as the log of total enrollment ratio. Particularly for enrollment at two-year schools, these estimates indicate enrollment is responsive to tuition changes. A $1,000 increase in tuition at flagship universities is associated with a 6 percent decline in enrollment at two-year public institutions.[33] Yet this estimation is likely to be significantly misspecified with the omission of the related cohort size as an independent variable; cohort size is both correlated with tuition levels chosen within state and directly related to enrollment levels at a rate that is known to be less than one-to-one (see Bound and Turner 2007). What we observe in the remaining columns of table 5.3 is that including the size of the college-age population reduces the magnitude of the tuition effect appreciably. Although some of the enrollment effects presented in columns 4 through 6 are negative and statistically significant, the effects are relatively small in magnitude, suggesting that tuition per se has not been

Table 5.3   Effects of Tuition on Enrollment Ratios Within States, Estimates from Institutional Measures of Enrollment

Tuition Variables	(1)	(2)	(3)	(4)	(5)	(6)
Four-year college	0.028	–0.024	–0.068	0.000	–0.010	–0.048
	(0.022)	(0.017)	(0.033)	(0.016)	(0.017)	(0.041)
Flagship university	0.010	–0.030	–0.057	–0.016	–0.026	–0.051
	(0.017)	(0.010)	(0.021)	(0.013)	(0.013)	(0.031)
Community college	0.064	–0.039	–0.091	0.014	–0.008	–0.047
	(0.038)	(0.030)	(0.061)	(0.035)	(0.037)	(0.089)
Type of enrollment	Overall	Public	Two-year	Overall	Public	Two-year
Includes Ln Population eighteen to twenty-four	No	No	No	Yes	Yes	Yes
With state trends?	No	No	No	No	No	No

Notes: Each coefficient is from a separate regression with the indicated covariates and type of enrollment. Data on enrollment are from WebCaspar database by the NSF and include the years 1977 to 2000. Data on tuition from the same years are from the Washington State Higher Education Coordinating Board. Tuition is in thousands of constant 2003 dollars. The dependent variable is the natural log of the ratio of enrollment to population in a state. Standard errors are clustered at the state level. The regressions use the square root of a state's population age eighteen to twenty-four as weights. Regressions include year and state fixed effects, the annual state unemployment rate, and the indicated tuition variable. When indicated (columns 4–6), the regressions also include the natural log of the population age eighteen to twenty-four (from the census) as controls. Overall enrollment is defined as enrollment at any type of institution, public enrollment is enrollment at any public institution, and two-year enrollment is enrollment at any two-year institution.

the primary factor affecting the enrollment decisions of recent high school graduates over the last three decades. What we focus on somewhat later in this section is how the effect of changes in tuition prices varies by age. Still, in concluding that changes in tuition charges at public universities have been a modest determinant of collegiate enrollment, we want to be clear in stating that this finding *does not* imply that total college costs are unimportant in explaining the timing and intensity of enrollment decisions. As discussed later, there is evidence that total college costs (including living expenses) do affect the timing and intensity of college-going. Also, the results presented here are limited to the range of observed tuition changes, such as the doubling tuition at public institutions.

Paying for College: Total College Costs and Family Circumstances

In making the point that there appears to be little strong empirical evidence identifying changes in tuition as the "culprit" in the changes in the overall enrollment or time to degree, we do not want to leave the reader with the impression that there have been no changes in the capacity of families to pay for colleges. Quite the contrary: changes in the structure of earnings and the living expenses associated with college completion have probably had dramatic effects on college choices, particularly for students from low-income families.

Although tuition increases have been episodic over the last two decades, the change in the structure of earnings has been more sustained: the real family income of those in the bottom quartile (with children age seventeen to nineteen still living at home) has fallen 17 percent during much of the 1980s and the 1990s, while the real family income of those in top quartile rose 22 percent over the same period.[34]

Compounding the erosion of family income are rising overall living costs, particularly for housing in urban areas. Of course, young people would be expected to pay for food or housing independent of enrollment decisions. Yet, to attend full-time (even at a low-tuition public institution) presupposes a source of financing for housing and food. To illustrate, while average tuition and fees for attendance at a public two-year school were $2,191, the College Board (2005b) estimates that the total annual cost of attendance was $11,692 with the inclusion of expenditures on rent, food, and books. Although total expenses are unavailable more than a few years back, some evidence can be gleaned by looking at the costs of room and board at postsecondary institutions that offer such services. Tuition, fees, and room and board at four-year public institutions cost $6,462 (2005 dollars) in 1976. By 2005–2006, these costs had nearly doubled to $12,127.[35]

Going Back to School as an Adult

Much attention has been focused on the question of how cyclical economic changes affect the enrollment and persistence of traditional college-age students, following an implicit assumption that school-leaving is a once-and-for-all decision. Empirical analysis of the educational investments of youth shows a large positive effect of the unemployment rate on high school graduation, a modest effect on college enrollment, and no effect on degree attainment (Card and Lemieux 2000; Kane 1994). Yet those most likely to seek postsecondary training in response to cyclical shocks may be outside the set defined as traditional college students, especially if it is possible for students to combine work and school. For those already in the labor force, on-the-job training opportunities are likely to decline in cyclical downturns (Lynch 1992), and postsecondary institutions may serve as an important channel for further skill development. In theory, workers seek further training during economic downturns because the opportunity costs of time are less. In addition, shocks to labor demand may be tied to technological changes that make some skills obsolete (or open new opportunities in emerging industries). We therefore first explore the question of whether older students are more likely to enroll in response to an economic downturn than are recent high school graduates.

One test of the proposition that the cyclicality of the postsecondary enrollment response is concentrated among those beyond the immediate high school years is to examine how college enrollment changes with variation within states in the October unemployment rate (corresponding to the October CPS). Table 5.4 presents results from 1977 to 2002. In the specification where the dependent variable is the overall enrollment rate (column 1), we find higher unemployment rates are associated with decreases in the college enrollment of those age twenty-three and younger. For those twenty-four and older, postsecondary enrollment is demonstrably and positively responsive to cyclical shocks; a one-per-centage-point change in the local unemployment rate produces about a 0.7-percentage-point change in enrollment for those between the ages of twenty-eight and thirty-five.

While these results are clear in demonstrating a greater enrollment response to cyclical shocks for those in their mid-twenties, the central question in this chapter concerns the causes of the broader increase in college enrollment of those in their mid- and late twenties who are on the "boundary" of adulthood. We put forward the hypothesis that since the early 1970s educational offerings and financing have changed in ways

Table 5.4   Estimates of the Effect of State Unemployment on College Enrollment, by Age

	(1)	(2)	(3)
Eighteen to twenty-year-olds	−0.009	−0.009	−0.005
	(0.002)	(0.001)	(0.001)
Twenty-one- to twenty-three-year-olds	−0.006	−0.006	−0.003
	(0.001)	(0.001)	(0.001)
Twenty-four- to twenty-seven-year-olds	0.003	0.002	0.000
	(0.001)	(0.001)	(0.001)
Twenty-eight- to thiry-five-year-olds	0.007	0.005	0.001
	(0.001)	(0.001)	(0.001)
Type of enrollment	Overall	Public	Two-year

Note: Each column indicates the coefficients on the interaction of the indicated age and the state-level unemployment rate. In addition to unemployment, each regression includes tuition at community colleges in the state (from Washington State Higher Education Coordinating Board), the natural log of the population age eighteen to twenty-four in the state, and state, year, and age group fixed effects. The observations are weighted by the square root of the population age eighteen to twenty-four (from the census). Other data are from the October CPS, 1977 to 2003.

that facilitate the enrollment in higher education of individuals who have already entered the labor force. The opening of Pell grants, tax credits, and student loans under Title IV to independent students is one channel of increased access to college for these students. What is more, the relative growth in nonresidential programs has also opened the supply of opportunities in the collegiate sectors to those who wish to combine labor force participation and college.[36]

Ideally, we would examine the enrollment response to cyclical shocks by age over distinct intervals, for example, 1950 to 1975 and 1976 to 2000. Yet microdata at the state level do not afford such comparisons, and in fact we are only able to look at the effect of cyclical shocks on enrollment behavior *after* the introduction of the Pell grant, with these regressions using 1977 as the starting year. That Pell grant receipt also varies with cyclical shocks supports this basic proposition. Sarah Turner (2003) finds that across all types of postsecondary options, increases in state-level unemployment produce significant increases in the number of Pell grant recipients, on the order of a 4.7 to 5.9 percent increase in the unemployment rate, with these effects concentrated among public colleges and for-profit institutions.

Evidence in this section and the more general observation that students often combine work and school (figure 5.4), particularly those in their mid- to late twenties, suggests that any firm demarcation between "work" and "college" that may have existed thirty-five years ago has been eroded. Students in their mid- to late twenties move between college and work and often combine these activities based on opportunities in the labor market.

Conclusion

College students are getting older, and undergraduate enrollment is no longer confined to the immediate post–high school years. More than 45 percent of undergraduates are over age twenty-one, compared with little more than 25 percent of undergraduates three decades ago. Beyond the simple aging of the undergraduate population, it is clear that the time spent enrolled has lengthened and that more students are combining work and school.

There is no single explanation for this blurring of the boundary between college enrollment and other activities. The one dimension of this change that is clear is the transformation of the enrollment behavior of women in the 1970s to equal (and then exceed) the levels of men at all ages. Reproductive control and the postponement of childbearing and marriage surely facilitated the college enrollment of women at both traditional and older ages.

By the mid-1980s, men and women enrolled in college in their mid-twenties were likely to also be participating in the labor force, with the enrollment of these age groups moving up steadily through the late 1980s and the 1990s. What we do not yet understand clearly is the mechanism for this pattern. We do not yet know how much of the combination of work and college is an adjustment to credit constraints (implicitly extending time to completion) and how much is a choice to acquire skills that may substitute for on-the-job training or complement employment persistence.

In concluding this analysis, we want to caution readers against making strong statements about the welfare implications of the evidence we have presented. Whether the blurring of the boundary between college enrollment and traditional indicators of adulthood such as full-time employment and family formation is a policy success or a policy failure is ambiguous. The explanation for the rise in adult collegiate participation is not unicausal. There is sufficient evidence to support the proposition that credit constraints may extend the period of enrollment, limiting the rate of college attainment; such effects have clearly negative welfare implications. At the same time, adjustments in federal financial aid and the structure of collegiate opportunities have plainly changed the college participation decision: no longer seen as a once-and-for-all window, returning to college is now viewed by many as a meaningful opportunity to respond to labor market shocks, to invest in training not provided by firms, or to deal with changes in personal circumstances. Surely this expansion of choice and opportunities is a positive feature of the U.S. market for higher education.

We would like to thank Susan Dynarski, Sheldon Danziger, and Cecilia Rouse and the participants in the "Conference on the Economics of the Transition to Adulthood" for helpful comments. Any errors are our own.

Notes

1. Most traditional economic models of investment in education consider it to be a full-time investment in human captial (e.g. Mincer 1970). Although such models also allow for "on-the-job training" (which occurs at work and after an individual has left school), they assume opportunity costs increase with age, producing a negative link between age and the probability of full-time schooling, as well as the expectation that investments in education will decrease with age. If market failures or barriers exist, students may be forced to attend school part-time or postpone their full-time investment in human capital.

2. Figure 5.2 also presents a second line showing the computation accounting for part-time enrollment. Both calculations produce similar qualitative re-

sults, and the distance between these lines does not change appreciably over the interval.

3. Other data sources enforce this finding: over 45 percent of BA degree recipients in 1977 finished in four years or less, while about 31 percent of degree recipients in 1993 finished in this time frame (McCormick and Horn 1996). Yet some caution should be exercised in comparing time-to-degree among different entering cohorts of students, as larger (smaller) recent cohorts will attenuate (extend) time-to-degree measured among those completing in a given year.

4. Although we do not want to overestimate the importance of BA receipt to the exclusion of other forms of collegiate attainment, such as the completion of certificate programs or associate degrees, it is nevertheless the case that considerable economic rewards are associated with BA degree receipt. What some have called "sheepskin effects," representing the wage advantage associated with degree receipt net of years of schooling, are empirically large; estimates from David Jaeger and Marianne Page (1996) find a return to a BA net of years of education of about 31 percent.

5. For references in the economics literature, see Brian Jacob (2002) and Patricia Anderson (2002). For recent documentation in the popular literature, see the cover article of the January 30, 2006, *Newsweek* by Peg Tyre entitled "The Trouble with Boys."

6. The importance of the widespread introduction of oral contraceptives in changing the educational and career decisions of women is well documented in Claudia Goldin and Lawrence Katz (2000) and Bailey (2006a).

7. Using the October CPS allows us to observe all women enrolled in school, even those who are working while enrolled. Bailey's (2006a) estimates use a variable based on "not in the labor force because in school," which may understate the effects on older students if this group is most likely to combine work and school. What is more, the question of how the family planning services available at age eighteen affect enrollment at older ages has the advantage of concentrating the variation in somewhat later years of the CPS for which all states are identified (1977 and after). To be clear, what we estimate is:

$$E_{isct} = \alpha + \beta_1 ELA + \beta_2 UnemRate + \beta_3 Black + \delta_1 Age25 + \delta_2 Age26 \\ + \delta_3 Age27 + \delta_4 Age28 + \delta_5 Age29 + \gamma_s + \lambda_t + \eta_c + \varepsilon_{isct}$$

where s indicates state, t indicates year, and c indicates cohort.

We estimate this separately for men and women because it is likely that state, time, and cohort effects do differ for men and women over this interval. We also add age parameters, since it is well established that undergraduate enrollment rates decline with age. The specification and the organization of the data lead to the assumption that current state is the same as the state at age eighteen.

8. We estimate the same specification for men, which can be interpreted as a falsification exercise if the supply of postsecondary opportunities is either elastic or a test for whether women's entry "crowded out" men. The results are consistently negative, but not statistically different from zero (second

column of table 5.1). We also consider the extent to which these effects differ by type of institution (bottom panel of table 5.1). Although these results suggest that the enrollment effects are concentrated at public two-year institutions and public four-year schools, we are limited in our capacity to make strong inferences about these estimates.

9. The enrollment rates reported are based on the authors' calculations using the CPS October supplement; these rates indicate the fraction enrolled among the population with at least a high school diploma but no college degree.

10. For further discussion of the development of the ideas of "transition to adulthood" and the changing nature of the transition, see Furstenberg, Rumbaut, and Settersten (2005).

11. According to the Centers for Disease Control and Prevention (CDC), most of that decrease happened in the 1970s (Martin et al. 2002; see also CDC, National Center for Health Statistics, table 1.7, "Total Fertility Rates and Birth Rates, by Age of Mother and Race of Child: United States, 1940–1980," accessed at http://www.cdc.gov/nchs/data/statab/t981x07.pdf).

12. In addition to increases in employment, Bound, Lovenheim, and Turner (2007) document increases in hours worked among those age eighteen to twenty-one. They find that these increases are particularly pronounced among students attending public universities.

13. To determine how much the changes in enrollment were related to changes in the demographic makeup of the population rather than changes in behavior, we did a simple Oaxaca decomposition. The results mimic the discussion here and are available from the authors upon request.

14. Early estimates (Meyer and Wise 1982; Ruhm 1997) suggest that the effects of working while in high school on future earnings are positive. However, Joseph Hotz and his colleagues (2002) show that the effects on earnings go to zero when structural modeling techniques, including modeling employment and enrollment decisions, are used to control for sample selection and endogeneity issues.

15. Anna Sjogren and Maria Saez-Marti (2004) present a model of investment in education that uses uncertainty about the opportunity cost of one's time to generate an optimal strategy of delaying school enrollment, particularly for those students for whom the returns to education are low. It may be that similar uncertainties are driving the decision to work while in school.

16. The GI Bill, which provided collegiate funding for veterans returning from World War II, is an example of an early categorical program. Notably, both the GI Bill and the Social Security student benefit program had generally significant effects on both collegiate enrollment and completion (Bound and Turner 2002; Dynarski 2003). The GI Bill and the Social Security student benefit program share several design features, including the transparency of eligibility determination—potential beneficiaries knew their eligibility and the level and duration of benefits without having to make additional calculations or wait for the results of a bureaucratic process—and the substantial size of the benefits, which often covered the majority of college costs.

17. Under Title IV of the Higher Education Act, federal financial aid policy

makes a statutory distinction between "dependent" and "independent" students in determining their program eligibility. Eligibility for independent students rests only on the financial position of the applicant and his or her spouse, relative to direct college costs and other demands on resources, including the number of children in the family. To be eligible for aid as an independent student, an individual must not have been claimed as a dependent in the prior or current year for tax purposes and may receive only limited cash and in-kind contributions from parents. Eligibility for students claiming independent status has become more restrictive since the inception of the program. The 1986 amendments to the Higher Education Act require students to be at least twenty-four years old, to be married, or to have children to qualify for aid as an independent student.

18. Still, symbolic attachment to these programs is considerable. In the 2004 presidential debate on domestic policy, both candidates invoked the Pell grant as a policy tool: Senator John Kerry mentioned the program twice, and President Bush mentioned it six times.

19. In one of the initial assessments of the program using time-series data, W. Lee Hansen (1983, 93) examined the relative enrollment rates of more and less affluent students before and after the introduction of the Pell program. From his review of the evidence, Hansen writes: "These data force one to conclude that the greater availability of student financial aid, targeted largely toward students from below-median-income families, did little if anything, to increase access. The results certainly do not accord with expectations that access would increase for lower income dependents relative to higher income dependents."

20. Ngina Chiteji (this volume) finds little change over the last forty years in the fraction of households of indebted adults age twenty-five to thirty-four. Most young adults appear to have manageable debt loads.

21. Kane (1999, figure 4.1) demonstrates a high degree of stacking in the distribution of student loans, with many students apparently constrained at the lower-division limit of $2,625 and the upper-division limit of $4,000.

22. Private borrowing for college increased from $1 billion in the 1995–96 academic year to $5 billion in 2001–2002 (Chaker 2007). This type of financing might not be available, however, to low-income families or older students who do not have sufficient credit or collateral to borrow in the private market.

23. The Hope Credit, the first arm of the 1997 tax credit program, provides a tax credit equal to 100 percent of the first $1,000 of qualified tuition expenses and 50 percent of the second $1,000 for the first two years of postsecondary education. The Lifetime Learning Tax Credit, the second arm of the program, covers 20 percent of the first $5,000 in tuition expenditures up to $1,000 and is available for upper-level undergraduates, adults upgrading their skills, or graduate and professional students. The College Board (2005a) estimates that the implicit tax expenditures through this program rose from $3.3 billion in 1998–99 to $6.3 billion in 2003–2004.

24. The allocation of Title IV aid is more generous for students enrolled at least half-time, while receipt of the Hope Credit requires at least six credits of enrollment per term.

25. Victoria Choitz, Laura Dowd, and Bridget Long (2004) examine the extent to which the tax benefits were received by middle-income parents or working adults. In 2001 nearly 80 percent of the Lifetime Learning Tax Credits were received by the primary filer or spouse rather than on behalf of a dependent (relative to about 58 percent for the Hope Credits). As we would expect, the benefits of these credits appear to accrue to moderate-income people, since fewer than 20 percent of Lifetime Learning Tax Credit recipients for 2001 earned less than $40,000 annually.

26. In 2003, U.S. Representatives John A. Boehner and Howard P. "Buck" McKeon, in a congressional analysis entitled "The College Cost Crisis," reported that the increases in tuition at public and private four-year institutions were threatening to put college "out of reach" for low- and middle-income students. However, they missed the point that 40 percent of students, as calculated from the Integrated Postseconday Data System (IPEDS) enrollment survey, are at institutions where the highest degree attainable is a two-year degree.

27. In 2004 the average tuition for a resident student at a public four-year institution was $5,132, while the average total expenses (including room and board, transportation, books, and supplies) for such students was $14,640. Average total expenses are even higher for those who commute or are from out of state (College Board 2005c).

28. One of the most commonly cited literature review pieces on the responsiveness of enrollment to changes in tuition (Leslie and Brinkman 1988) is limited by the combination of estimates from very different markets. We would expect the enrollment response to a change in tuition at one institution (when there are a number of collegiate substitutes) to be much larger than the price response to a change across a more broadly defined market.

29. In our analysis (and the within-state estimates produced by Kane [1995]), regressions of enrollment rates on tuition with state and year fixed effects often produce small and insignificant effects of college price on enrollment. We present our regressions weighting by the square root of a state's college-age population (defined as those between ages eighteen and twenty-four). Doing so generally leads to predicted effects of tuition hikes that are somewhat larger in absolute value than those obtained without such weighting.

30. It is worth remembering that the doubling of tuition at public institutions has occurred over the course of the last three decades. Also, we make no argument as to the impact of repeated large increases in the real cost of tuition on enrollment. Because this is not the case over the time of our data, doing so would involve predicting out of sample.

31. The largest outliers were for two increases in the average community college tuition in California. From 1991 to 1992, community college tuition increased from $120 to $210, and the following year it increased again to $390 (in constant 2003 dollars). Enrollment rates at two-year institutions also dropped over the period, from 13.2 to 11.7 to 11.3 percent.

32. While we believe that these institutional measures give quite accurate counts of enrollment, we are very skeptical about the interpretation of these measures as exactly comparable to CPS-style enrollment rates, for the following reasons. First, because the age structure of college enrollment differs

across states, over time, and within states over time, some variation in a measure such as Enrollment/Pop18–24 will be generated by changes in the enrollment of potential students over the age of twenty-four rather than changes in the true enrollment rate of a defined age group (such as those age eighteen to twenty-four). In addition, we might prefer a denominator based on high school graduates and excluding those with completed collegiate attainment when examining the link between undergraduate enrollment and tuition, which is not possible with the combination of institutional measures and population counts.

33. In many respects, these results parallel other results reported in the literature. For example, Donald Heller (1999) estimates that an increase in community college tuition of $1,000 would result in a (statistically significant) 2.1 percent drop in enrollment at public institutions. Thomas Kane (1995) finds a similar estimate, –2.9 percent. These estimates are produced by including the cohort size only in the denominator of the dependent variable, rather than also including it as an explanatory variable. However, this is the equivalent of including population as an explanatory variable and restricting the coefficient to be –1, which implies a perfectly elastic supply-side response.

34. Reported amounts are in constant dollars (2000) and are based on the authors' calculations from the 1980 and 2000 decennial census 5 percent samples. Richard Fry, Sarah Turner, and Anthony Carnevale (2000) report similar changes using other datasets.

35. The increases in the full cost of going to college could be behind the increase in recent decades of young adults living with their parents, as reported in Robert Schoeni and Karen Ross (2005).

36. Moreover, as suggested by Christopher Taber (2004), it may be that firms are increasingly recognizing postsecondary training as a substitute for on-the-job training.

References

Anderson, Patricia M. 2002. "Where the Boys No Longer Are: Recent Trends in U.S. College Enrollment Patterns." Unpublished paper. Dartmouth University, Hanover, N.H.

Avery, Christopher, and Caroline M. Hoxby. 2004. "Do and Should Financial Aid Decisions Affect Students' College Choices?" In *College Choices: The New Economics of Choosing, Attending, and Completing College*, edited by Caroline M. Hoxby. Chicago, Ill.: University of Chicago Press.

Bacolod, Marigee, and V. Joseph Hotz. 2006. "Cohort Changes in the Transition from School to Work: Evidence from Three NLS Surveys." *Economics of Education Review* 25(4): 351–73.

Bailey, Martha. 2006a. "From the Baby Boom to Sex and the City: Fertility Control and Women's Changing Careers." Unpublished paper. University of Michigan, Ann Arbor.

———. 2006b. "More Power to the Pill: The Impact of Contraceptive Freedom on

Women's Life-Cycle Labor Supply." *Quarterly Journal of Economics* 121(1): 289–320.

Baum, Sandy. 2003. "The Role of Student Loans in College Access." Research report 5. Washington: College Board.

Bound, John, and Sarah E. Turner. 2002. "Going to War and Going to College: Did World War II and the GI Bill Increase Educational Attainment for Returning Veterans?" *Journal of Labor Economics* 20(4): 784–815.

———. 2007. "Cohort Crowding: How Resources Affect Collegiate Attainment." *Journal of Public Economics* 91(5/6): 877-99.

Bound, John, Michael Lovenheim, and Sarah E. Turner. 2007. "Understanding the Increased Time to the Baccalaureate Degree." Population Studies Center Research Report 07-626.

Briggs, Tracey Wong. 2001. "Student Loans for All Income Levels Increase." *USA Today*, December 2. Accessed at http://www.usatoday.com/life/2001-12-03-student-loans.htm.

Card, David, and Thomas Lemieux. 2000. "Dropout and Enrollment Trends in the Postwar Period: What Went Wrong in the 1970s?" In *An Economic Analysis of Risky Behavior Among Youth*, edited by Jonathan Gruber. Chicago, Ill.: University of Chicago Press.

Chaker, Anne Marie. 2007. "Parents Use Bank Loans to Cover Tuition Bills." Accessed at Wall Street Journal Online, http://www.collegejournal.com/aid admissions/financialissues/20030109-chaker.html.

Choitz, Victoria, Laura Dowd, and Bridget Long. 2004. "Getting Serious About Lifelong Learning: Improving the Use and Value of the Hope and Lifetime Learning Credits for Working Adult Students." Policy brief. Arlington, Mass.: FutureWorks (March).

College Board. 2005a. *Trends in Higher Education*. New York: College Board Publications.

———. 2005b. *Trends in Student Aid*. New York: College Board Publications.

———. 2005c. *Trends in College Pricing.* New York: College Board Publications.

Dynarski, Susan. 2003. "Does Aid Matter? Measuring the Effect of Student Aid on College Attendance and Completion." *American Economic Review* 93(1): 279–88.

Fry, Richard, Sarah E. Turner, and Anthony P. Carnevale. 2000. "Growing Inequality in Collegiate Attainment: Evidence on the Role of Family Income." Unpublished paper. University of Virginia, Charlottesville.

Furstenberg, Frank F., Jr., Rubén Rumbaut, and Richard A. Settersten Jr. 2005. "On the Frontier of Adulthood: Emerging Themes and New Directions." In *On the Frontier of Adulthood: Theory, Research, and Public Policy*, edited by Richard A. Settersten Jr., Frank F. Furstenberg Jr., and Rubén Rumbaut. Chicago, Ill.: University of Chicago Press.

Goldin, Claudia, and Lawrence F. Katz. 2000. "The Power of the Pill: Oral Contraceptives and Women's Career and Marriage Decisions." Working paper 7527. Cambridge, Mass.: National Bureau of Economic Research.

Goldin, Claudia, Lawrence F. Katz, and Illyana Kuziemko. 2006. "The Homecoming of American College Women: Reversal of the College Gender Gap."

Working paper 12139. Cambridge, Mass.: National Bureau of Economic Research.

Hansen, W. Lee. 1983. "Impact of Student Financial Aid on Access." In *The Crisis in Higher Education*, edited by Joseph Froomkin. New York: Academy of Political Science.

Heller, Donald E. 1999. "The Effects of Tuition and State Financial Aid on Public College Enrollment." *Review of Higher Education* 23(1): 65–89.

Hotz, V. Joseph, Lixin Colin Xu, Marta Tienda, and Avner Ahtiv. 2002. "Are There Returns to the Wages of Young Men While Working in School?" *Review of Economics and Statistics* 84(2): 221-36.

Ionescu, Felicia. 2006. "The Effect of the Federal Student Loan Program on College Enrollment and Default Rates." Unpublished paper. University of Iowa, Ames.

Jacob, Brian. 2002. "Where the Boys Aren't: Noncognitive Skills, Returns to School, and the Gender Gap in Higher Education." *Economics of Education Review* 21(6): 589–98.

Jaeger, David, and Marianne E. Page. 1996. "Degrees Matter: New Evidence on Sheepskin Effects in the Returns to Education." *Review of Economics and Statistics* 78(4): 733–40.

Kane, Thomas J. 1994. "College Entry by Blacks Since 1970: The Role of College Costs, Family Background, and the Returns to Education." *Journal of Political Economy* 102(5): 878–911.

———. 1995. "Rising Public College Tuition and College Entry: How Well Do Public Subsidies Promote Access to College?" Working paper 5164. Cambridge, Mass.: National Bureau of Economic Research.

———. 1999. *The Price of Admission: Rethinking How Americans Pay for College*. Washington: Brookings Institution Press.

Leslie, Larry L., and Paul T. Brinkman. 1988. *The Economic Value of Higher Education*. New York: Macmillan.

Long, Bridget. 2004. "The Impact of Federal Tax Credits for Higher Education." In *College Choices: The Economics of Where to Go, When to Go, and How to Pay for It*, edited by Caroline M. Hoxby. Chicago, Ill.: University of Chicago Press.

Lynch, Lisa M. 1992. "Private-Sector Training and the Earnings of Young Workers." *American Economic Review* 82(1): 299–312.

Martin, Joyce A., Brady E. Hamilton, Stephanie J. Ventura, Fay Menacker, and Melissa M. Park. 2002. "Births: Final Data for 2000." *National Vital Statistics Report* 50(5, February 12). Accessed at http://www.cdc.gov/nchs/data/nvsr/nvsr50/nvsr50_05.pdf.

McCormick, Alexander C., and Laura J. Horn. 1996. *A Descriptive Summary of 1992–93 Bachelor's Degree Recipients One Year Later, with an Essay on Time to Degree*. NCES 96-158. Washington: U.S. Government Printing Office for U.S. Department of Education, National Center for Education Statistics.

Meyer, Robert H., and David A. Wise. 1982. "The Transition from School to Work: The Experiences of Blacks and Whites." Working paper 1007. Cambridge, Mass.: National Bureau of Economic Research.

Mincer, Jacob. 1970. "The Distribution of Labor Income: A Survey with Special Reference to the Human Capital Approach." *Journal of Economic Literature* 8(1): 1–26.

Orfield, Gary. 1992. "Money, Equity, and College Access." *Harvard Educational Review* 62: 337–72.

Ruhm, Christopher J. 1997. "Is High School Employment Consumption or Investment?" *Journal of Labor Economics* 15(4): 735–76.

Schoeni, Robert, and Karen Ross. 2005. "Material Assistance Received from Families During the Transition to Adulthood." In *On the Frontier of Adulthood: Theory, Research, and Public Policy*, edited by Richard A. Settersten Jr., Frank F. Furstenberg Jr., and Rubén G. Rumbaut. Chicago, Ill.: University of Chicago Press.

Seftor, Neil, and Sarah E. Turner. 2002. "Federal Student Aid and Adult College Enrollment." *Journal of Human Resources* 37(2): 336–52.

Sjogren, Anna, and Maria Saez-Marti. 2004. "On the Timing of Education." Working paper 614. Stockholm, Sweden: Research Institute of Industrial Economics.

Strach, Patricia. 2005. "The Politics of Policy Design: Federal Funding for Higher Education." Unpublished paper. State University of New York, Albany.

Taber, Christopher. 2004. "Comment on 'Going to College and Finishing College: Explaining Different Educational Outcomes' by Sarah Turner." In *College Choices: The Economics of Where to Go, When to Go, and How to Pay for It*, edited by Caroline M. Hoxby. Chicago, Ill.: University of Chicago Press.

Turner, Sarah. 2003. "Pell Grants as Fiscal Stabilizers." Unpublished paper. University of Virginia, Charlottesville.

———. 2004. "Going to College and Finishing College: Explaining Different Educational Outcomes." In *College Choices: The Economics of Where to Go, When to Go, and How to Pay for It*, edited by Caroline M. Hoxby. Chicago, Ill.: University of Chicago Press.

Tyre, Peg. 2006. "The Trouble with Boys." *Newsweek* (January).

U.S. Bureau of the Census. n.d. "College Enrollment of Students Fourteen Years Old and Over, by Type of College, Attendance Status, Age, and Gender: October 1970 to 2004." *Current Population Survey*, table A-7. Accessed at http://www.census.gov/population/www/socdemo/school.html, last updated January 11, 2007.

PART II

LIVING WITH PARENTS LONGER AND STARTING FAMILIES LATER

Chapter 6

Labor Market Experiences and Transitions to Adulthood

CAROLYN J. HILL AND HARRY HOLZER

R ichard Settersten, Frank Furstenberg, and Rubén Rumbaut (2005, 5) recently concluded that today "entry into adulthood has become more ambiguous and generally occurs in a gradual, complex, and less uniform fashion" than in the recent past. This more protracted and complex transition to adulthood is often the focus of media and other reports that describe it as a "failure to launch" or a prolonged "adultolescence" in which youth simply refuse to assume the responsibilities of adulthood. Others have argued that perhaps the economy is the reason why more youth live longer at home with parents or delay marriage. Real wages stagnated or declined for many American workers during the 1970s and 1980s (although they recovered modestly afterwards), and less-educated young men experienced the largest declines (Katz and Autor 1999). Employment rates among young, less-educated white and Hispanic men declined slightly in the 1980s and stabilized in the 1990s; those of young black men (especially those without a high school diploma) continued to decline fairly sharply throughout this period, however, while their incarceration rates rose.[1] Could these declines have contributed to the protracted transition into adulthood as young men found it hard to earn sufficient wages to support themselves or a family?

In addition to labor market opportunities, the decisions of young people may reflect their family backgrounds and situations (including parental income and whether or not they themselves are parents), as well as a range of personal attitudes and behaviors. These decisions are likely to reflect their relative maturity, independence, and responsibility, as well as their expectations about longer-term labor market opportunities and success. Higher expectations and more positive attitudes are likely to be reflected earlier in life in a range of "productive" behaviors, such as both academic success and labor market experiences during the high school years. In contrast, lower expectations and more negative attitudes may be reflected in risky behaviors during those years, including substance use and illegal activities. Although previous research has analyzed the effects of high school academic and job histories as well as crime and incarceration on future labor market outcomes, how these factors affect young people's choices about their living arrangements and marriage more broadly has received less attention.[2]

This chapter examines the extent to which labor market changes and other personal characteristics explain changes over time in young adults' living arrangements (living with parents or marrying). The estimates are not necessarily causal—that is, we are not arguing that labor market changes caused the changes in living arrangements. Rather, the results are only a starting point for considering how transitions to adulthood are affected by labor market trends and other behaviors of youth. Our chapter builds on the work of David Card and Thomas Lemieux (2000), who analyzed Current Population Survey (CPS) data on wages and hours worked across regions and over time to account for changes in living arrangements and other outcomes among youth and young adults age sixteen to twenty-four in the United States. It also draws on work by Valerie Oppenheimer and Alisa Lewin (1999), who used the National Longitudinal Survey of Youth (1979 cohort) to examine the relation between schooling and labor market conditions and marriage decisions for young adults through age thirty-three. Finally, we draw on research by Mary Corcoran and Jordan Matsudaira (2005), who used the Panel Study of Income Dynamics (PSID) to document differences among youth age twenty-seven to thirty-four in leaving home, education, and employment between 1986 and 1996.

Data

We use data from the 1979 and 1997 cohorts of the National Longitudinal Survey of Youth (NLSY-79 and NLSY-97). The NLSY collects information annually on labor market outcomes, school experiences and academic performance, family income, criminal behavior, family relationships, and living arrangements for a group of individuals. All of these factors are likely to be related to labor market behavior. The NLSY also includes data on some young people who are incarcerated at the time of the survey, and we have included them in our sample (though we have also checked to make sure that our results are not driven by their inclusion). We impose a few restrictions on the full NLSY-79 and NLSY-97 samples, detailed in the appendix. The final sample for this study was roughly 4,000 young adults who were age twenty to twenty-two in 1984 (cohort 1) or 2002 (cohort 2). The sample sizes vary somewhat (owing to missing data), depending on the variables examined.

We focus on three living arrangements at the time of the survey: living at home with parents, being married, or cohabiting with an intimate partner. Roughly 80 percent of NLSY youth lived in one of these three arrangements. The remainder lived alone, with other relatives, or with roommates. We also assess hours worked, weeks worked, and hourly wages, both at the time of the survey and during high school (at ages sixteen and seventeen). To achieve comparability across the two NLSY cohorts, the wage rate includes tips and bonuses as well as regular wages. We adjust nominal wages for inflation using the Consumer Price Index Research Series (CPI-RS), which is the Bureau of Labor Statistics' most complete effort to measure inflation and eliminate upward biases in the consumer price index over time.[3]

Behaviors and outcomes during high school include grade point average (GPA) and whether the individual drank alcohol, smoked cigarettes, or smoked marijuana. Supplementary analyses also incorporated results from the Armed Services Vocational Aptitude Battery (ASVAB) and arrest and illegal activities before age eighteen for sample members in the NLSY-97 (because these variables are available for the high school years only in the NLSY-97; see also Michael 2001). The appendix contains further information about the definition and construction of our variables, and table 6A.1 presents summary statistics on the variables used as explanatory variables in the regression models.

We present two kinds of results: (1) summary statistics on labor market outcomes and living arrangements and (2) regression equations in which the outcomes are our three categories of living arrangements. The summary statistics are presented separately for the two NSLY cohorts and by enrollment/education status and race and/or gender within each cohort. The main regression equations, estimated using ordinary least squares (OLS), appear separately by gender and use pooled samples across the two cohorts. The basic models contain cohort dummies to capture trends over time between 1984 and 2002 and controls for age, education/enrollment, race-ethnicity, and parental income during the sample members' teenage years. Then two sets of variables are added sequentially to the models to ascertain the extent to which they can account for observed changes over time or differences across education and race/gender groups. First, variables are added that capture contemporaneous employment outcomes as reflections of sample members' labor market opportunities. Next, educational and employment outcomes and risky behaviors of young people during high school are added to the model as reflections of sample members' independence, maturity, and future expectations of success.[4] Higher GPAs (as well as college enrollment) should capture expectations of future labor market success. Whether or not the sample member already has a child is also included among the latter variables, since this might be associated with a greater likelihood of marriage or cohabitation and less likelihood of living with parents. We also present some estimated regression models separately by cohort to decompose the changes over time into those attributable to changes in variable means versus those attributable to changes in coefficients. Sample weights are used in the summary statistics but not in the regression analyses.

Several limitations of this analysis should be noted. First, the timing of the NLSY cohorts is not ideal. Real wages of less-educated workers stagnated or declined over the period extending from 1973 to 1995 and rose thereafter. By comparing outcomes in 1984 and 2002, we combine periods of modestly declining and then significantly rising wages. However, changes in living arrangements between 1985 and 2003 might still reflect lagged responses to the long-term deterioration in labor market opportunities for young workers that began in the 1970s.

Second, self-reports of risky behavior and crime might not be accurate given the stigma associated with these actions (people tend to not report stigmatized actions). The results, therefore, may underreport risky behavior, especially for blacks, among whom self-reported crime rates appear to be especially downward-biased (Abe 2001; Hindelang, Hirschi, and Weis 1981; Viscusi 1986). The ways in which some of these variables are measured—such as whether or not one ever engaged in the behaviors rather than with what frequency—also create limitations. All in all, these measurement issues are likely to bias our estimated regression relationships toward zero.[5]

Finally, it is well known (see, for example, Ellwood 1982; Gardecki and Neumark 1998; Meyer and Wise 1982) that estimates of the effects of early labor market outcomes on later ones will be upwardly biased owing to the presence of omitted variables. Estimates of earlier risky behaviors on later labor market outcomes or living arrangements might be similarly biased, since these behaviors often reflect self-selection by individuals according to unobserved personal attitudes or attributes. In estimated regressions that measure the effects of current employment outcomes on living arrangements, the independent variables might well be endogenous with respect to the dependent variables. Because of these limitations, we can only speculate about interpretations, while deferring strong claims about causal relationships to future research.

Descriptive Statistics on Employment and Living Arrangements

Table 6.1 presents average hourly wages, hours worked, and weeks worked for young people at ages twenty to twenty-two in the two NLSY

Table 6.1   Employment Outcomes of Young Adults Age Twenty to Twenty-two in 1984 and 2002

	Hourly Wages		Total Hours Worked		Weeks Worked	
	1984	2002	1984	2002	1984	2002
Full sample	$8.77	$9.94	1,240	1,286	33.2	35.3
By education level						
Not enrolled						
High school dropout or GED	8.47	9.16	1,167	1,176	28.4	28.4
High school degree	8.94	10.03	1,467	1,478	36.0	35.9
Some college or college degree	9.66	10.98	1,445	1,616	36.0	39.7
Enrolled						
Two-year college	8.37	9.99	1,070	1,304	35.9	38.5
Four-year college	7.84	9.62	754	955	29.6	35.2
By gender and race-ethnicity						
Male						
White	9.61	10.50	1,369	1,410	34.4	36.0
Black	8.61	10.14	1,143	1,118	28.7	28.6
Hispanic	9.55	10.38	1,326	1,402	33.7	34.3
Female						
White	8.12	9.53	1,221	1,247	35.0	37.7
Black	7.10	8.73	779	1,012	23.0	29.3
Hispanic	8.28	9.63	1,020	1,216	29.2	34.8

Sources: Authors' calculations using the NLSY-79 and NLSY-97.
Notes: Hourly wages are in 2002 dollars, adjusted for inflation using the CPI-RS. Full sample sizes for 1984 and 2002 are, respectively: 2,994 and 3,341 for hourly wages; 4,008 and 4,290 for total hours worked; and 4,039 and 4,420 for weeks worked.

cohorts. Females and blacks tend to have lower wages, hours worked, and weeks worked than males or whites. Among those who did not go on to college, persons with lower educational attainment lag behind those with more education in both wages and work effort.

Between 1984 and 2002, real wages for all respondents as a group increased on average by 13 percent, from $8.77 to $9.94; annual hours worked increased by 4 percent, to 1,286 hours; and average weeks worked rose 6 percent, to 35.3 weeks a year.[6] The trends over time show relatively constant or mildly increasing real wages and work effort for most groups, with black males and black females exhibiting the largest percentage increases in wages. Other studies using the CPS (for example, Juhn 2000; Katz and Autor 1999) have shown declining real wages and employment among less-educated young men between 1987–88 and 1995. Presumably, the earnings gains experienced by these groups after 1995 counteracted those prior declines. Nevertheless, real earnings and employment for these groups in 2002 did not achieve the earning levels reached in the early 1970s, before the lengthy period of declining real wages among less-educated men began.[7]

Increases in wages and work effort are largest (in both absolute and percentage terms) for those enrolled in either a two-year or a four-year college and for those who are not enrolled but have some college experience. Specifically, real wages rose by 23 percent over this eighteen-year period for persons enrolled in four-year colleges, by 12 percent for high school graduates, and by just 8 percent for high school dropouts. Among the less-educated, increases are generally larger among women than men (results available from the authors). Together, these patterns suggest that labor market inequality between more- and less-educated young adults, but not between genders, continued to widen overall during the period.

Black and Hispanic females show the largest increases in work effort, perhaps owing to welfare reform and the growth of work supports for low-income families, such as the Earned Income Tax Credit (Blank 2002). In contrast, black males show modest declines in total hours worked over this time period; these declines (in data not reported in the table) are quite dramatic among high school dropouts. When incarcerated persons are removed from the sample, hours for black males increase very slightly over time (by seven hours), yet black male dropouts still show declines over time in hours and weeks worked. The decline is less dramatic, but remains statistically significant.[8]

Table 6.2 shows that between 1985 and 2003 the percentage of young adults living with their parents increased from 45.4 to 56.8 percent, the percentage married dropped dramatically from 23.6 to 10.3 percent, and the percentage cohabiting increased sharply from 6.7 to 14.4 percent.

The increasing propensity of young adults to live with their parents or to cohabit with a partner and their decreasing propensity to marry are evident across almost all subgroups. Marriage rates declined most dramatically for black females (12.3 percentage points, or 71 percent) and for black males (5.2 percentage points, or 63 percent).[9] Declines of similar magnitude remain when incarcerated persons are removed from the sample. The increased tendency to live at home with parents is most pronounced among those with only a high school degree (increasing by 24 percent) and those enrolled in four-year colleges (increasing by 27 percent). By 2002–2003, one-half of those with only a high school degree lived with parents at age twenty to twenty-two, and three-fourths of those in a traditional four-year college were living at home while in school. Cohabitation rates at least doubled for everyone but white and black females, whose rates of increase were still quite high (84 and 74 percent, respectively). Those enrolled in college are generally more likely to live at home and less likely to marry than the non-college-enrolled. Young women are less likely to live at home and more likely to be married than young men, presumably because on average they marry men

Table 6.2   Living Arrangements of Young Adults Age Twenty to Twenty-two in 1984 and 2002

	Lived with Parents		Married		Cohabiting	
	1985	2002 to 2003	1985	2002 to 2003	1985	2002 to 2003
Full sample	45.4%	56.8%	23.6%	10.3%	6.7%	14.4%
By education level						
Not enrolled						
High school dropout or GED	40.4	42.1	28.8	14.1	11.7	24.1
High school degree	41.0	50.7	31.3	12.3	7.2	18.5
Some college or college						
degree	40.7	47.9	25.5	15.5	6.1	14.7
Enrolled						
Two-year college	62.0	66.7	10.0	7.4	4.0	9.7
Four-year college	58.8	74.6	7.1	3.7	1.5	5.5
By gender and race-ethnicity						
Male						
White	49.4	61.0	17.7	7.6	4.3	12.3
Black	56.6	62.8	8.3	3.1	5.5	12.4
Hispanic	53.2	63.8	21.7	8.6	6.8	13.4
Female						
White	37.1	51.8	33.3	14.8	9.1	16.7
Black	52.4	52.5	17.3	5.0	7.3	12.7
Hispanic	45.4	51.7	33.9	19.9	7.9	20.1

Sources: Authors' calculations using the NLSY-79 and NLSY-97.
Notes: Full sample sizes for 1984 and 2002 are, respectively: 4,035 and 4,420 for lived with parents; and 4,039 and 4,416 for married and cohabiting.

who are somewhat older. Blacks tend to marry less than whites or Hispanics, with black men being the least likely to marry.

Equations for Living Arrangements

Tables 6.3, 6.4, and 6.5 show how various personal characteristics and behaviors affect the probability that young people will live with their parents, get married, or cohabit.[10] All estimates presented are from linear probability models.[11] For these models, we present separate estimates by gender, pooling the two cohorts. Appendix table 6A.2 will further divide the samples by cohort.

We present three specifications in these tables: model 1 includes a year (or cohort) dummy, plus variables for age, education, race, and parental income during the sample members' teenage years (entered as a set of quintile dummies, to allow for possible nonlinear effects).[12] These variables are clearly exogenous to living arrangement decisions. Model 2

(Text continues page 154)

Table 6.3 Linear Probability Models Predicting Living with Parents for Young Adults Age Twenty to Twenty-two in 1984 and 2002

	Males			Females		
	Model 1	Model 2	Model 3	Model 1	Model 2	Model 3
Constant	2.232*** [0.198]	2.087*** [0.201]	2.083*** [0.204]	1.985*** [0.199]	1.853*** [0.203]	1.788*** [0.207]
Year = 2002 (omitted category: year = 1984)	0.079*** [0.016]	0.084*** [0.016]	0.095*** [0.017]	0.052*** [0.015]	0.052*** [0.016]	0.068*** [0.017]
Age	-0.083*** [0.009]	-0.074*** [0.009]	-0.064*** [0.009]	-0.075*** [0.009]	-0.071*** [0.009]	-0.060*** [0.009]
Education level (omitted category: not enrolled, some college or college degree)						
Not enrolled, high school dropout or GED	0.008 [0.024]	-0.006 [0.024]	0.028 [0.026]	-0.100*** [0.024]	-0.111*** [0.025]	-0.051** [0.026]
Not enrolled, high school degree	0.002 [0.023]	0.001 [0.023]	0.004 [0.023]	-0.017 [0.022]	-0.023 [0.022]	-0.008 [0.022]
Enrolled, two-year college	0.123*** [0.033]	0.103*** [0.032]	0.092*** [0.032]	0.161*** [0.032]	0.154*** [0.032]	0.130*** [0.031]
Enrolled, four-year college	0.151*** [0.025]	0.112*** [0.026]	0.105*** [0.026]	0.240*** [0.023]	0.225*** [0.024]	0.175*** [0.025]
Race-ethnicity (omitted category: white)						
Black	0.083*** [0.019]	0.075*** [0.019]	0.065*** [0.019]	0.135*** [0.019]	0.130*** [0.019]	0.128*** [0.020]
Hispanic	0.075*** [0.020]	0.074*** [0.020]	0.077*** [0.020]	0.094*** [0.020]	0.098*** [0.020]	0.086*** [0.020]
Parents' average income (omitted category: fifth quintile)						
First quintile	-0.070* [0.027]	-0.082*** [0.027]	-0.086*** [0.027]	-0.077*** [0.027]	-0.088*** [0.027]	-0.071*** [0.027]
Second quintile	-0.031 [0.027]	-0.040 [0.027]	-0.057** [0.026]	-0.052* [0.027]	-0.059** [0.027]	-0.04 [0.027]
Third quintile	-0.025 [0.028]	-0.030 [0.027]	-0.042 [0.027]	-0.056** [0.028]	-0.058** [0.028]	-0.042 [0.028]
Fourth quintile	0.037 [0.027]	0.030 [0.027]	0.022 [0.027]	-0.057* [0.028]	-0.058** [0.028]	-0.049* [0.027]

Labor market variables	(1)	(2)	(3)	(4)
Hours worked (hundreds of hours)	-0.004*** [0.001]	-0.003*** [0.001]	-0.001 [0.001]	-0.002* [0.001]
Hourly wage (omitted category: fifth quintile)				
First quintile	0.106*** [0.028]	0.089*** [0.027]	0.115*** [0.029]	0.107*** [0.029]
Second quintile	0.102*** [0.027]	0.083*** [0.026]	0.093*** [0.029]	0.092*** [0.029]
Third quintile	0.044 [0.027]	0.040 [0.027]	0.070** [0.031]	0.065** [0.030]
Fourth quintile	0.052** [0.025]	0.044* [0.025]	0.077** [0.030]	0.082*** [0.030]
Had a child by 1984 (1979 cohort) or 2002 (1997 cohort)		-0.220*** [0.020]		-0.207*** [0.018]
GPA in high school		-0.041*** [0.011]		-0.018 [0.011]
Hours worked, ages 16 and 17 (hundreds of hours)		-0.003*** [0.001]		-0.004*** [0.001]
Substance use before age 18				
Drank alcohol		-0.018 [0.018]		0.014 [0.018]
Smoked cigarettes		-0.029 [0.018]		-0.027 [0.018]
Smoked marijuana		-0.052*** [0.017]		-0.025 [0.018]
Number of observations	4,281	4,281	4,170	4,170
R-squared	0.073	0.116	0.118	0.156

Sources: Authors' calculations using the NLSY-79 and NLSY-97.

Notes: Robust standard errors, clustered for siblings, are shown in brackets. Missing data dummies were included for all explanatory variables except for cohort and age.

* p < 0.10; ** p < 0.05; *** p < 0.01

Table 6.4 Linear Probability Models Predicting Being Married for Young Adults Age Twenty to Twenty-two in 1984 and 2002

	Males			Females		
	Model 1	Model 2	Model 3	Model 1	Model 2	Model 3
Constant	-0.734***	-0.609***	-0.397***	-0.505***	-0.549***	-0.334**
	[0.125]	[0.126]	[0.123]	[0.160]	[0.163]	[0.165]
Year = 2002 (omitted category: year = 1984)	-0.084***	-0.085***	-0.094***	-0.126***	-0.121***	-0.132***
	[0.009]	[0.009]	[0.010]	[0.012]	[0.013]	[0.014]
Age	0.043***	0.037***	0.023***	0.039***	0.041***	0.028***
	[0.006]	[0.006]	[0.006]	[0.007]	[0.008]	[0.007]
Education level (omitted category: not enrolled, some college or college degree)						
Not enrolled, high school dropout or GED	0.008	0.018	-0.017	0.045**	0.035	-0.009
	[0.017]	[0.017]	[0.017]	[0.022]	[0.022]	[0.023]
Not enrolled, high school degree	0.002	0.004	-0.002	0.039**	0.036*	0.019
	[0.016]	[0.016]	[0.015]	[0.019]	[0.019]	[0.019]
Enrolled, two-year college	-0.058***	-0.046**	-0.034*	-0.096***	-0.103***	-0.082***
	[0.019]	[0.019]	[0.018]	[0.023]	[0.023]	[0.023]
Enrolled, four-year college	-0.079***	-0.055***	-0.045***	-0.163***	-0.170***	-0.124***
	[0.015]	[0.015]	[0.015]	[0.017]	[0.018]	[0.018]
Race-ethnicity (omitted category: white)						
Black	-0.093***	-0.087***	-0.106***	-0.155***	-0.159***	-0.185***
	[0.011]	[0.011]	[0.011]	[0.014]	[0.014]	[0.015]
Hispanic	0.005	0.006	-0.009	-0.001	-0.002	-0.012
	[0.014]	[0.014]	[0.013]	[0.018]	[0.018]	[0.018]
Parents' average income (omitted category: fifth quintile)						
First quintile	0.027	0.036**	0.021	0.011	0.009	-0.019
	[0.017]	[0.017]	[0.016]	[0.021]	[0.021]	[0.021]
Second quintile	0.038**	0.044***	0.045***	0.019	0.016	-0.006
	[0.017]	[0.017]	[0.016]	[0.021]	[0.021]	[0.020]
Third quintile	0.001	0.004	0.008	0.030	0.031	0.017
	[0.016]	[0.016]	[0.015]	[0.022]	[0.022]	[0.021]
Fourth quintile	-0.002	0.001	0.003	0.013	0.013	0.005
	[0.016]	[0.016]	[0.015]	[0.021]	[0.021]	[0.020]

	(1)	(2)	(3)	(4)	(5)	(6)
Labor market variables						
Hours worked (hundreds of hours)	0.002***	0.002***	0.002***	0.002***	-0.002*	0.000
	[0.001]	[0.001]	[0.001]	[0.001]	[0.001]	[0.001]
Hourly wage (omitted category: fifth quintile)						
First quintile		-0.061***	-0.057***		0.015	0.004
		[0.018]	[0.017]		[0.022]	[0.022]
Second quintile		-0.085***	-0.071***		0.043*	0.031
		[0.016]	[0.015]		[0.023]	[0.022]
Third quintile		-0.055***	-0.050***		0.036	0.032
		[0.018]	[0.017]		[0.025]	[0.024]
Fourth quintile		-0.032*	-0.030*		0.034	0.027
		[0.018]	[0.017]		[0.025]	[0.024]
Had a child by 1984 (1979 cohort) or 2002 (1997 cohort)			0.271***			0.215***
			[0.017]			[0.016]
GPA in high school			0.022***			0.009
			[0.007]			[0.009]
Hours worked, age 16 and 17 (hundreds of hours)			0.001			0.002***
			[0.000]			[0.001]
Substance use before age 18						
Drank alcohol			0.004			-0.032**
			[0.011]			[0.015]
Smoked cigarettes			0.005			0.011
			[0.011]			[0.014]
Smoked marijuana			-0.021**			-0.044***
			[0.010]			[0.015]
Number of observations	4,281	4,281	4,281	4,170	4,170	4,170
R-squared	0.069	0.082	0.180	0.118	0.120	0.174

Sources: Authors' calculations using the NLSY-79 and NLSY-97.
Notes: Robust standard errors, clustered for siblings, are shown in brackets. Missing data dummies were included for all explanatory variables except for cohort and age.
* p < 0.10; ** p < 0.05; *** p < 0.01

Table 6.5   Linear Probability Models Predicting Cohabiting for Young Adults Age Twenty to Twenty-two in 1984 and 2002

	Males			Females		
	Model 1	Model 2	Model 3	Model 1	Model 2	Model 3
Constant	-0.287** [0.118]	-0.231* [0.122]	-0.136 [0.123]	-0.037 [0.142]	0.013 [0.146]	-0.051 [0.153]
Year = 2002 (omitted category: year = 1984)	0.081*** [0.009]	0.080*** [0.009]	0.089*** [0.010]	0.093*** [0.011]	0.088*** [0.011]	0.078*** [0.012]
Age	0.014*** [0.006]	0.011* [0.006]	0.005 [0.006]	0.005 [0.007]	0.002 [0.007]	0.001 [0.007]
Education level (omitted category: not enrolled, some college or college degree)						
Not enrolled, high school dropout or GED	0.067*** [0.014]	0.074*** [0.014]	0.034** [0.016]	0.059*** [0.018]	0.073*** [0.019]	0.058*** [0.020]
Not enrolled, high school degree	0.015 [0.013]	0.018 [0.013]	0.011 [0.013]	0.020 [0.016]	0.025 [0.016]	0.024 [0.016]
Enrolled, two-year college	-0.031* [0.017]	-0.023 [0.017]	-0.017 [0.017]	-0.052*** [0.020]	-0.044** [0.020]	-0.037* [0.020]
Enrolled, four-year college	-0.059*** [0.012]	-0.039*** [0.012]	-0.023* [0.013]	-0.084*** [0.014]	-0.070*** [0.015]	-0.058*** [0.016]
Race-ethnicity (omitted category: white)						
Black	-0.025** [0.011]	-0.014 [0.011]	-0.021* [0.011]	-0.068*** [0.013]	-0.061*** [0.013]	-0.047*** [0.014]
Hispanic	0.000 [0.013]	0.001 [0.013]	-0.005 [0.013]	-0.020 [0.015]	-0.019 [0.015]	-0.007 [0.015]
Parents' average income (omitted category: fifth quintile)						
First quintile	0.032** [0.014]	0.040*** [0.014]	0.036*** [0.014]	0.072*** [0.017]	0.076*** [0.017]	0.078*** [0.017]
Second quintile	0.049*** [0.014]	0.052*** [0.014]	0.057*** [0.014]	0.059*** [0.017]	0.062*** [0.017]	0.060*** [0.017]
Third quintile	0.025* [0.014]	0.027** [0.014]	0.030** [0.014]	0.053*** [0.018]	0.050*** [0.018]	0.046*** [0.017]
Fourth quintile	0.013 [0.013]	0.015 [0.013]	0.018 [0.013]	0.033** [0.017]	0.032* [0.017]	0.030* [0.016]

Labor market variables

Hours worked (hundreds of hours)	0.002*** [0.001]	0.002*** [0.001]	0.002*** [0.001]	0.002*** [0.001]	0.002*** [0.001]	0.002*** [0.001]
Hourly wage (omitted category: fifth quintile)						
First quintile		-0.038** [0.017]	-0.031* [0.017]		-0.040* [0.022]	-0.031 [0.022]
Second quintile		-0.015 [0.017]	-0.007 [0.017]		-0.038* [0.021]	-0.032 [0.021]
Third quintile		0.000 [0.018]	0.000 [0.017]		-0.031 [0.023]	-0.027 [0.023]
Fourth quintile		-0.011 [0.017]	-0.010 [0.016]		-0.028 [0.023]	-0.028 [0.023]
Had a child by 1984 (1979 cohort) or 2002 (1997 cohort)			0.114*** [0.016]		0.040*** [0.014]	0.040*** [0.014]
GPA in high school			-0.008 [0.006]		0.010 [0.008]	0.010 [0.008]
Hours worked, age 16 and 17 (hundreds of hours)			0.001 [0.000]		0.001** [0.001]	0.001** [0.001]
Substance use before age 18						
Drank alcohol			0.010 [0.010]			0.017 [0.012]
Smoked cigarettes			0.006 [0.010]			0.022* [0.012]
Smoked marijuana			0.032*** [0.010]			0.019 [0.013]
Number of observations	4,281	4,281	4,281	4,170	4,170	4,170
R-squared	0.046	0.058	0.085	0.046	0.050	0.061

Sources: Authors' calculations using the NLSY-79 and NLSY-97.
Notes: Robust standard errors, clustered for siblings, are shown in brackets. Missing data dummies were included for all explanatory variables except for cohort and age.
* $p < 0.10$; ** $p < 0.05$; *** $p < 0.01$

adds variables for contemporaneous labor market outcomes (that is, hours worked in the previous year and hourly wages entered as a set of quintile dummies), which might be partly endogenous but which also might constrain the choice of living arrangements. Finally, model 3 adds a set of variables that reflect current needs as well as a set of underlying attitudes and behaviors that might be more or less associated with independence, maturity, future orientation, and risk. These variables include whether the individual had a child,[13] high school grade point average, hours worked while ages sixteen and seventeen, and substance use (alcohol, cigarettes, or marijuana) by age eighteen. At least a few of these variables, such as high school GPA, might also be a proxy for long-term labor market expectations or potential, to augment our contemporaneous (and therefore more short-term) labor market outcomes.

The regression analyses confirm the trends in living arrangements over time shown in table 6.2: namely, young adults are living with their parents and cohabiting more frequently than two decades ago and marrying less frequently. Furthermore, the magnitude of the change is similar to that observed in table 6.2. The tendency to live with parents now rises between the two time periods by eight to ten percentage points for males and by five to seven points for females; marriage rates fall by eight to nine points for males and about thirteen points for females, while cohabitation rises eight to nine points for both groups. The estimated changes over time in tables 6.3 to 6.5 also do not vary greatly across the different models. Together, these findings suggest that our ability to account for the trends we observe over time with this set of explanatory variables is quite limited, even with the set of controls that we have included for demographic characteristics, parental income, contemporaneous labor market characteristics, and high school behaviors.

Several cross-sectional findings are also worth noting. Not surprisingly, marriage rates rise with age, while the tendency to live with parents falls. Those who are enrolled in a two-year college and especially those enrolled in a four-year college are more likely than others to live with their parents and less likely to marry or cohabit; since enrollment rates have risen over time, these developments probably contribute to the observed trends in living arrangements (although table 6.2 shows the trend occurring among the non-college-enrolled as well). The tendency to live at home is greater among blacks and Hispanics than whites, while marriage and cohabitation rates are lower among blacks. The effects of parental income are notable as well: those from higher-income families are more likely to live at home and less likely to marry or cohabit than those from lower-income families. Perhaps their parents' greater ability to "feather their nests" enhances the appeal of living at home for more affluent young adults.

Overall, higher wages and more hours worked reduce the tendency to live at home and raise the tendency to marry or cohabit. The magnitude of the effect of hours worked, however, is relatively small, although differences across hourly wage quintiles seem somewhat more substantial. For instance, earning in the lower wage quintiles (the bottom 80 percent of earners) increases the probability for young men of living with their parents by four to nine percentage points compared with earning in the top quintile. Neither hours worked nor wages are statistically significant predictors of being married for females, while both are significant for males. Results for cohabitation are more mixed. Finally, in all cases, labor market variables do little to explain the changes (measured by the changes in R-squared between models 1 and 2), and the change in magnitude for the cohort dummy is negligible.[14] The potential endogeneity of the labor market outcomes with respect to living arrangements may account for these apparently modest effects, but this seems unlikely for two reasons. First, the effects of living arrangement choices on wages and work effort should go in the same direction, and second, other studies that use more aggregated labor market outcomes to avoid the endogeneity problems (see also Card and Lemieux 2000) generate magnitudes of effects that are quite similar to our own.[15]

Stronger explanations for the living arrangements are found in other variables. In particular, having a child significantly reduces the likelihood of living at home and increases the odds of either marrying or cohabiting. Productive behavior in high school—either academically (as measured by GPA) or in the labor market (as measured by hours worked at ages sixteen and seventeen)—tends to reduce living at home and increase marriage, even after accounting for current labor market impacts.

The estimated effects of productive behavior probably reflect youths' higher expectations for longer-term earnings, or they may reflect greater individual independence, maturity, and responsibility. In contrast, early substance use is likely to reflect a different set of personal traits—perhaps less orientation to the future and less aversion to risk. Although the estimated effects are small (and often not statistically significant), there is some evidence of reduced tendencies to live at home or marry and greater tendency to cohabit among young adults who use substances. We also find that ASVAB math/verbal aggregate scores had virtually no effects on living arrangements, and that participation in a range of illegal activities before age eighteen (results available from the authors on request) had only modest effects that resemble those of substance use. That is, illegal activity early in life reduces the tendency to live at home or marry (especially for those who have been arrested), but increases the tendency of some (those who attacked others or carried handguns) toward cohabitation.[16]

Given our inability to account for observed trends in living arrangements, we explored whether the pooled results in tables 6.3 through 6.5

might be masking some changes over time that would better help us account for these trends (see table 6A.2 for separate estimates of model 3 for the NLSY-79 and NLSY-97). In general, the patterns are quite similar as before, with a few exceptions. For instance, young men in the bottom quintile of the wage distribution are much more likely to live at home (relative to those in the top quintile) in the later period. But the positive effects of four-year college enrollment on living with parents become stronger over time, while the negative effects of GPA become weaker. These latter findings imply a shift toward living at home at the *higher* end of the educational spectrum and argue against the notion that expectations of weak future labor market outcomes are driving the changes in living arrangements. Regarding marriage and cohabitation, we find that high school graduates and dropouts are clearly marrying less, but that is also true for those with somewhat more positive labor market outcomes. The negative income effects on cohabitation weaken over time, while the positive labor market effects become stronger. And those with children are now less likely to marry and somewhat more likely to cohabit than before.

In short, the trends observed over time seem to apply to a variety of groups with different future prospects and circumstances. To what extent does the pattern of changing estimated effects over time help account for observed trends in living arrangements? We have decomposed these overall changes into those accounted for by changes in the values of the explanatory variables versus those accounted for by changes in coefficients, using the well-known Blinder-Oaxaca decomposition (Blinder 1973; Oaxaca 1973).

The results strongly suggest that changes in the outcomes over time are being driven by changes in the relationships between observable characteristics and outcomes (that is, the coefficients) rather than by changes in the characteristics and experiences of the young adults themselves.[17] But no single set of changes—including those on contemporaneous labor market outcomes—can account for much of the observed changes in outcomes. The growing tendency of young men in the lowest wage quintile to live with their parents can account for less than 1.5 percentage points of the overall increase.[18] For females and for the other living arrangements, these effects generally go in the opposite direction. And as noted, many of the changes can be observed in the future for those who had high GPAs in high school or were in college, and therefore have relatively higher earnings, as well as for those who have less achievement or education and lower earnings.

Conclusion

Overall, we find that in 2002 young people tended to live at home with their parents more frequently, cohabit more frequently, and marry less frequently than was the case in 1984. These trends differ little by education, race-ethnicity, or gender. We also find that changes in wages and employment explain very little of the increased tendency to live with parents or the declining tendency to marry, either over time or by education, race-ethnicity, or gender.

However, at a point in time, higher grades, more work experience, and higher wages in high school are better explanations for the choice of marriage and living arrangements. We also find some evidence that risky behaviors during high school increase the tendency to cohabit a few years later, while these behaviors lessen the tendency to live at home. These findings at least suggest that personal attitudes and behaviors that reflect independence and maturity are associated with later living arrangements, although not necessarily with changes in outcomes over time.

In short, the long-term declines in labor market opportunities for less-educated young workers cannot account for much of the growing tendency of young adults to live at home or cohabit, nor for their reduced tendency to marry. Of course, it is possible that our measures do not fully capture the effects of changes in labor market opportunities. For one thing, the labor market outcomes might reflect transitory, rather than permanent, employment behaviors and outcomes, and perhaps it is the more permanent behaviors that have a greater impact on living arrangements. Perhaps rising costs of living are more influential (especially for housing in some regions of the country; see Yelowitz, this volume). The data may also fail to capture the effect of rising expectations. Still, the fact that we observe similar trends over time in living arrangements across different education, racial-ethnic, and gender groups reinforces the notion that these trends are not largely driven by changes in labor market opportunities, which have diverged greatly across education and gender groups in the past two or three decades.

As for the relation between high school outcomes and subsequent living arrangements, this is more likely to capture a range of unobserved personal expectations and behaviors across people and opportunity sets over time, all of which influence living arrangements in the short term—above and beyond the effects that express themselves in current labor market outcomes. Those individuals who earned good grades or worked more in high school can afford more independence and have better marriage prospects than those with weaker histories. Those who engaged in risky behaviors during high school are perhaps less welcome or less comfortable living at home with their parents, and they also might have weaker preferences for and worse prospects for marriage. For these individuals, cohabitation might be the preferred route, at least in the short term. Of course, even for the latter set of findings, estimated effects are quite small. Thus, we emphasize that these findings and interpretations are simply a starting point and only suggestive at best.

Appendix

Data Description

The NLSY-79 is a nationally representative survey of persons age fourteen to twenty-one as of December 31, 1978, and the NLSY-97 is a nationally representative survey of youth age twelve to sixteen as of December 31, 1996. The original sample sizes were 12,686 and 8,984, respectively.

We imposed three restrictions on the sample for our analysis. First, we included only young adults who turned twenty to twenty-two in 1984 and 2002, respectively. This subsample of the NLSY-79 was born in 1962 to 1964, and the subsample of the NLSY-97 was born in 1980 to 1982. The youngest sample members in the NLSY-79 turned twenty in 1984, and the oldest sample members in the NLSY-97 turned twenty-two in 2002; thus, in 1984 and 2002, the two cohorts overlapped for members who turned twenty to twenty-two in these years. These young adults were old enough to have completed high school but not yet old enough to have completed college. We focus on the years 1984 and 2002 because they represent similar points in the business cycle at which young adults of the same ages in the two cohorts can be observed. While unemployment rates in 1984 were somewhat higher than those in 2002 (7.5 versus 5.8 percent), labor market tightness seems comparable across the two years after adjusting for changing demographics. The labor market was recovering from a steep recession in 1984 while approaching the trough of a more modest downturn in 2002.

For the second sample restriction, we exclude any persons who were still enrolled in high school in 1984 or 2002 and persons enrolled in college for whom the type (two-year or four-year) could not be reliably determined. Enrolled in high school were 132 persons in our NLSY-79 sample and 49 in our NLSY-97 sample; the numbers of college enrollees in our samples for whom it was not possible to determine the type of college were 115 and 4, respectively.

For the third sample restriction, we include only the largest racial-ethnic subgroups: white non-Hispanics, black non-Hispanics, and Hispanics.

As noted in the chapter, the NLSY includes data on some young people who were incarcerated at the time of the survey. We measured incarceration status using the type of residence variable in the NLSY-79 and the type of dwelling variable in the NLSY-97. A respondent was considered incarcerated if rounds 1984 or 1985 of the NLSY-79 indicated incarceration or if rounds 5 (2001–2002) or 6 (2002–2003) of the NLSY-97 indicated incarceration. During the 2002–2003 survey year of the NLSY-97, a total of 81 individuals in our sample were incarcerated, while an additional 22 were incarcerated during the previous survey period. Comparable numbers for the NLSY-79 in the 1985 survey year are 42 and 23. Incarcerated individuals account for about 2 percent of our full sample in either the NLSY-79 or NLSY-97 cohorts, but nearly 5 percent of young black men in the 1979 cohort and 10 percent of young black men in the 1997 cohort.

The Bureau of Justice Statistics reports that 12 percent of young black men between the ages of sixteen and thirty-four are incarcerated at any time, while about twice that number are on parole or probation. Given the very high rates of incarceration among young black men, other analyses of this population are based on data that are seriously truncated. Undercounts in the CPS and elsewhere of non-incarcerated young black men are discussed in John Bound (1986) and various census reports.

Of course, the labor market outcomes and living arrangements of incarcerated men are somewhat predetermined, and including them might skew results in ways that would make them unrepresentative for those who truly have choices to make. In addition to the estimates presented here, we have a full set of estimates that do not include them (available from the authors on request). Virtually no qualitative result is changed by their inclusion or omission from the sample, though a few magnitudes are changed.

Variable Construction

Lived with Parents, Married, or Cohabited   These statuses are constructed from the household rosters and are measured at the time of the 1985 survey (January to June 1985) for NLSY-79 sample members and at the time of the round 6 survey (November 2002 to July 2003) for NLSY-97 sample members. "Parents" are defined as biological, step, adopted, or foster parents. Cohabiting relationships include only opposite-sex relationships.

Enrollment and Education Level   These variables are measured as of September of the corresponding year (1984 or 2002). Some values were imputed using information about enrollment status and education level at the time of the interview in rounds prior to and following these dates. Enrollment levels are "not enrolled" (and include separate categories for high school dropouts, GED, high school degree, some college, or college graduate) and "enrolled" (with separate categories for two-year college, including vocational and technical schools, and four-year colleges and universities, including graduate school).

Table 6A.1   Means for Control Variables

	Male		Female	
	NLSY-79	NLSY-97	NLSY-79	NLSY-97
Age on December 31, 1984 (1979 cohort) or 2002 (1997)	21.54	21.49	21.54	21.49
Race-ethnicity				
White	78.5%	69.5%	78.8%	71.4%
Black	14.7	16.0	14.6	16.1
Hispanic	6.9	14.5	6.5	12.6
Enrollment status and education level				
Not enrolled, high school dropout or GED	24.7	20.4	17.3	14.8
Not enrolled, high school degree	30.9	31.3	32.6	25.0
Not enrolled, some college or college degree	19.8	15.8	24.9	18.5
Enrolled, two-year college	6.3	8.3	5.9	10.2
Enrolled, four-year college	18.3	24.3	19.3	31.5
Parents' average income (average within quintile)				
First quintile	$16,051	$6,348	$15,474	$6,375
Second quintile	33,437	25,003	32,833	24,911
Third quintile	48,191	44,427	48,303	44,061
Fourth quintile	64,243	67,272	64,399	66,887
Fifth quintile	100,498	132,364	99,141	132,503
Hourly wage in 1984 or 2002 (average within quintile)				
First quintile	$4.94	$5.75	$4.92	$5.70
Second quintile	6.35	7.27	6.28	7.24
Third quintile	7.43	8.51	7.46	8.51
Fourth quintile	9.11	10.15	9.16	10.18
Fifth quintile	14.61	16.47	13.27	16.15
Had child by 1984 or 2002	14.5%	13.9%	29.5%	27.3%
GPA in high school	2.3	2.7	2.6	3.0
Hours worked, ages sixteen and seventeen	1,173	1,116	897	1,016
Substance use prior to age eighteen				
Drank alcohol	78.1%	72.8%	68.0%	74.0%
Smoked cigarettes	76.3	60.6	71.5	60.7
Smoked marijuana	52.5	42.1	42.4	38.2

Source: Authors' calculations from the NLSY-79 and NLSY-97.

Parental Income   We averaged values over three years when the sample member turned sixteen, seventeen, and eighteen. If income information in all three years was not available, then information for the subset of available years was used. For the 1997 cohort, in the first round we used the NLSY-constructed variable for income, along with the constructed variable for income source (to identify parental information); we used the income updates from parents in subsequent rounds. For the 1979 cohort, we used the created variable for total net family income and used only cases that had completed version A of the screener (indicating that parental income, not that of independent youth, was included in this variable). Quintiles were calculated separately by cohort, pooling across gender.

Hourly Wages   Hourly wages are measured in 2002 dollars, adjusted for inflation using the CPI-RS. When observed wages were nonzero but less than $2 or greater than $50, the value for this variable was set to missing. Fifty-one observations in our NLSY-79 sample and forty-five observations in our NLSY-97 sample had nonzero wages less than $2. No observations in our NLSY-79 sample and forty observations in our NLSY-97 sample had wages greater than $50. Wages were used from the job worked as of December 31 of the corresponding year (1984 or 2002) or from the last known job in the year if the sample member was not employed on December 31. To ensure comparability between the NSLY-79 and NLSY-97 measures, we used a measure of hourly earnings, or hourly compensation. This is the hourly wage plus any overtime, tips, or bonuses. (An hourly wage variable is not available in the NLSY-79 for this year.) Quintiles were calculated separately by cohort, pooling across gender.

Total Hours Worked   Total hours worked were measured for calendar years 1984 and 2002. We used created variables in the NLSY-79 and NLSY-97.

Had a Child by 1984 or 2002   For the 1997 cohort, we used created variables that provide the date of each child's birth, along with the round 6 interview date. For the 1979 cohort, we used information from the fertility and relationship history taken in the 1985 round of the survey.

Grade Point Average   We used course grades from transcript data for NLSY-79 sample members and course grades from self-reports for NLSY-97 sample members. (At the time the analysis was conducted, transcript data were not yet available for all sample members in the NLSY-97.) We calculated GPA by converting grades to a numeric four-point scale (A = 4.0).

Hours Worked, Ages Sixteen and Seventeen   We summed hours worked for all weeks between the youth's sixteenth and eighteenth birth dates.

Table 6A.2   Linear Probability Models Predicting Living Situation for Young Adults Age Twenty to Twenty-two in 1984 and 2002, Separately by Cohort

	Live with Parents			
	Male		Female	
	NLSY-79	NLSY-97	NLSY-79	NLSY-97
Constant	1.734***	2.515***	1.639***	1.963***
	[0.298]	[0.281]	[0.300]	[0.288]]
Age	–0.043***	–0.083***	–0.053***	–0.066**
	[0.014]	[0.013]	[0.013]	[0.013]
Education level (omitted category: not enrolled, some college or college degree)				
Not enrolled, high school dropout or GED	0.035	–0.010	–0.038	–0.065*
	[0.036]	[0.037]	[0.036]	[0.039]]
Not enrolled, high school degree	–0.001	0.002	–0.030	0.016
	[0.031]	[0.032]	[0.030]	[0.032]
Enrolled, two-year college	0.111**	0.082*	0.166***	0.119***
	[0.052]	[0.042]	[0.052]	[0.041]
Enrolled, four-year college	0.065	0.126***	0.148***	0.185***
	[0.040]	[0.035]	[0.038]	[0.034]
Race-ethnicity (omitted category: white)				
Black	0.071**	0.051*	0.172***	0.083***
	[0.028]	[0.028]	[0.029]	[0.027]
Hispanic	0.076***	0.075***	0.096***	0.073***
	[0.029]	[0.027]	[0.029]	[0.028]
Parents' average income (omitted category: fifth quintile)				
First quintile	–0.073*	–0.090**	–0.064	–0.069*
	[0.039]	[0.038]	[0.040]	[0.036]
Second quintile	–0.057	–0.041	–0.014	–0.057
	[0.039]	[0.036]	[0.041]	[0.036]
Third quintile	–0.010	–0.061*	–0.015	–0.066*
	[0.040]	[0.036]	[0.043]	[0.037]
Fourth quintile	0.044	0.006	–0.054	–0.050
	[0.041]	[0.035]	[0.042]	[0.036]
Labor market variables				
Hours worked (hundreds of hours)	–0.003**	–0.003***	0.001	–0.003**
	[0.001]	[0.001]	[0.002]	[0.001]
Hourly wage (omitted category: fifth quintile)				
First quintile	0.048	0.121***	0.127***	0.096**
	[0.041]	[0.037]	[0.045]	[0.038]
Second quintile	0.087**	0.081**	0.093**	0.091**
	[0.038]	[0.036]	[0.044]	[0.038]
Third quintile	0.047	0.033	0.091**	0.043
	[0.038]	[0.037]	[0.045]	[0.042]]
Fourth quintile	0.019	0.067*	0.089*	0.071*
	[0.035]	[0.035]	[0.046]	[0.040]

Table 6A.2 (*Continued*)

| | Married | | | | Cohabit | | |
| | Male | | Female | | Male | | Female | |
NLSY-79	NLSY-97	NLSY-79	NLSY-97	NLSY-79	NLSY-97	NLSY-79	NLSY-97
−0.291	−0.607***	−0.365	−0.386**	0.048	−0.245	−0.077	−0.040
[0.199]	[0.143]	[0.271]	[0.196]	[0.143]	[0.195]	[0.203]	[0.227]
0.017*	0.029***	0.026**	0.028***	−0.002	0.014	0.004	0.002
[0.009]	[0.007]	[0.012]	[0.009]	[0.006]	[0.009]	[0.009]	[0.010]
−0.001	−0.037*	−0.005	−0.024	0.030	0.041	0.076***	0.063*
[0.026]	[0.021]	[0.034]	[0.031]	[0.018]	[0.027]	[0.024]	[0.034]
0.018	−0.023	0.051*	−0.024	−0.001	0.026	0.034*	0.022
[0.024]	[0.018]	[0.028]	[0.025]	[0.014]	[0.022]	[0.018]	[0.026]
−0.093***	−0.006	−0.082*	−0.091***	−0.026*	−0.003	0.002	−0.052*
[0.024]	[0.024]	[0.044]	[0.026]	[0.016]	[0.027]	[0.028]	[0.030]
−0.059**	−0.042**	−0.158***	−0.116***	−0.018	−0.021	−0.039**	−0.061**
[0.024]	[0.019]	[0.029]	[0.023]	[0.013]	[0.020]	[0.018]	[0.025]
−0.142***	−0.072***	−0.211***	−0.151***	−0.012	−0.029	−0.030	−0.061***
[0.018]	[0.012]	[0.025]	[0.018]	[0.013]	[0.018]	[0.019]	[0.020]
−0.004	−0.007	−0.035	0.016	0.004	−0.014	−0.023	0.008
[0.021]	[0.015]	[0.028]	[0.022]	[0.016]	[0.019]	[0.019]	[0.023]
0.018	0.036**	−0.027	−0.011	0.038**	0.019	0.100***	0.047*
[0.025]	[0.018]	[0.035]	[0.024]	[0.017]	[0.021]	[0.022]	[0.026]
0.081***	0.022	−0.019	0.006	0.028*	0.072***	0.065***	0.049*
[0.027]	[0.017]	[0.035]	[0.024]	[0.015]	[0.022]	[0.022]	[0.026]
0.001	0.018	0.031	0.003	0.020	0.032	0.016	0.070***
[0.025]	[0.017]	[0.037]	[0.024]	[0.016]	[0.021]	[0.020]	[0.026]
0.025	−0.013	−0.004	0.009	−0.006	0.033*	0.035	0.027
[0.027]	[0.016]	[0.037]	[0.022]	[0.014]	[0.020]	[0.023]	[0.023]
0.003**	0.001	0.000	0.000	0.001	0.003***	0.001	0.003**
[0.001]	[0.001]	[0.002]	[0.001]	[0.001]	[0.001]	[0.001]	[0.001]
−0.062**	−0.036*	0.049	−0.027	−0.016	−0.058**	−0.047	−0.023
[0.028]	[0.019]	[0.039]	[0.025]	[0.021]	[0.026]	[0.033]	[0.029]
−0.088***	−0.041**	0.086**	−0.01	0.004	−0.032	−0.040	−0.026
[0.025]	[0.018]	[0.039]	[0.026]	[0.020]	[0.026]	[0.032]	[0.029]
−0.075***	−0.018	0.095**	−0.025	−0.009	0.002	−0.054*	−0.002
[0.027]	[0.020]	[0.041]	[0.028]	[0.020]	[0.028]	[0.032]	[0.034]
−0.034	−0.027	0.091**	−0.014	0.005	−0.026	−0.063*	−0.004
[0.027]	[0.019]	[0.042]	[0.028]	[0.019]	[0.027]	[0.032]	[0.032]

Table 6A.2   *(Continued)*

	Live with Parents			
	Male		Female	
	NLSY-79	NLSY-97	NLSY-79	NLSY-97
Had a child by 1984 (1979 cohort)	-0.238***	-0.204***	-0.191***	-0.215***
or 2002 (1997 cohort)	[0.027]	[0.030]	[0.025]	[0.026]
GPA in high school	-0.077***	-0.021	-0.035**	-0.002
	[0.017]	[0.015]	[0.017]	[0.015]
Hours worked, ages sixteen and	-0.002	-0.003***	-0.006***	-0.003**
seventeen (hundreds of hours)	[0.001]	[0.001]	[0.001]	[0.001]
Substance use before age eighteen				
Drank alcohol	-0.028	-0.024	0.022	-0.014
	[0.028]	[0.025]	[0.025]	[0.026]
Smoked cigarettes	-0.026	-0.035	-0.043	-0.015
	[0.027]	[0.024]	[0.026]	[0.025]
Smoked marijuana	-0.087***	-0.017	-0.045*	-0.002
	[0.023]	[0.024]	[0.025]	[0.025]
Number of observations	2,064	2,217	1,971	2,199
R-squared	0.116	0.122	0.150	0.155

Sources: Authors' calculations using the NLSY-79 and NLSY-97.
Notes: Robust standard errors, clustered for siblings, are shown in brackets. Missing data dummies were included for all explanatory variables except for age.
* $p < 0.10$; ** $p < 0.05$; *** $p < 0.01$

Drank Alcohol Before Age Eighteen   This measure was constructed from a series of questions in the NLSY-97 and NLSY-79. With information about the sample member's birth date as well as the date at which he or she started drinking, we created a binary variable indicating whether the sample member had started drinking before his or her eighteenth birthday.

Smoked Cigarettes Before Age Eighteen   This measure was constructed in a similar way to that described for drinking alcohol before age eighteen.

Smoked Marijuana Before Age Eighteen   This measure was also constructed in a similar way to that described for drinking alcohol before age eighteen.

Weights   We used the 1985 survey year weights for the NLSY-79 and the round 6 (November 2002 to July 2003) weights for the NLSY-97. These weights were used only in tables showing means and proportions, not in any regression analyses.

Missing Data Indicators   These are included in all regressions for any explanatory variables that have missing values.

Table 6A.2   (*Continued*)

| | Married | | | | Cohabit | | | |
| | Male | | Female | | Male | | Female | |
NLSY-79	NLSY-97	NLSY-79	NLSY-97	NLSY-79	NLSY-97	NLSY-79	NLSY-97
0.367***	0.161***	0.274***	0.157***	0.040**	0.198***	−0.032*	0.108***
[0.025]	[0.022]	[0.024]	[0.021]	[0.017]	[0.027]	[0.016]	[0.021]
0.024**	0.021***	0.017	−0.003	−0.005	−0.011	0.012	0.012
[0.012]	[0.008]	[0.015]	[0.012]	[0.008]	[0.010]	[0.010]	[0.012]
0.001	0.001	0.004***	0.001	0.000	0.001	0.001	0.002*
[0.001]	[0.001]	[0.001]	[0.001]	[0.001]	[0.001]	[0.001]	[0.001]
0.000	0.011	−0.046**	−0.019	0.014	0.003	0.009	0.034*
[0.019]	[0.012]	[0.023]	[0.018]	[0.012]	[0.016]	[0.016]	[0.019]
0.015	0.006	0.004	0.017	−0.013	0.019	0.035**	0.001
[0.018]	[0.013]	[0.023]	[0.017]	[0.011]	[0.016]	[0.015]	[0.020]
−0.021	−0.024*	−0.037	−0.056***	0.038***	0.027	0.021	0.018
[0.016]	[0.012]	[0.023]	[0.018]	[0.010]	[0.017]	[0.017]	[0.021]
2,066	2,215	1,973	2,197	2,066	2,215	1,973	2,197
0.223	0.110	0.171	0.124	0.051	0.113	0.049	0.082

We gratefully acknowledge financial support from the Smith-Richardson Foundation, the Upjohn Institute for Employment Research, and the MacArthur Foundation. We also thank Henry Chen for excellent research assistance.

Notes

1. The declining real and relative wages of less-educated young men helps to explain their diminishing work effort (Juhn 1992). The rising participation of young black men in crime during the 1980s, and the large increases in their incarceration rates, help to account for their diminishing work effort (Holzer et al. 2005).
2. See David Neumark (2002) for recent evidence on how early employment outcomes affect later ones for youth. The effects of crime and incarceration on future labor market outcomes are reviewed in Jeffrey Kling, David Weiman, and Bruce Western (2000) and Harry Holzer et al. (2005), as well as Richard Freeman (1999). For the effects of smoking, drinking, and marijuana use on employment outcomes see Robert Kaestner (1991, 1996) and Frank Chaloupka et al. (1999).
3. See Katharine Abraham (2003) for a discussion of these issues, and http://www.bls.gov/cpi/cpiurstx.htm for further information. The CPI-RS eliminates some, though not all, of the upward bias in the CPI. Over the relevant time period, it is comparable to the Gross Domestic Product (GDP)

Deflator for Personal Consumption Expenditures, which has been used by others (for example, Katz and Autor 1999) in analyzing real wage trends.

4. We also explored the effects of a set of variables for self-reported expectations regarding educational attainment, having a child, and getting married, but these generally showed little change over time, and little explanatory power in the regressions, so we omitted them from the regression specifications shown in this chapter.

5. Classical measurement error in independent variables, which is uncorrelated with other observed characteristics, tends to generate downward biases (toward zero, in absolute value) in estimated coefficients. The errors in measurement of the relevant variables in these models, such as underreporting of criminal activity, might not have that characteristic, and thus might generate biases that are harder to ascertain.

6. Appendix Table 6A.1 shows average hourly wages within quintiles. The largest percentage increases (for both males and females) between 1984 and 2002 were for those in the bottom and top quintiles.

7. For instance, Lawrence Katz and David Autor (1999) show that the real wages of young men with only five years of labor market experience declined sixteen percent between 1971 and 1987, and about nineteen percent among high school graduates with five years of experience. Chinhui Juhn's (1992, 2000) work has emphasized declining employment and labor force activity in response to these relative and real wage declines.

8. Including incarcerated persons, mean hours for black male dropouts decline by 318 hours (from 1,198 in 1984 to 880 in 2002); when incarcerated persons are removed from the sample, mean hours for this group decline by 251 hours (from 1,292 in 1984 to 1,041 in 2002).

9. Declines for black male high school dropouts were even more dramatic: 7.4 percentage points, or 91 percent).

10. According to table 6.2, these three arrangements comprise roughly 80 percent of the living arrangements of the young adults in our sample. A fourth category might include living alone or with others, including roommates or other relatives. One can infer the effects of any of our independent variables on the probability that individuals choose this latter arrangement by summing the coefficients on this variable in the other three equations and subtracting that sum from zero.

11. For binary dependent variables like the ones examined in tables 6.3 to 6.5, logit or probit models are appropriate because they provide nonlinear coefficient estimates and correct standard errors. However, inferences using OLS are generally the same, especially for samples in which the means of the dependent variables are not very close to zero or one in magnitude and when evaluated for independent variables near their means. Given that the coefficients in OLS models are easier to interpret, we present them here. Estimates from corresponding logit models (either as a series of binomial models or as one multinomial model) show similar results and are available from the authors.

12. Family income is averaged over three years, to generate a measure that is closer to the family's permanent rather than transitory income. See the appendix.

13. We tested a measure of whether the sample member had a child before age 18. Using this variable did not substantively change the results, so we chose to include the measure of having children closer to the time that living arrangements were measured.

14. Of course, the distribution of individuals across wage quintiles between the two cohorts is unchanged by definition, though the returns to being in lower versus higher quintiles might change over time as inequality in the labor market has widened. We explore this possibility in appendix table 6A.2.

15. Findings from Card and Lemieux (2000, Table 9) indicate that a 10 percent decline in real wages would increase the tendency to live at home by 1.3 percentage points, while a 10 percent decline in employment would raise this tendency by 0.4 percentage points.

16. ASVAB scores were measured as age-adjusted percentiles. The illegal activities measured were damaged property, physical attacks/carried a handgun, sold drugs or joined a gang, and were ever arrested. A few anomalous results were found, such as positive effects of attacks/handguns on marriage for males.

17. Specifically, the results indicate that changes in living with parents (for females), marriage (for both males and females), and cohabiting (for males) are almost completely explained by changes in the coefficients over time. Living with parents (for males) and cohabiting (for females) show more mixed results, depending on whether the changes in coefficients and variables are weighted by earlier or later variable and coefficient values.

18. This computation is based on the fact that 20 percent of all young men are in each quintile and that the coefficient on this quintile rises from 0.048 to 0.121 in appendix table 6A.2.

References

Abe, Yasuyo. 2001. "Changes in Gender and Racial Gaps in Adolescent Antisocial Behavior: The NLSY-97 Versus the NLSY-79." In *Social Awakening: Adolescent Behavior as Adulthood Approaches*, edited by Robert T. Michael. New York: Russell Sage Foundation.

Abraham, Katharine G. 2003. "Toward a Cost-of-Living Index: Progress and Prospects." *Journal of Economic Perspectives* 17(1): 45–58.

Blank, Rebecca. 2002. "Evaluating Welfare Reform in the United States." *Journal of Economic Literature* 40(4): 1105–66.

Blinder, Alan S. 1973. "Wage Discrimination: Reduced Form and Structural Estimates." *Journal of Human Resources* 8(4): 436–55.

Bound, John. 1986. "NBER-Mathematica Survey of Inner-City Youth: Analysis of the Undercount of Older Youth." In *The Black Youth Employment Crisis*, edited by Richard B. Freeman and Harry J. Holzer. Chicago, Ill.: University of Chicago Press.

Card, David, and Thomas Lemieux. 2000. "Adapting to Circumstances: The Evolution of Work, School, and Living Arrangements Among North American Youth." In *Youth Employment and Joblessness in Advanced Countries*, edited by

David G. Blanchflower and Richard B. Freeman. Chicago, Ill.: University of Chicago Press.

Chaloupka, Frank J., Michael Grossman, Warren K. Bickel, and Henry Saffer, editors. 1999. *The Economic Analysis of Substance Use and Abuse: An Integration of Econometric and Behavioral Economic Research.* Chicago, Ill.: University of Chicago Press.

Corcoran, Mary, and Jordan Matsudaira. 2005. "Is It Getting Harder to Get Ahead? Economic Attainment in Early Adulthood for Two Cohorts." In *On the Frontier of Adulthood: Theory, Research, and Public Policy*, edited by Richard A. Settersten Jr., Frank F. Furstenberg Jr., and Rubén G. Rumbaut. Chicago, Ill.: University of Chicago Press.

Ellwood, David. 1982. "Teenage Unemployment: Permanent Scars or Temporary Blemishes?" In *The Youth Labor Market*, edited by Richard B. Freeman and David A. Wise. Chicago, Ill.: University of Chicago Press.

Freeman, Richard B. 1999. "The Economics of Crime." In *Handbook of Labor Economics*, Volume 3, edited by Orley Ashenfelter and David Card. Amsterdam: North-Holland.

Gardecki, Rosella, and David Neumark. 1998. "Order from Chaos? The Effects of Early Labor Market Experience on Adult Labor Market Outcomes." *Industrial and Labor Relations Review* 51(2): 299–322.

Hindelang, Michael J., Travis Hirschi, and Joseph G. Weis. 1981. *Measuring Delinquency.* Beverly Hills, Calif.: Sage Publications.

Holzer, Harry, Steven Raphael, and Michael Stoll. 2005. "How Do Employer Perceptions of Crime and Incarceration Affect Employment Prospects of Young Black Men?" In *Black Males Left Behind*, edited by Ronald B. Mincy. Washington: Urban Institute Press.

Juhn, Chinhui. 1992. "Decline of Male Labor Market Participation: The Role of Declining Market Opportunities." *Quarterly Journal of Economics* 107(1): 79–121.

———. 2000. "Black-White Employment Differential in a Tight Labor Market." In *Prosperity for All? The Economic Boom and African Americans*, edited by Robert Cherry and William M. Rodgers III. New York: Russell Sage Foundation.

Kaestner, Robert. 1991. "The Effects of Illicit Drug Use on the Wages of Young Adults." *Journal of Labor Economics* 9(3): 332–54.

———. 1996. "The Effects of Illicit Drug Use on the Labor Supply of Young Adults." *Journal of Human Resources* 29(1): 123–36.

Katz, Lawrence, and David Autor. 1999. "Changes in the Wage Structure and Earnings Inequality." In *The Handbook of Labor Economics*, Volume 3a, edited by Orley Ashenfelter and David Card. Amsterdam: North-Holland.

Kling, Jeffrey, David Weiman, and Bruce Western. 2000. "The Labor Market Consequences of Mass Incarceration." Paper presented to the Urban Institute "Roundtable on Offender Reentry." Washington (October).

Meyer, Robert, and David Wise. 1982. "High School Preparation and Early Labor Force Experience." In *The Youth Labor Market*, edited by Richard B. Freeman and David A. Wise. Chicago, Ill.: University of Chicago Press.

Michael, Robert T., editor. 2001. *Social Awakening: Adolescent Behavior as Adulthood Approaches.* New York: Russell Sage Foundation.

Neumark, David. 2002. "Youth Labor Markets in the U.S.: Shopping Around Versus Staying Put." *Review of Economics and Statistics* 84(3): 462–82.

Oaxaca, Ronald. 1973. "Male-Female Wage Differentials in Urban Labor Markets." *International Economic Review* 14(3): 693–709.

Oppenehimer, Valerie K., and Alisa Lewin. 1999. "Career Development and Marriage Formation in a Period of Rising Inequality: Who Is at Risk? What Are Their Prospects?" In *Transitions to Adulthood in a Changing Economy: No Work, No Family, No Future?* edited by Alan Booth, Ann C. Crouter, and Michael J. Shanahan. Westport, Conn.: Praeger.

Settersten, Richard A., Jr., Frank F. Furstenberg Jr., and Rubén G. Rumbaut, editors. 2005. *On the Frontier of Adulthood: Theory, Research, and Public Policy.* Chicago, Ill.: University of Chicago Press.

Viscusi, W. Kip. 1986. "Market Incentives for Criminal Behavior." In *The Black Youth Employment Crisis*, edited by Richard B. Freeman and Harry J. Holzer. Chicago, Ill.: University of Chicago Press.

Chapter 7

Young Adults Leaving the Nest: The Role of the Cost of Living

AARON S. YELOWITZ

Time magazine article published January 24, 2005, and entitled "They Just Won't Grow Up" discusses the widely held perception that the transition to adulthood has become longer. The article describes the emergence of "twixters," young adults in their twenties who refuse to settle down. In response to the question "What makes you an adult?" people age eighteen to twenty-nine answered: having a first child (22 percent), moving out of the parents' home (22 percent), getting a good job with benefits (19 percent), getting married (14 percent), and finishing school (10 percent). Despite the fact that such perceptions about adulthood are quite standard, only 61 percent of survey respondents viewed themselves as adults. Thirty-five percent of respondents who did not consider themselves adults claimed that they were "just enjoying life the way it is," and one-third stated that they were "not financially independent enough" to be an adult.[1]

These responses motivated this study of trends in living arrangements and the role of the cost of living in the transition to adulthood. Many twixters who were "enjoying life" were living with their parents, and those who said they were not financially independent highlighted the importance of housing costs, transportation costs, and child care costs. This chapter describes the living arrangements of young adults age eighteen to thirty-four from 1970 to 2000 and explores the role of the cost of living, particularly housing and rental costs, in explaining these trends between 1980 and 2000.[2] The analysis sheds light on the broader implications of the housing boom and slowdown that many local markets have experienced in recent years.[3] Dramatic changes in housing

170

costs might disproportionately affect young adults, who are more mobile and usually entering the housing market for the first time.

After a brief review of previous work that examines young adults leaving the nest, I describe the census data and a framework for examining living arrangements. This is followed by descriptions of the cost-of-living variables used, an overview of trends from 1970 to 2000, and the results from the empirical analysis. I conclude with a discussion of some possible implications of these findings on the transition to adulthood.

Previous Research

Many existing studies of the living arrangements of youth focus on those personal and family characteristics that influence determinants of living arrangements.[4] Testing for the effects of economic variables has been quite limited (Haurin, Hendershott, and Kim 1993). The studies that do examine economic variables—such as housing costs—offer mixed evidence on the effects on living arrangements; they also suffer serious difficulties in isolating the effect of housing costs. This section highlights some of the findings from several key publications.

Donald Haurin, Patric Hendershott, and Dongwook Kim (1993, 1994) use a cross-sectional dataset of young adults in 1987 to examine the effect of housing costs and economic factors on living arrangements. In one study, the authors find that higher rents cause fewer young adults to live outside of the parental home and more young adults to live in groups. In the other, they find that the relative cost of homeownership is important to a young adult's own-versus-rent decision.[5] Both studies rely on a single dataset that has small sample sizes. More importantly, by relying on a single cross-section, the authors are unable to account for other factors that vary across localities and could be correlated with both housing costs and living arrangements.

In contrast to those studies, a more recent study by Steven Garasky, Jean Haurin, and Donald Haurin (2001) finds that economic variables have little impact on the decision to leave a living arrangement or not, whether a large arrangement (more than one other nonspouse or nonpartner adult) or a small one (one nonspouse or nonpartner adult), while sociodemographic variables do matter.

This study offers a number of innovations relative to previous work. First, the previous studies were based on relatively small samples. This analysis uses census data from 1970 to 2000 with millions of observations. This study also examines changes in market conditions over long periods, whereas earlier studies examined shorter time periods (often a single point in time). Finally, this study emphasizes metropolitan-level variables (such as economic conditions) rather than focusing only on individual or family variables.

Study Sample and Methodology

Living Arrangements and Sample

The sample for this analysis was drawn from the census public use data from 1970, 1980, 1990, and 2000 (U.S. Department of Commerce 1971, 1985, 1995, 2003; for more detail on the data and sample, see appendix A). The young adults in the sample are age eighteen to thirty-four. I created four mutually exclusive living arrangements that are comparable across the 1970 to 2000 censuses.[6] Each young adult is assigned to one of these categories:[7]

> *Independent.* The young adult is either the head or the spouse, and the only members of the household are the head, the spouse, and natural, adopted, or stepchildren under the age of eighteen. For example, a married couple with young children would be included in this category, as would a young adult living by herself or himself. A single mother would also fit into this category, but a cohabiting couple would not.
>
> *Economic arrangement.* The young adult resides only with same-generation family members (siblings, cousins, and so forth) or same-generation others who are not family members (or both). Households with children under age eighteen or members of an older generation (parents, grandparents, uncles, aunts, and so forth) are excluded. For example, two adult siblings sharing an apartment together would fall into this arrangement, as would two unrelated college students living in an apartment.[8]
>
> *Not independent (parental arrangement).* The young adult lives in a household with only family members, and at least one of those family members is of an older generation (such as parents, grandparents, uncles, and aunts). For example, a young man living with his parents or his grandparents would fall into this category.
>
> *Other.* Some household arrangements are a hybrid of these three types of arrangements and are difficult to characterize in terms of the transition to adulthood. These fall under the "other" category and are excluded from the analysis. For example, a married couple with children who rent out a room to an unrelated individual are in a living arrangement that might be considered either independent or economic. The same would be true of a single mother with a roommate. Living arrangements for a young adult male who lives with his parents and has an unmarried female partner are likewise difficult to classify. Would the unmarried female partner be classified as living in an economic arrangement, an independent arrangement, or a non-independ-

ent arrangement? Across the four census decades, approximately 10 percent of young adults fall into this category, and there is very little variation by age.[9]

Although this study treats independent living arrangements, economic living arrangements, and parental living arrangements as different degrees of moving into adulthood, richer microdata, if available, could be more informative. For example, a young man with wealthy parents might receive a large subsidy to live in his own apartment, yet such a subsidy suggests that he is not independent of his parents. Unfortunately, the census provides no information on intrafamily transfers for individuals living in separate households, so there is no way to detect such arrangements.

In addition to restricting the sample to individuals age eighteen to thirty-four, I excluded those living in group quarters. Because the cost-of-living variables vary at the metropolitan statistical area (MSA) level, I also required that the individual live in a uniquely identified MSA for the 1980 to 2000 census years (for more detail on the MSA restrictions, see appendix A). Overall, 57 MSAs had complete information on house price indices, fair market rents, and median house prices, yielding a final sample size of 3,636,296, with around 1.3 million observations on young adults in each census year.

I was unable to create categories of living arrangements that combined housing tenure (owning or renting) with household composition—that is, the simultaneous decision of housing tenure and household composition (see appendix A for details). The motivation for combining the two is to gain a more detailed characterization of the transition to adulthood. For example, most people would agree that a homeowner living independently represents a greater transition to adulthood than a renter living independently.

Analysis

A key contribution of this study is to carefully incorporate local cost-of-living variables that vary over time and across metropolitan areas, providing a more compelling empirical framework for estimating these costs than previous studies. Given the recent real estate boom, particular attention is given to modeling the impact of housing costs. Housing prices, rental costs, transportation expenses, child care costs, and labor market conditions can all affect whether young adults can afford to live independently, and understanding those factors can help us sort out the question of whether economic conditions or other factors, such as individual preferences, are associated with their decisions to remain living with their parents or in other dependent situations.

For housing prices, I use the house price index (HPI), a broad measure of the movement of single-family house prices, available from the Office of Federal Housing Enterprise Oversight (OFHEO) on a quarterly basis (for more on this index, see appendix A). The index is based on single-family, detached properties using data on conventional conforming mortgages obtained from the Freddie Mac and Fannie Mae. The HPI gives only relative changes, not absolute changes, in values for housing prices. To obtain price levels, I use median home prices from the National Association of Realtors (NAR) quarterly report on metropolitan-area existing-home prices.[10] This report reflects sales prices of existing single-family homes by MSA. I account for the quality of the stock of homes over time (see appendix A for details) and also calculate the tax deductions for mortgage interest and the changing mortgage interest rates and "points" paid on a mortgage. Interest rates and points (combined) varied between 7.25 percent and 17.21 percent during the period under study.

In addition to housing prices, I also estimate the effects of rent, as measured by the fair market rent series of the U.S. Department of Housing and Urban Development (HUD). I also estimate the separate impact of transportation costs. Although transportation costs are often thought of in terms of expenditures on vehicles, insurance, maintenance, and fuel, longer commuting times are likely to be positively correlated with more intensive vehicle use. Moreover, the opportunity cost of an individual's time is itself a cost of commuting. Because it is difficult to obtain direct expenditure measures on transportation that vary across locality and over time, I use commuting time to proxy for these expenditures. Likewise, I include child care costs, controlling for fixed differences across MSAs and over time (see appendix A for details on these calculations).

The motivation for including housing costs, rents, transportation costs, and child care costs separately is that they may act differently on the transition to adulthood. For example, we might expect higher child care costs to affect a woman's transition differently than a man's, while there is little reason to believe that higher rents would have a different impact on women's and men's transitions. In addition, cost-of-living measures are likely to be positively correlated with each other. Localities with high housing costs tend to have longer commuting times and higher child care costs. If transportation costs or child care costs were excluded, the empirical framework would incorrectly attribute their effects on living arrangements to housing costs.

Another important factor to consider is labor market conditions. It is possible that we could find that higher housing costs or rents lead to greater independence of young adults, but that correlation could reflect the fact that healthy labor markets tend to have greater housing demand, higher incomes, and more independence. Thus, I include the statewide unemployment rate for each MSA in each census year. I use the state-wide rather than the MSA-wide unemployment rate because the latter was not easily obtainable prior to 1990 (for more detail on each of these variables and their measurement, see appendix A).

To estimate the effect of each of these cost measures on a young adult's choice of living arrangement (living independently, economic arrange-ment, or non-independent living), I created a model that accounts for ei-ther the monthly house payment or the median house price, the fair market rent, commuting times in minutes, average estimated child care costs, and the statewide unemployment rate. I also include covariates that are believed to affect living arrangements, including controls for age (dummy variables for single years of age), sex, race-ethnicity, educa-tional attainment, current school enrollment, U.S. citizenship, current marital status, whether the individual lived in the same state five years prior to the census, and the prior year's earnings. Finally, I include dummy variables for MSA (fifty-seven separate localities, as shown in table 7A.1) and year (1980, 1990, and 2000; for more detail on the model, see appendix B).

Trends in Living Arrangements by Age from 1970 to 2000

Figure 7.1 examines how each of the four living arrangements described here evolved between 1970 and 2000, by age of the young adult.

Figure 7.1 shows that the percentage of young adults who live inde-pendently has declined dramatically during the last thirty years. Further tabulations (not shown) reveal that independent living also declined from one decade to the next, and for all ages. Most notable is the decline in independent living among those in their mid-twenties. Among twenty-four-year-olds, for example, the percentage living independently fell by more than thirty percentage points. In contrast, there has been a much less dramatic change for young adults at either end of the age spectrum. One hypothesis that could explain this age pattern and time pattern is that a greater percentage of those in their early twenties are go-ing to college and staying in school longer.

This schooling hypothesis is also consistent with the percentage of young adults living in an "economic arrangement." The fraction living with either unrelated individuals or family members of the same gen-eration peaks in the early twenties and then declines. Over the decades (not shown), these patterns became more dramatic. For ex-ample, the percentage of twenty-one-year-olds living in an economic arrangement doubled in the last thirty years, from 10 to 21 percent.

Figure 7.1 also seems to support one of the key points of the *Time*

Figure 7.1   Changes from 1970 to 2000 in Living Arrangement, by Age

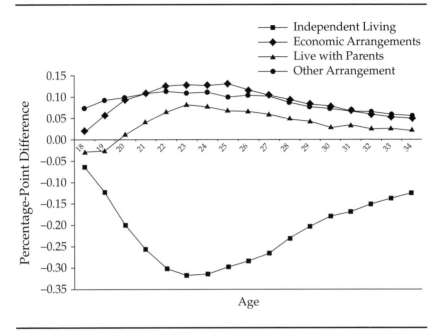

Source: Author's calculations.

magazine article—that more adult children (especially those in their mid-twenties) live with their parents than in earlier generations. However, this trend appears to have started earlier than *Time*'s "twixters" article would suggest. Most of the living-with-parents increase was among twenty-three- to twenty-seven-year-olds between 1980 and 1990 (figure 7.1 shows only the 1970 to 2000 change), when the percentage living with their parents increased from 18 to 25 percent. Apparently today's twixters are not much different from other cohorts of young adults since 1990.

Finally, figure 7.1 shows a steady rise over time in "other living arrangements." Between 1970 and 2000, the percentage living in this arrangement roughly doubled, from 7 to 15 percent. Yet the fraction of young adults living in this arrangement remained fairly low, even in 2000, and there is no obvious trend by age.

Results from Empirical Model from 1980 to 2000

Summary Statistics

Table 7.1 presents summary statistics for the full sample of 3.6 million young adults and also breaks out the sample by census year and whether the individual is over or under age twenty-five. On average, 55 percent of young adults lived in "independent" arrangements, but there was a ten-percentage-point drop between 1980 and 2000, with roughly equal percentage-point rises in economic living arrangements and non-independent arrangements. Age plays a critical factor: those age twenty-five to thirty-four are nearly fifty percentage points more likely to be living independently than those age eighteen to twenty-four (72 and 25 percent, respectively). More than half of the sample is female, and nearly 70 percent are white. A number of characteristics changed over the twenty-year horizon. For example, the percentage of individuals of Hispanic ethnicity doubled from 8 to 17 percent. The number of dropouts remained fairly constant at about 17 percent, but there was a decrease in individuals with a high school diploma, from 32 to 24 percent, and an increase in individuals with at least some college, from 51 to 59 percent. By 2000 nearly one-quarter of young adults were still enrolled in school. Therefore, a shift from high school to college educational attainment between 1980 and 2000 is evident both in terms of years of schooling and school enrollment.

Individual annual earnings (which includes nonworkers) rose in real terms, from $18,000 to $22,000, between 1980 and 2000, and the unemployment rate fell from 7.2 to 4.1 percent. The percentage who were U.S. citizens declined from 94 percent to 87 percent, and the percentage who were married fell from 48 percent to 41 percent. Mobility increased dramatically over this period. The fraction who had lived in the same state five years earlier fell from one-half to one-third.

Over the entire period, the median house price was $157,320. It rose in real terms between 1980 and 1990 and then declined.[11] The monthly housing payment—which accounts for credit market conditions and tax deductibility and also keeps housing quality constant—fell dramatically, from $1,476 to $1,092, a 26 percent drop.[12] In contrast, monthly rental payments rose slightly during this period, from $726 to $741. Commuting time increased from twenty-three to twenty-seven minutes, but there was no clear trend in child care costs.

Main Results

Table 7.2 summarizes the results from the model estimating the effect of housing and other costs on the probability of living independently (see table 7A.2 for full results). The first three columns examine housing values, which are measured in $10,000 increments. As the first cell shows, there is a statistically significant, negative relationship between house values and independent living arrangements. For every $10,000 increase in house value, there is a 0.61-percentage-point decline in independent living. In contrast, as housing costs rise, so does the number of youth living in an economic arrangement or living non-independently.

Table 7.1   Summary Statistics for Young Adult Sample Used in Regression Analysis

	1980	1990	2000	Age Less than Twenty-five	Age Twenty-five or Older
Independent	0.60	0.53	0.50	0.25	0.72
Economic	0.12	0.15	0.17	0.17	0.13
Not independent	0.29	0.33	0.32	0.58	0.15
Age	25.9	26.6	26.5	21.1	29.5
	(4.8)	(4.8)	(4.9)	(2.0)	(2.8)
Male	0.49	0.49	0.49	0.49	0.49
White	0.75	0.71	0.60	0.66	0.70
African American or black	0.14	0.13	0.14	0.15	0.13
Hispanic	0.08	0.12	0.17	0.13	0.11
Other nonwhite	0.03	0.05	0.09	0.05	0.05
High school dropout	0.17	0.16	0.17	0.23	0.12
High school graduate	0.32	0.27	0.24	0.31	0.26
Some college	0.51	0.57	0.59	0.46	0.61
Enrolled in school	0.19	0.23	0.24	0.38	0.12
U.S. citizen	0.94	0.92	0.87	0.92	0.91
Currently married	0.48	0.44	0.41	0.21	0.60
Lived in same state five years ago	0.50	0.35	0.33	0.46	0.36
Individual earnings in prior year, including nonworkers	17,985	20,843	22,266	10,954	25,850
	(18,395)	(22,736)	(28,099)	(12,638)	(26,151)
Year is 1980	1.00	0.00	0.00	0.41	0.35
Year is 1990	0.00	1.00	0.00	0.30	0.34
Median house price	141,387	169,370	163,984	155,994	158,125
	(42,548)	(83,809)	(65,809)	(65,149)	(67,174)
Monthly house payment based on market conditions	1,476	1,399	1,092	1,337	1,330
	(444)	(692)	(438)	(553)	(563)
Monthly fair market rent	726	734	741	731	734
	(113)	(156)	(162)	(141)	(145)
Average travel time in MSA in minutes	22.9	24.0	26.9	24.4	24.6
	(2.6)	(2.5)	(3.0)	(3.1)	(3.2)

Higher rents seem to have no impact on living independently; perhaps surprisingly, higher rent levels lead to fewer young adults living with parents and more young adults living in economic arrangements. Higher commuting costs slow the transition to adulthood: the likelihood of living with parents goes up one percentage point for every two additional commuting minutes.[13]

The results for child care costs are not intuitive: higher child care costs

Table 7.1 *(Continued)*

	1980	1990	2000	Age Less than Twenty-five	Age Twenty-five or Older
Average hourly wage of child care workers in MSA	8.81 (1.06)	8.04 (1.26)	9.15 (0.85)	8.68 (1.15)	8.66 (1.17)
Statewide unemployment rate	7.2 (1.5)	5.6 (0.8)	4.1 (0.7)	5.8 (1.7)	5.7 (1.7)
Median house price at age twenty-five		149,900 (61,859)	155,038 (62,392)		152,396 (62,172)
Monthly house payment at age twenty-five		1,444 (557)	1,049 (434)		1,252 (539)
Monthly fair market rent at age twenty-five		731 (130)	743 (165)		737 (148)
Sample size: all ages	1,350,065	1,164,891	1,121,340	1,374,110	2,262,186
Sample size: age twenty-five or older		758,512	716,400		1,474 912

Source: Author's calculations.
Note: Standard deviations in parentheses. "Independent" is defined as a living arrangement in which the young adult is living either alone or with a spouse and/or natural, adopted, or stepchildren under eighteen only. "Economic" is defined as a living arrangement in which the young adult is living with unrelated individuals and/or same-generation family members (for example, a spouse, siblings, or cousins), but no members of older generations (for example, parents, grandparents, or uncles/aunts); in addition, no children under eighteen are present. "Dependent" is defined as a living arrangement in which the young adult is living in a household with only family members and at least one of those family members is a member of an older generation (for example, parents, grandparents or uncles/aunts). If a young adult did not fit into one of these three categories (for example, a single mother with roommates), he or she was excluded from the regression analysis. All dollar amounts (individual earnings, median house price, monthly house payment, monthly fair market rent, average wage of child care workers, and their equivalents at age twenty-five) are expressed in constant 2000 dollars. The MSA-level measures of housing market conditions at age twenty-five are calculated only in the 1990 and 2000 census years. The sample includes MSAs that meet the following criteria: (1) the MSA was defined in the 1980, 1990, and 2000 census PUMS; (2) median house price data were available from recent National Association of Realtors publications (see www.realtor.org); (3) house price index data were available from 1980 onward from the Office of Federal Housing and Enterprise Oversight (www.ofheo.gov); (4) fair market rent data were available from the U.S. Department of Housing and Urban Development (www.huduser.org); and (5) the MSA had more than 20,000 individual observations on young adults from the 1980 to 2000 period.

lead to more independent living. This may suggest that the measure being used—child care wages—is reflecting characteristics besides the child care market. For example, markets with higher child care wages may also have higher wage levels in general. If this is the case, those higher wage levels may foster independence.[14]

Table 7.2 Summary of Results from "Differences-in-Differences" Specification

	(1) Independent	(2) Economic	(3) Not Independent	(4) Independent	(5) Economic	(6) Not Independent
Median house price ($10,000 change)	-0.0061*.	0.0011*	0.0021*	—	—	—
Monthly house payment ($1,000 change)	—	—	—	-0.0584*	0.0221*	0.0041
Monthly fair market rent ($1,000 change)	0.0072	0.0453*	-0.0824*	-0.0457	0.0362*	-0.0371
Average travel time (one-minute change)	-0.0050*	-0.0026	0.0048*	-0.0065*	-0.0023*	0.0052*
Average wage of child care workers ($1 hourly increments)	0.0058*	0.0015	-0.0070*	0.0057*	0.0007	-0.0059*
Statewide unemployment rate (one percentage point)	-0.0091*	-0.0029*	0.0098*	-0.0101*	-0.0018*	0.0090*

Source: Author's calculations.
Notes: See appendix B for full results. Asterisk indicates variable is statistically significant at a 95 percent level of confidence.

Finally, adverse labor market conditions delay the transition to adulthood. A one-percentage-point increase in the unemployment rate lowers the probability of living independently by 0.9 percentage points.

The individual characteristics (presented in table 7A.2) show that males, Hispanics (relative to whites), other nonwhites (relative to whites), students, and individuals who lived in the same state five years prior are all significantly less likely to be in an independent living arrangement.[15] In contrast, African Americans, the currently married, the college-educated, U.S. citizens, and high earners are all significantly more likely to be living independently.

Using housing payments rather than housing values (columns 4, 5, and 6) finds a similar story. Every $100 increase in the monthly housing payment leads to a 0.58-percentage-point decline in living independently. In contrast to housing values, monthly housing payments seem to have no effect on living with parents, but they increase the likelihood of living in an economic arrangement. Higher rents significantly increase the likelihood of living in an economic arrangement but have insignificant effects on other living arrangements. Other than those differences, the results are similar to the calculations with housing values.

A number of variables in the previous specification could be criticized on the grounds that they are determined at the same time as living arrangements, meaning they are endogenous to the empirical model. One could argue that location is endogenous; that is, when an individual wants to "settle down" and live independently, he or she moves to a more affordable MSA.[16] Some of the individual characteristics could also be viewed as problematic, especially school enrollment, marital status, and earnings. The role of earnings has been addressed in previous studies. Garasky, Haurin and Haurin (2001, 332) argue that "participation in the paid labor force is a decision that occurs jointly with the decision on household formation. For example, a youth may not work because he or she is subsidized in the parental household." As a result, they use a predicted wage. I reestimated the models excluding individual earnings. The results on the cost-of-living variables are similar to the main specification. For example, a $10,000 increase in house prices leads to a statistically significant 0.49-percentage-point drop in independent living rather than the 0.61-percentage-point drop in table 7.2.[17] The statistical significance disappears for non-independent living arrangements, but all of the directions are similar to the full specification.

An important question about the main results is whether the impact of the cost-of-living variables is economically meaningful in addition to being statistically significant. To figure this out, table 7.3 shows the results of two exercises. The first exercise is moving each economic variable from the twenty-fifth percentile to the seventy-fifth. Such a movement spans a realistic range of cost-of-living values that an individual

Table 7.3 Evaluating the Effects Using the Main Specification

	Independent	Economic	Not Independent	Independent	Economic	Not Independent
Are the Coefficients Meaningful? Move from 25th to 75th Percentile for Each Independent Variable						
Median house price	-0.051	0.009	0.018	-0.044	0.017	0.003
Monthly house payment	—	—	—	—	—	—
Monthly fair market rent	0.001	0.007	-0.013	-0.007	0.006	-0.006
Average travel time in minutes	-0.025	-0.013	0.024	-0.033	-0.012	0.026
Average wage of child care workers	0.009	0.002	-0.011	0.009	0.001	-0.009
Statewide unemployment rate	-0.022	-0.007	0.023	-0.024	-0.004	0.021
Mean of dependent variable	0.545	0.143	0.312	0.545	0.143	0.312
Can the Cost of Living Explain the Time-Series Trends? Change 1980 Values to 2000 Values						
Median house price	-0.014	0.002	0.005	—	—	—
Monthly house payment	—	—	—	0.022	-0.008	-0.002
Monthly fair market rent	0.000	0.001	-0.001	-0.001	0.001	-0.001
Average travel time in minutes	-0.020	-0.010	0.019	-0.026	-0.009	0.021
Average wage of child care workers	0.002	0.000	-0.002	0.002	0.000	-0.002
Statewide unemployment rate	0.028	0.009	-0.031	0.032	0.006	-0.028
Dependent variable, 1980	0.597	0.116	0.287	0.597	0.116	0.287
Dependent variable, 2000	0.504	0.173	0.324	0.504	0.173	0.324
Change over time	-0.093	0.057	0.037	-0.093	0.057	0.037

Source: Author's calculations.

might face. The second is examining the actual change in each economic variable between 1980 and 2000.

The first exercise shows that housing prices or monthly housing payments may affect living arrangements. If an individual faced housing costs in the seventy-fifth percentile rather than the twenty-fifth percentile (equivalent to facing Washington, D.C., housing costs rather than Houston housing costs), independent living falls by five percentage points, from a baseline of 55 percent. Although housing costs matter, they explain only a small part of the 9.3-percentage-point decline in independent living between 1980 and 2000. Increasing housing costs from the 1980 to the 2000 value leads to a 1.4-percentage-point drop in independent living. Housing costs are therefore a small factor in the drop in independent living.

The other two noteworthy economic variables are transportation costs and labor market conditions. Moving from the first to the third quartile in travel time leads to a 2.5-percentage-point decline in independent living; a similar movement in the unemployment rate leads to a 2.2-percentage-point decline. However, labor market conditions do a poor job of explaining the time trends, because the labor market improved between 1980 and 2000 at the same time that independent living decreased. On the other hand, increased travel times can explain two percentage points of the 9.3-percentage-point decline in independent living—a larger share than housing costs.

I also estimated the model by gender, by age, and by race (results available on request). Changes in credit markets, for example, may have increased the opportunities to enter the housing market for minority youth relatively more than for whites, and these changes may also have interacted with the included cost-of-living variables. Specifically, the greater reliance by lenders on credit scoring—where race and ethnicity are not factors—would lead to relatively greater changes in opportunities for minorities to live independently and a greater responsiveness to changing market conditions.[18] Nonwhites are considerably more responsive to changing market conditions than whites. A $10,000 increase in the price of housing leads to a 0.9-percentage-point drop in independent living for nonwhites, an effect that is more than double that for whites. In addition, the effects of housing costs on living with parents (non-independent living) show up significantly for nonwhites but not for whites.

I found virtually identical marginal effects for males and females. The results by age show more responsiveness for those older than twenty-five than for younger adults, which should be expected since older adults are more likely to have completed their schooling. Nonetheless, the difference is relatively modest. A $10,000 increase in house price leads to a 4.3-percentage-point decline in independent living for older individuals, and a 3.6-percentage-point decline for younger ones.

Finally, we need to recognize that marriage, fertility, and living arrangements may be jointly determined. Living independently could facilitate marriage or children, and marriage or children could press a young adult to move out of the parents' home. In defining independent, non-independent, other, and economic living arrangements, a household with children could only fall into the first three categories.

I reran the basic specifications, attempting to control for marriage and childbearing more carefully. In particular, I reestimated the models including the number of children as an additional control, and I also estimated models separately for young adults with any children or no children. The first exercise—including number of children as an additional control—had no effect. Perhaps more interesting, the response to housing prices was virtually identical for young adults with or without children. Among those without children, the probability of independent living fell by 0.58 percentage points for every $10,000 increase in house value. For those with children, it fell by 0.62 percentage points. If anything, we would expect young adults without children to be more responsive to changes in housing prices, since they are less constrained by issues like overcrowding, schools, and neighborhood quality. The fact that the responses are the same suggests that family structure does not interact with housing prices in an important way to bias the results.

Table 7.4 summarizes results for the thirteen MSAs that experienced significant volatility in housing prices (increases in real housing costs of 30 percent in a three-year period) (full results are presented in table 7A.3). Here again, housing costs are rather limited in explaining the time-series trends. The results suggest that the impact of a $10,000 change in housing prices is about one-tenth that found in the main specification.

Before dismissing the idea that housing costs matter based on these thirteen MSAs, we should consider the possibility that many individuals did not live in the same MSA during the census year (when living arrangements were recorded) as they did at age twenty-five (when the market conditions were measured). Two-thirds of all young adults in the 2000 census lived in a different state in 1995 (the same was true for young adults in the 1990 census). By measuring the individual's locality at age twenty-five with error, the effect of housing costs is too small. Also, the sample examines MSAs with rapid rises in housing appreciation. It is possible that individuals based their decision to live independently on both current housing costs and their expectation of future housing costs. When housing prices rise rapidly in a short time period, individuals may be concerned about getting "priced out" of the market and thus respond by quickly purchasing a home. In contrast, in the primary specification with fifty-seven MSAs, housing costs are measured at a time when we are certain the individual lived in the MSA, and because prices were not

Table 7.4 Summary of Results from "Differences-in-Differences-in-Differences" Specification

	Independent	Economic	Not Independent	Independent	Economic	Not Independent
Median house price at age twenty-five ($10,000 change)	-0.0005	0.0002	-0.0 010	—	-0.0020	0.0009
Monthly house payment at age twenty-five ($1,000 change)	—	—	—	-0.0031		
Monthly fair market rent at age twenty-five ($1,000 change)	0.0222	0.0187	-0.0440*	0.0198	0.0215*	-0.0461*

Source: Author's calculations.

appreciating as rapidly, the concern about being priced out is much smaller. Overall, the results from rapidly appreciating MSAs lend support to the idea that the role of housing costs is relatively minor, but because of some severe measurement error issues, it seems that the primary specification that includes all localities is more compelling.

Conclusion

This study explored the role of the cost of living on the living arrangements of young adults. Between 1970 and 2000, dramatically fewer young adults lived independently, with more living with parents, in economic arrangements with others of their generation, or in other arrangements. The differences across decade are most dramatic in the mid-twenties, but even at older ages the percentage living independently has declined. Several factors unrelated to the cost of living, such as marital status and school enrollment, also changed during this time and may help explain these trends.

The main goal of this chapter, however, was to assess how changes in the costs of housing, transportation, and child care have affected these living decisions. The results suggest that housing and transportation costs do impede independent living, although the effects of child care costs are counterintuitive. Nonetheless, these factors appear to explain little of the aggregate changes over the time period analyzed. Rising real housing costs can explain perhaps 15 percent of the total change in independent living arrangements between 1980 and 2000.

As more young adults are "failing to launch," many have suggested that the recent run-up in housing costs is a likely contributor. However, the decline in independent living appears to have started much earlier than the most recent rise in housing costs. What do the empirical results on housing costs mean for the transition to adulthood going forward from 2000? Although the empirical analysis stops in 2000, the results suggest that it is possible that housing costs will play a far greater role in future analysis.

Between 2000 and 2005, as table 7.5 shows, many areas experienced a real estate boom, with rises in real housing costs that went well beyond the rise from 1980 to 2000. In twenty-five MSAs—almost all in California and Florida—nominal housing prices rose by at least 100 percent. House prices increased 51 percent nationally, while general prices increased by just 13 percent. The median house price in the United States rose by $65,000 in real terms over this period (National Association of Realtors 2007).

The estimates in this chapter suggest that such large changes in housing costs would lead to fairly sizable changes in living arrangements among young adults. For example, the main results suggest a drop in in-

Table 7.5   House Price Appreciation from the First Quarter of 2000 to the First Quarter of 2005

1	Santa Barbara–Santa Maria–Goleta, CA	125%
2	Yuba City, CA	124
3	Merced, CA	120
4	Modesto, CA	120
5	San Diego–Carlsbad–San Marcos, CA	119
6	Salinas, CA	119
7	Riverside–San Bernardino–Ontario, CA	118
8	Sacramento–Arden–Arcade–Roseville, CA	114
9	Stockton, CA	113
10	Fresno, CA	112
11	Port St. Lucie–Fort Pierce, FL	111
12	Vallejo–Fairfield, CA	110
13	San Luis Obispo–Paso Robles, CA	109
14	Santa Ana–Anaheim–Irvine, CA	109
15	Los Angeles–Long Beach–Glendale, CA	108
16	Chico, CA	107
17	Oxnard–Thousand Oaks–Ventura, CA	107
18	Fort Lauderdale–Pompano Beach–Deerfield Beach, FL	107
19	Madera, CA	107
20	Napa, CA	106
21	Redding, CA	104
22	Bakersfield, CA	104
23	West Palm Beach–Boca Raton–Boynton Beach, FL	104
24	Ocean City, NJ	103
25	Barnstable Town, MA	102
26	Palm Bay–Melbourne–Titusville, FL	99
27	Miami–Miami Beach–Kendall, FL	98
28	Naples–Marco Island, FL	97
29	Punta Gorda, FL	95
30	Washington–Arlington–Alexandria, DC-VA-MD-WV	95
31	Providence–New Bedford–Fall River, RI-MA	94
32	Vero Beach, FL	93
33	Nassau–Suffolk, NY	92
34	Cape Coral–Fort Myers, FL	92
35	Sarasota–Bradenton–Venice, FL	91
36	Las Vegas–Paradise NV	91
37	Kingston, NY	91
38	Bethesda–Frederick–Gaithersburg, MD	90
39	Oakland–Fremont–Hayward, CA	89
40	Carson City, NV	88
41	Santa Rosa–Petaluma, CA	88
42	Edison, NJ	87
43	Reno–Sparks, NV	87
44	Poughkeepsie–Newburgh–Middletown, NY	86
45	Hanford-Corcoran, CA	85
46	Deltona–Daytona Beach–Ormond Beach, FL	84

47 Atlantic City, NJ	83
48 Winchester, VA-WV	80
49 Visalia–Porterville, CA	80
50 Fort Walton Beach–Crestview–Destin, FL	79
National housing appreciation	51
CPI = U over same period	13

Source: Author's calculations, based on data from the National Association of Realtors.

dependent living of four percentage points from a baseline rate of 50 percent (in the year 2000), with increases in both living in economic arrangements and non-independently.[19] In addition, minorities were found to be much more responsive to changes in house prices than whites, so independent living should fall by a greater percentage after 2000. The results would also imply that independent living among youth should fall the most in California and Florida, the states that experienced the most dramatic rises in housing costs. These consequences for independent living, unfortunately, cannot be easily tested until the 2010 census is conducted.

Appendix A: Data and Sample

Sample

The 1970 census used two long-form questionnaires, one for a 15 percent sample of the population, the other for a 5 percent sample. For each questionnaire, a 1-in-100 sample was drawn with three different geographic identifiers: county groups, states, and geographic divisions with neighborhood identifiers. I use the 5 percent sample with state identifiers. The 1970 sample does not easily provide MSA identifiers, so there was no compelling reason to use the sample with county-group identifiers rather than state identifiers. Moreover, none of the relevant cost-of-living variables examined here date back as early as 1970. Therefore, young adults from 1970 are not included in the regression analysis but are included to illustrate long-term trends.

I use the 1-in-20 sample for 1980, 1990, and 2000 and restrict the sample to young adults age eighteen to thirty-four in uniquely identified MSAs. This yields a sample size in excess of 4 million observations (before other exclusions).

Living Arrangements

For several reasons, I was unable to create categories of living arrangements that combined housing tenure—owning or renting—with household composition. First, previous studies, such as Frances Goldscheider and Julie DaVanzo (1985), Roger Avery, Frances Goldscheider, and Alden Speare (1992), and Frances Goldscheider, Arland Thornton, and Linda Young-DeMarco (1993), focus exclusively on the household composition of young adults leaving the nest and do not combine this with housing tenure. Even research that emphasizes economic factors such as local housing costs (for example, Garasky, Haurin, and Haurin 2001) examines only living arrangements, not ownership. William Clark and Clara Mulder (2000) focus more on housing tenure and less on household composition among nest-leavers. They model the decision of young adults who leave their parents' home to own a home, own a trailer, or rent. The authors also separately examine the choice to rent independently or share a rental unit with roommates. Yet none of these studies have examined the simultaneous decision about housing tenure and household composition.

A second possibility is to focus separately on the own-versus-rent decision among young adults. I rejected this approach because it is not always possible to assign the correct ownership status to each of the young adults in the household, especially in households for which there is an economic arrangement. For example, the census 2000 long form (available at http://www.census.gov/dmd/www/pdf/d02p.pdf) defines the head of household (person 1) as "the person, or one of the people living here who owns, is buying, or rents this house, apartment, or mobile home. If there is no such person, start with any adult living or staying here." Although it is easy to assign housing tenure to those in "independent" living arrangements (married couples or single individuals living alone), assigning housing tenure to young adults in economic arrangements is more difficult. It is possible that two individuals, related or unrelated, jointly own a home or that one of them is paying rent to the other. Because the census asks these housing questions only at the household level, not the individual level, it is impossible to tell. For this reason, it did not seem worthwhile to pursue this approach.

Metropolitan Statistical Areas

The 1980, 1990, and 2000 censuses identified 272, 273, and 297 MSAs, respectively, with approximately 2.2 million young adults in each of those years. For an MSA to be included, it had to be identified in all three censuses, which narrowed the sample to 224 MSAs. From there, the MSA had to have complete information on the cost-of-living variables. For example, only 139 MSAs have a house price index that dates back to 1980. Similarly, a number of MSAs were missing information on fair market rents or median house prices.

Overall, 91 MSAs had complete information on house price indices, fair market rents, and median house prices, with around 1.3 million observations on young adults in each census year. Unfortunately, with such a large sample, I did not have the computational power to estimate the probit models while including MSA fixed effects. I found, however, that by eliminating smaller MSAs (those with fewer than 20,000 observations across the three censuses), I could estimate the models. This criterion leaves 57 MSAs. I have estimated the models at the MSA-year level of aggregation, using all 91 MSAs and three census periods. The basic conclusions on housing prices are unchanged; the models use the individual data in order to compare the effects based on several demographic criteria like race and education. Although a substantial number of MSAs are eliminated, nearly 90 percent of the young adults remain in the sample, yielding a final sample size of 3,636,296.

Estimating Cost-of-Living Variables

Housing Prices   As noted, this analysis uses the housing price index. The HPI has several advantages over other available indices. First, it is constructed from a sample of millions of repeat transaction pairs going back thirty years (including both home sales and refinances). In contrast, the constant-quality home price index published by the Commerce Department is based on a sample of only around 12,000 transactions annually.

Second, the HPI is available for many MSAs, whereas the indices published by Fannie Mae or Freddie Mac are available only at the national level and census-division level or for fewer MSAs. OFHEO produces indices for 379 MSAs, with different starting points. The starting points vary because an MSA must have at least 1,000 total transactions before it can be published. In addition, an MSA must have experienced at least ten transactions in any given quarter for that quarterly value of the HPI to be published.

Third, OFHEO describes the HPI as a "constant-quality" house price index. The index for each geographic area is estimated using repeated observations of housing values for individual, single-family residential properties on which at least two mortgages have been originated and subsequently purchased by either Freddie Mac or Fannie Mae since January 1975. In December 1995, the database held more than 6.9 million repeat transactions; more recently, it held 30.7 million transactions. The index is updated each quarter as additional mortgages are purchased by Fannie Mae and Freddie Mac. The new mortgage acquisitions are used to identify repeat transactions for the most recent quarter and for each quarter since the first quarter of 1975. The use of repeat transactions on the same physical property units helps to control for observed and unobserved differences in housing quality. Moreover, lack of information on property characteristics in historical government-sponsored enterprises data precludes the estimation of hedonic house price indexes. The

HPI methodology is a modified version of the Case-Shiller geometric weighted repeat sales procedure (Case and Shiller 1987, 1989).

Excluded Housing Transactions   As indicated in the chapter, many housing transactions are included. However, several are not. The conforming mortgage loan limit for single-family homes in 2006 is $417,000. Loans whose principal is in excess of this limit (known as "jumbo loans") are excluded. Mortgages on properties financed by government-insured loans, such as the Federal Housing Administration (FHA) or Veterans Administration (VA) mortgages, are also excluded, as are mortgages on condominiums or multi-unit properties. To the extent that the excluded properties exhibit similar changes in appreciation over time, the HPI should be an accurate measure of housing prices (for more detail, see appendix A). In the regression analysis that follows, I restricted the sample to MSAs that had continuously available HPI data from the first quarter of 1980 to the first quarter of 2000.

Median House Prices   With both the HPI and median house prices, the MSAs are as defined according to the U.S. Office of Management and Budget (OMB) and include the specified city or cities and surrounding suburban areas. The median house price data, unlike the HPI, do not control for housing quality. To obtain nominal price levels from 1980 to 2000, I deflate median NAR house prices for the fourth quarter of 2004 by the HPI. Thus, the series of prices is of constant quality, reflecting the quality of the stock of homes sold in 2004. This series of nominal housing prices was then converted into constant 2000 dollars using the Consumer Price Index for all Urban Consumers (CPI-U).

Converting Housing Prices into Monthly Payments   One innovation in this study is to recognize the importance of credit market conditions and the federal tax code. Although local housing prices are clearly the main driver of affordability, both interest rates and tax rates play important roles. According to Freddie Mac, interest rates on conforming thirty-year fixed mortgages varied between 6.94 percent in 1998 and 16.63 percent in 1981; the points associated with the mortgages varied between 0.99 points in 1999 and 2.50 points in 1985. These interest rates are available at the national level only. I converted these combinations of interest rates and points into a single interest rate by assuming that 0.90 of a point translated into a 0.25 percent higher interest rate.[20] Making this adjustment leads to a time series of interest rates that vary between 7.25 percent and 17.21 percent.

It is also important to recognize that much of the interest on home mortgages is tax-deductible, and that this deduction is more valuable the higher the individual's marginal tax rate. In the period studied, the highest federal marginal tax rate varied between 28 and 70 percent. Of course, it is unrealistic to assume that a typical homeowner—especially a young adult—would face such high marginal rates (and therefore face lower effective housing payments). Although I was unable to find information on marginal tax rates for the median (young) taxpayer, I did obtain from the Congressional Budget Office information on "effective (average) tax rates" on earned income for nonelderly, childless adults from 1979 onward. Although replacing marginal rates with effective rates could dramatically affect monthly housing payments, the empirical results are fairly robust when using either the median house price or the monthly payment computed here. Despite large changes in the tax schedule and taxable income base, effective rates at the federal level stayed in a fairly narrow range, varying from a low of 11.4 percent in 1984 to 13.8 percent in 1981.

Given interest rates and tax rates, I then computed the time series of after-tax monthly payments per $1,000 of housing value. I relied on first-year amortization calculators from "Mortgage Professor" (http://www.decisionaide.com/mpcalculators/ExtraPaymentsCalculator/Extra Payments1.asp). The monthly payment nets out the tax savings from the deductibility of mortgage interest, a factor that should be fairly important during the initial years of homeownership. On the basis of these schedules, the after-tax monthly payment per $1,000 of housing value varied between $6.08 in 1998 and $12.45 in 1981. I then applied these year-specific payments to each MSA's housing value to obtain the monthly payment.

Fair Market Rents

To control for conditions in the rental market, which may trend differently from housing prices, I obtained the Department of Housing and Urban Development's fair market rent series for two-bedroom apartments, available for many metropolitan areas from 1983 through the present. I use fair market rents (FMRs) to gauge gross rent estimates (rent plus all utilities except telephone). I use rents from all units occupied by renters who moved to their present residence within the past fifteen months. HUD combines data from the census, the American Housing Survey, and random digit dialing telephone surveys to determine the FMR.

FMRs are expressed as a percentile point within the distribution of standard-quality rental units. Currently, the fortieth percentile of rent is used, but before 1996 the forty-fifth percentile was used. Because HUD provided both the fortieth and forty-fifth percentiles of rents for each MSA in 1995, I can convert FMRs after 1995 to the forty-fifth percentile by multiplying that year's FMR by the MSA's ratio of rents in the forty-fifth and fortieth percentiles from 1995. Across all MSAs, rents in the forty-fifth percentile were 2.8 percent higher than in the fortieth; the largest difference was 6.7 percent. Because FMRs are unavailable before 1983, I deflate the 1983 numbers for the years 1980 to 1982. Finally, I convert all monthly rents to constant 2000 dollars using the CPI-U.

Transportation Costs

This study controls for transportation costs by deriving commuting-time measures from the 1980 to 2000 public use microdata samples (PUMS). Although transportation costs are often thought of in terms of expenditures on vehicles, insurance, maintenance, and fuel, longer commuting times are likely to be positively correlated with more intensive vehicle use. Moreover, the opportunity cost of an individual's time is itself a cost of commuting. Because it is not possible to obtain expenditures on transportation by locality over time, I use commuting time as a proxy. The census has detailed information on commuting patterns. In each MSA for each census year, I extracted all individuals who drove to work alone in a private vehicle, who worked at least 1,500 hours per year, and who left their home between 6:00 and 10:00 A.M. These restrictions impose a more uniform measure of transportation costs across MSAs and over time. In reality, when congestion goes up, workers find alternative means to avoid these costs, including moving closer to work, relying on public transportation or carpools, and changing their work schedules. Yet these optimizing responses to congestion, which in turn reduce congestion, entail costs in terms of convenience for workers.

I did not measure the direct, out-of-pocket costs of transportation; I speculate that relative to congestion costs, the variation across MSAs is quite minimal. Without data on direct, out-of-pocket transportation costs by MSA, I can only speculate on how they would affect the results. Explicit transportation costs are likely to be positively correlated with the implicit time costs because longer commuting times involve higher fuel consumption, greater wear and tear on vehicles, and higher insurance costs. The inclusion of MSA fixed effects will eliminate permanent fixed differences in commuting costs across localities.

Child Care Costs

To measure child care costs, I extracted all workers from the 1980 to 2000 PUMS who reported their occupation as child care and computed the average hourly wage rate in each MSA and year. I excluded individuals whose imputed wage rate was less than $1 per hour or greater than $100 per hour and converted all wage rates into constant 2000 dollars.

Although the wage rate of child care workers is admittedly a rough measure of the costs facing parents, we would expect that higher wage rates are positively correlated with higher out-of-pocket costs for parents. An advantage of using a measure derived from the census, rather than relying on measures published elsewhere, is that wage rates vary within an MSA over time. Thus, I control for fixed differences across MSAs and over time. Virtually all published measures of child care costs are at only one point in time, are at the state level rather than the metro level, or sample only a handful of MSAs.

Appendix B: Model and Identification Strategy

The basic model estimates an equation of the form:

$$LIVING\_ARR^*_{imt} = \beta_0 + \beta_1 HOUSE\_PAY_{imt} + \beta_2 FMR_{imt} + \beta_3 TRAV_{imt} +$$

$$\beta_4 CCARE_{imt} + \beta_5 ST\_URATE_{imt} + \beta_6 X_{imt} + \beta_7 D_{im} + \beta_8 D_{it} + \varepsilon_{imt} \quad (7A.1)$$

where equation 7A.1 is the underlying index function for the probit model (and i indexes individuals, m indexes MSAs, and t indexes time). I estimate separate probit models for each living arrangement. Although, in principle, estimating a multinomial logit or multinomial probit would be more desirable (since the living arrangement outcomes are not independent of each other), this was computationally impossible with 3.6 million observations. In the model, $LIVING\_ARR_{imt}$ is the young adult's living arrangement (independent, economic, or non-independent), $HOUSE\_PAY_{imt}$ is either the monthly house payment or the median house price, FMR_{imt} is the fair market rent, $TRAV_{imt}$ is the travel time in minutes, $CCARE_{imt}$ is the average wage of child care workers, and ST_URATE_{imt} is the statewide unemployment rate. Each of the economic variables varies by geographic area and time but not by individual circumstances. X_{imt} contains other covariates that are hypothesized to affect living arrangements and includes controls for age (dummy variables for single years of age), sex, race-ethnicity, educational attainment, current school enrollment, U.S. citizenship, current marital status, whether the individual lived in the same state five years prior to the census, and prior year's earnings. The vectors D_{im} and D_{it} are dummy variables for MSA (fifty-seven separate localities, as shown in table 7A.1) and year (1980, 1990, and 2000). In practice, we do not observe the underlying value of $LIVING\_ARR^*_{imt}$; instead, we observe only the discrete outcome:

$$LIVING\_ARR_{imt} = 1 \; if \; LIVING\_ARR^*_{imt} \geq 0$$

$$LIVING\_ARR_{imt} = 0 \; if \; LIVING\_ARR^*_{imt} < 0 \quad (7A.2)$$

Assuming that $\varepsilon_{imt} \sim N(0,1)$ and denoting $\Phi(\bullet)$ as the cumulative normal function gives the following probability:

$$prob(LIVING\_ARR_{imt}) = \Phi\begin{pmatrix} \beta_0 + \beta_1 HOUSE\_PAY_{imt} + \beta_2 FMR_{imt} + \beta_3 TRAV_{imt} \\ + \beta_4 CCAR_{imt} + \beta_5 ST\_URATE_{imt} + \beta_6 X_{imt} + \beta_7 D_{im} + \beta_8 D_{it} \end{pmatrix} \quad (7A.3)$$

When the economic variables and additionally D_{im} and D_{it} are included, the coefficients on $\beta_1 - \beta_5$ provide the difference-in-differences estimate of the impact of the cost of living on living arrangements. The dummy variables for metropolitan area account for long-standing, time-invariant differences between the different metropolitan areas. For example, some areas—such as San Francisco or Boston—persistently have a high cost of living and also tend to have high-paying job opportunities for young adults. Unless these long-standing differences in job opportunities can be adequately controlled for in the empirical models, the likely impact is to bias the effect of housing costs on deterring independent living. That is, good job opportunities, which in this instance are positively correlated with housing costs, also facilitate independent living arrangements. Although the statewide unemployment rate may partially control for these long-standing differences, it is unlikely to fully control for the differences. Thus, without MSA fixed effects, it is possible that the expected negative effect of housing costs on independent living arrangements may not emerge.

The same sorts of arguments could be made about the inclusion of time dummies. For example, national-level credit market conditions have changed over the twenty-year analysis period. The Federal Reserve Bank of San Francisco reports that subprime mortgage lending has grown tremendously since the early 1990s and now constitutes a significant fraction of the overall mortgage market.[21] Since their short credit histories may make young adults high credit risks, this is a potentially significant change that could facilitate greater independence. In the analysis, real housing prices trended upward by 16 percent from 1980 to 2000; as a result, fewer young adults may be able to afford living independently (and this is borne out). Yet we would expect that the drop in independent living would be even more dramatic if the changing credit market conditions at the national level were accounted for. The inclusion of time dummies accounts for unobserved or hard-to-measure national factors such as this.

With the inclusion of both MSA and time dummies, the estimated impact of the cost of living comes from within-MSA changes in housing costs (and other economic variables) over time. An analysis of variance reveals that roughly 15 percent of the variation in median housing costs comes from the within-MSA variation over time; the remainder is subsumed by MSA and time dummies. A similar analysis reveals that 11 percent of the variation in monthly housing payments and 15 percent of the variation in fair market rents comes from the within-MSA variation over time.

Although much of the variation is subsumed by the fixed effects, it may be inappropriate to use such variation to identify the effects of the cost of living on living arrangements in the first place. For example, when I estimate the impact of median house prices on independent living, I find that the coefficient estimate is around one-third smaller without the inclusion of MSA and time dummies.

Although a difference-in-differences estimator provides more compelling evidence than either cross-sectional or time-series estimates, it does have limitations. In particular, if there are factors that change differently across MSAs over time, then it is difficult to distinguish the effect of the cost of living from those other factors. There is no perfect way to address this problem, but as a specification check, I modify the model. In particular, for young adults age twenty-five to thirty-four, I consider how the housing market conditions when they turned twenty-five affected their current living arrangement. This approach can be estimated only for 1990 and 2000 given that housing market information is unavailable prior to 1980. In this case, the variation in the cost of living comes from MSA, year, and age. The motivation for this exercise is twofold. First, other authors, in particular Garasky, Haurin, and Haurin (2001, 333), have noted that an apparent interaction between housing costs and age has an impact on living arrangements. They state that "for older youths (25+), we expect both economic and socio-demographic variables to play significant roles" in living arrangements. Most young adults turning twenty-five have completed their schooling, so it is likely that they are in a position to become independent. Second, I restrict my attention to thirteen of the fifty-seven MSAs that experienced rapid bursts in housing prices, defined as real increases of 30 percent or more in median house prices over a three-year-period. Table 7A.1 indicates these MSAs with an asterisk. Many of these localities are in the Northeast or in California.

Figure 7A.1 shows the trajectories for six of the thirteen MSAs. Some MSAs, such as Honolulu, experienced rapid appreciation and then steep declines in housing prices.[22] Others, such as Philadelphia, experienced a burst of appreciation and relatively flat prices thereafter. Notice that these bursts of appreciation occurred at different times in different locations.

Another key point—the intuition behind this identification strategy—is that some young adults might be "in the right place at the right time." Consider a twenty-five-year-old living in San Francisco in 1986 who was deciding whether to live independently, in an economic arrangement, or with his parents. He would have faced a market in which the median house price was $260,991. A similar twenty-five-year-old in 1989 would have faced a market in which the median house price was $399,916, a 50 percent increase. If the cost of living is an important factor for living arrangements, we are likely to observe higher percentages of independent living for the cohorts that happened to face dramatically lower housing prices when they turned twenty-five. Except for differences in initial

Table 7A.1   MSAs Used in Regression Analysis

    80—Akron, OH
   520—Atlanta–Sandy Springs–Marietta, GA
  *640—Austin–Round Rock, TX
   720—Baltimore–Towson, MD
  1000—Birmingham–Hoover, AL
*1120—Boston–Quincy, MA
  1280—Buffalo–Niagara Falls, NY
  1520—Charlotte–Gastonia–Concord, NC-SC
  1600—Chicago–Naperville–Joliet, IL
  1640—Cincinnati–Middletown, OH-KY-IN
  1680—Cleveland–Elyria–Mentor, OH
  1840—Columbus, OH
  1920—Dallas–Plano–Irving, TX
  2000—Dayton, OH
  2080—Denver–Aurora, CO
  2160—Detroit–Livonia–Dearborn, MI
  3000—Grand Rapids–Wyoming, MI
  3120—Greensboro–High Point, NC
*3320—Honolulu, HI
  3360—Houston–Baytown–Sugar Land, TX
  3480—Indianapolis, IN
  3600—Jacksonville, FL
  3760—Kansas City, MO-KS
  4120—Las Vegas–Paradise, NV
*4480—Los Angeles–Long Beach–Glendale, CA
  4520—Louisville, KY-IN
  4920—Memphis, TN-MS-AR
  5000—Miami–Miami Beach–Kendall, FL
  5080—Milwaukee–Waukesha–West Allis, WI
  5120—Minneapolis–St. Paul–Bloomington, MN-WI
  5360—Nashville–Davidson–Murfreesboro, TN
*5380—Nassau–Suffolk, NY
  5560—New Orleans–Metairie–Kenner, LA
*5600—New York–Wayne–White Plains, NY-NJ
*5640—Newark–Union, NJ-PA
  5720—Virginia Beach–Norfolk–Newport News, VA-NC
  5880—Oklahoma City, OK
  5960—Orlando, FL
*6160—Philadelphia, PA
  6200—Phoenix–Mesa–Scottsdale, AZ
  6280—Pittsburgh, PA
  6440—Portland–Vancouver–Beaverton, OR-WA
  6760—Richmond, VA
  6780—Riverside–San Bernardino–Ontario, CA
  6840—Rochester, NY
*6920—Sacramento–Arden–Arcade–Roseville, CA

7040—St. Louis, MO-IL
*7160—Salt Lake City, UT
7240—San Antonio, TX
*7320—San Diego–Carlsbad–San Marcos, CA
*7360—San Francisco–San Mateo–Redwood City, CA
*7600—Seattle–Bellevue–Everett,WA
8160—Syracuse, NY
8280—Tampa–St. Petersburg–Clearwater, FL
8400—Toledo, OH
8520—Tucson, AZ
8840—Washington–Arlington–Alexandria, DC-VA-MD-WV

Source: Author's calculations.
*An MSA that experienced rapidly rising housing prices over a three year period. Overall, of the 91 MSAs that satisfied other criteria, these MSAs also had at least 20,000 young adults in them when combining the 1980 to 2000 census PUMS files.

Figure 7A.1   Examples of Rapid Escalation in Housing Prices (30 Percent or More Real Appreciation over Three Years)

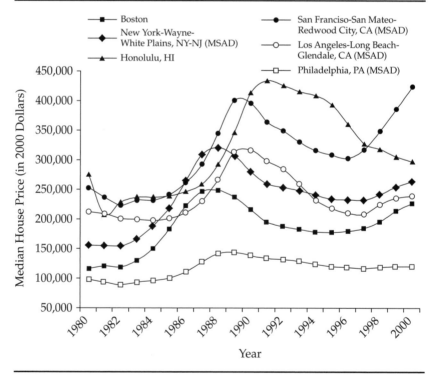

Source: Author's calculations, based on data from the National Association of Realtors and Office of Federal Housing Enterprise Oversight.

Table 7A.2   Full Results: Probit Models on Living Arrangements, Differences-in-Differences Specification

	(1) Independent	(2) Economic	(3) Not Independent	(4) Independent	(5) Economic	(6) Not Independent
Median house price	-0.0156 (0.0020) [-0.0061]	0.0076 (0.0021) [0.0011]	0.0072 (0.0028) [0.0021]	—	—	—
Monthly house payment	—	—	—	-0.1493 (0.0303) [-0.0584]	0.1570 (0.0234) [0.0221]	0.0139 (0.0396) [0.0041]
Monthly fair market rent	0.0184 (0.0944) [0.0072]	0.3215 (0.1007) [0.0453]	-0.2794 (0.1309) [-0.0824]	-0.1169 (0.1198) [-0.0457]	0.2567 (0.0831) [0.0362]	-0.1259 (0.1367) [-0.0371]
Average travel time in minutes	-0.0127 (0.0051) [-0.005]	-0.0185 (0.0047) [-0.0026]	0.0163 (0.0080) [0.0048]	-0.0166 (0.0053) [-0.0065]	-0.0164 (0.0044) [-0.0023]	0.0178 (0.0081) [0.0052]
Average wage of child care workers	0.0149 (0.0065) [0.0058]	0.0105 (0.0071) [0.0015]	-0.0238 (0.0094) [-0.007]	0.0146 (0.0077) [0.0057]	0.0049 (0.0068) [0.0007]	-0.0200 (0.0101) [-0.0059]
Statewide unemployment rate	-0.0231 (0.0064) [-0.0091]	-0.0205 (0.0053) [-0.0029]	0.0331 (0.0082) [0.0098]	-0.0258 (0.0072) [-0.0101]	-0.0128 (0.0047) [-0.0018]	0.0304 (0.0084) [0.009]
Male	-0.3949 (0.0068) [-0.1536]	0.1248 (0.0083) [0.0176]	0.2786 (0.0099) [0.0823]	-0.3946 (0.0069) [-0.1535]	0.1248 (0.0083) [0.0176]	0.2784 (0.0099) [0.0822]
Hispanic	-0.1566 (0.0290) [-0.0618]	-0.0644 (0.0275) [-0.0088]	0.2252 (0.0386) [0.0707]	-0.1577 (0.0290) [-0.0622]	-0.0640 (0.0275) [-0.0087]	0.2260 (0.0386) [0.0709]
African American or black	0.1323 (0.0145)	-0.3955 (0.0143)	0.1784 (0.0182)	0.1325 (0.0146)	-0.3960 (0.0144)	0.1786 (0.0182)

Table 7A.2 *(Continued)*

	(1) Independent	(2) Economic	(3) Not Independent	(4) Independent	(5) Economic	(6) Not Independent
Other nonwhite	[0.0512]	[-0.0453]	[0.0552]	[0.0512]	[-0.0453]	[0.0553]
	-0.1950	-0.1547	0.3093	-0.1977	-0.1535	0.3110
	(0.0216)	(0.0223)	(0.0334)	(0.0217)	(0.0223)	(0.0335)
	[-0.0772]	[-0.0197]	[0.1004]	[-0.0782]	[-0.0196]	[0.101]
Currently married	1.9048	-1.6005	-1.2476	1.9042	-1.6007	-1.2473
	(0.0196)	(0.0237)	(0.0318)	(0.0197)	(0.0237)	(0.0318)
	[0.6381]	[-0.2244]	[-0.3426]	[0.638]	[-0.2244]	[-0.3426]
High school dropout	-0.0108	-0.0367	0.0230	-0.0109	-0.0366	0.0231
	(0.0112)	(0.0112)	(0.0119)	(0.0113)	(0.0112)	(0.0119)
	[-0.0042]	[-0.0051]	[0.0068]	[-0.0043]	[-0.0051]	[0.0069]
Some college	0.0781	0.1630	-0.2165	0.0784	0.1632	-0.2168
	(0.0042)	(0.009)	(0.0084)	(0.0041)	(0.0090)	(0.0083)
	[0.0306]	[0.0227]	[-0.0644]	[0.0307]	[0.0227]	[-0.06451]
Enrolled in school	-0.1263	-0.0558	0.1211	-0.1264	-0.0557	0.1213
	(0.0064)	(0.0101)	(0.0115)	(0.0064)	(0.0101)	(0.0115)
	[-0.0497]	[-0.0077]	[0.0367]	[-0.0497]	[-0.0077]	[0.0367]
Lived in same state five years ago	-0.3650	-0.5981	0.7473	-0.3654	-0.5986	0.7479
	(0.0348)	(0.0575)	(0.0655)	(0.0348)	(0.0574)	(0.0654)
	[-0.1429]	[-0.0785]	[0.2304]	[-0.1431]	[-0.0786]	[0.2306]
U.S. citizen	0.2198	-0.4846	0.1905	0.2203	-0.4836	0.1893
	(0.0203)	(0.0190)	(0.0198)	(0.0203)	(0.019)	(0.0198)
	[0.0870]	[-0.0898]	[0.0527]	[0.0872]	[-0.0895]	[0.0524]
Individual earnings	7.5313	1.5193	-12.3256	7.5025	1.5073	-12.2892
	(0.4220)	(0.1877)	(0.4609)	(0.4218)	(0.1859)	(0.4609)
	[2.9453]	[0.2141]	[-3.6365]	[2.9341]	[0.2124]	[-3.6261]

Source: Author's calculations.
Notes: Sample size in all specifications is 3,636,296. All models estimated as probit models. Standard errors in parentheses and marginal effects in brackets. In addition to the variables shown, all models include single-year-of-age dummies, MSA dummies, year dummies, and a constant term and correct for clustering at the MSA-year level. Median house price is divided by 10,000, monthly house payment and fair market rent are divided by 1,000, and individual earnings are divided by 1,000,000.

Table 7A.3 Full Results: Housing Market Conditions at Age 25—Rapid Appreciation, Differences-in-Differences-in-Differences Specification

	Independent	Economic	Not Independent	Independent	Economic	Not Independent
Median house price at age twenty-five	-0.0013 (0.0009) [-0.0005]	0.0010 (0.0011) [0.0002]	-0.0010 (0.0011) [-0.0002]	—	—	0.0043 (0.0128) [0.0009]
Monthly house payment at age twenty-five	—	—	—	-0.0085 (0.0115) [-0.0031]	-0.0116 (0.0130) [-0.002]	—
Monthly fair market rent at age twenty-five	0.0619 (0.0374) [0.0222]	0.1099 (0.0594) [0.0187]	-0.2075 (0.0524) [-0.044]	0.0550 (0.0372) [0.0198]	0.1267 (0.0573) [0.0215]	-0.2175 (0.0503) [-0.0461]
Male	-0.3806 (0.0076) [-0.1363]	0.2266 (0.0088) [0.0387]	0.2659 (0.0083) [0.0566]	-0.3806 (0.0076) [-0.1363]	0.2266 (0.0088) [0.0387]	0.2659 (0.0083) [0.0566]
Hispanic	-0.1466 (0.0147) [-0.0537]	-0.0808 (0.0148) [-0.0133]	0.2782 (0.0212) [0.0650]	-0.1466 (0.0147) [-0.0537]	-0.0807 (0.0148) [-0.0133]	0.2781 (0.0212) [0.0649]
African American or black	0.0750 (0.0172) [0.0266]	-0.3839 (0.0120) [-0.0531]	0.2642 (0.0138) [0.0628]	0.0750 (0.0172) [0.0266]	-0.3839 (0.0120) [-0.0531]	0.2642 (0.0138) [0.0628]
Other nonwhite	-0.2957 (0.0115) [-0.1109]	-0.0988 (0.0165) [-0.016]	0.4605 (0.0172) [0.1175]	-0.2957 (0.0115) [-0.1109]	-0.0988 (0.0165) [-0.016]	0.4604 (0.0172) [0.1175]
Currently married	1.765 (0.0185) [0.5837]	-1.6213 (0.0203) [-0.3067]	-0.9954 (0.0175) [-0.2192]	1.765 (0.0185) [0.5837]	-1.6213 (0.0203) [-0.3067]	-0.9954 (0.0175) [-0.2192]

Table 7A.3 *(Continued)*

	Independent	Economic	Not Independent	Independent	Economic	Not Independent
High school dropout	-0.0221	-0.0001	0.0155	-0.0221	-0.0001	0.0155
	(0.0103)	(0.0118)	(0.0106)	(0.0103)	(0.0118)	(0.0106)
	[-0.008]	[-0.0001]	[0.0033]	[-0.008]	[-0.0001]	[0.0033]
Some college	0.0944	0.1277	-0.2026	0.0944	0.1277	-0.2026
	(0.0073)	(0.0092)	(0.0081)	(0.0073)	(0.0092)	(0.0081)
	[0.0341]	[0.0212]	[-0.0445]	[0.0341]	[0.0212]	[-0.0445]
Enrolled in school	-0.0459	0.0101	0.0267	0.0459	0.0101	0.0268
	(0.0069)	(0.0075)	(0.0096)	(0.0069)	(0.0075)	(0.0096)
	[-0.0166]	[0.0017]	[0.0057]	[-0.0166]	[0.0017]	[0.0057]
Lived in same state five years ago	-0.4748	-0.7996	1.0341	-0.4748	-0.7996	1.0341
	(0.0199)	(0.03)	(0.0308)	(0.0199)	(0.03)	(0.0308)
	[-0.1755]	[-0.114]	[0.2653]	[-0.1755]	[-0.114]	[0.2653]
U.S. citizen	0.2087	-0.4081	0.1055	0.2087	-0.4081	0.1055
	(0.0152)	(0.0137)	(0.0128)	(0.0152)	(0.0137)	(0.0128)
	[0.0771]	[-0.0824]	[0.0215]	[0.0771]	[-0.0824]	[0.0215]
Individual earnings in prior year	4.8308	-0.0066	-9.0739	4.8308	-0.066	-9.0739
	(0.1662)	(0.1212)	(0.2665)	(0.1662)	(0.1212)	(0.2665)
	[1.7355]	[-0.0011]	[-1.9252]	[1.7355]	[-0.0011]	[-1.9252]

Source: Author's calculations.

Notes: Sample size in all specifications is 50,593. Sample is restricted to young adults who are age twenty-five to thirty-four in one of the thirteen MSAs that experienced rapid price appreciation (30 percent or more in real terms over three years) and are in the 1990 or 2000 census PUMS: Boston–Quincy, MA, Honolulu, HI, Los Angeles–Long Beach–Glendale, CA, Nassau–Suffolk, NY, New York–Wayne–White Plains, NY-NJ, Newark–Union, NJ-PA, Philadelphia PA, Austin–Round Rock, TX, Sacramento–Arden-Arcade–Roseville, CA, Salt Lake City, UT, San Diego–Carlsbad–San Marcos, CA, San Francisco–San Mateo–Redwood City, CA, and Seattle–Bellevue–Everett, WA. Standard errors in parentheses and marginal effects in brackets. In addition to the variables shown, all models include MSA* year interactions, MSA* age interactions, year* age interactions, and a constant term and correct for clustering at the MSA* year* age level. Median house price is divided by 10,000, and monthly house payment and fair market rent are divided by 1,000. The average travel time to work, average wage of child care workers, and state unemployment rates are not included because the specification already includes MSA* year interactions.

housing costs, most other factors, such as the current health of the local job market or lending market conditions at the national level, should be quite similar when we observe young adults in 1990 or 2000.

By using housing conditions at age twenty-five rather than during the census year, equation 7A.1 is now modified as:

$$LIVING\_ARR^*_{imt} = \beta_0 + \beta_1 HOUSE\_PAY\_25_{imt} + \beta_2 FMR\_25_{imt}$$
$$+ \beta_3 X_{imt} + \beta_4 D_{im}D_{it} + \beta_5 D_{it}D_{ia} + \beta_6 D_{it}D_{ia} + \varepsilon_{imt} \quad (7A.1)$$

This specification includes MSA*time interactions, as well as MSA*age and time*age interactions (D_{ia} represents age dummies). The variation in travel time, child care costs, and the unemployment rate are subsumed by the MSA*time interactions. The coefficients $\beta_1 - \beta_2$ now represent the "triple differences" estimate of the impact of the cost of living.

The author would like to thank Sandy Korenman, Sheldon Danziger, Ceci Rouse, and conference participants for helpful comments.

Notes

1. See Time Poll, "Inside the World of the Twixters," available at: http://www .time.com/time/covers/1101050124/graphic/.
2. Much of the study focuses on housing costs rather than child care or transportation costs because of the availability of high-quality data. These other costs are probably important for the transition to adulthood as well, but the lack of a long time series makes it more difficult to come to firm conclusions.
3. By ending in 2000, however, the analysis stops short of the recent escalation in housing prices.
4. Roger Avery, Frances Goldscheider, and Alden Speare (1992) find that the effects of parental resources on leaving-home decisions differ depending on the route out of the home (marriage versus living alone or with roommates). Goldscheider, Arland Thornton, and Linda Young-DeMarco (1993) find that the transition to full residential independence among Detroit youth is gradual. Finally, William Clark and Clara Mulder (2000) find that independence in the housing market is closely related to the size and regional location of the housing market. In addition, the young adult's resources are an important influence on housing-market entry.
5. Specifically, a 10 percent increase in the relative cost of ownership reduces the likelihood of ownership by 7.1 percent.
6. Other authors in this volume (in particular, Hill and Holzer) define "living arrangements" somewhat differently, as does Jordan Matsudaira (2006). For example, Matsudaira's key dependent variable is "fraction of young adults living with at least one parent." This is very similar to my category "not independent." Living away from parents need not signal a complete transi-

tion to adulthood, however, and it is unclear ex-ante whether higher housing costs affect only living with parents. Later results show that higher housing costs reduce the likelihood of living in a nuclear family arrangement and increase the likelihood of living in an economic arrangement. This type of household adjustment would be missed by a focus only on whether a young adult is living with parents.

7. I tried classifying young adults by both living arrangements and homeownership status. For reasons discussed later, I abandoned this approach and focused exclusively on living arrangements.

8. Although the "economic arrangement" group could be thought of as roommates, cohabitors without children would fall into this group as well. I put cohabitors with children into the "other" category and exclude them from the analysis. If, instead, cohabitors with children are classified as "independent," then the empirical findings hardly change.

9. The fraction of young adults who fall into the "other" category uniformly increases over time, from about 7 to 15 percent; most of the increase occurred between 1980 and 2000. Some of this change is due to cohabitors with children. This classification does not, however, affect the empirical results.

10. Many young adults probably buy starter homes or condominiums that cost less than the median house price. Unfortunately, the NAR data do not have other percentiles in the housing distribution. Changes in house prices by percentile are correlated with each other, so the differential responsiveness may be because of socioeconomic status.

11. For the sample of MSAs I examine, holding quality constant and adjusting for inflation, prices fell in real terms. Consider the OFHEO data for the entire United States (http://www.ofheo.gov/media/pdf/3q06_hpi_reg.xls). In the first quarter of 1990, the index was 170.83. By the first quarter of 2000, this quality-constant index had increased to 231.86. Thus, nominal appreciation over the decade for the entire country was 35.7 percent (or an annual nominal appreciation of 3.1 percent). According to table B-60 of *The Economic Report of the President 2006* (accessed at http://www.whitehouse.gov/cea/erp06.pdf, page 351), the CPI stood at 130.7 in 1990 and at 172.2 in 2000. This represents a 31.7 percent increase in prices, or 2.7 percent annual inflation. Thus, for the entire United States, there was a trivial change in real housing prices. Since the actual sample used in this study includes a number of metropolitan areas that had run-ups in housing prices going into 1990 (and severe falls in the early to mid-1990s), it is plausible that real, constant-quality prices fell.

12. It may appear surprising that housing payments fell, given the rise in nominal house prices, but interest rates fell from 14.2 percent in 1980 to 8.3 percent in 2000. In addition, *real* housing prices rose only modestly over the period.

13. The results on commuting time appear to be implausibly large. A $15,000 increase in house prices has the same effect on independence as a two-minute increase in commuting time. The results on housing prices are unaffected, however, by excluding commuting time. For example, a $10,000 change in median house price leads to a 0.64-percentage-point decline in independent living, rather than 0.61 percentage points.

14. It could also be the case that the unemployment rate, commuting times, and child care wages all tend to be correlated with each other in a way that affects the living arrangements of young adults.
15. Although same-state-of-residence is arguably endogenous, the results on house prices actually get larger by excluding it. A $10,000 change in house price leads to a 0.70-percentage-point decline in independent living.
16. One approach to dealing with the endogeneity of location is to construct an instrumental variable based on the person's birthplace. Unfortunately, this is hard to do in my analysis since I would need to know the MSA, not the state, where the individual was born. The census asks only for state of birth, not city of birth.
17. The results for all alternative specifications are available from the author.
18. According to the credit service FICO (http://www.myfico.com), credit scores do not explicitly incorporate race, color, religion, national origin, sex, marital status, or age.
19. One mitigating factor would be the fall in interest rates since 2000. As a consequence, the monthly housing payment would not rise as rapidly as median house prices.
20. This trade-off between the interest rate and points is justified by casual inspection of thirty-year mortgage loan combinations on www.eloan.com.
21. See Lederman 2001.
22. Although Honolulu may be different from other localities for a variety of reasons, the specifications include MSA fixed effects to account for those differences.

References

Avery, Roger, Frances Goldscheider, and Alden Speare Jr. 1992. "Feathered Nest/Gilded Cage: Parental Income and Leaving Home in the Transition to Adulthood." *Demography* 29(3, August): 375–88.
Case, Karl E., and Robert J. Shiller. 1987. "Prices of Single Family Real Estate Prices." *New England Economic Review* (September): 45–56.
———. 1989. "The Efficiency of the Market for Single-Family Homes." *American Economic Review* 79(1): 125–37.
Clark, William, and Clara H. Mulder. 2000. "Leaving Home and Entering the Housing Market." *Environment and Planning A* 32(9, September): 1657–71.
Garasky, Steven, R. Jean Haurin, and Donald R. Haurin. 2001. "Group Living Decisions as Youths Transition to Adulthood." *Journal of Population Economics* 14(2): 329–49.
Goldscheider, Frances, and Julie DaVanzo. 1985. "Living Arrangements and the Transition to Adulthood." *Demography* 22(4): 545–63.
Goldscheider, Frances, Arland Thornton, and Linda Young-DeMarco. 1993. "A Portrait of the Nest-Leaving Process in Early Adulthood." *Demography* 30(4): 683–99.
Haurin, Donald R., Patric H. Hendershott, and Dongwook Kim. 1993. "The Impact of Real Rents and Wages on Household Formation." *Review of Economics and Statistics* 75(2): 284–93.

————. 1994. "Housing Decisions of American Youth." *Journal of Urban Economics* 35(1): 28–45.

Lederman, Elizabeth. 2001. "Subprime Mortgage Lending and the Capital Markets." Federal Reserve Bank of San Francisco. FRBSF Economic Letter 2001-38. December 28, 2001. Accessed at http://www.frbsf.org/publications/economics/letter/2001/el2001-38.pdf.

Matsudaira, Jordan. 2006. "Economic Conditions and the Living Arrangements of Young Adults." Network on Transitions to Adulthood Working Paper, May 2006. Accessed at http://www.transad.pop.upenn.edu/downloads/matsudaira.pdf.

National Association of Realtors. 2007. "Median Sales Price of Existing Single-Family Homes for Metropolitan Areas." Accessed at http://www.realtor.org/Research.nsf/files/MSAPRICESF.pdf/$FILE/MSAPRICESF.pdf.

U.S. Department of Commerce. Bureau of the Census. 1971. *Census of Population and Housing, 1970 (United States): Public Use Samples* (computer file). Washington: U.S. Bureau of the Census (producer); Ann Arbor, Mich.: Inter-university Consortium for Political and Social Research (distributor, 1991).

————. 1985. *Census of Population and Housing, 1980 (United States): Public Use Microdata Sample (a Sample): 5 Percent Sample (Puerto Rico)* (computer file). ICPSR version. Washington: U.S. Bureau of the Census (producer); Ann Arbor, Mich.: Inter-university Consortium for Political and Social Research (distributor, 1997).

————. 1995. *Census of Population and Housing, 1990 (United States): Public Use Microdata Sample: 5 Percent Sample* (computer file). 3rd ICPSR release. Washington: U.S. Bureau of the Census (producer); Ann Arbor, Mich.: Inter-university Consortium for Political and Social Research (distributor, 1996).

————. 2003. *Census of Population and Housing, 2000 (United States): Public Use Microdata Sample: 5 Percent Sample* (computer file). ICPSR release. Washington: U.S. Bureau of the Census (producer); Ann Arbor, Mich.: Inter-university Consortium for Political and Social Research (distributor, 2003).

Chapter 8

Sticking Around: Delayed Departure from the Parental Nest in Western Europe

KATHERINE NEWMAN AND SOFYA APTEKAR

Most of the chapters in this volume focus on the transition to adulthood in the United States, yet some of the most dramatic changes in pathways to independence are unfolding beyond U.S. borders. In some Catholic countries of western Europe, young adults are marrying later or not marrying at all. Below-replacement fertility has produced pressures to open the gates to immigration in countries with little or no history of incorporating newcomers. Changing patterns of household formation have wide-ranging implications for intergenerational economic support and are taking place against the backdrop of divergent national policies for old-age support, labor market protection, national investment in higher education, and child care benefits.

This chapter examines the delayed departure of young adults from the parental (natal) home in western Europe, where, in some countries, more than 50 percent of men age thirty still reside with their parents. In others, the age of independence is considerably younger than it is in the United States. We focus on the role of employment, housing barriers, and social policy in shaping patterns of home-leaving and then consider whether delayed departure has affected the life satisfaction of young adults in Europe.

Sociologists who study this issue in the United States note that an abrupt change in the timing of independence creates tension as new generations of adolescents violate the norms and expectations of those who

207

came before them (Newman 1993). The resulting confusion over when, in normative terms, it is appropriate to make major life transitions can lead to widespread concern about "defective" generations that do not abide by social conventions. However, this is not the only conceivable outcome. In some countries—for example, Italy—general well-being and satisfaction seem to be enhanced by long stays in the family home, and in countries where youth face high economic uncertainty, the family can be a critical (and welcome) buffer in the face of instability.

We hypothesize that as the stay-at-home pattern shifts from being one confined to a small group to one that is a recognizable pathway, the social anxiety over delayed departure will diminish. It is the "against the grain" nature of new patterns that is disruptive or transgressive. Once a new norm is evident, it becomes more socially acceptable and possibly even a source of pleasure rather than a source of internal unhappiness or intergenerational tension. Indeed, the comfort factor with delayed departure may make it difficult for social policies (such as family allowances, pension benefits based on marital status, and so on) to stimulate either marriage or childbearing, a problem for countries facing low fertility rates.

We pursue our analysis in three steps. First, we draw on the European Quality of Life Survey (EQLS) of 2003 (European Foundation for the Improvement of Living and Working Conditions 2003) to show the diversity of patterns in home-leaving across western Europe. Second, we use data from the Organization for Economic Cooperation and Development (OECD) to explore the effect of youth unemployment, housing barriers, and specific domains of social policy on the proportion of young people age eighteen to thirty-four who reside with their parents. Finally, using the EQLS survey, we examine how delayed departure is associated with life satisfaction among young adults. We test the hypothesis that the "normative status" of independence influences the depth of dissatisfaction among youths living with their parents and their social role as "aging dependents."

Sticking Around

The age at which young people leave the parental home has been rising in all developed nations. Yet southern Europe stands out as a region that has seen a pronounced delay in home-leaving develop over a short period of time (Alders and Manting 1999; Cherlin, Scabini, and Rossi 1997; Cordon 1997). At present, the median age of departure from the parental home ranges from twenty for Finnish women to thirty for Italian men.[1]

Figure 8.1, based on recent data from the EQLS, shows that only approximately 10 percent of those age eighteen to thirty-four reside with their parents in Scandinavian countries. Rates in northern European

Figure 8.1   Percentage of Young People (Eighteen to Thirty-four) Living with
Their Parents, Without a Partner or Children

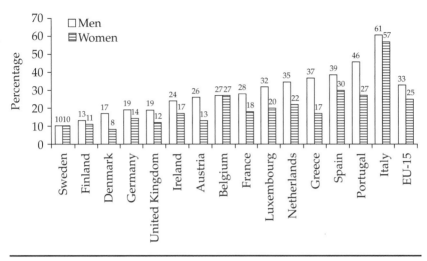

Source: European Foundation for the Improvement of Living and Working Conditions
(2003).

countries range between 15 and 30 percent. In southern Europe, as many
as 60 percent of young adults live with their parents.[2] Southern Europe
also differs from other countries in that more young people move directly from being single, childless, and living with their parents to living
with a spouse and soon thereafter with children.[3] As table 8.1 shows, di-
verse and extended intermediate stages, such as living alone or cohabi-
tating, flourish elsewhere (Billari 2004; Billari, Philipov, and Baizan 2001;
Cook and Furstenberg 2002; Iacovou 2002; Mulder and Manting 1994;
Rossi 1997).

Market Conditions, Social Policy, and Variation in Home-Leaving

Housing Markets

European countries vary on many social policy and labor market dimensions, and these variations provide possible explanations for the proportion of young adults living with their parents. For example, housing
market conditions can affect home-leaving. Housing costs have been rising as a proportion of all consumer expenditures throughout Europe
(Boelhouwer and van der Heijden 1993). Public policies have affected

Table 8.1   Household Arrangements of Eighteen- to Thirty-four-Year-Old Men

	With Parents	Alone	Coupled (With or Without Children)	Other
Denmark	17%	33%	48%	1%
Sweden	10	44	39	7
Finland	13	39	44	4
Belgium	27	28	40	6
Austria	26	35	27	11
France	28	36	31	6
Germany	19	40	31	11
Luxembourg	32	12	38	18
Netherlands	35	27	31	6
United Kingdom	19	34	30	17
Ireland	24	10	29	36
Italy	62	11	19	8
Greece	37	33	17	14
Spain	39	5	35	21
Portugal	46	7	36	11
EU-15	33	26	29	12

Source: OECD (2006).

housing availability.[4] In the Netherlands, 42 percent of the total housing stock is in the public sector (European Foundation for the Improvement of Living and Working Conditions 2004), and some housing is built specifically for young students and workers (Mulder and Hooimeijer 2002). Austria and the United Kingdom also have considerable municipal housing, with 26 percent each (European Foundation for the Improvement of Living and Working Conditions 2004). Denmark saw a construction boom in the 1980s, much of it in the public rental sector (Boelhouwer and Heijden 1993). Nearly three-fourths of rented dwellings in the United Kingdom are public compared with 37 percent in France and 8 percent in Spain (Holdsworth and Solda 2002; Jurado Guerrero 2001). More public housing tends to lower rental prices, making the move out of the parental home easier, at least where single young adults are eligible (as they tend to be in the Nordic welfare states).

Unique situations have shaped some European housing markets. West Germany faced an acute housing shortage following reunification as many East Germans migrated to areas with more jobs and a higher standard of living. The government responded by encouraging deregulation of rents (Boelhouwer and Heijden 1993), which created affordability problems for youth. Spain experienced a construction boom after entering the European Union (EU), but the boom aggravated the housing situation of most Spaniards through price hikes while increasing the housing stock of high-end dwellings, second residences, and tourist accommodations.

The economic crisis that swept much of Europe in the 1980s prompted many governments to deregulate, abolish rent control, sell public housing, and encourage homeownership. This altered the housing landscape in Spain (Holdsworth 2000; Holdsworth and Solda 2002), France, Belgium, and the United Kingdom (Boelhouwer and Heijden 1993). Italy instituted a "just rent" scheme that resulted in a bifurcated rental market, with affordable but oversubscribed rentals, on the one hand, and accessible but unaffordable housing, on the other (Castles and Ferrera 1996). In 1991 Sweden raised caps on rent by 20 percent but continued to provide generous tax relief on mortgage interest (Boelhouwer and Heijden 1993).

In countries where homeownership is dominant, young adults are less able to leave the parental home unless the government provides assistance for first-time buyers (relatively rare). In Spain and Italy, more than 70 percent of people own their dwellings (European Foundation for the Improvement of Living and Working Conditions 2004), and there is no public provision for new entrants to the private housing market.[5] More than one-half (54 percent) of primary residences are owner-occupied in France, and 65 percent are owner-occupied in the United Kingdom (Holdsworth and Solda 2002; Jurado Guerrero 2001). Most Spaniards buy a house *before* leaving the parental home (Holdsworth 2000), with only one-fourth moving to a rented dwelling. This compares with three-quarters of the French (Jurado Guerrero 2001).

Using OECD data on the shares of owner-occupied housing across the fifteen original countries of the European Union (EU-15) (*OECD Economic Review* 2004), we find a clear relationship between the proportion of the market that is privately owned and the proportion of young adults living with their parents (figure 8.2). A 10 percent increase in owner-occupied housing is associated with about a 3 percent increase in the proportion living with parents. Approximately 14 percent of the variance among countries in the prevalence of coresidence with parents is explained by the proportion of owner-occupied housing.[6]

The Labor Market

Changes in the labor market prospects of young Europeans, particularly increases in unemployment or temporary employment, have also contributed to the prolonged stay in the family home. Two seemingly opposite aspects of labor regulation are at work. One occurs when a previously protectionist regime shifts in such a way that the change has the most profound effect on new entrants to the labor market—who tend to

Figure 8.2   Proportion of Eighteen- to Thirty-four-Year-Olds Living with Their Parents, by Percentage of Owner-Occupied Housing

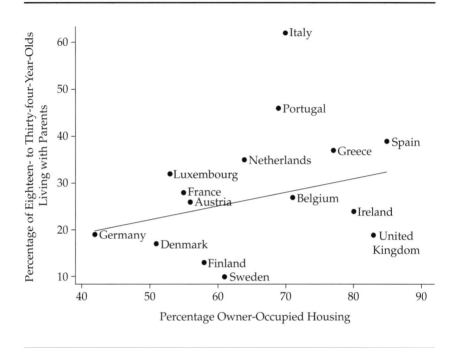

Source: OECD Economic Review 38 (2004c).
Note: Linear fit without Italy, r = 0.37.

be young. Complaints surrounding the rigidity of European labor markets, particularly the difficulty of laying workers off, led some countries to permit temporary contracts. Beginning in 1984, for instance, new legislation allowed Spanish firms to offer short-term employment contracts, a sharp departure from past practices. Today one-third of Spanish workers are governed by short-term agreements, the highest level in western Europe. Older workers, who had permanent jobs before the reforms, had more bargaining power to protect their insider status, leaving new entrants to the labor market more vulnerable to temporary contracts. Not surprisingly, the percentage of twenty-five- to twenty-nine-year-old Spanish male workers in temporary employment rose from 20 percent in 1987 to more than 50 percent less than ten years later (Golsch 2003). Figure 8.3 shows that as temporary employment rises, the proportion of eighteen- to thirty-four-year-olds living with their parents grows as well.

Figure 8.3   Proportion of Eighteen- to Thirty-four-Year-Olds Living with Their Parents, by Proportion of Young Workers (Age Twenty-five to Thirty-nine) in Temporary Employment

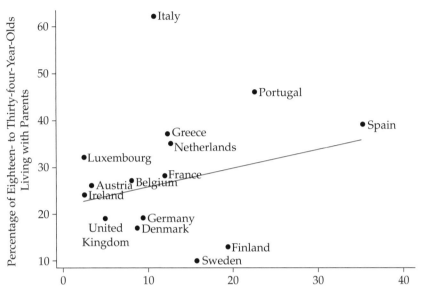

Percentage of Workers Age Twenty-five to Thirty-nine in Temporary Employment

Source: Eurostat (2003).
Note: Linear fit without Italy, r = 0.35.

The opposite of looser labor policies—continued rigidity—also disproportionately affects youth. The OECD (2004b) classifies countries' labor market policies by protection of regular workers against individual dismissal, regulation of temporary forms of employment, and requirements for collective dismissals. Figure 8.4 shows that as employment protections strengthen, youth unemployment rises. Employers hesitate to offer positions to young and inexperienced workers if they cannot terminate them. France is a case in point. To address barriers to youth employment, the French government proposed new regulations in March 2006 that would have permitted employers to fire workers under age twenty-six with no notice or severance. Nearly one-fourth (23 percent) of French citizens under age twenty-six are jobless, and in the immigrant districts outside major cities the figure rises to nearly 50 percent. The proposal sparked enormous street demonstrations and caused the shutdown of more than half of France's public universities (Sciolina

Figure 8.4   Youth Unemployment Rate, by Employment Protection Scale (0 to 6)

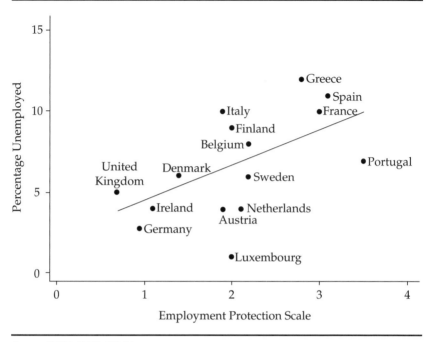

Source: OECD (2003, 2004b).
Note: r = 0.53.

2006). The proposal was withdrawn a month later, just in time to avert what many analysts predicted would have been the collapse of the Chirac government.

There is also a strong relationship between employment protection and the incidence of temporary contracts among young workers. Figure 8.5 shows that an increase of one point on the employment protection scale is associated with about an 8 percent increase in the proportion of twenty-five- to thirty-nine-year-old workers with temporary contracts. Forty-six percent of the variance in temporary employment in this age group is explained by employment protection.

These two trends—youth unemployment and temporary employment—increase the likelihood that young people will remain with their parents, whose resources (housing, income, and so forth) buffer their earnings instability (Eurostat 2002).[7] Moving up a point in the employment protection scale is correlated with an additional 9 percent of young

Figure 8.5   Proportion of Young Workers (Age Twenty-five to Thirty-nine) in Temporary Employment, by Employment Protection Scale (0 to 6)

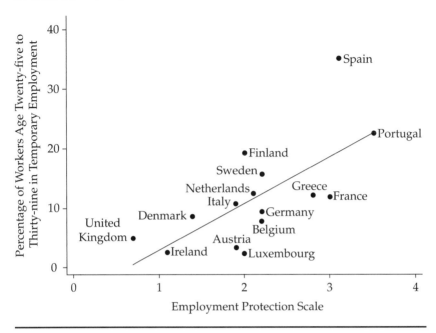

Source: Eurostat (2003).
Note: r = 0.68.

people living with their parents (see figure 8.6). This relationship is stronger than the one between the proportion of owner-occupied housing and living arrangements: 17 percent of the variance in the proportion living with parents is explained by the employment protection scale.

Although unemployment rates have remained largely stable, the rates of "idleness" (defined as neither at work nor in school) among young people have been on the rise everywhere in Europe, but much more dramatically in the south (Cordon 1997). Figure 8.7's employment-to-population ratio reveals this trend (OECD 2003). The negative relationship shown in figure 8.7 is as expected: as more young people are in the labor force, the proportion living with their parents decreases. A 10 percent increase in the employment ratio is associated with a 4 percent decrease in the proportion living with parents. The relationship is rather weak, although stronger than that for unemployment and living arrangements (not shown here).

One potential explanation for the relatively weak relationship be-

Figure 8.6   Proportion of Eighteen- to Thirty-four-Year-Olds Living with Their Parents, by Employment Protection Scale (0 to 6)

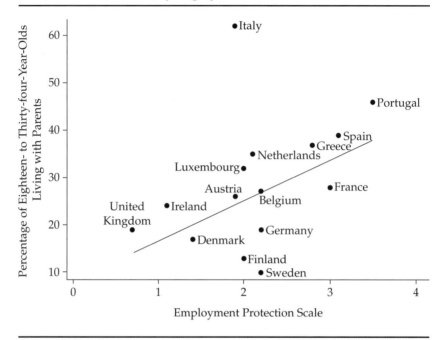

Source: OECD (2004b).
Note: Linear fit without Italy, r = 0.64.

tween unemployment and delayed departure from the family home lies in variations in the sources of income that youth receive. A combination of joblessness and lack of unemployment insurance produces pressures for youth to rely on family resources (or refrain from venturing far from them in the first place) unless social policy has made alternative resources available.[8] Figure 8.8 looks at the sources of support for the young unemployed across countries, as reported by respondents to the Eurobarometer Survey in 2001. In southern Europe, parent or family resources are virtually all that is available to support jobless youth. In the Nordic countries and some liberal democracies, such as Ireland and the United Kingdom, unemployment and social security provide the lion's share of support for unemployed youth. Continental regimes, such as France, Germany, and Belgium, fall in the middle.

In countries with substantial benefits for out-of-work young people or for those who have never worked, the capacity to become (or remain) independent of parental resources is greater than in countries where these

Figure 8.7   Proportion of Eighteen- to Thirty-four-Year-Olds Living with Parents, by Employment-to-Population Ratio

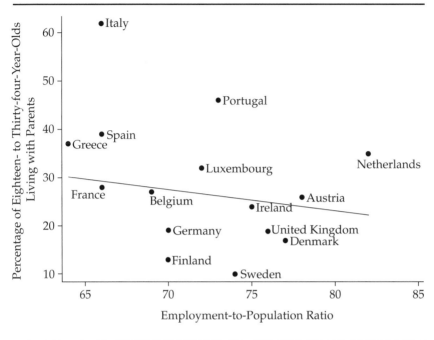

Source: OECD (2003).
Note: Linear fit without Italy, r = 0.21.

benefits are closed to young people. As expected, the average percentage of eighteen- to thirty-four-year-olds living at home rises when benefits are available (OECD 2004a) (see figure 8.9). Where benefits are available, on average 14 percent fewer young people live with parents. Benefit availability explains 28 percent of the variance in percentage living with parents.[9]

The Impact of Delayed Departure on Life Satisfaction

Does delayed departure make young people feel out of step with others in their society? We hypothesize that for the current generation of young adults in Europe, delayed departure has taken a toll on their sense of life satisfaction. This is partly because the pattern of independence differs from that of their parents, who may be unaware of (or choose to ignore) the structural factors that make leaving home now

Figure 8.8   Sources of Support for Unemployed Eighteen- to Tweny-four-Year-Olds in 2001

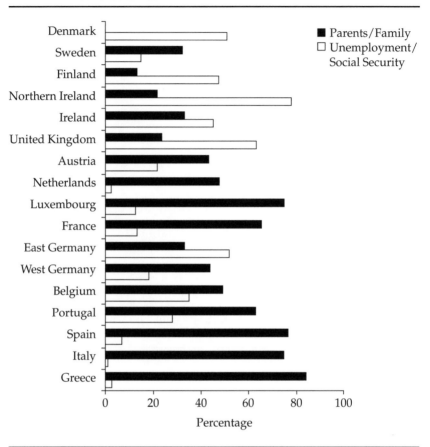

Source: Christensen (2001), from the question: "Where do you get most of your money from? Choose all that apply: regular job, unemployment/social security benefits, training allowance/educational grant, family, casual work, partner, work in the 'black economy,' and other."

more difficult (for an American parallel, see Newman 1993). Yet, as this pattern grows more common, we might expect to see accommodations in households, which may lead to acceptance and more positive relations between generations who live together. Of course, cultural and political influences can "retard" this adjustment by publicly defining delayed departure as a default on the social contract. In this case, the growing proportion of young adults at home may lead to positive relations inside the household but a continued discomfort in the public sphere and a dissonance with norms.

Figure 8.9   Percentage of Eighteen- to Thirty-four-Year-Olds Living at Home, by Availability of Unemployment Benefits for Twenty-Year-Old with No Working Experience

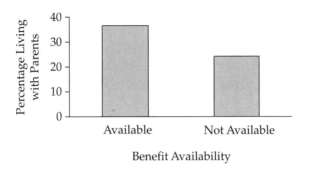

Benefit Availability

Source: OECD (2004).

We examine the relationship between living arrangements of young adults and their satisfaction with their lives using a large multinational dataset. The European Quality of Life Survey of 2003 is a cross-sectional survey of 26,257 Europeans over the age of eighteen in twenty-eight European countries and Turkey. For this chapter, we examine data for the fifteen member states of the European Union before 2004. There were about 1,000 respondents for each country, with the exception of Luxembourg, which had 600. Restricting our analysis to people age eighteen to thirty-four yields a sample size of 4,096.

We examine the effect of coresidence with parents and other predictors on life satisfaction using a random-effects, hierarchical linear regression model. The hierarchical model allows us to decompose the variance into individual and macro levels. Table 8.2 describes the variables used in this analysis. We examine the effect of living with one's parents and of the percentage of young people who live at home after adjusting for potential contributing factors such as age, sex, marital status, whether the young adult is a parent, employment and its precariousness, student status, income, economic hardship, number in household, homeownership, and number of rooms in the parental home.[10] The interaction term, between living at home and percentage of young people at home in the country, is included to test the hypothesis that the effect of living at home is mediated by how widespread this status is in the given country.

From the simple means, it appears that young people living with parents score about the same on life satisfaction. However, there is significant national variation in life satisfaction, which warrants multilevel modeling (see table 8.3). As we noted earlier, the rates of living with

Table 8.2 Variables Used and Means, by Residential Status

		Mean	
Variable	Definition	Living With Parents (N = 1,194)	Living Without Parents (N = 2,902)
Life satisfaction	How satisfied you are with your life these days (1 to 10)	7.42	7.47
Age	Years	22.7	27.7
Male	Sex = male	0.51	0.39
Married	Married or living with a partner	0.06	0.56
Employed	Currently working for pay	0.45	0.67
Student	Enrolled in higher education	0.42	0.12
Lives with parents	Mother and/or father in the same household	—	—
Home is owned	Own without mortgage or own with mortgage	0.64	0.40
Rooms	Number of rooms in the dwelling, excluding kitchen, bathroom, hallways	4.62	3.37
Number of people in the household	Including the respondent	3.76	2.33
Second income quartile (household)	Quartiles of OECD-equivalent household income per country (first quartile as reference category)	0.12	0.17
Third income quartile (household)		0.16	0.21
Fourth income quartile (household)		0.12	0.20
Hardship	Household in arrears when paying bills in the last twelve months	0.03	0.07
Percentage at home	Percentage of eighteen- to thirty-four-year-olds living with parents in given country	34.5	26.9
Living with parents × percentage at home	Interaction term between living with parents and percentage of eighteen- to thirty-four-year-olds living with parents	34.5	—

Source: European Foundation for the Improvement of Living and Working Conditions (2003).

Table 8.3   Mean Differences in Life Satisfaction, by Country and Residential Status

	Without Parents	With Parents
Austria	7.78	7.48
Belgium	7.41	7.18
Denmark	8.31	8.28
Finland	8.09	8.11
France	6.79	6.78
Germany	7.31	7.98
Greece	7.50	6.96
Ireland	7.61	7.96
Italy	7.33	7.43
Luxembourg	7.61	7.24
Netherlands	7.43	7.42
Portugal	6.20	7.06
Spain	7.67	7.71
Sweden	7.77	7.66
United Kingdom	7.14	7.27

Source: European Foundation for the Improvement of Living and Working Conditions (2003).

parents vary greatly by country, with very high levels of coresidence in southern Europe and very low levels in Scandinavia (see figure 8.1).

The bivariate correlations between percentage living at home and life satisfaction across the fifteen EU countries is statistically significant but weak ($r = .053$). For a more powerful analysis, table 8.4 presents results from a two-level linear regression model[11] with an interaction effect between living with parents and percentage living with parents in the country.[12] In this analysis, the effect of living at home is much more striking.

The model predicting life satisfaction supports our hypothesis that the more widespread the practice of living with parents, the less toll it takes on personal satisfaction. On average, living with parents decreases life satisfaction substantially. Moreover, living in a country where more young people are at home is associated with lower life satisfaction. To be more specific, a 10 percent increase in the proportion of young adults living with their parents is associated with a reduction of 0.12 points in life satisfaction, holding all other variables constant. However, the interaction term between living at home and the percentage of young adults living at home has a positive coefficient. This implies that the toll that living at home takes on life satisfaction eases as that status becomes more common. The magnitude of the interaction effect is almost identical to that on the aggregate coresidence measure but with the opposite sign, which indicates that for young adults living with their parents, the "normalcy" of

Table 8.4   Results from Two-Level Linear Regression Model with Random Effects Predicting Life Satisfaction

	Life Satisfaction
	β
Age	−0.026***
Male	−0.064
Married	0.426***
Own child(ren)	0.138
Employed (reference category not working)	0.515***
Student (reference category not working)	0.736***
Lives with parents	−0.466**
Home is owned	0.361***
Number of rooms	0.068***
Number of people in household	−0.028
Second income quartile	−0.071
Third income quartile	0.117
Fourth income quartile	0.241***
Hardship	−1.583***
Percentage living at home	−0.012***
Lives with parents × percentage at home	0.013**
Constant	7.478
Level 2 country effect (not exponentiated) (Standard deviation)	0.130 (0.023)
Log likelihood	−7891.841

Source: European Foundation for the Improvement of Living and Working Conditions (2003).
**p ≤ .01; ***p ≤ .001

this arrangement in their country almost exactly counterbalances the negative effect of living in a country with a higher prevalence of coresidence.

All three coefficients are significant. Therefore, we reject the hypothesis that there is no difference in life satisfaction between those who are living with their parents and those who are not, and between those who live in a country where it is more common to live with one's parents and those who do not; we also reject the idea that the "normalcy" of living with one's parents does not moderate the individual effect of living with them.

The same model also shows that being married, employed, or a student had a large positive effect on life satisfaction. Young adults living in a home that was owner-occupied or had more rooms were also significantly more likely to be satisfied with their lives. Predictably, economic hardship was associated with a much reduced score on life satisfaction. Income seems to have a nonlinear effect, given that only those in the highest earnings quartile had a statistically significant and positive association with life satisfaction. Few young adults are earning enough to place them in the top quartile of the overall income distribution for the working population. Those who are, however, score 0.24 points higher on life satisfaction. Having one's own children, gender, and the number of people in the household have no significant effect on life satisfaction, once other factors are taken into account.

All in all, we can say that the subjective "disadvantage" of living with one's parents decreases as the proportion of people in the country living at home increases. The growing normalcy of coresidence positively mediates the effect of living with parents in young adulthood.

Conclusion

The rate at which young people are able to move into their own homes or apartments clearly varies across Europe. The evidence presented here suggests that employment and unemployment benefit policies that protect older workers at the expense of new entrants to the labor market make it harder for young adults to move out of their family homes. Housing markets play a key role in the pattern of home-leaving as well. In countries with a large rental sector, the proportion of young adults living at home is relatively small, while in countries with a high rate of homeownership, the barriers to residential independence are high, particularly if there are no first-time home buyer programs and labor market conditions make finding a long-term job problematic (and therefore reduce the ability of young people to acquire mortgage financing).

When we consider the relatively steep down payments expected of European buyers (generally nearer 50 percent of the value of the home versus 10 to 20 percent in the American context), it seems clear that young people will be at a disadvantage in joining the ranks of homeowners. In short, market conditions and social policies seem to have a significant impact on the age at which young Europeans separate from their parents' homes.

What, if any, societal consequence does this constraint have? To what extent does delayed departure affect the more subjective experience of life satisfaction? As we predicted, the more prevalent the practice of delayed departure, the less troublesome it becomes. As the pattern of living with parents into the late twenties and thirties spreads, the negative effects of coresidence on life satisfaction diminish. This suggests that social anxiety declines as the new residential arrangement becomes a more clearly defined pathway. Living with parents is no longer seen necessarily as a sign of personal failure or a harbinger of difficult family dynamics.

The development of new demographic patterns rarely proceeds

smoothly, particularly when they have such significant consequences for bedrock questions of national fertility rates, labor supply, and the viability of social security systems. Even if these structural problems were not at issue, sharp divergence between generations in the pathway to adulthood can arouse controversy to the extent that residential and financial autonomy remain important landmarks on the way to personal independence and full-fledged adulthood. Yet there is no self-evident reason why these facets must remain as tightly interlocked as they have been in the past. Indeed, it may be that we are witnessing the emergence of a new developmental stage, one we might term "in-house adulthood." Living with one's parents at age fifteen is likely to imply a very different set of constraints on privacy, freedom of action, sexual expression, and subordination to parental control than may be in place at age thirty. Young people who crest into their thirties while still at home may find that they develop relationships with their parents that are characterized less as ones between an authoritative parent and a submissive child and more as ones between equals who reside together and enjoy one another's company and support and who have relegated to the past the constraints, enforced through parental surveillance, that once restricted the younger generation—particularly girls—to parentally approved behavior.

The growth of two-income households and the attendant time pressures on parents may mean that they have less time for their children's early years and hence less of an "itch" to see them depart. They may come to feel that they have not had their fill of their children at age eighteen and are not as ready to let them go as previous generations might have been. Parents are delaying childbearing, having fewer children, and investing more of their resources in those they have. Changes in the transition to adulthood are part and parcel of much broader changes in family arrangements. Hence, the change we investigate here in the transition to adulthood may be more fruitfully investigated as an elongation of the entire family system, which has consequences for the social roles of all generations. Teresa Jurado Guerrero (2001) reports on a different Eurobarometer survey for 1993 that found that more than one-half of all Europeans think it is a good thing that adult children live longer with parents, although the variation is considerable: only one-third of Spaniards agreed, while 70 percent of Greeks did so. Giovanna Rossi (1997) argues that a participatory model of family is predominant in Italy, characterized by egalitarian communication between parents and children. Parents and adult children living with them are satisfied with the arrangement and continue to be satisfied as children age (Scabini and Cigoli 1997). In fact, both parents and children feel that the main disadvantage of leaving home is emotional loss. A full 60 percent of parents do not see any advantages in a child's departure (Dalla Zuanna 2001).

Moreover, children are pleased with their levels of autonomy within the family (Scabini and Cigoli 1997). They have egalitarian relationships with their parents characterized by reciprocal emotional dependence (Cook and Furstenberg 2002).[13] Under these circumstances, leaving the parental home is not seen as an important marker of adulthood the way steady employment is. It is clearly possible to be a responsible adult while living under the parental roof.

It remains to be seen whether other countries will develop a similar form of in-house adulthood, but the data we have analyzed here give us reason to think this may come to pass. The more delayed departure becomes normative, the less stigma will be associated with the practice. As Margaret Mead showed us many decades ago, there are many ways to organize family life, each with its own logic. And although tension may go with this territory, it is a malleable sentiment whose flip side, affection and intimacy, may be valued just as much as autonomy.

This may not be the news that social policy analysts want to hear given that there are clearly significant and problematic consequences to delayed departure. When young people stay home into their thirties, they do not marry early enough to have many children. The "birth dearth" is causing serious perturbations in the social security system of countries like Italy, Spain, and Japan. Particularly in conservative welfare regimes, which rely on families to care for their own before the state steps in, the capacity of young people to "graduate" to adulthood in time to husband the resources to take care of their own parents may be compromised. This may be responsible for the unprecedented interest shown by the elderly in Japan in retirement homes, which barely existed in years past (Campbell and Campbell 2003). It may be that their children are not in a position to take care of them in the ways that elders could have expected as a birthright in the past.

No doubt it will take time for social policy to catch up to demographic reality. Along the way, we will see some serious strains in welfare states around the globe. Yet absent a sharp change in the economic fortunes of young people or the development of a widespread change in sentiment that would underwrite Scandinavian-style supports for the residential autonomy of youth, it is hard to imagine the trend toward delayed departure abating.

Appendix A: Response Rates in the European Quality of Life Survey

Although this dataset collects extensive information about a range of quality-of-life measures, response rates varied greatly across the countries, ranging from 30 percent in Spain to 91 percent in Germany. Although this is troublesome, a comparison of household income distribution within the sample and OECD indicators conducted by the European Foundation for the Improvement of Living and Working Conditions (2005) concluded that the EQLS data do not deviate enough from national indicators to merit adjustments. This was true for median incomes (the correlation between country median of EQLS household income and GDP per capita is 0.92) as well as for income dispersion. Two deviations that are noted concern Denmark and Germany. The EQLS data for Denmark show wider income dispersion than data from other sources. Data for Germany have a median income in the bottom income quartile that is lower than outside estimates. If there is an overrepresentation of those in the bottom of the lowest quartile, it may skew our results by including a disproportionate number of young people who are in extremely difficult financial situations. Nevertheless, the authors of the report did not deem these two deviations severe enough to require correction.

Appendix B: Country-Level Indicators of Housing and Labor Markets

Variable	Definition	Source
Percentage in owner-occupied housing	Share of owner-occupied housing, 2002	OECD Economic Review 38 (2004a)
Availability of unemployment benefits (dichotomous)	Benefits available in 2002 for a twenty-year-old unemployed single person, living alone with no family responsibilities and no employment record	OECD (2004a)
Unemployment rate (percentage)	Unemployment rate for twenty- to thirty-four-year-olds in 2003	OECD (2003)
Employment/population ratio	Ratio of employed twenty- to thirty-four-year-olds to total population twenty- to thirty-four-year-olds in 2003	OECD (2003)

Country-Level Indicators of Housing and Labor Market (*Continued*)

Variable	Definition	Source
Employment/protection scale	Overall strictness of employment protection legislation, an eighteen-item scale that includes indicators of (1) employment protection of regular workers against individual dismissal; (2) specific requirements for collective dismissals; and (3) regulation of temporary forms of employment	OECD (2004b)
Percentage in temporary employment	Temporary employees as percentage of total employees for twenty-five- to thirty-nine-year-olds	Eurostat (2003)

Source: Authors' compilation.

We gratefully acknowledge the support of the MacArthur Foundation Research Network on Transitions to Adulthood and the Woodrow Wilson School Faculty Research Fund. We thank the European Foundation for the Improvement of Living and Working Conditions, which gave us permission to analyze the European Quality of Life Survey of 2003 for this chapter. Special thanks to Sheldon Danziger, Paul Attewell, and Scott Lynch for their input and advice.

Notes

1. Young people in the Nordic countries are the most likely to live away from their parents, while young southern Europeans are the least likely (Iacovou 2002). The proportion of twenty-five- to twenty-nine-year-olds living with their parents in southern Europe is higher than the proportion of twenty- to twenty-four-year-olds living with their parents in central Europe, and this gap has been widening (Cordon 1997).
2. Measures of variability in ages at home-leaving show diversity within countries as well. Scandinavian countries are more homogeneous than southern European countries (Billari 2004; Billari, Philipov, and Baizan 2001).

3. Southern Europeans are also less likely than their northern counterparts to return home once they have left (Holdsworth and Solda 2002).

4. The underground economy complicates the picture significantly in southern Europe. As much as 50 percent of housing in Italy, for instance, is illegal (Castles and Ferrera 1996).

5. Southern European countries have historically high savings rates and few other ways to invest, coupled with a cultural propensity to invest in housing. Nevertheless, these differences should be kept in perspective because until the 1970s homeownership levels in Italy and Spain were at the OECD average (Castles and Ferrera 1996).

6. In bivariate analyses involving the percentage living at home, Italy is excluded as an extreme outlier (figures 8.2, 8.3, 8.6, and 8.7).

7. Unemployment rates are quite varied within the European Union. Southern European countries have the highest unemployment rates across age groups, ranging from 15 percent in Greece to 28 percent in Spain, compared with 5 percent in Austria and 7 percent in the Netherlands (Lippman 2002). However, the impact of unemployment has been concentrated disproportionately among young workers, particularly in the south. More than 70 percent of the unemployed in Italy are under age twenty-nine (Cook and Furstenberg 2002).

8. Policies governing employment protection also influence the options for youth. Social democratic and conservative welfare regimes have stronger employment protection legislation than liberal regimes, and that creates difficulties for young people because employers are unwilling to hire them, especially during economic downswings (Breen and Buchmann 2002). This is the case in Italy, where the government protects the high-paying jobs of older workers and sponsors their subsequent retirement on the basis of their incomes before retirement (Cook and Furstenberg 2002).

9. Without Italy, it actually explains less (23 percent).

10. Unfortunately, we are unable to include an indicator of educational attainment in our analysis because that variable had serious problems and EQLS recommends using number of years of education instead. In addition to the variation in meaning that the latter indicator has across different countries, the fact that many young respondents are still in school poses a significant problem, and we chose not to use that variable either.

11. A more accurately specified model is a hierarchical ordered logit. Because the ordered logit results were very similar to linear regression results, we present the latter here for ease of interpretation.

12. One might imagine that men and women would react differently to the constraint of living with parents, since traditionally women were kept under closer watch and more restricted by their parents. However, gender is statistically insignificant in this analysis.

13. Adult children in southern Europe may be satisfied with their levels of self-determination, but Chiara Saraceno (2004) points out that individual decisions affecting the transition to adulthood are really intergenerational and kin decisions, whether this is admitted or even fully realized.

References

Alders, Maarten, and Dorien Manting. 1999. "Household Scenarios for the European Union: Methodology and Main Results." *Netherlands Official Statistics* 14: 17–27.

Billari, Francesco C. 2004. "Becoming an Adult in Europe: A Macro(/Micro)-Demographic Perspective." *Demographic Research* (Max Planck Institute for Demographic Research) S3(April 17): 15–44.

Billari, Francesco C., Dimiter Philipov, and Pau Baizan. 2001. "Leaving Home in Europe: The Experience of Cohorts Born Around 1960." *International Journal of Population Geography* 7(5): 339–56.

Boelhouwer, Peter, and Harry van der Heijden. 1993. "Housing Policy in Seven European Countries: The Role of Politics in Housing." *Netherlands Journal of Housing and the Built Environment* 8(4): 383–404.

Breen, Richard, and Marlis Buchmann. 2002. "Institutional Variation and the Position of Young People: A Comparative Perspective." *Annals of the American Academy of Political and Social Science* 580: 288–305.

Campbell, John, and Ruth Campbell. 2003. "Adapting to Long-Term Care Insurance: Where to Live?" *Social Science Japan* 6(1): 3–5.

Castles, Francis G., and Maurizio Ferrera. 1996. "Homeownership and the Welfare State: Is Southern Europe Different?" *South European Society and Politics* 1(2): 163–85.

Cherlin, Andrew J., Eugenia Scabini, and Giovanna Rossi. 1997. "Still in the Nest: Delayed Home-Leaving in Europe and the United States." *Journal of Family Issues* 18(6): 572–75.

Christensen, Thomas, European Commission. 2001. Eurobarometer 55.1OVR: Young Europeans [computer file]. ICSPR version. Brussels: European Opinion Research Group EEIG [producer]; Cologne, Germany: Zentralarchiv fur Empirische Sozialforschung/Ann Arbor, Mich.: Inter-university Consortium for Political and Social Research [distributors].

Cook, Thomas D., and Frank F. Furstenberg Jr. 2002. "Explaining Aspects of the Transition to Adulthood in Italy, Sweden, Germany, and the United States: A Cross-Disciplinary, Case Synthesis Approach." *Annals of the American Academy of Political and Social Science* 580: 257-87.

Cordon, Juan Antonio Fernandez. 1997. "Youth Residential Independence and Autonomy: A Comparative Study." *Journal of Family Issues* 18(6): 576–607.

Dalla Zuanna, Gianpiero. 2001. "The Banquet of Aeolus: A Familistic Interpretation of Italy's Lowest Low Fertility." *Demographic Research* (Max Planck Institute for Demographic Research) 4(5): 133-62.

European Foundation for the Improvement of Living and Working Conditions. 2003. *European Quality of Life Survey*, edited by J. D. Jens Alber, Wolfgang Keck, and Ricarda Nauenburg. Berlin: Social Science Research Center (WZB).

———. 2004. *Quality of Life in Europe: First Results of a New Pan-European Survey.* Luxembourg: Office for Official Publications of the European Communities.

———. 2005. "Income Inequalities and Deprivation." In *Quality of Life in Europe*, edited by C. T. W. Tony Fahey and Bertrand Maître. Luxembourg: Office for Official Publications of the European Communities.

Eurostat. 2002. *European Social Statistics: Labour Force Survey Results 2002*. Luxembourg: Office for Official Publications of the European Communities.

————. 2003. *European Social Statistics: Labour Force Survey Results 2003*. Luxembourg: Office for Official Publications of the European Communities.

Golsch, Katrin. 2003. "Employment Flexibility in Spain and Its Impact on Transitions to Adulthood." *Work, Employment, and Society* 17(4): 691–718.

Holdsworth, Clare. 2000. "Leaving Home in Britain and Spain." *European Sociological Review* 16(2): 201–22.

Holdsworth, Clare, and Mariana Irazoqui Solda. 2002. "First Housing Moves in Spain: An Analysis of Leaving Home and First Housing Acquisition." *European Journal of Population* 18(1): 1–19.

Iacovou, Maria. 2002. "Regional Differences in the Transition to Adulthood." *Annals of the American Academy of Political and Social Science* 580: 40–69.

Jurado Guerrero, Teresa. 2001. *Youth in Transition: Housing, Employment, Social Policies, and Families in France and Spain*. Aldershot, England: Ashgate.

Lippman, Laura. 2002. "Cross-National Variation in Educational Preparation for Adulthood: From Early Adolescence to Young Adulthood." *Annals of the American Academy of Political and Social Science* 580: 70–102.

Mulder, Clara H., and Pieter Hooimeijer. 2002. "Leaving Home in the Netherlands: Timing and First Housing." *Journal of Housing and the Built Environment* 17(3): 237–68.

Mulder, Clara H., and Dorien Manting. 1994. "Strategies of Nest-Leavers: 'Settling Down' Versus Flexibility." *European Sociological Review* 10(2): 155–72.

Newman, Katherine. 1993. *Declining Fortunes: The Withering of the American Dream*. New York: Basic Books.

Organization for Economic Cooperation and Development. 2003. *Employment and Labor Market Statistics*. Paris: OECD.

————. 2004a. *Benefits and Wages: OECD Indicators*. Paris: OECD.

————. 2004b. *Employment Outlook*. Paris: OECD.

————. 2004c. *Economic Review*. Paris: OECD.

————. 2006. *Employment Outlook*. Paris: OECD.

Rossi, Giovanna. 1997. "The Nestlings: Why Young Adults Stay at Home Longer: The Italian Case." *Journal of Family Issues* 18(6): 627–44.

Saraceno, Chiara. 2004. "The Reproductive Paradox of 'Weak' and 'Strong' Families in Contemporary Europe." In *Das Europäische Sozialmodell*, edited by Hartmut Kaelble and Gunther Schmidt. Berlin: Jahrbuch-WZB.

Scabini, Eugenia, and Vittorio Cigoli. 1997. "Young Adult Families: An Evolutionary Slowdown or a Breakdown in the Generational Transition." *Journal of Family Issues* 18(6): 608–26.

Sciolina, Elaine. 2006. "French Students Step Up Protests Against New Job Law." *New York Times*, March 15.

Chapter 9

To Have and to Hold: An Analysis of Young Adult Debt

NGINA S. CHITEJI

Researchers have long recognized the importance of studying young adults' experiences in labor markets, in the educational arena, and within the family. These three domains are considered key to shaping the transition to adulthood in the United States (Settersten, Furstenberg, and Rumbaut 2005). Young adults' experiences in credit markets have received less attention in the scholarly literature. Given their stage in the life cycle, however, we would expect young people to have much to gain from participation in credit markets. Moreover, we would expect their use of credit to be connected to their experiences in other markets.

Credit markets exist to mobilize funds and make them available to individuals who have productive uses for the funds. Uses that are expected to generate a positive revenue stream in the future are one example, but credit markets also exist simply to allow individuals to transfer purchasing power across time so that they may control the timing of purchases of the goods and services they want to attain in life. One obvious link across markets that results is that young adults may find it desirable to borrow when facing a rising earnings profile in the labor market. Young adults typically are at a point in life when their earnings are lower than average. Accordingly, the ability to transfer purchasing power across time may be particularly important to them. For example, an individual who knows that she will have high earnings in a few years once she becomes a practicing physician may not want to endure limited consumption while she is in training as a resident simply because her income is low during that residency. Instead, she can borrow against future

231

income to stabilize or to "smooth" her consumption over time. Similarly, young adults can benefit from credit markets when they want to acquire an item whose purchase price is too large to be paid for out of regular, weekly, or monthly income. A classic example of this "indivisible good" problem is a home purchase.

The labor market is not the only market that bears on decisions about borrowing. Credit market outcomes can be tied to individuals' experiences in the educational arena. More specifically, economic theory predicts that it can be advantageous for young adults to borrow for schooling because expenditures on schooling facilitate the acquisition of skills and knowledge, that is, "human capital," which boosts wages. Individuals can then use the earnings stream that higher education gives them access to in order to repay their education loans.

This chapter examines young adult debt, with an emphasis on both the total amount of debt that today's young adults have and the types of debt they hold. It compares the situation of contemporary young adults with that of all U.S. households and offers some historical context by presenting data for young adults of the 1960s and 1980s. Largely descriptive, the chapter aims to discuss borrowing patterns and summarize some existing debates about young adult debt. However, it also examines the relationship between debt and the attainment of some traditional markers of adult status. One key theme that emerges from the research is that, as a group, today's young adults do not appear to have an unusual or distinctly troublesome amount of debt. As with most human experiences, however, there is variation within the group.

Borrowing by Today's Young Adults

How many young adults are in debt, how much debt do they have, and why are young adults borrowing money? This section examines rates of indebtedness among young adults, the magnitude of their debt, and the allocation of this debt across different debt categories.

Rates of Indebtedness

As shown in figure 9.1, about 85 percent of young adult households—defined as those whose head is age twenty-five to thirty-four—hold some type of debt. This statistic comes from analysis of data from the 2001 Survey of Consumer Finances (SCF), a nationally representative survey of U.S. households conducted under the auspices of the Federal Reserve.[1] In addition to providing information about total debt, the SCF breaks down household debt into six categories: mortgage or housing debt, lines of credit other than home equity lines, residential debt other than that associated with the primary residence, credit card debt, installment debt, and

Figure 9.1   Rates of Indebtedness Among Young Adults Age Twenty-five to Thirty-four (2001 Data)

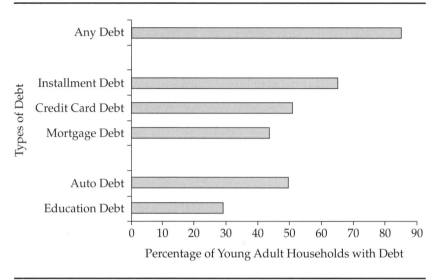

Source: Author's analysis of data from the 2001 Survey of Consumer Finances.

other debt. The survey's additional details about the purposes of household borrowing allow us to isolate funds borrowed for educational purposes and for automobiles. For more information on the datasets used in this study and the study's methodology, see the appendix.

Figure 9.1 shows rates of indebtedness for types of debt that are important to young adults.[2] About 43.6 percent of today's young adult households carry mortgage debt. Borrowing to finance the purchase of a home typically is considered to be a good reason for assuming debt. Aside from providing a roof over one's head, housing is an investment good. In fact, for many U.S. households housing is the primary component of household wealth (Charles and Hurst 2002). Debt accumulated to secure a home often is viewed as debt that ultimately should facilitate wealth creation, particularly when housing market conditions are such that housing is appreciating rapidly. The SCF data also indicate that about 65 percent of young adult households age twenty-five to thirty-four carry installment loans, that about 51 percent have credit card debt, that almost 50 percent have auto debt, and that about 29 percent have education debt.

Table 9.1 compares young adults with all U.S. households. As shown, the rate of indebtedness among young adult households (85 percent) is somewhat higher than the proportion of all U.S. families that are in-

Table 9.1   Rates of Indebtedness of Young Adult Households for Different Types of Debt

Debt Category	2001 Young Adults Holding	2001 All U.S. Families Holding	1983 Young Adults Holding	1963 Young Adults Holding
Any debt	85.1%	75.1%	83.2%	85.0%
Installment debt	65.1	45.2	62.9	71.8
Credit card debt	51.0	44.4	2.8	n.a.
Mortgage debt	43.6	44.6	39.3	36.88
Other residential debt	3.3	4.7		1.6
Lines of credit other than home equity	1.7	1.5	15.1	n.a.
Other debt	9.4	7.2	18.8	41.9
Auto debt	49.5	36.4	38.9	45.1
Educational debt	29.0	14.6	11.1	n.a.

Notes: Column 2 is based on author's independent analysis of 2001 SCF data. Column 3, rows 2 to 9, is based on Aizcorbe et al. (2003, 23) and author's own calculations using 2001 SCF data for auto debt and educational debt. Column 4 is based on author's independent analysis of 1983 SCF data, with some of the debt categories reported in the 1983 survey reconfigured to match the 2001 debt categories. For column 5, data reflect author's analysis of data from the 1963 Survey of Financial Characteristics of Consumers (SFCC). All data, from all surveys and all survey years, are weighted.

debted (about 75 percent). This is not surprising, however, given the standard motives for borrowing and young adults' stage in life, as noted earlier. For four of the SCF debt categories reported in table 9.1—mortgage debt, other residential debt, lines of credit other than home equity lines, and "other debt"—the proportion of young adults in debt is similar to that of all U.S. households. Yet elsewhere there are differences: the fraction of young adults with auto debt (49.5 percent) is higher than the fraction of all U.S. households (36.4 percent), and young adults are also more likely to have education loans—again, not surprising given their stage in life. Older households are more likely to have completed their schooling, and they will have had more time to pay off any loans they acquired for this purpose. Young adults also are more likely to hold credit card debt (51 percent versus 44 percent of all U.S. households) and installment loans (65 percent compared with 45 percent of all U.S. households).

It is interesting to consider the higher rates of installment debt and credit card indebtedness among young adults given the recent concern about young adult borrowing expressed in popular discourse (Manning 2000; Stewart 2005; Time 2005; USA Today 2006). Installment credit and credit cards both can be used to acquire indivisible goods, such as furniture, which a young adult might need when setting up an independent residence. The need to finance indivisible goods is probably an important explanation for the higher incidence of installment debt, especially given that the SCF installment debt category includes auto loans and education debt. Accordingly, the twenty-percentage-point difference in installment debt holding might be attributable to young adults' desire to borrow for purposes that would not be deemed surprising or inappropriate.

The difference in rates of holding credit card debt is about 7 percent. While not small, the figure is also not incredibly large. Because credit cards can be used for numerous purposes, it is difficult for a researcher to extrapolate when viewing these data on households' reasons for borrowing. Without additional information, it is impossible to know whether the greater incidence of credit card debt among young adults reflects a more relaxed attitude toward spending or a desire to finance expenditures that economic theory deems normal or practical for young adults.

Amounts of Debt Held

How much debt do young adults have? Table 9.2 presents the mean (average) level of debt held by young adults in 2001 and the means for different types of debt. On average, the amount of debt held by young adults regardless of type ($55,616 in 2001 dollars) is similar to that for all U.S. families (about $54,501). Table 9.2 also reports median values because the distribution of debt is highly uneven. The figures characterizing the average household (the means) are appreciably higher than the medians for each of the debt categories. When a distribution is highly skewed, a focus on the mean values can lead one to overstate the indebtedness of the typical household. For example, although the average amount of debt held by young adults is $55,616, the median (or typical) young adult household holds about $25,000 of debt. The young adult median is higher, however, than the median level of debt for the population at large. The typical U.S. household holds only about $14,300 of debt.

As table 9.2 reveals, for several types of debt the typical young adult household has zero debt. For mortgage debt, the zero median is consistent with the moderate rate of homeownership among young adults. The SCF data indicate that only 48.4 percent of young adult households own homes (not shown). This compares with 67.7 percent for the population at large (Aizcorbe, Kennickell, and Moore 2003, 17). When more than half of young adults do not own their own home, it is not surprising that the median young adult household has no mortgage debt.

What is more surprising, perhaps, is that the typical young adult

Table 9.2   Amount of Debt Held by Young Adult Households, by Type of Debt

Variable	All U.S. Households 2001	Young Adult Households 2001 Mean [median]	Young Adult Households 1983 Mean [median]	Young Adult Households 1963 Mean [median]
Total debt	$54,501 [$14,300]	$55,616 [$25,000]	$32,610 [$8,168.42]	$26,562.38 [$1,543.00]
Mortgage debt	$41,006 [$0]	$41,054 [$0]	$22,233.23 [$0]	$20,579.50 [$0]
Installment debt	$6,736 [$0]	$9,640 [$3,800]	$5,134.13 [$650]	$4,446.99 [$315]
Credit card debt	$1,837 [$0]	$2,246 [$70]	$638.45 [$0]	n.a.
Auto debt	$4,169 [$0]	$5,495 [$0]	$2,448.07 [$0]	$2,978.87 [$0]
Education loans	$1,860 [$0]	$3,478 [$0]	$659.95 [$0]	n.a.

Source: Based on author's analysis of data from the 2001 and 1983 SCF and the 1963 SFCC.
Notes: All dollar values are in 2001 dollars. All data are weighted. Data for the SCF's "other residential debt," "other lines of credit," and "other debt" categories have been suppressed, since the incidence of holding these types of debt is low for young adults and the balances held are not appreciably large. In 2001 the mean for "other lines of credit" was $79, with a median of $0; the mean for "other residential debt" was $2,056 (median $0); and the mean for "other debt" was $540 (median $0). The figures for 1983 and 1963 were similarly small. Tables with these categories are available from the author upon request. The sum of mean values for the different debt categories may exceed the mean reported for total debt because auto debt and education loans are actually subcategories of installment debt.

household holds less than $100 in credit card debt. Some scholars and policymakers have expressed concern about young adults' use of credit cards and about their ability to manage such debt (Draut 2006; Manning 2000; USA Today 2006; U.S. GAO 2001). Yet it is here that the consequences of having a distribution that is highly uneven are most apparent. Because some young adult households have a lot of credit card debt while others have little, the group's average level of credit card debt (over $2,000) is much higher than the $70 held by the typical young adult household. Moreover, because many young adult households (close to 50 percent) have *no* credit card debt, when we examine the levels held by those who have *positive* amounts, we find a mean and a median that greatly exceed the mean and median for young adults as a group. That is to say, there are big differences between the average young adult household (which holds about $2,246 of credit card debt) and the average among those who carry balances from month to month (about $4,000). Similarly, there is a big difference between the typical young adult household (which holds about $70 in credit card debt) and what is typical among those who fail to pay off their balances each month (with the typical young adult revolver holding about $2,400 of credit card debt). We therefore must be careful when choosing statistics to characterize young adults. Should we take our statistic from the distribution of all young adults, or should we limit the sample to those who fail to pay off their credit card balances each month? Because this chapter is interested in young adults as a group, it focuses on the mean and median for *all* young adult households. Relying instead on the statistics derived from analysis of the subsample of young adults who carry balances from month to month can be misleading. For example, as noted earlier, $4,000 is the average we get from an analysis of credit card debt revolvers, yet fewer than 20 percent of all young adults actually have credit card debt that is this large.[3]

The Allocation of Young Adult Debt

Table 9.3 presents data on the distribution of young adult debt by different types of debt. Almost three-quarters of young adult debt is held in the form of mortgage or home-related debt. This is comparable to the share that this category represents for the U.S. population at large, suggesting that most young adult debt is held for the same reasons that other U.S. families hold debt. The fraction of total young adult debt that is credit card debt (about 4 percent) is also similar to that of all U.S. households (about 3.4 percent). Installment debt is a slightly larger share of total debt for young adults than for the U.S. population at large (17.3 percent compared with 12.3 percent). The shares for auto debt and educational debt are also slightly higher for young adults.

Sizing Up Young Adults' Debt Obligations

How burdensome is debt for young adults? Researchers typically answer this question by examining a household's debt in relationship to its resources. Four measures can be used to perform this assessment: the debt-to-income ratio, the debt-to-net-worth ratio, the degree to which households fall behind making payments on debt, and the percentage of monthly income that must be allocated to making payments on existing debts.

As shown in table 9.4, comparing young adults' debt to their income yields a groupwide debt-to-income ratio of 1.11, which is higher than the comparable ratio for the population at large. The 1.11 figure indicates that, as a group, young adults could not retire all of their existing debt using their current income. In comparison, the debt-to-income ratio for all U.S. households lies below unity, indicating that the total value of outstanding debts does not outstrip income. The debt-to-net-worth ratio for

Table 9.3   Debt Type as a Share of Total Debt for Young Adults and for All U.S. Households

	All U.S. Households	Young Adult Households		
	2001	2001	1983	1963
Mortgage debt	75.1%	73.8%	68.2%	77.5%
Other residential debt	6.4	3.7	12.7	3.7
Installment debt	12.3	17.3	15.7	16.7
Credit card debt	3.4	4.0	2.0	n.a.
Lines of credit other than home equity loans	0.5	0.14	1.3	n.a.
Other debt	2.3	1.0	3.4	5.9
Auto debt	7.8	9.9	7.5	11.2
Educational debt	3.1	6.3	2.0	n.a.

Notes: For column 2, data are from tables 10 and 12 of Aizcorbe et al. (2003, 21, 25). Column 3 is based on author's analysis of data from the 2001 SCF. Column 4 is based on author's analysis of data from the 1983 SCF. Column 5 is based on author's analysis of data from the 1963 SFCC. All data are weighted. Only the rows for the six broad SCF categories are expected to sum to 100. The two additional rows (for auto and education debt) represent subcomponents of the SCF's installment debt category. Note, however, that data may not sum to 100, owing to rounding error.

young adults is 0.57. This too is higher than the comparable figure for all U.S. households. Interestingly, however, this ratio does not appear to have changed dramatically for young adults since 1963, suggesting that the dramatic rise in debt over this thirty-eight-year period was matched by a growth in family resources when wealth is used as the measure of available family resources. With income as the measure of family resources, however, the story is different. Table 9.4 shows that the young adult debt-to-income ratio rose from about 0.733 to 1.11 between 1963 and 2001.

Table 9.4 also shows the percentage of households that have problems making payments on time. In 2001 about 11 percent of young adult households experienced payment problems, defined in the SCF as having fallen at least two months behind on debt payments. This compares with 7 percent for the nation as a whole, according to data reported in Aizcorbe and others (2003, 29).

A final indicator that researchers examine to determine whether debt is burdensome is how much of a household's monthly income must be used to service the household's debt. The average monthly payment-to-income ratio for young adults is 0.19, indicating that the average young adult household uses about nineteen cents of every dollar earned for debt payments. A payment-to-income ratio exceeding 0.40 is considered to be high, signaling financial distress (Aizcorbe et

Table 9.4 Size of Young Adults' Debt Obligations and Their Experiences with Debt

	Young Adults in 2001	All U.S. Households	Young Adults in 1983	Young Adults in 1963
Holding any debt	85.1%	75.1%	83.2%	85.0%
Average amount of debt held	$55,616	$54,501	$32,610	$26,562
Median amount of debt held	$25,000	$14,300	$8,168	$1,543
Debt-to-income ratio	1.11	0.789	0.66	0.733
Debt-to-net worth ratio	0.57	0.138	0.491	0.566
Average debt payment–to-income ratio	0.19	0.125	n.a.	n.a.
Young adult households experiencing financial distress	9.3%	11%	n.a.	n.a.
Making late payments on debt	11%	7%	#	n.a.
Ever bankrupt	7.7%	10.0%	n.a.	n.a.
Young adult resources, mean values (medians in brackets)				
Total assets	$153,125	$449,600	$91,695.45	n.a.
	[58,750]	[135,800]	[15,838]	
Net worth	$97,509	$395,500	$73,138	$46,929.40
	[19,045]	[86,100]	[19,505]	[7,909]
Family income	$50,109	$68,000	$41,089	$36,261.9
	[39,061]	[39,900]	[36,800]	[34,068]
Households with negative net worth	15.14%	6.8%	10.2%	10.9%

Source: Data for column 3, rows 2, 8, 10, 11, 15, and 16 are taken from Aizcorbe et al. (2003, 23, 28, 29, 29, 5, and 7, respectively). Data for all U.S. households in all other cells of column 3 come from author's own analysis of SCF data.

Notes: All dollar values are expressed in 2001 dollars. # = late payment rates are not exactly comparable across time. The 2001 survey asks about being late by at least sixty days (roughly two months), while the 1983 survey simply asks about payments that were late (no time period mentioned) or missed. Accordingly, we do not report the 1983 figure. Total asset values for 1963 are unavailable owing to lack of comparability across surveys. See the appendix for additional discussion of this issue.

al. 2003). Our analysis reveals that about 9.3 percent of young adult households have a payments-to-income ratio in the distress range.[4] This is actually lower than the rate for the U.S. population at large: about 11 percent of all U.S. households experience financial distress (Aizcorbe et al. 2003, 29). Young adults also have slightly lower bankruptcy rates than the population at large, about 7.7 percent compared with 10 percent, according to the 2001 SCF data. In combination, these data suggest that some young adult households have negative experiences with debt, but that most have debt loads that are not worrisome.

Trends over Time

Comparing young adults with the population at large is one way to contextualize their behavior. Examining trends over time is another. In this section, data from the 1983 SCF and data from the Federal Reserve's 1963 Survey of Financial Characteristics of Consumers are used to compare today's young adults with their counterparts in the 1980s and the 1960s.[5]

The Trend for Total Debt

As shown in table 9.1, the proportion of young adults holding debt has remained fairly stable over time—in the realm of 80 to 85 percent—suggesting that, as a group, today's young adults are no more likely to be in debt than young adult cohorts of the past. The amount of debt held, however, has changed. Total debt has increased for young adults both at the mean and at the median (table 9.4). Additionally, despite increases in income over time, the debt-to-income ratio rose slightly between 1963 and 2001 (table 9.4). The growth in debt that occurred between 1983 and 2001 is particularly striking. The average young adult household held $32,610 in debt in 1983 (measured in 2001 dollars). By 2001 it held $55,616. The change at the median was similarly striking. Although the typical young adult household held a little more than $8,000 in debt in 1983 (measured in 2001 dollars), by 2001 this figure had grown to $25,000. These increases coincide with an era of significant expansion in financial markets' ability to extend credit (Laibson 1997). The growth in indebtedness at the median was also substantial in the earlier period (1963 to 1983). In addition, comparison of medians to means for the three time points suggests that the distribution of debt has become less uneven over time. The ratio of median debt to the mean level has risen for young adults. This too is consistent with a story of widening availability of credit and a transition from a world in which a few, unusual individuals held large amounts of debt to one in which typical, "regular Joe" young adult households have begun to borrow non-negligible sums.

Trends by Different Types of Debt

Although the rate of overall indebtedness has changed little over time for young adults, in some debt categories we do see change. As shown in table 9.1, the fraction of young adults holding mortgage debt has risen slightly over time, from 36.9 percent in 1963 to about 39 percent in 1983 to 43.6 percent in 2001. This increase is mirrored by a slight increase in homeownership rates, which rose from 45.3 percent to 48.4 percent during, for example, the 1983 to 2001 time period (data not shown). The level of mortgage or home-related debt held shows a pattern of modest change on average between 1963 and 1983, but it grew rapidly between 1983 and 2001, when the average amount held almost doubled (table 9.2). The average home price rose about 36 percent during this period (U.S. Bureau of the Census 2006, 622).

Table 9.2 reveals that the amount of credit card debt held by young adults has risen substantially—at the mean—since 1983 (the earliest year for which data are available). Yet the median level of credit card debt rose only from $0 to $70 for young adults. This is a rather modest change in levels. The proportion of young adult households holding credit card debt rose somewhat over the period, from about 43 percent to 51 percent (table 9.1).

Table 9.1 shows that the proportion of young adult households with education debt rose from about 11 percent in 1983 to 29 percent in 2001 (1983 is the earliest year for which data are available). This increase comes with a five-percentage-point increase in the proportion of young adults completing a college degree (U.S. Bureau of the Census 2005).[6] Yet the increase also undoubtedly reflects changes in college funding and in tuition costs that have caused more students to borrow to finance their educations than was true for previous generations (U.S. Department of Education 1998; College Board 2004a, 2004b). The data are consistent with an argument that rising tuition costs and falling grant opportunities have caused today's young adults to turn to credit markets to pay for schooling, a hypothesis that recently has captured the attention of policymakers and advocates (for example, see Draut 2006). The large increase in the average amount of education debt held by young adults evident in table 9.2—from less than $1,000 to almost $3,500—adds further weight to the argument. How society should view these findings is unclear, however. They raise a question about who should pay to educate the nation's young. Should it be the young adults themselves, given that they stand to benefit from higher earnings upon the completion of their schooling? Or should it be the taxpayer, given that taxpayers heavily subsidized some earlier generations of young adults (for example, through the GI Bill)?

The amount of installment debt held by young adults increased both at the mean and at the median from 1963 to 2001 (table 9.2). This change has not been accompanied by a large increase in the fraction of young adults holding this type of debt (table 9.1). About 70 percent of young adult households had some installment debt in 1963. This figure dropped in later years, to between 63 and 65 percent. The relative stability in the fraction of young adult households holding this type of debt in the latter portion of the period suggests that the increases in these levels reflect greater borrowing by individual young adults than in the past. This growth in borrowing—about a doubling of amounts at the mean and close to a tenfold increase at the median—is not easy for an analyst to judge. Does the fact that today's typical young adult has about $3,800 in installment debt, while the equivalent household held only about $650 in 1983, suggest that today's young adults have more furniture and appliances while young adults of the past lived more modestly? If so, would more than $3,000 in furniture and appliances be acceptable given today's social norms? Installment debt provides an example of the difficulty in attempting to discern whether the borrowing decisions of young adults are sensible or misguided. Even if one had detailed information about the types of items purchased on installment credit (for example, knowledge that it was a $3,800 stereo system instead of $3,800 spent on a dishwasher, bed, and a used car), such purchases of indivisible goods are consistent with a hypothesis that today's young adults are smoothing consumption—meaning that the rise in installment debt cannot be unambiguously labeled as "bad" or irrational. Instead, the increase in sums borrowed could be evidence that borrowing constraints have been lifted as the credit market has evolved over time. If households of the past had lower balances because they were credit-constrained, the change would signal a rational response to those constraints having been lifted, and the change would imply that today's young adults are better off than previous generations, even though they have higher debt loads. If their lifetime incomes or financial positions can support the increased debt loads, the increase in debt by itself is no cause for worry.

The overall trends discussed in this section suggest that being in debt is not something that is new to young adults, although the amounts borrowed have increased over time. Much of the increase has occurred for categories of debt that we would expect young adults to benefit from holding. Although the increase in total debt held has not been matched by an equivalent rise in current income, causing the young adult debt-to-income ratio to rise somewhat, it is difficult to judge the increases in debt as "good" or "bad." The rise in borrowing could reflect the lifting of credit constraints for households.

Table 9.5   The Uneveness of the Distribution of Young Adult Debt: Means, Medians, Total Debt, and Share of Young Adult Debt Held at Different Points Along the Debt Distribution, 2001

Debt Quintile	Average Amount of Debt Held for the Group	Median Amount Held for the Group	Share of Total Debt Held by the Group
Bottom 20 percent of debt holders	$90.09	$0	0.03%
Second quintile of debt holders	$5,288.47	$5,160	1.93%
Middle 20 percent of debt holders	$25,751.54	$24,800	9.41%
Fourth quintile of debt holders	$72,036.06	$72,000	25.8%
Top 20 percent of debt holders	$174,071.60	$138,400	62.8%

Source: Author's calculations based on data from the 2001 SCF.
Notes: All data are weighted. Data in column 4 may not sum to 100 owing to rounding error.

Debt and Different Types of Young Adults

As noted earlier, debt is distributed unevenly among young adults. This section examines different groups of young adults. The analysis reveals that there is substantial variation by debt quintile, and that there are also differences by income, education, and race.

Examining the Debt Distribution

Although 85 percent of young adults have some debt, the analysis of the 2001 SCF data indicates that the top 20 percent of young adult debtors hold more than 60 percent of the group's debt and that the bulk of young adult debt is concentrated in the hands of 40 percent of the population (see table 9.5). The middle quintile (the middle 20 percent) hold just under 10 percent of the group's debt.

Young Adult Debt by Income

Table 9.6 shows the levels of debt held at different points along the income distribution, with young adult households assigned to an income quintile on the basis of cutoff points from the national distribution.[7] As expected, young adult debt generally rises with income. The average amount of debt held by high-income households is about twelve times the amount held by the average low-income young adult household. At the median, the ratio between the top and bottom is almost 146-to-1.

In addition to the higher balances, high-income households have much higher monthly payment levels on average than the lower-income groups. High-income young adults do not hold more debt relative to their incomes, however, than lower-income households. The debt-to-in-

Table 9.6   Young Adult Debt by Income Quintile, 2001

	Bottom Quintile	Second Quintile	Middle Quintile	Fourth Quintile	Top Quintile
Total debt	$13,219.62 [$810]	$21,963.86 [$7,400]	$45,295.35 [$26,560]	$76,699.59 [$64,280]	$157,346.83 [$118,700]
Total monthly payments on debt	$196.54 [$3.19]	$346.09 [$233.47]	$662.20 [$570.00]	$1,011.64 [$985.27]	$1,819.58 [$1,657.22]
Debt-to-income ratio for group	1.22	.84	1.07	1.17	1.16
Debt-to-net-worth ratio for group	0.54	0.75	0.73	0.80	0.41
Household-level debt-to-income ratio (mean)	1.53	0.86	1.07	1.17	1.28
Households in financial distress	18.2%	10.7%	9.5%	5.1%	1.5%
Monthly payment-to-income ratio (mean)	0.249	0.162	0.188	0.186	0.185
Mortgage debt	15.9%	20.4%	44.5%	64.8%	86.4%
Credit card debt	31.2%	49.5%	67.2%	58.7%	40.3%

Source: Author's calculations using data from the 2001 SCF.
Notes: All data are weighted. Median values in brackets. Income quintile groupings are based on census data on the distribution of income for the national population at large.

come ratio is lower for the former. Moreover, the rate of financial distress is much higher for lower-income households. Almost one in five low-income young adults (18.2 percent) spend more than 40 percent of their monthly income servicing their debt. Fewer than 2 percent of households in the top quintile are in a similar position.

Debt by Levels of Education

When examining debt held by young adults in different educational categories, we find that total debt is highest for the college-educated (table 9.7). The average amount of debt held by young adult households whose head is college-educated is $90,315. This is much higher than the amounts held at lower levels of education. The general pattern is one of debt rising with education, although some sample sizes are small enough that caution should be exercised when interpreting any differences. At the median, amounts of debt held appear to rise with education as well, from $6,830 to $13,000 to $25,110 to $50,000. This pattern of rising debt undoubtedly reflects the higher income prospects of highly educated individuals, specifically their greater prospects for future wage growth. Two pieces of data suggest that the higher debt levels do not come with a greater strain on resources: the debt-to-net-worth ratio is lowest for the

Table 9.7 Borrowing by Education Level, 2001

Variable	No High School Degree	High School Graduates	Some College	College or More
Total debt	$32,660.88	$37,718.22	$47,422.55	$90,315.42
	[$6,830]	[$13,000]	[$25,110]	[$50,000]
Total monthly payments	$439.04	$574.19	$692.75	$1,054.23
	[$222]	[$350]	[$561.11]	[$754.72]
Debt-to-income ratio for group	1.11	.98	1.07	1.19
Debt-to-net-worth ratio for group	1.05	.84	.76	.43
Mean household-level debt-to-income measure	.97	1.21	.994	1.318
	[.250]	[.4554]	[.663]	[.995]
Households experiencing financial distress	9.4%	13.6%	7.3%	7.1%
Amount of education debt	$552.43	$1,258.95	$3,347.28	$7,064.17
	[0]	[0]	[0]	[0]
Mortgage debt	38.5%	37.4%	42.3%	52.8%
Credit card debt	27.3%	52.0%	62.2%	52.2%

Source: Author's calculations using data from the 2001 SCF.
Notes: All data are weighted. Median values are in brackets.

highly educated and highest for those without a high school degree, and the rate of financial distress among highly educated young adults is no higher than the rate of distress among the least educated.

Interestingly, levels of mortgage or home-secured debt are similar for high school graduates and those who failed to complete high school, as are rates of mortgage holding (38.5 percent compared with 37.3 percent). On average, high school dropouts have about $26,725 in mortgage debt, while young adults with high school degrees hold $25,558 in housing debt on average (not shown). As individuals move to obtain a college degree, however, both the amounts of mortgage debt held and the rates of holding mortgage debt rise. These data are consistent with other research suggesting that the plight of the less skilled is not great (for example, see Mishel, Bernstein, and Allegretto 2007). Their worsening position in the labor market may affect their prospects for owning homes. The college-educated appear to fare better in mortgage markets than individuals who have only a high school degree (if we go by the proportion obtaining a mortgage). This outcome may be related to the former's better income prospects, or it could stem from their greater financial sophistication (knowledge) and greater ability to navigate mortgage markets as a consequence.

Our analysis finds that the average young adult household whose head has at least a college degree has about $7,064 outstanding in educational loans.[8] In recent years there has been a boisterous discussion of the rising costs of a college education, the changing way in which college educations are financed, and the loan burdens that individuals who wish to obtain a degree must assume (College Board 2004a, 2004b; Draut and Silva 2004; Gertner 2006; Monks 2001; U.S. Senate 2006). Recent research finds that despite rising tuition costs, the payoff to obtaining a college degree remains high, with estimates putting the average lifetime benefit from attending college at around $300,000 (Barrow and Rouse 2005).

Debt by Race and Ethnicity

Richard Settersten, Frank Furstenberg, and Rubén Rumbaut (2005) note that experiences in early adulthood can differ greatly by race and ethnicity. Young adults' experiences in credit markets are no exception. The rate of indebtedness among white households is greater than it is among nonwhite young adults—90.1 percent compared with 73.5 percent (table not shown). This pattern largely holds across the several different types of debt. Approximately 70 percent of white young adult households hold installment debt compared with 53.9 percent of nonwhites. For mortgage debt the rates are 47.9 percent and 33.5 percent, respectively. Among whites, 54.6 percent have auto debt compared with 37.7 percent of nonwhites. Finally, for credit card debt the estimates of rates of possession are numerically quite different (about 54 percent for whites and 45 percent for nonwhites), but sample size limitations require that we view this estimated difference with caution.

In what other ways do whites and nonwhites differ? Levels of total debt held are higher for whites than for nonwhites, with the race difference being particularly pronounced at the median. The average white young adult household possesses $65,296 of debt, while the average nonwhite young adult holds $33,165 in debt. The typical (median) white young adult household holds $37,020 of debt, while the typical nonwhite young adult holds only $6,000 of debt. While the shares of total outstanding debt held in the form of mortgages, credit card debt, and other lines of credit are substantively similar by race, the shares held in the form of installment debt, education debt, auto debt, and other residential debt differ at least slightly.

The debt-to-income ratio is also higher for whites as a group than for nonwhites: 1.16 compared with 0.942. This may reflect differences in prospects for future wage growth by race. For example, many researchers argue that the labor market prospects of African Americans have declined with the falling fortunes of less-skilled workers. If nonwhites' prospects for wage growth are limited, we would expect them to be less likely to borrow against future income. When examining debt-to-net-worth ratios, however, it is white young adults who have the lower value. Their deb-to-net-worth ratio is about 0.54, while nonwhites (who have lower levels of wealth) have a higher debt-to-net-worth ratio of about 0.82.

Differences aside, there are interesting similarities between whites and nonwhites. Payment delinquency rates are somewhat similar, with almost 10 percent of whites and 11 percent of nonwhites having made late payments. Rates of financial distress are also similar, and there is no substantive difference in the fraction of white and nonwhite households that have negative net worth (15.5 percent and 14.2 percent, respectively).

Trouble Within the Young Adult Group?

As noted in previous sections, comparisons of young adults' indebtedness with the population at large and with young adults of the past do not indicate that today's young adults are in a unique or precarious situation as a group. Yet the analysis points to variation within the group, with some households bearing greater debt loads than others. This section identifies households whose debt might be considered troublesome. Because viewing borrowing behavior in isolation may not provide an accurate picture of the extent to which debt poses a problem for some young adults, this section asks not whether debt per se is a problem, but whether there are young adults whose overall financial position is weak.

Financially At-Risk Households

To identify households that are financially at risk, we first examine debt-to-income ratios for individual households. The groupwide average of 1.11 reported in table 9.4 allows us to compare young adults (as a group) to the U.S. population at large and to determine how fast debt has grown relative to income over time; however, it does not indicate how many young adults have debt loads that vastly exceed their income, which is one measure we might use to determine whether a household is mired in debt. Accordingly, this section also constructs debt-to-income measures for individual households. For this analysis, young adults with zero income were coded as having one dollar of income so that a finite debt-to-income ratio could be computed.[9]

For at least 10 percent of young adult households, the debt-to-income ratio is zero. Moreover, for 20 percent of all young adult households the amount of debt held represents less than 4 percent of their income, and 25 percent of young adults have debt-to-income ratios below 0.10 (or 10 percent). At the thirtieth percentile, the amount of debt held begins to approach one-fifth of household income: the debt-to-income ratio is

0.175. Household debt-to-income ratios begin to rise more quickly around this point. The household at the fortieth percentile has a debt-to-income ratio of 0.367. For the median or typical household, debt represents about 63 percent of income, while a household at the sixtieth percentile would need almost 95 percent of its current income to retire its existing debt. By the seventieth percentile, the debt-to-income ratio is 1.37. At the eightieth percentile it is 1.84, making debt equivalent to almost twice the household's income. At the ninetieth percentile, it is about 2.56, and finally, at the most extreme, about 1 percent of young adult households have a total debt load that is more than seven times their income.

We also asked what fraction of young adults have a debt level that is too large to be maintained given the household's existing savings. It is savings that individuals typically turn to when their income flow stops, and accordingly, we can argue that young adults who do not have sufficient savings to offset their debt are at risk. There are several ways in which we might measure the household's total available savings. The most appropriate measure here is the value of total assets held, given that a household has an option to liquidate all its assets to pay off its existing debt. Our analysis indicates that about 15 percent of young adults would be unable to pay off their existing debt obligations with their assets (see table 9.8).

Because most household debt is financed over time, however, it is also appropriate to ask what proportion of young adult households would have difficulty making monthly payment obligations on their outstanding debt if they lost their job. To answer this question we borrow Robert Haveman and Edward Wolff's (2005) "asset-poor" concept and apply it to the total monthly debt payments of young adult households. Haveman and Wolff characterize a household as asset-poor if its existing net worth is too low to allow it to sustain a minimum level of consumption for more than three months when it has no income flowing into the household. In our analysis, we asked what percentage of households would exhaust their current savings in just under three months by making monthly payments on their outstanding debt. We use three different measures of savings for the analysis. Like Haveman and Wolff, we construct the first measure (asset poor-1) using net worth to measure household savings. However, because liquidating any assets financed with debt is one way to reduce one's liabilities, we also construct a measure that uses total assets to gauge household savings (asset poor-2). Finally, we compare each household's monthly payment obligations to the value of its financial assets (asset poor-3). We do this because many households may not wish to sell their homes, vehicles, and other physical assets to pay their bills, since they remain likely to need a place to live and a source of transportation even if they are unemployed.

Table 9.8   Measures of Large Debt Burdens: Young Adult Households That Might Be Considered Financially at Risk, 2001

Measure of Risk	Percentage of Young Adult Households at Risk
Households whose debt exceeds the value of their assets	15.1%
Households that could not make three months of debt payments out of existing savings (with net worth used to measure savings)	16.5
Households that could not make three months of debt payments if they were to liquidate all existing assets	1.1
Households that could not make three months of debt payments using their current financial assets	17.5
Households with no wealth	19.2
Households with no financial assets	8.5

Indebtedness Among Young Adult Households with No Wealth[a]	Value
Mean amount of total debt outstanding	$24,761.66
Median amount of total debt outstanding	$14,650
Mean amount of total monthly debt payments	$381.45
Median for total monthly debt payments	$300

Source: Author's calculations using the 2001 SCF.
a. No-wealth households are those with zero or negative net worth. All data are weighted.

As shown in table 9.8, when using net worth to measure savings, we find that 16.5 percent of young adults are asset-poor. The proportion of households whose situation is troublesome is lower when we use total assets to measure available savings. However, if we restrict the analysis to highly liquid assets (financial assets such as cash, bank accounts, and stocks), we find that about 17.5 percent of young adults could not meet three months' worth of existing debt repayment obligations with their current stock of savings. It is worth noting that Asena Caner and Edward Wolff (2004) find that about 44 percent of young households age twenty-five to thirty-four have net worth that is insufficient to allow them to remain above the poverty line for at least three months. (The figure actually rises to 65 percent when the authors exclude home equity from the measure of savings.) The Caner and Wolff data are instructive because our measures of "asset-poor" consider only young adults' need to meet repayment obligations on existing debt. In practice, an income disruption means that one also has to finance daily living expenses from one's existing stock of savings.

Table 9.8 also reveals that about 8.5 percent of young adults have no financial assets. In addition, the average amount of debt held by young adult households with negative or zero net worth is about $24,762, and the average total monthly repayment obligation is $381.

Debt and Delayed Transitions into Adulthood

Although economic theory suggests that some debt can ease the transition to adulthood, others have asked whether debt may hinder the transition (Draut 2006; Manning 2000; *USA Today* 2006). Empirical research indicates that young adults today are taking more time to transition to adulthood as they extend their educations, delay marriage and childbearing, and delay leaving their parents' homes (Furstenberg, Rumbaut, and Settersten 2005; Yelowitz, this volume). Those who argue that debt causes young adults to delay movement into adulthood start with this empirical observation and attempt to link the trend to debt. Using data from the Panel Study of Income Dynamics (PSID) and regression analysis, we analyze the relationship between debt and two events often thought of as key markers of adulthood: becoming a parent and becoming a homeowner. We start by defining a young adult household as having transitioned into a state (such as parenthood) if it began the period of interest not in that state (sans children) but had attained the adult marker being examined by the end of the period. We then used regression analysis to identify factors that are associated with this transition. The regressions include a variety of economic and demographic variables that previously have been identified as important determinants of the transition in question, to which we add different measures of debt (for more details about the analysis, see the appendix).

Table 9.9 displays the results for young adults' transition into parenthood. As the table shows, we found no consistent evidence of a negative association between preexisting debt and becoming a parent. Better predictors of achieving the markers of adulthood are age, income, and race-ethnicity. As shown in the table (model 1), age is positively associated with moving into parenthood (though at a diminishing rate), increases in income increase the probability of becoming a parent, and being nonwhite reduces the probability of transitioning into parenthood (by about 2.8 percent). Each subsequent model in the table adds to the regression a different measure of indebtedness, such as noncollateralized debt (model 2) and mortgage debt (model 3). Although the coefficient for noncollateralized debt has the predicted sign, with debt being negatively associated with the transition into parenthood (model 2), the variable is not statistically significant. Model 3 uses mortgage debt at the start of the period to measure indebtedness. Again, the estimated coefficient has the expected sign; however, it is not statistically significant.

Table 9.9   Debt and the Transition into Parenthood: Marginal Effects from Probit Regressions (*t*-stats in Parentheses)

	Base Model (1)	(2)	Models That Include Debt Measures (3)
Age	.094*	.093	.086
	(1.62)	(1.59)	(1.47)
Age squared	−0.002**	−.002**	−.002
	(−1.69)	(−1.67)	(−1.53)
Average income (in $10,000s)	.009**	.009**	.010**
	(4.08)	(4.14)	(3.94)
Race (nonwhite = 1)	−.028**	−.029**	−.029**
	(−1.70)	(−1.75)	(−1.62)
Marital status (married = 1)	.016	.016	.020
	(1.05)	(1.06)	(1.33)
Measures of prior indebtedness			
Noncollateralized debt (in $10,000s)		−.003	
		(−1.03)	
Mortgage debt (in $10,000s)			−.001
			(−1.23)
Number of observations	3,192	3,191	3,116
Wald statistic	28.00	28.80	27.87

Notes: Regressions reported here use data from a sample of pooled time periods from the Panel Study of Income Dynamics. See appendix for further discussion of the dataset and the years included in the analysis. All regressions are weighted and include a constant term. Debt values are reported in 2001 dollars. Average income takes three years of household labor income from years prior to the transition period.
*p = 0.106; **p = .10

In addition to the analyses measuring indebtedness in levels (reported in the table), we ran regressions using dummy variables indicating (1) whether a young adult had noncollateralized debt or not, (2) whether a young adult had mortgage debt or not, and (3) whether a young adult had negative net worth. This was done as a check on the earlier analysis, since some might argue that it is not the amount of debt that an individual has that would matter for the transition to adulthood, but whether the individual has any debt or not. While the results of these analyses are not shown, they failed to support the hypothesis that prior indebtedness has negative effects on the transition into parenthood. Our analysis of the transition into homeownership also failed to produce consistent support for a hypothesis that debt depresses young adults' ability to transition into adulthood (table not shown).

Conclusions and Caveats

This chapter has examined young adults' behavior in credit markets and the relationship between their credit market outcomes and their experiences in other markets. We find little to suggest that, as a group, today's young adults have troublesome debt levels. In fact, their behavior in credit markets does not appear to be remarkably different from that of other families in the nation or from that of young adults in the past. There are, however, some young adult households whose situations are worrisome. Moreover, this study finds that there are several interesting debates surrounding the debt of young adults that policymakers and scholars have yet to resolve.

Whether debt impedes young people's ability to transition into adulthood is one such debate. Although our analysis does not support this hypothesis, there are markers of adult status that we did not examine, such as attaining a full-time job, marriage, and living independently of one's parents. The PSID largely contains information about young adults who have established independent households, and these households may be more financially stable (or savvy) than others, making it possible that they would not be sidetracked by debt while others might be. Unfortunately, the two major national datasets commonly used to analyze debt, the PSID and the SCF, share this trait. One interesting avenue for future research would be to obtain a dataset of all young adults, regardless of living status, with debt information for them, and to determine whether debt hampers some young adults' ability to leave home.

Appendix: The Data Used in This Study

The analysis relied on four different datasets: the 2001 Survey of Consumer Finances (SCF), the 1983 Survey of Consumer Finances (SCF), the 1963 Survey of Financial Characteristics of Consumers (SFCC), and the Panel Study of Income Dynamics (PSID). This data appendix discusses the major features of each dataset and guides the reader to additional readings for more information.

The 2001 Survey of Consumer Finances

The 2001 SCF is a survey of 4,449 households that is nationally representative when its data are weighted using the survey weights. We define households with heads age twenty-five to thirty-four as young adult households. Note that like most other national datasets covering wealth and family finances, the SCF is a household-level survey. This means that it is not possible to ascertain the specific individual in the household who incurred the debts recorded. It also means that the young adults in the survey are young adults who have set up independent households, either as the head of their own household or as a spouse. Any individuals age twenty-five to thirty-four who live with their parents and are financially dependent on them would not be captured in the sample. (Their information would be part of the information about their parents' household.) Much of the background demographic information provided in the SCF is for the household head. For example, levels of education are reported for household heads only, so when we identify college-educated young adult households, we make this delineation on the basis of the heads' characteristics. Note also that a multiple imputation procedure is used in the construction of the 2001 SCF dataset. In addition to correcting for oversampling of high-income households, the survey weights can be used to adjust for the presence of the implicates that result from the multiple imputation. The presence of implicates means that special care must be taken when computing standard errors. For a thorough discussion of these and related issues, see Aizcorbe and others (2003) and the 2001 SCF codebook (Federal Reserve 2001).

Although we construct some of our debt measures from the raw data, the chapter also relies heavily on six debt categories preconstructed by the SCF; these data are reported in the Federal Reserve's regular triennial reports on its survey results (as in, for example, Aizcorbe et al. 2003). The "mortgage debt" category in the 2001 SCF is really a "housing" or "home-secured debt" category. It largely comprises home mortgages (on a household's principal residence) but also includes home equity loans and home equity lines of credit. The other residential debt category includes land contracts, mortgage debt for residential property other than the principal residence (such as vacation homes), and installment debt for cottages or vacation homes. Other lines of credit are those other than home equity loans. The installment debt category represents consumer loans with fixed terms and fixed payment periods, such as automobile loans, student loans, and loans for furniture or other household durable goods. The "other" debt category includes loans against pensions, loans against life insurance, margin loans, and other miscellaneous debt.

The 1983 Survey of Consumer Finances

The 1983 SCF is a nationally representative (with weights) sample of 4,262 U.S. households. Because not all the debt categories presented in the 1983 wave of the SCF were the same as those that appeared in 2001, we reconfigured some of the 1983 categories to match the 2001 categories. Additional information about this survey is contained in the Federal Reserve (1997) codebook and in Robert Avery, Gregory Elliehausen, and Glenn Canner (1984a, 1984b).

The 1963 Survey of Financial Characteristics of Consumers

The Survey of Financial Characteristics of Consumers is a survey that was conducted in 1963 by the Federal Reserve Board, with assistance from the Census Bureau and the Internal Revenue Service. The SFCC, which surveyed 3,551 U.S. households, is regarded as the precursor to the contemporary Survey of Consumer Finances. Restricting the dataset to households whose heads are between age twenty-five and thirty-four yields 362 observations.

The documentation for this survey indicates that the survey's total debt measure consists of debts secured by a family's home and by its investment assets, along with personal debt and debt on life insurance (Projector and Weiss 1966, 47). Our total debt measure was constructed somewhat similarly. It combines debt on the following variables: debt on principal residence (variable 104); debt associated with any second family residence (variable 106); debt associated with real estate investments (variable 108); debit balances on brokerage accounts (variable 110); loans secured by stocks and bonds (variables 115 and 116); the four SFCC installment debt categories of debt for automobiles (variable 117); home repair and renovations (variable 118); other consumer goods (variable 119); other purposes (variable 120); and the SFCC's four non-installment debt categories: debt owed to banks (variable 121), other financial institutions (variable 122), medical providers (variable 123), and private individuals (variable 124). These variables are all reported at the family level.

The SFCC also reports data covering loans secured by life insurance for heads, spouses, and other family members. These data were not included in our total debt measure. The SFCC documentation indicates that investments in life insurance were not incorporated into the wealth measure that it used in the Dorothy Projector and Gertrude Weiss report owing to concerns about the reliability of the data (see Projector and Weiss 1966, 48). Because of this, we also omitted the debt secured by life insurance from our total debt measure.

Where necessary, we combined individual SFCC debt categories to create measures that could be compared with the different debt categories presented in the 2001 SCF. Two of the broad debt categories available in the 2001 SCF are not relevant for the 1960s. Accordingly, we cannot use the 1963 SFCC to construct 1963 equivalents for credit card debt and other lines of credit.

Following the SFCC guidelines, we constructed our wealth measure by adding up the different components of wealth available in the survey. For many items, the valuation concept involves taking equity in the asset (the market value of the asset minus any debt secured by the asset). This is true for housing, for example. For business interests, however, the

SFCC recorded the book value of the business (farm and nonfarm) minus any debts. The technical report indicates that the market value estimates were deemed unreliable because many families were not able to determine the price for which their business might be sold (Projector and Weiss 1966). The wealth measure includes assets held in formal trust (variable 176), but not capital gains and losses. As noted in the Federal Reserve's codebook, the Fed did not include capital gains and losses in its published wealth estimates. Accordingly, we also excluded these variables to allow comparability as a check on our work. Also omitted from the wealth estimates were the data covering equity in annuities and retirement plans. As noted in Projector and Weiss (1966, 49), a substantial number of respondents who had this item did not provide amounts. Accordingly, the SFCC deems these data too unreliable to use.

The Panel Study of Income Dynamics

The Panel Study of Income Dynamics is a nationally representative survey of nearly 8,000 U.S. families that began in 1968. Since then, it has followed the original families surveyed over time, along with their offspring as they have set up families of their own. Because of this design, this dataset allows us to examine a young adult household in two different time periods to determine whether the characteristics of the household have changed over time.

Our analysis of PSID data uses two different samples. We first analyzed young adults who appeared in the dataset in 1994 and 1999 to determine whether they transitioned into parenthood or homeownership during this time period. We identified households across time by imposing the restriction that the household have the same head in 1999 as in 1994. This ensured that we had the "same" household in each time period. Imposing this constraint, along with the constraint that the household head had to be between ages twenty-five and thirty-four in the initial period, resulted in a sample of 569 young adult households. To increase the sample size, we constructed a second sample that pooled young adult households from three different periods: those who could have transitioned into parenthood or homeownership between 1994 and 1999; those who could have transitioned between 1999 and 2001; and those who could have transitioned between 2001 and 2003. The pooled sample yields a dataset with more than 3,000 young adult observations.

It is important to note that the PSID's list of debt measures is less comprehensive than the SCF's. In the PSID, direct information is available only about noncollateralized debt and mortgage debt. (Our mortgage debt variable merges the information about first and second mortgages, which are reported separately in the PSID.) There are also data about net worth levels. The latter are used to construct two dummy variables for whether a household has negative net worth (one using the PSID's wealth-1 measure and the second using the PSID's wealth-2 measure). The negative net worth dummies are used as an additional measure of indebtedness. For additional information about the PSID, see http://psidonline.isr.umich.edu.

Notes

1. Like most other national datasets covering wealth and family finances, the SCF is a household-level survey, that is, most of its data—for debt, assets, and wealth, for example—are measured at the household level. For additional discussion of this dataset, see the appendix.

2. The analysis of SCF data indicates that only about 3 percent of young adult households have "other residential debt," that fewer than 2 percent of young adult households carry "other lines of credit," and that only about 9 percent hold "other debt." This chapter thus does not analyze these categories of debt, since they are not salient for young adults.

3. Economists characterize an analysis that focuses narrowly on borrowers as analysis of the conditional distribution, that is, the distribution conditional on having a positive level of debt. The statistics from this distribution typically are called the "conditional mean" and the "conditional median." Intuitively, they are different from the mean and the median of the entire distribution, which characterize *all* young adults (not just those with positive amounts of credit card debt).

4. Our 9.3 percent figure is lower than that reported in Tamara Draut and Javier Silva (2004), who find that about 13 percent of twenty-five- to thirty-four-year-olds experience debt hardship. These authors restrict their analysis to indebted households, however, rather than examining all young adults.

5. The SFCC is the precursor to the modern Survey of Consumer Finances. For a discussion of the evolution of the SCF and the SFCC, see Arthur Kennickell (2000) and Projector and Weiss (1966). Note that the 2001 SCF, the 1983 SCF, and the SFCC each report families' liabilities differently. We reclassify the data from the latter two to create debt categories that are similar to those in the 2001 SCF whenever possible. All dollar value comparisons use constant 2001 dollars.

6. Current Population Survey data indicate that the fraction of individuals age twenty-five to thirty-four completing at least four years of college rose from 12.9 percent in 1962 to 24.41 percent in 1983 to 29.65 in 2001.

7. About 18 percent of young adult households are among the poorest 20 percent of all U.S. households; 24 percent fall in the second-lowest income quintile, and 23 percent are middle-income households; another 23 percent are in the fourth-highest income quintile. Thirteen percent of young adults have incomes high enough to place them in the top quintile of U.S. households.

8. Our figure is much lower than the $19,300 reported in Draut (2006, 94–95). Draut's data come from studies of recent graduates and therefore reflect the amounts held by young adults as they are exiting college. Because our analysis covers young adults later in life, it is possible that some of the discrepancy

is explained by the fact that our young adults have had time to pay down some of their outstanding student debt. A study of National Center for Education Statistics data suggests that the discrepancy also could be due to lower starting balances for our cohort of young adults (Choy and Li 2005, iv). These authors find that mean balances held by exiting seniors rose from $12,826 to $20,458 (in 2001 dollars) between 1993 and 2000.

9. It is standard to construct debt-to-income and debt-to-net-worth ratios that divide the total debt held by a group of individuals by the group income or group net worth, and such aggregate-level measures are informative. However, because they represent groupwide information, they can obscure the position of individual households whose debt vastly exceeds their income or wealth. The calculations of debt-to-income ratios at various percentiles are available from the author upon request.

References

Aizcorbe, Anna, Arthur Kennickell, and Kevin Moore. 2003. "Recent Changes in U.S. Family Finances." *Federal Reserve Bulletin* (January).

Avery, Robert, Gregory Elliehausen, and Glenn Canner. 1984a. "Survey of Consumer Finances, 1983." *Federal Reserve Bulletin* (September).

———. 1984b. "Survey of Consumer Finances, 1983: A Second Report." *Federal Reserve Bulletin* (December).

Barrow, Lisa, and Cecilia Rouse. 2005. "Does College Still Pay?" *The Economists' Voice* 2(4): 1–8. Accessed at http://www.bepress.com/ev/vol2/iss4/art3.

Caner, Asena, and Edward Wolff. 2004. "Asset Poverty in the United States, 1984–1999." *Review of Income and Wealth* 50(4): 493–518.

Charles, Kerwin, and Erik Hurst. 2002. "The Transition to Homeownership and the Black-White Wealth Gap." *Review of Economics and Statistics* 84(2): 281–97.

Choy, Susan P., and Xiaojie Li. 2005. *Debt Burdens: A Comparison of 1992–93 and 1999–2000 Bachelor's Degree Recipients a Year After Graduating*. NCES 2005-170. Washington: U.S. Government Printing Office.

College Board. 2004a. *Trends in College Pricing, 2004*. New York: College Board.

———. 2004b. *Trends in Student Aid, 2004*. New York: College Board.

Draut, Tamara. 2006. *Strapped: Why America's 20- and 30-Somethings Can't Get Ahead*. New York: Doubleday.

Draut, Tamara, and Javier Silva, 2004. *Generation Broke: The Growth of Debt Among Young Americans*. New York: Demos. Accessed at http://www.demos.usa.org.

Federal Reserve. 1997. *Codebook for 1962 Survey of Financial Characteristics of Consumers and 1963 Changes in Family Finances*. Accessed December 19, 2005, at http://www.federalreserve.gov/pubs/oss/oss2/6263/codebk6263.txt.

———. 2001. *2001 Survey of Consumer Finances*. Accessed at http://www.federal-reserve.gov/pubs/oss/oss2/2001/scf2001home.html.

Furstenberg, Frank, Jr., Rubén Rumbaut, and Richard Settersten. 2005. "On the Frontier of Adulthood." In *On the Frontier of Adulthood: Theory, Research, and Policy*, edited by Richard Settersten, Frank Furstenberg Jr., and Rubén Rumbaut. Chicago, Ill.: University of Chicago Press.

Gertner, Jon. 2006. "Forgive Us Our Student Debts." *New York Times Magazine* (June 11): 60–68.

Haveman, Robert, and Edward Wolff. 2005. "The Concept and Measurement of Asset Poverty." *Journal of Economic Inequality* 2(2): 145–69.

Kennickell, Arthur. 2000. "Wealth Measurement in the Survey of Consumer Finances: Methodology and Directions for Future Research." Paper presented to the annual meeting of the American Association for Public Opinion Research (May). Accessed October 2005 at http://www.federalreserve.gov/pubs/oss/oss2/method.html.

Laibson, David. 1997. "Golden Eggs and Hyperbolic Discounting." *Quarterly Journal of Economics* 112(2): 443–77.

Manning, Robert. 2000. *Credit Card Nation*. New York: Basic Books.

Mishel, Lawrence, Jared Bernstein, and Sylvia Allegretto. 2007. *The State of Working America, 2006–2007*. Ithaca, N.Y.: Cornell University Press.

Monks, James. 2001. "Loan Burdens and Educational Outcomes." *Economics of Education Review* 20(6): 545–50.

Projector, Dorothy, and Gertrude Weiss. 1966. "Survey of Financial Characteristics of Consumers." Federal Reserve technical paper (August). Accessed at http://www.federalreserve.gov/pubs/oss/oss2/6263/sfcc6263home.html.

Settersten, Richard, Frank Furstenberg, Jr., and Rubén Rumbaut, editors. 2005. *On the Frontier of Adulthood: Theory, Research, and Policy*. Chicago, Ill.: University of Chicago Press.

Stewart, Janet Kidd. 2005. "Generation IOU." *Chicago Tribune*, April 27.

Time. 2005. "Time Poll: Over One-Half of Young Adults 'in Debt' When They Finish College" (January 16). Accessed at http://www.time.com/time/press_releases/article/0,8599,1018036,00.html.

U.S. Bureau of the Census. 2005. "Table A-1: Years of School Completed by People 25 Years and Over, by Age and Sex: Selected Years 1940 to 2004." *Current Population Survey*. Accessed at http://www.census.gov/population/socdemo/education/cps2006/tabA-1.xls.

———. 2006. *Statistical Abstract of the United States*. Washington: U.S. Government Printing Office. Accessed at http://www.census.gov/compendia/statab.

U.S. Department of Education. National Center for Education Statistics. 1998. "Trends in Student Borrowing." *Education Statistics Quarterly* 1(3). Accessed at http://nces.ed.gov/programs/quarterly/vol_1/1_3/4-esq13-c.asp.

U.S. General Accounting Office. 2001. *Consumer Finance: College Students and Credit Cards*. Washington: GAO.

U.S. Senate. 2006. "Tax Exemptions and Incentives for Higher Education." Finance Committee hearings, December 5.

USA Today. 2006. "Young and in Debt" (series). November 20 to December 29. Accessed at http://www.usatoday.com/money/perfi/credit/young-debt-digest.htm.

PART III

Family Background, Incarceration, and the Transition to Adulthood

Chapter 10

Family Background and Children's Transitions to Adulthood over Time

MELANIE GULDI, MARIANNE E. PAGE, AND
ANN HUFF STEVENS

The transition to adulthood is almost by definition a process of breaking away from one's family of origin. Nevertheless, family background has an impact on the success of this transition. For example, Gary Sandefur, Jennifer Eggerling-Boeck, and Hyunjoon Park (2005) and David Ellwood and Thomas Kane (2000) show that parental education and family income are positively correlated with the probability that a young adult will pursue postsecondary education, and Tom Hertz (2005) estimates that a son born into a family whose income is in the top 10 percent of the income distribution is twenty-three times more likely to end up in the top 10 percent as an adult than a son born into the bottom 10 percent.

Over the past thirty years, several social and economic changes may have altered the impact of parents on the success with which their children approach adulthood. In this chapter, we look at whether the importance of family background has changed over time. We compare various "markers" of adulthood for two groups who were coming of age in the mid-1970s and early 1990s. We look at whether early adult income levels, educational attainment, and the probability of starting one's own family differ by parental income and education, and we ask how these differences have changed over time. Knowing the extent to which family influences are changing is an important part of understanding why today's youth are taking longer to reach traditional markers of adulthood than previous generations. There may be important policy considerations as well. For example, if the association between parental income and the economic success of their children is becoming stronger over time, and if this association is due to the changing impact of income itself rather than the effects of other family characteristics correlated with income, then policies aimed at increasing the financial resources of poor families may also affect trends in outcomes for youths.

We come to three conclusions. First, a successful transition to adulthood differs markedly across individuals who grew up in high- and low-income families and with high- and low-educated parents.[1] Second, there is little evidence that the influence of characteristics associated with parental income has changed over time. An exception is that those who grew up in high-income families seem to be delaying childbearing more than they did in the past. Third, the relationship between young adults' education and that of their parents appears to have become stronger over time. This is in marked contrast to the lack of a significant change between parental education and the next generation's income, and it is somewhat surprising given the large increases in the wage returns to schooling that took place over this period.

Why Might Family Background Affect Youth Outcomes?

Many studies have documented a strong relationship between family background characteristics—particularly parental education and income—and young adults' socioeconomic outcomes (see, among many examples, Duncan and Brooks-Gunn 1997; Settersten, Furstenberg, and Rumbaut 2005). Ellwood and Kane (2000) report that youth with similar academic credentials enroll in college at very different rates depending on their parents' income and education. Gary Solon (1992) and others show that the incomes of young men in their mid- to late twenties are highly correlated with their father's income during childhood.

Table 10.1 shows the likelihood of attaining several markers of adulthood by age thirty according to the quartile distribution of family income when the individual was age fourteen to seventeen, for two groups of young adults, the first born between 1954 and 1957 and the second born between 1970 and 1973.[2] For both cohorts, young adults' income and education increase dramatically as their family's income increases. Adult income is nearly twice as high among those whose parents' income was in the top quartile of earners than among those whose parents' income was in the bottom quartile. Similarly, the probability that a child from the top quartile will complete college is approximately four to seven times larger (depending on the cohort) than the probability that a child from the bottom quartile will complete college. Marriage probabilities also increase with family income, although less steeply. The probability of becoming a parent, however, falls with parental income. This makes sense given the positive education correlation across generations; it is well known that more highly educated women delay childbearing.

There is also a strong association between parental education and young adults' outcomes. Family income and education among young adults increase monotonically with parental education. Among those born in the mid-1950s, those whose parents had at least sixteen years of education had a 56 percent chance of completing college, whereas those whose parents were high school dropouts had a 10 percent chance of reaching this milestone. This pattern persists among individuals born fifteen years later. For both cohorts, marriage and fertility patterns across parental education categories are very similar to those for parental income.

Why does family socioeconomic status matter? Exactly how family background affects the transition to adulthood is largely unknown, but likely includes role modeling, labor market connections, neighborhood influences, and parents' ability to make monetary investments in their children, such as paying for high-quality elementary and secondary schools (either by paying the higher cost of housing in neighborhoods with good public schools or by purchasing private schooling), paying for postsecondary education, or helping children with down payments for their own homes. Wealthier families may also be able to provide a better safety net for their children if they fall into trouble through either bad luck or bad choices. Finally, the correlation between parents' socioeconomic status and young adult outcomes may also reflect genetic traits such as intelligence or motivation.

Why Might the Importance of Family Background Be Changing over Time?

Our two cohorts are approximately fifteen years apart, and the economic and social conditions under which they grew up and ultimately entered adulthood were very different. In particular, the late 1970s and 1980s was a period of increasing globalization and technological change, which has been associated with widening income inequality and increasing returns to skill. At the end of the 1970s, male college graduates had earnings that were 35 percent higher than the earnings of those with a high school diploma; by the end of the 1980s, the earnings differential was 53 percent (Gottschalk 1997). This translated into a fall in the share of income going to individuals at the bottom of the income distribution and a rise in the share going to those at the top. High-income parents tend to provide more resources to their children than low-income parents (Schoeni and Ross 2005), so when inequality increases, we might expect a widening in the dispersion of investments that parents can make

Table 10.1   Young Adult Outcomes by Age Thirty According to Household Head's Education Level and Family income Quartile

	Cohort 1 (Born 1954 to 1957) (Old)				
	Average Family Income[a]	Less Than 12 Years of Education	16 Years of Education or More	Are Parents	Currently Married
Family income quartile					
Bottom 25 percent	$38,062	24.4%	6.5%	76.0%	54.4%
25 to 50 percent	49,238	39.4	15.7	68.5	62.2
50 to 75 percent	61,124	43.0	22.5	65.5	71.6
Top 25 percent	69,673	68.4	42.7	57.6	73.7
Household head's education					
Not a high school graduate	46,147	27.3	9.9	75.8	58.1
High school graduate (including GED)	56,226	45.5	20.3	66.7	69.7
Some college[b]	63,406	55.6	32.2	64.4	74.9
BA degree or more	71,720	84.6	56.1	41.5	73.0

in their children. Solon (2004) shows that if these investments are important to children's future success, then, holding all else equal, rising inequality will result in a decline in intergenerational mobility. In other words, young adults from disadvantaged families will have a harder time escaping their parents' economic legacy.

Because this prediction rests on the assumption that all else is equal, it is important to consider the possible influence of other family background characteristics that were changing at the same time that family incomes were becoming more unequal. Not only did the return to education change dramatically during the mid-1970s and 1980s, but the level of education nearly doubled. Recent research by Janet Currie and Enrico Moretti (2003), Philip Oreopolous, Marianne Page, and Ann Huff Stevens (forthcoming), and Bruce Sacerdote (2005) suggests that childhood birthweight, grade-for-age, and other childhood outcomes that are predictive of socioeconomic success later in life are positively related to parents' education levels. Changes in parents' schooling may therefore have affected both the level and nature of parental investments that ultimately affect the success with which young adults make the transition into adulthood.

The probability of growing up in a single-parent family also rose steadily over this period (Wu and Li 2005). Adolescents who have spent time in non-intact families fare more poorly on average than those who grew up in a household with both of their biological parents (McLana-

Table 10.1   *(Continued)*

	Cohort 2 (Born 1970 to 1973) (Young)			
Average Family Income[a]	Less Than 12 Years of Education	16 Years of Education or More	Are Parents	Currently Married
$42,980	32.7%	14.8%	70.8%	54.1%
51,372	60.5	28.2	59.3	59.1
64,936	70.4	37.1	48.1	59.1
83,613	76.9	58.0	37.6	60.6
43,197	28.1	5.4	74.5	63.5
54,208	52.0	19.7	60.2	54.4
63,511	64.2	44.3	46.4	60.0
81,064	90.4	66.7	37.4	57.6

Source: Authors' tabulations from the PSID.
a. Average family income is in 2005 dollars and has been computed using the Consumer Price Index All Urban Consumers (series CUUROOOOSAO), accessed at http://data.bls .gov/cgi-bin/surveymost?cu.
b. More than twelve but less than sixteen years of education.

han and Sandefur 1994), and this may subsequently affect their prospects as young adults. Other changes in children's family environments include declines in family size, increases in mothers' labor force participation, and the deterioration of inner-city neighborhoods.

All of these changes may have affected parents' desires and abilities to invest in their children. At the same time, there have been enormous increases in government expenditures on behalf of children, which may have counteracted some of the disadvantages of growing up in a low-income family. Examples of such programs include Head Start, the Special Supplemental Nutrition Program for Women Infants and Children (WIC), Medicaid, and the school lunch and school breakfast program. The federal government has also become more involved in education. Between the early 1970s and early 1990s, per pupil spending on public education increased by more than 50 percent and became more equally distributed across school districts. The Pell grant program, which provides need-based grants for postsecondary education, began in 1972. If these programs were successful in their missions, then we would expect family background to become a less important predictor of educational attainment over time.

Measuring Changes in the Importance of Family Background

We estimate changes in the predictive power of family background on transitions to adulthood by estimating the slope coefficient in regressions of young adults' socioeconomic outcomes on measures of parents' socioeconomic status, specifically family income and parental education. The results from these regressions capture both the causal effect of parental income and education and the effect of all other background characteristics that are correlated with parental income or education. To estimate the extent to which the association between these outcomes and family socioeconomic status has changed over time, we compare the outcomes of our two cohorts. Our family background measures are by no means all-encompassing, but they are easily observable and can be directly tied to theories about intergenerational mobility (for example, as outlined by Becker and Tomes 1979). As a result, they are the measures most commonly used in cross-generational studies.

Data

We use data from the Panel Study of Income Dynamics (PSID). Individuals in the "old" group (born between 1954 and 1957) turned twenty in the mid-1970s, whereas those in the "young" cohort entered their twenties at the beginning of the 1990s. We chose these groups because they span a period when income inequality was widening in the United States, returns to education were increasing, marriage rates were declining, and more women were entering the workforce. In addition, the young cohort is the youngest group for which we can observe young adult outcomes in the dataset, using the most recently released survey wave from 2003. We attempted to select cohorts that experienced similar business-cycle conditions for the period during which we measure family background variables.

To measure changes in income, we use the average of the log of family income for each year the child was age fourteen to seventeen, adjusted for the current unemployment rate and gross domestic product and the age of the household head. This allows us to approximate a measure of "permanent" income that abstracts from both business-cycle and parents' life-cycle effects. Our measure of parental education is based on the educational attainment of the household head. We use several variables to capture the successful transition to adulthood. Young adults' family income is the average of the adult child's family income when he or she is between the ages of twenty-five and thirty (see the appendix for specific years used), measured in logs. Measuring each generation's income in logs makes it easier to interpret their estimated relationship. The second outcome is educational attainment, which we measure in two ways. The first variable is the individual's years of education by age thirty, and the second variable measures whether the individual has completed college by age thirty. Finally, we construct indicators for whether the individual is married or a parent by age thirty. More specific details on the measurement of these variables are available in the appendix.

Results

Table 10.2 summarizes our estimates of the relationship between family background and young adults' outcomes. Many studies have estimated the association between the income of parents and their adult children (for a review, see Solon 1999); the upper half of the first column summarizes our estimates of this relationship when the children are in early adulthood. Because income in each generation is measured in logs, these estimates can be interpreted as percentage effects. We find that nearly half (0.471) of the variance in young adults' income can be attributed to factors correlated with the level of income in their family of origin. This estimate is very similar to those in previous studies. We also see that individuals born during the early 1970s have incomes that are about 11 percent higher than the incomes of those born fifteen years earlier.[3] We find no evidence that the importance of family income has changed over time.

In the next column, we look at the relationship between family income and young adults' educational attainment. Consistent with known trends, on average, the younger cohort has completed more schooling (nearly one additional year) than the older cohort. We also see that family income has a strong positive effect on young adults' educational attainment: a 10 percent increase in family income is associated with an additional 0.15 of a year of schooling. Evidence that this effect is changing over time, however, is weak. Similarly, we find no evidence that the association between family income and college completion has changed.

Mary Corcoran and Jordan Matsudaira (2005), Tom Hertz (2005), and Chul-In Lee and Gary Solon (2005) also find limited evidence that intergenerational mobility has changed over time. As noted in our earlier discussion, Solon's (2004) analysis suggests that, all else being constant, the increases in income inequality that occurred during the latter third of the twentieth century should have led to an increase in the intergenerational income correlation. The fact that we find no evidence of such a change suggests that all else was not constant, and that some countervailing factor probably changed as well. One possibility is that government programs aimed at young children, such as Head Start and the school lunch and school breakfast program, may have made up for some parents' reduced ability to make both cognitive and nutritional investments in their

Table 10.2 Estimated Relationships Between Family Background Variables and Young Adult Outcomes

	Family Income (Measured in Logs)	Years of Education	Completed College	Has Children	Ever Married	Currently Married
Family background measure: family income						
Young (born 1970 to 1973)	0.103**	0.668**	0.128**	-0.131**	-0.169**	-0.072*
	[0.039]	[0.145]	[0.032]	[0.033]	[0.030]	[0.033]
Family income	0.471**	1.539**	0.232**	-0.096**	0.068**	0.153**
	[0.045]	[0.142]	[0.028]	[0.034]	[0.023]	[0.032]
Additional effect of family income for the young cohort	-0.037	-0.347	-0.008	-0.109*	-0.028	-0.091
	[0.069]	[0.233]	[0.049]	[0.052]	[0.049]	[0.056]
Number of observations	1,484	1,407	1,407	1,468	1,467	1,467
Family background measure: head's education						
Young (born 1970 to 1973)	-0.056	-0.161	-0.04	-0.046	-0.148	-0.060
	[0.047]	[0.179]	[0.033]	[0.039]	[0.033]	[0.039]
Head's education	0.057**	0.282**	0.042**	-0.031**	0.000	0.019**
	[0.006]	[0.023]	[0.005]	[0.005]	[0.004]	[0.005]
Additional effect of head's education for the young cohort	0.022	0.124*	0.039**	-0.012	-0.010	-0.022
	[0.014]	[0.053]	[0.011]	[0.012]	[0.010]	[0.012]
Number of observations	1,476	1,399	1,399	1,460	1,459	1,459

Notes: All analyses are based on data from the PSID. Robust standard errors in brackets.
* significant at 5%; ** significant at 1%

children. Eliana Garces, Duncan Thomas, and Janet Currie (2002) and Jens Ludwig and Douglas Miller (2005) find some evidence that Head Start has positive long-run effects on individuals' educational attainment. Increases in financial assistance for postsecondary education (such as the Pell grant) may have increased access to higher education among older youth, although evidence on the efficacy of tuition assistance programs is mixed.[4]

We also examine changes in the relationship between parental income and marriage and fertility. Consistent with well-documented trends, table 10.2 shows that the probability of being married and having a child by age thirty has declined over time across the family income spectrum. For example, the probability that men and women born in the early 1970s had become parents by age thirty was 13 percent less than the probability for the older cohort. Similarly, the probability that the young cohort had married by age thirty was 17 percent lower. Family income during childhood is also significantly related to these outcomes. Children from high-income families are more likely to be married by age thirty, which is consistent with economists' theories about marriage markets. *All else being equal*, men and women with more income and education make more desirable marriage partners.

At the same time, young adults from high-income families are more likely to delay childbearing, and this relationship has grown stronger over time. Individuals from financially advantaged families who came of age during the early 1990s were twice as likely to delay childbearing as those who turned twenty during the late 1970s. Because marriage and fertility often go hand in hand, these results may at first seem surprising. However, our results are reminiscent of patterns found by David Ellwood, Ty Wilde, and Lily Batchelder (2004) and Ellwood and Christopher Jencks (2004), who find that highly educated women are marrying and having children later than they were a generation ago, whereas women with less education are also marrying later but not delaying childbearing.

The second panel of table 10.2 presents our estimates of the relationship between household head's education and young adults' socioeconomic outcomes. The results largely echo those in the top panel, with little evidence of systematic change in the importance of family background. There does appear to be a strengthening of the relationship between parents' and children's educational attainment, however, and the magnitude of this change is nontrivial. The gap in the probability of completing college between those whose parents' highest level of education was a high school diploma and those whose parents completed college has grown by nearly 16 percent (4 years*0.039). For both cohorts, the average level of education among those whose parents have only a high school diploma is 13.4 years. Among members of the older cohort, who would have finished high school during the early 1970s, those whose parents completed college have an average education level of 14.5 years, whereas individuals from similar families who would have graduated from high school during the late 1980s average 15 years of schooling.

Taken together, the results in the top and bottom panels of table 10.2 are somewhat surprising, given that individuals' education and income are positively correlated, and we find no evidence that family income has become more important over time. If the introduction and strengthening of government programs aimed at children was undoing the increasing disparity in parents' ability to invest in their children, then we would not expect to see such a large increase in the predictive power of parental education. Furthermore, we see no change in the relationship between parental education and young adults' own income despite the large increases in wage returns to education that occurred between the time periods when the two cohorts entered the labor market.[5]

Discussion

We find limited evidence that the importance of family background (as measured by parental income and education levels) has changed over time. Although our estimates suggest an increase in the association between an individual's educational attainment and that of his or her parents, we find no evidence that this has translated into a changing dynamic between young adult income and parental education. This is particularly puzzling in light of the fact that returns to education have been increasing. If parents' education is becoming a more important determinant of youth's human capital, then we would expect to see this effect play out in the incomes of young adults. Of course, these differences may appear later in life. We have focused here on the outcomes of young adults, and changes in the effect of family background on long-run income may not show up until later in young people's lives.

We find no evidence that the relationship between family income and young adults' human capital *or* income has increased. This mix of empirical results makes it difficult to relate the increase in inequality to a strengthening relationship between parents' and children's education and suggests that caution should be applied when interpreting the estimated changes in particular relationships. Recent research on trends in intergenerational mobility has produced wildly divergent results, which Lee and Solon (2005) argue stem from inefficient use of available data. We are also limited by small sample sizes.

As with previous studies, we find that young adults' socioeconomic outcomes differ dramatically by family income and education. Ellwood and Kane (2000) show that differences in educational attainment result from more than differences in families' ability to afford postsecondary schooling, and that the parents' education levels have an effect on a youth's probability of entering college that is independent of the effect of family income. The positive education correlation across generations may thus reflect some combination of genetic similarities across generations, differences in parenting skills, and different access to information about educational opportunities between more- and less-educated parents. It is possible that the importance of these family background characteristics is increasing over time even as the importance of family income per se stays the same. Determining optimal policies for overcoming these gaps will be challenging indeed.

We also uncover suggestive evidence of a widening gap in out-of-wedlock fertility between young adults from different family backgrounds. Although all young adults are delaying marriage, only those from high-income families are delaying parenthood. This growing gap in the propensity to form single-parent families is troubling because it means that an increasing fraction of American children are being born to young single mothers from economically disadvantaged families. Many studies have documented that children who grow up in such families have worse economic outcomes than children whose parents are better off. These trends may therefore result in a substantial widening in future generations' outcomes.

Although we find evidence that some measures of family socioeconomic status have a larger impact on some youth outcomes than they used to, we find no evidence of a systematic change in the importance of parental income and education over time. It does not necessarily follow that the influence of these characteristics on long-term outcomes has remained the same. As we noted, the young adults in our study are still in early adulthood, when earnings differences between individuals with different levels of education are relatively small. Over time, these differences are likely to grow, and a change in the relationship between children's income and their parents' income and education may become more evident. Likewise, there may be changes in the relationship between family background and the next generation's marital stability or completed family size—outcomes that cannot be measured accurately before age thirty. A more complete understanding of the mechanisms by which families influence their children at all stages of life and the effect of changing economic and social conditions on these mechanisms is certainly warranted.

Appendix

Our data primarily come from the Panel Study of Income Dynamics (PSID), a longitudinal survey that began in 1968 with a nationally representative sample of about 5,000 U.S. families. Survey respondents were reinterviewed every year between 1968 and 1997, and they have been surveyed every other year since then. An advantage of the PSID is that it has followed children of the originally sampled households from 1968 through the present, even after they left home to start their own families, making it possible to link measures of the children's socioeconomic status as young adults to measures of their parents. A disadvantage of this dataset, however, is that the number of children of a given age is small. We therefore boost our sample size by combining children born in adjacent years into groups.

Family background characteristics are observed during two periods: 1968 to 1974 ("old" cohort) and 1984 to1990 ("young" cohort). Adult transition outcomes are observed in the periods 1983 to 1987 and 1999 to 2003. More detail is given in table 10A.1.

The two cohort groups examined were age fourteen in 1968 to 1971 (old cohort) and in 1984 to 1987 (young cohort). Birth cohorts are formed by choosing individuals who were age fourteen in each year. For example, persons who were age fourteen in 1970 form the 1956 cohort.

Persons for whom we can observe both family background characteristics and adult transition outcomes form our sample. Owing to the move to biennial collection of data by the PSID beginning in 1997, adult transition outcomes cannot be observed for every cohort precisely at age thirty. Most of these outcomes are observed when a person is age twenty-nine or thirty, as shown in table 10A.1. Adult income is averaged over multiple waves, as shown in table 10A.2.

Family Background Characteristics

Family income is the income of the family in 1982 to 1984 dollars. It is obtained using PSID variables for total family money income and converted to 1982 to 1984 dollars using the CPI. As with most recent studies, we use multiyear measures of parental income, because existing research (Solon 1992; Zimmerman 1992) has shown that using single-year measures of parental income to proxy for lifetime income leads to attenuated estimates of the intergenerational relationship.

Ideally, each child's family background characteristics would be observed for each age between fourteen and seventeen (four waves total). The top codes for income are set much lower (even in real terms) before 1980 than after 1980. To address the non-observability of high earners in the earlier period, we trim observations with the top 1 percent and bottom 1 percent of family income. (Observations here are defined on the child-wave dimension, leaving four observations per child.) After trimming the data in this fashion, if family income is observed for fewer than three of the four possible waves, we drop the child from the sample.

We recode *head's age* to be a missing value when an age is not reported for the PSID variable (code 999) or when it is between 0 and 16. In the first-stage regression, head's age is assigned one of forty age dummies defined using the following age groupings: seventeen to twenty-one, twenty-two to twenty-five, twenty-six to twenty-nine, a separate dummy for each age from thirty to sixty-five, and age sixty-six or older.

Table 10A.1   **Observations of Family Background Characteristics and Adult Transition Outcomes**

Adult Age	Birth Cohort	Year Adult Outcomes Observed	Years Family Background Characteristics Observed
Twenty-nine	1954	1983	1968 to 1971
Thirty	1955	1985	1969 to 1972
Twenty-nine	1956	1985	1970 to 1973
Thirty	1957	1987	1971 to 1974
Twenty-nine	1970	1999	1984 to 1987
Thirty	1971	2001	1985 to 1988
Twenty-nine	1972	2001	1986 to 1989
Thirty	1973	2003	1987 to 1990

Source: Authors' compilation from the PSID.
Note: The regressions performed in this analysis are weighted using the PSID individual weight assigned in the year the person is observed as an adult.

Education is the number of years of education (one to seventeen, with twelve equal to a high school degree or GED). When education is missing (codes 96, 97, 98, 99) or reported as zero years, we assigned it a missing value. Because the PSID does not update information on individuals' schooling every year, we cannot accurately identify parents' exact years of education when the child was age fourteen to seventeen. Instead, we use the 1972 value of the head's education for the old cohort and the 1988 value of the head's education for the young cohort. When the 1972 value is missing, provided the head is the same in 1975, we assign the 1975 value. When the 1972 and 1975 values are missing, we assign the 1968 value. When the 1988 value is missing, we assign the 1989 value. Next, we follow a similar procedure for 1990, then 1987, 1986, 1985, and 1984. It is possible that a child could have a different head in each of the waves when family background characteristics are observed. When this is the case, we average the education reported by all heads associated with a child to obtain one value of head's education per child. To facilitate interpretation, we use the deviation of the head's education from the sample mean.

Adult Transitions Outcomes

Adult family income is obtained by averaging family income over at least two of three waves of data, as shown in table 10A.2.

For each cohort, we obtain *adult education* using the education variable described earlier for the year when adult transition outcomes are observed (see table 10A.1).

Using year of first birth and age, we create an indicator for whether the individual had become a *parent by age thirty (twenty-nine)*. The PSID does not collect fertility information for all individuals. This leads to

Table 10A.2   Observations of Adult Family Income

Adult Age	Birth Cohort	Year Adult Family Income Observed
Twenty-five, twenty-seven, twenty-nine	1954	1981, 1983, 1985
Twenty-six, twenty-eight, thirty	1955	1981, 1983, 1985
Twenty-five, twenty-seven, twenty-nine	1956	1983, 1985, 1987
Twenty-six, twenty-eight, thirty	1957	1983, 1985, 1987
Twenty-five, twenty-seven, twenty-nine	1970	1997, 1999, 2001
Twenty-six, twenty-eight, thirty	1971	1997, 1999, 2001
Twenty-five, twenty-seven, twenty-nine	1972	1999, 2001, 2003
Twenty-six, twenty-eight, thirty	1973	1999, 2001, 2003

Source: Authors' compilation from the PSID.

some individuals being dropped from the regressions with parenthood as the adult outcome. Of those with fertility information, some of the individuals in our sample report fertility information prior to reaching age thirty (twenty-nine). Of individuals who last reported fertility information prior to reaching age thirty (twenty-nine), only 0.25 percent reported being childless.

Using marriage status, we create an indicator for whether the individual was *ever married*, which is defined as being married, widowed, divorced (including annulment), or separated. Alternatively, using the same raw data, we create another marriage indicator for whether the individual is *currently married* (not separated).

Economic Data

Gross domestic product is GDP in current dollars, obtained from the Bureau of Economic Analysis (http://www.bea.gov/national/xls/gdplev.xls), and converted to 1982 to 1984 dollars using the CPI. The *unemployment rate* was obtained from the Bureau of Labor Statistics (ftp://ftp.bls.gov/pub/special.requests/lf/aat1.txt). The *consumer price index* (CPI) in 1982 to 1984 dollars was obtained from the Bureau of Labor Statistics (series ID: CUUR0000SA0).

First-Stage Regression

The first-stage regression examines family income during childhood with controls for the unemployment rate, gross domestic product, and head's age. Three or four income residuals are obtained for each child. These residuals are averaged for each child and used as a control in the second-stage adult income regressions.

Notes

1. Throughout this chapter, we measure parental education using the reported education of the household head.
2. Our data source, the Panel Study of Income Dynamics, moved from yearly to biennial collection of data beginning in 1997. Therefore, outcomes are observed at age twenty-nine for some cohorts.
3. Because "young" is a binary variable, the percentage change in income is calculated as $e^\beta - 1$, where β is the coefficient on young.
4. For example, Susan Dynarski (2000) and Thomas Kane (2003) find large enrollment effects of targeted assistance programs, but Lee Hansen (1983), Kane (1994), and Charles Manski and David Wise (1983) find little evidence that the Pell grant program has affected enrollment or college completion among low-income youth.
5. We considered the possibility that our model was too simple to capture important changes taking place at the top or bottom of the income or education distributions. Specifically, we ran separate regressions of children's outcomes on indicators for whether their parents' incomes were in the bottom quartile or the top quartile and regressions of children's outcomes on indicators for whether their parents had a high school education or less or a college degree (sixteen or more years of schooling). These regressions produced no evidence of nonlinear changes among children from families with very high or very low socioeconomic status. We have also conducted our analyses separately by race (white versus nonwhite) and gender, but the estimates produced by most of these analyses are too imprecise to draw any conclusions. One exception to this is that the predictive power of parental income and education on nonwhite youth's education levels appears to be becoming stronger over time relative to whites. The estimates are too imprecise to draw strong conclusions, but the pattern is suggestive of a widening disparity of opportunities between the most advantaged minorities and the least advantaged minorities. Note that our older cohort of black youth was coming of age during the civil rights movement. Since the early 1980s, labor market opportunities for blacks appear to have stagnated.

References

Becker, Gary, and Nigel Tomes. 1979. "An Equilibrium Theory of the Distribution of Income and Intergenerational Mobility." *Journal of Political Economy* 87(6): 1153–89.

Corcoran, Mary, and Jordan Matsudaira. 2005. "Is It Getting Harder to Get Ahead? Economic Attainment in Early Adulthood for Two Cohorts." In *On the Frontier to Adulthood: Theory, Research, and Public Policy*, edited by Richard A. Settersten Jr., Frank F. Furstenberg Jr., and Rubén G. Rumbaut. Chicago, Ill.: University of Chicago Press.

Currie, Janet, and Enrico Moretti. 2003. "Mother's Education and the Intergenerational Transmission of Human Capital: Evidence from College Openings." *Quarterly Journal of Economics* 118(4): 1495–532.

Duncan, Greg J., and Jeanne Brooks-Gunn. 1997. *Consequences of Growing Up Poor.* New York: Russell Sage Foundation.

Dynarski, Susan M. 2000. "Hope for Whom? Financial Aid for the Middle Class and Its Impact on College Attendance." *National Tax Journal* 53(3): 629–61.

Ellwood, David T., and Christopher Jencks. 2004. "The Spread of Single-Parent Families in the United States Since 1960." In *The Future of the Family*, edited by Daniel Patrick Moynihan, Lee Rainwater, and Timothy Smeeding. New York: Russell Sage Foundation.

Ellwood, David, and Thomas J. Kane. 2000. "Who Is Getting a College Education?" In *Securing the Future*, edited by Sheldon Danziger and Jane Waldfogel. New York: Russell Sage Foundation.

Ellwood, David T., Ty Wilde, and Lily Batchelder. 2004. "The Mommy Track Divides: The Impact of Childbearing on Wages of Women of Differing Skill Levels." Working paper. New York: Russell Sage Foundation.

Garces, Eliana, Duncan Thomas, and Janet Currie. 2002. "Longer-Term Effects of Head Start." *American Economic Review* 92(4): 999–1012.

Gottschalk, Peter. 1997. "Inequality, Income Growth, and Mobility: The Basic Facts." *Journal of Economic Perspectives* 11(2): 21–40.

Hansen, W. Lee. 1983. "Impact of Student Financial Aid on Access." In *The Crisis in Higher Education*, edited by Joseph Froomkin. New York: Academy of Political Science.

Hertz, Tom. 2005. "Attrition and Age-Bias-Corrected Estimates of the Trend in the Intergenerational Persistence of Family Income." Unpublished paper. Washington: American University.

Kane, Thomas J. 1994. "College Attendance by Blacks Since 1970: The Role of College Cost, Family Background, and the Returns to Education." *Journal of Political Economy* 102(5): 878–911.

———. 2003. "A Quasi-experimental Estimate of the Impact of Financial Aid on College-Going." Working paper 9703. Cambridge, Mass.: National Bureau of Economic Research (May). Accessed at www.nber.org/papers/W9703.

Lee, Chul-In, and Gary Solon. 2005. "Trends in Intergenerational Income Mobility." Unpublished paper. Ann Arbor, Mich.: University of Michigan.

Ludwig, Jens, and Douglas L. Miller. 2005. "Does Head Start Improve Children's Life Chances? Evidence from a Regression Discontinuity Design." Working paper 11702. Cambridge, Mass.: National Bureau of Economic Research (October). Accessed at http://papers.nber.org/papers/W11702.

Manski, Charles F., and David A. Wise. 1983. *College Choice in America.* Cambridge, Mass.: Harvard University Press.

McLanahan, Sara, and Gary Sandefur. 1994. *Growing Up with a Single Parent: What Hurts, What Helps.* Cambridge, Mass.: Harvard University Press.

Oreopolous, Philip, Marianne Page, and Ann Huff Stevens. Forthcoming. "The Causal Effect of Parental Education on Children's Human Capital." *Journal of Labor Economics.*

Sacerdote, Bruce. 2005. "What Happens if We Randomly Assign Children to Families?" Unpublished paper. Hanover, N.H.: Dartmouth College.

Sandefur, Gary D., Jennifer Eggerling-Boeck, and Hyunjoon Park. 2005. "Off to a Good Start? Postsecondary Education and Early Adult Life." In *On the Frontier of Adulthood: Theory, Research, and Public Policy*, edited by Richard A. Settersten Jr., Frank F. Furstenberg Jr., and Rubén G. Rumbaut. Chicago, Ill.: University of Chicago Press.

Schoeni, Robert F., and Karen E. Ross. 2005. "Material Assistance from Families During the Transition to Adulthood." In *On the Frontier of Adulthood: Theory, Research, and Public Policy*, edited by Richard A. Settersten Jr., Frank F. Furstenberg Jr., and Rubén G. Rumbaut. Chicago, Ill.: University of Chicago Press.

Settersten, Richard A., Jr., Frank F. Furstenberg Jr., and Rubén G. Rumbaut. 2005. *On the Frontier of Adulthood: Theory, Research, and Public Policy*. Chicago, Ill.: University of Chicago Press.

Solon, Gary. 1992. "Intergenerational Income Mobility in the United States." *American Economic Review* 82(3): 393–408.

———. 1999. "Intergenerational Mobility in the Labor Market." In *Handbook of Labor Economics*, Volume 3A, edited by Orley Ashenfelter and David Card. Amsterdam: North-Holland.

———. 2004. "A Model of Intergenerational Mobility Variation over Time and Place." In *Generational Income Mobility in North America and Europe*, edited by Miles Corak. Cambridge: Cambridge University Press.

Wu, Lawrence L., and Jui-Chung Allen Li. 2005. "Historical Roots of Family Diversity: Marital and Childbearing Trajectories of American Women." In *On the Frontier of Adulthood: Theory, Research, and Public Policy*, edited by Richard A. Settersten Jr., Frank F. Furstenberg Jr., and Rubén G. Rumbaut. Chicago, Ill.: University of Chicago Press.

Zimmerman, David. 1992. "Regression Toward Mediocrity in Economic Stature." *American Economic Review* 82(3): 409–29.

Chapter 11

Early Incarceration Spells and the Transition to Adulthood

STEVEN RAPHAEL

Over the past three decades, the population of U.S. prisons and jails has more than quadrupled. In 1977 roughly 500,000 people were incarcerated in the nation's prisons and jails. As of 2004 this figure was more than 2.1 million, with the lion's share of these inmates incarcerated in state and federal prisons. The risk of incarceration is especially high for minority men. Between 1974 and 2001, the proportion of U.S. adults who were either currently or previously incarcerated increased from approximately 1.2 percent to 2.7 percent. For men the proportion increased from 2.3 percent to 4.9 percent, while for African American men the figure increased from 8.7 percent to 16.6 percent (Bonczar 2003). These increases are even larger for young minority men with relatively low levels of education (Raphael 2005).

Having served time early in one's life may lengthen the time until—or indefinitely forestall—the achievement of conventional markers of adulthood. If adulthood is characterized as being law-abiding, becoming economically self-sufficient, living in a stable relationship, and perhaps having children, it is fairly easy to see how early incarceration might arrest one's development. Newly released offenders often have little savings and are barred from receiving federal housing assistance, both factors that are likely to drive them into the homes of their parents or other relatives. In addition, employers are often averse to hiring former inmates, especially for service jobs involving customer contact (Holzer, Offner, and Sorensen 2005). This employer reluctance is compounded in many states and localities by legal restrictions against hiring felons for certain occupations.[1] Moreover, offenders accumulate little non-institutionalized work experience while incarcerated. Although young men and women who enter prison are just as likely to have children as those who do not, the likelihood of ever having been married is much lower for former offenders. Former inmates also have less to offer to potential spouses, with obvious consequences for marriage prospects.

Therefore, the rising prison and jail incarceration rates over the past three decades may be an increasingly common stumbling block along the path to adulthood, especially for minority men. As the MacArthur Foundation Network on Transitions to Adulthood has found, the path to adulthood has become more protracted and circuitous in recent years for the majority of youth (Settersten, Furstenberg, and Rumbaut 2005). Families are often called on today to support their children into their early twenties as social institutions struggle to catch up to the demographic and cultural shifts. Although many middle- and upper-class families can shoulder this added expense, both in time and money, many low-income or working-class families cannot.

In this chapter, I explore the effect of having served time on conventional measures of the transition to adulthood. Using data from the 1979 National Longitudinal Survey of Youth (NLSY-79) from 1979 through 1996, I test for a connection between prior jail or prison time (measured as having been interviewed for the survey while incarcerated) and four conventional markers of adulthood: living independently from parents, marriage, employment (measured as the proportion of the survey year employed), and hourly earnings. The NLSY interviews the same set of individuals each year. In the 1979 survey, the respondents were age fourteen to twenty-two, while in 1996 they were thirty to thirty-eight. Thus, the NLSY-79 provides an ideal dataset for studying the effects of prior incarceration spells during the time period when most youth transition from adolescence to adulthood.

A simple comparison of the four measures of adulthood over time reveals large differences between youth who have ever served time and those who have not, with those who have served time performing poorly on all measures. The key question in this analysis is whether prior incarceration experience causes these differences or is simply a proxy for other factors that might influence outcomes. Although it is quite difficult to establish causality, we can make use of the longitudinal nature of the NLSY to refine the empirical estimates and strengthen the case either way. The repeated annual observations permit us to assess whether serving time increases, say, the likelihood of living with one's parents relative to this likelihood before being incarcerated and to compare the individuals who have had this experience with those who have never been to prison or jail.

Bruce Western (2002) pursues an even more stringent strategy in his analysis of incarceration and wages. Specifically, he restricts his analysis to a subsample of youth who were at very high risk of incarceration and assesses whether wages for those who were incarcerated early in their adult lives fell behind those of high-risk youths who were incarcerated later or who were never incarcerated. By limiting the study to high-risk youth, Western is able to show that it was not other factors, such as education or income, that made the difference, because all the youth, by virtue of being high-risk, shared these attributes to a certain degree. Western finds a sizable relative decline in the hourly wages of formerly incarcerated high-risk youth relative to those of youth who did not serve time.

Here I pursue both empirical strategies to assess the effects of prior incarceration spells on key transitions to adulthood. Given that nearly 90 percent of state and federal prison inmates are male, incarceration will present more of a problem with the transition to adulthood for males than females. For this reason, I focus on the effect of incarceration for men only.

To summarize the results, I find large differences between young men with and without a prison record, and those differences widen with time for all four markers of adulthood. Moreover, I find a relative erosion of outcomes that correlates with the timing of the first incarceration spell. In other words, a first-time incarceration corresponds with a worsening of the performance on the outcome analyzed relative to the performance of those who did not experience an incarceration spell. In the more stringent empirical tests that restrict the analysis sample to youth who eventually serve time (à la Western), some of the effects fade. In particular, there is no evidence of an incarceration effect on wages or the likelihood of residing with one's parents. Nonetheless, there are sizable effects of prior incarceration on marriage and annual weeks worked.

Although the impact of incarceration does not survive the most stringent empirical tests on two of the transitions analyzed, the analysis does reveal the relatively poor performance of those who serve time. Those youth involved with the criminal justice system during adolescence and early adulthood are clearly a vulnerable population.

Documenting Recent Incarceration Trends

The rising risk of incarceration since the early 1970s has hardly been evenly distributed. As noted in the introduction, young African American men are particularly susceptible. Figure 11.1 presents estimates from the U.S. Bureau of Justice Statistics (BJS), reported in Bonczar (2003), of the percentage of adults incarcerated by age between 1974 and 2001. In 1974 the percentage incarcerated was a strictly increasing function of age (reflecting the greater cumulative incarceration risk as one ages as well as the effect of sentence length on the age-specific incarceration rate). However, over the subsequent twenty-seven years, incarceration rates

Figure 11.1   Percentage Incarcerated, by Age, 1974 to 2001

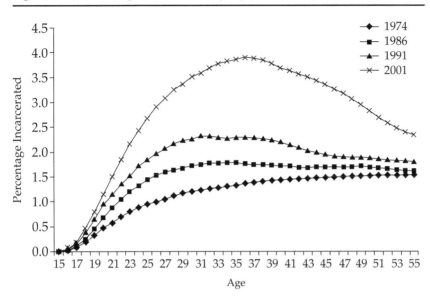

Source: Bonczar (2003).

rose disproportionately for young adults in their twenties and thirties. By 2001 the peak of the incarceration age profile occurred at age thirty-five (3.9 percent), while in previous years incarceration increased uniformly with age. There is also a large proportional difference between the incarceration rate at the peak and the rates for younger and older adults between 2001 and 1974.

Figure 11.2 presents first-time incarceration rates by age calculated by the BJS. The first-time incarceration rate nearly tripled between 1974 and 2001 for adults in their early twenties. This pattern is consistent with both a greater proportion of young adults serving time and earlier incarceration spells for those who eventually serve time.

Table 11.1 presents estimates of the proportion incarcerated by race, age, and educational attainment between 1980 and 2000.[2] The table shows that, first, although incarceration rates have increased for all groups, African American men experienced the largest absolute increase, while Hispanic men experienced the largest increase as a percentage of the 1980 level. The overall proportion incarcerated remained constant for white men between 1980 and 2000, while black men experienced a five-percentage-point increase (from 4 to 9 percent), Asian men experienced a one-percentage-point increase (from 0 to 1 percent), and Hispanic men saw a two-percentage-point increase (from 1 to 3 percent).

Figure 11.2   First-Time Incarceration Rates, by Age, 1974 to 2001

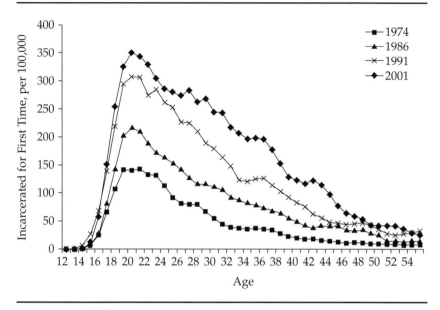

Source: Bonczar (2003).

Second, table 11.1 shows a strong relationship between education and incarceration, with an apparent interaction between education and race. For all racial and ethnic groups, less-educated men are considerably more likely to be incarcerated than more-educated men, but less-educated black men have the highest incarceration rates. Between 1980 and 2000, the proportion incarcerated among black high school dropouts more than tripled, from 6 to 21 percent. In addition, within education groups, incarceration rates peak for adults in their late twenties and early thirties (comparable to the patterns presented in figure 11.1).

Gauging the population of former prison inmates is more difficult than measuring current incarceration rates owing to the fact that none of the major household surveys in the United States asks respondents whether they have served time. Using an indirect method that combines population data, birth cohort estimates of the likelihood of entering prison for the first time at each age, and cohort- and age-specific mortality rates (Bonczar 2003), the BJS estimates that in addition to the 1.3 million current inmates in 2001, 4.3 million non-institutionalized persons had served a prison term in the past.[3] Combined, current and former prison inmates accounted for 4.9 percent of the adult male population in 2001.

Table 11.1 Proportion of Men Age Eighteen to Fifty-five Incarcerated, by Race-Ethnicity, Age, and Educational Attainment

	White		Black		Asian		Hispanic	
	1980	2000	1980	2000	1980	2000	1980	2000
All Men	0.01	0.01	0.04	0.09	0.00	0.01	0.01	0.03
Less than high school	0.02	0.05	0.06	0.21	0.01	0.02	0.02	0.04
Eighteen to twenty-five	0.03	0.04	0.08	0.22	0.02	0.04	0.03	0.04
Twenty-six to thirty-five	0.03	0.07	0.08	0.33	0.01	0.03	0.02	0.04
Thirty-six to forty-five	0.02	0.05	0.03	0.19	0.00	0.01	0.01	0.04
Forty-six to fifty-five	0.01	0.03	0.02	0.08	0.00	0.01	0.01	0.02
High school graduate	0.01	0.02	0.03	0.09	0.01	0.01	0.01	0.03
Eighteen to twenty-five	0.01	0.02	0.03	0.09	0.01	0.01	0.01	0.03
Twenty-six to thirty-five	0.01	0.02	0.04	0.12	0.01	0.02	0.01	0.04
Thirty-six to forty-five	0.00	0.02	0.02	0.09	0.00	0.01	0.01	0.03
Forty-six to fifty-five	0.00	0.01	0.01	0.04	0.00	0.01	0.01	0.02
More than high school	0.00	0.01	0.02	0.04	0.00	0.00	0.01	0.02
Eighteen to twenty-five	0.00	0.01	0.02	0.03	0.00	0.00	0.01	0.01
Twenty-six to thirty-five	0.00	0.01	0.03	0.05	0.00	0.00	0.01	0.02
Thirty-six to forty-five	0.00	0.01	0.01	0.05	0.00	0.00	0.01	0.02
Forty-six to fifty-five	0.00	0.00	0.01	0.03	0.00	0.00	0.00	0.01

Note: Figures tabulated from the 1980 and 2000 5 percent PUMS of the decennial Census of Population and Housing.

Of course, there are again large differences by race and ethnicity. The same set of estimates indicate that 2.6 percent of non-Hispanic white males, 16.6 percent of non-Hispanic black males, and 7.7 percent of Hispanic males have served prison time (figures that are roughly double the current institutionalization rates listed in table 11.1). The comparable figures for whites, blacks, and Hispanics for 1974 were 1.4, 8.7, and 2.3 percent, respectively.

The BJS also uses this method to calculate lifetime probabilities of entering either the state or federal prison system. Given that the risk of incarceration has increased over the past three decades, lifetime probabilities should exceed the current proportion of a specific population that is either currently incarcerated or formerly incarcerated.[4] These estimates indicate that a white male born in 1974 faced a 2.2 percent lifetime likelihood of going to prison. For those born in 2001, the risk had increased to 5.9 percent. For black males, this likelihood had increased from 13.2 percent to 32.2 percent, while for Hispanics the likelihood had increased from 4 percent to 17.2 percent.

There are also large differences within racial groups between less-educated and more-educated men and between groups of men stratified by age, which supports the recent work of Lance Lochner and Enrico Moretti (2004), who find a causal effect of education on the likelihood of going to prison. Although the BJS provides race-specific estimates of the proportion that have ever served time by age, there are no estimates of how this group varies by level of education. Moreover, the results presented earlier indicate that education is a stronger predictor of current incarceration than age; education is therefore also likely to be more strongly associated with ever having served time.

I am able to fill this gap to a certain degree with administrative prison data from California. Using administrative records on all prison terms served during the 1990s in a California state prison, I first calculate an unduplicated count of prisoners entering the system during the 1990s by race and by how old each prisoner would be in 2000.[5] I then use the 1997 Survey of Inmates in State and Federal Correction Facilities to estimate the distribution of inmates by age-education within racial and ethnic groups. I use these distribution estimates to allocate the number of unduplicated prisoners within each age-race group across education groups.[6] Dividing these counts by the estimated 2000 California population (institutional plus non-institutional) within each age-race-education group yields estimates of the proportion of males in each group serving a prison term during the 1990s.

Table 11.2 presents these results. The first column presents national estimates of the proportion who ever served time by race-ethnicity and age from the BJS. The second column presents comparable estimates of the proportion serving time in California. The final four columns present

Table 11.2   Bureau of Justice Statistics Estimates of the Proportion of the Male Population Who Ever Served Time in a State or Federal Prison, by Race-Ethnicity and Age, and California Department of Corrections Estimates of the Proportion Who Ever Served Time in a California State Prison During the 1990s, by Race, Age, and Educational Attainment

	Estimates for the Nation[a]	Estimates for California from CDC Administrative Records				
		All[b]	High School Dropouts[c]	High School Graduates[c]	College[c]	College or More[c]
Non-Hispanic white males						
Eighteen to twenty-four	0.01	0.01	0.03	0.00	0.00	0.00
Twenty-five to thirty-four	0.03	0.03	0.31	0.03	0.01	0.00
Thirty-five to forty-four	0.04	0.03	0.30	0.04	0.02	0.01
Forty-five to fifty-four	0.03	0.02	0.17	0.02	0.01	0.01
Fifty-five to sixty-five	0.03	0.01	0.04	0.01	0.00	0.00
Non-Hispanic black males						
Eighteen to twenty-four	0.09	0.04	0.19	0.02	0.01	0.00
Twenty-five to thirty-four	0.20	0.19	1.14	0.15	0.05	0.03
Thirty-five to forty-four	0.22	0.19	1.23	0.16	0.07	0.04
Forty-five to fifty-four	0.18	0.15	0.90	0.12	0.06	0.05
Fifty-five to sixty-five	0.13	0.05	0.18	0.04	0.01	0.02
Hispanic males						
Eighteen to twenty-four	0.04	0.01	0.02	0.00	0.00	0.00
Twenty-five to thirty-four	0.09	0.05	0.08	0.03	0.02	0.02
Thirty-five to forty-four	0.10	0.05	0.07	0.04	0.02	0.03
Forty-five to fifty-four	0.10	0.03	0.04	0.03	0.02	0.03
Fifty-five to sixty-five	0.07	0.01	0.02	0.02	0.01	0.01

a. Estimates drawn from Bonczar (2003, table 7).
b. Estimates calculated as follows: The administrative term-records for all terms served in California were sorted by a CDC internal ID number. The first term for each unique ID was selected out to construct a sample of unduplicated prisoners. For each prisoner, I calculate how old the prisoner would be in the year 2000. I then calculate counts of prisoners by age and race for 2000. Using the 2000 1 percent PUMS, I then estimate the California population size for each age-race cell listed in the table. The figures in the table are the ratio of the prisoner counts to the 2000 census population estimate for each cell.
c. Estimates calculated as follows: I first calculate the counts of unduplicated prisoners by age and race following the procedures outlined in note b. I then use data from the 1997 Survey of Inmates in State and Federal Corrections Facilities to estimate the educational attainment of prison inmates in the United States by race-ethnicity and age. I use these estimates to allocate the number of unduplicated prisoners within each age-race cell across the four educational groups. (The CDC administrative data do not contain information on educational attainment.) I then use the 2000 1 percent PUMS to estimate the California population size of each age-race-education cell in the table. The figures in the table are the ratio of the prisoner counts hypothetically allocated across education groups to the 2000 census population estimate for each cell.

estimates by level of education that allot prisoners within race-age groups across education groups according to the estimated educational distributions of inmates during the late 1990s.

The tabulations by age indicate that the California and BJS estimates are fairly similar for males between age eighteen and fifty-four. For older males, the California estimates indicate that a smaller proportion had ever served time. This is sensible considering that the California administrative records cover only the 1990s, and that former prisoners over age fifty-four in 2000 were likely to have served time prior to the 1990s. Both sets of estimates indicate that the proportion who ever served time increases with age through the late thirties and early forties and then declines. Black men between age twenty-five and forty-four have the highest rates of current or previous incarceration (roughly one-fifth of this group, using both the California and BJS estimates).

The estimates by race, age, and education reveal dramatic differences. For black high school dropouts between the ages of twenty-five and forty-four, the number of prisoners serving time during the previous decade exceeds census population counts (that is, the ratio is greater than one).[7] Ninety percent of black high school dropouts between ages forty-five and fifty-four are estimated to have served a prison term during the past decade. These figures suggest that for black California high school dropouts, serving time in prison is practically a certainty.

Although ratios in excess of one are clearly too large, Becky Pettit and Bruce Western (2004) estimate that for all African American men born between 1965 and 1969, the portion who had been to prison by 1999 was 20.5 percent overall, 30.2 percent for black men without a college degree, and 58.9 percent for black men without a high school degree. Although their estimates are lower than mine, Petit and Western still find that, by their thirties, black high school dropouts are more likely than not to have served time.

The proportion of blacks who have served prison time in the past decade is considerably lower for those with more education, although the figures for black high school graduates are still quite high (between 12 and 16 percent). By contrast, the comparable fractions of whites and Latinos are smaller for all comparisons.

Incarceration and the Transition to Adulthood

Conventional notions of adulthood generally involve being economically independent, law-abiding, and responsible. With regards to personal responsibility, it is often assumed that functional adults are in long-term relationships, that they are likely to be married, and, if they become parents, that they provide economically and emotionally for their children. That ex-inmates are delayed in adult transitions (as defined here) is not surprising. The extent to which having served time per se contributes to such arrested development, however, is an open question.

Perhaps the most direct avenue by which prior incarceration may affect the transition to adulthood is via employment prospects. Time in prison may impede an ex-offender's ability to secure employment as well as the quality of employment through a number of avenues. To start, former inmates are often legally barred from holding certain jobs under federal and state law and sometimes under local ordinances (Holzer, Raphael, and Stoll 2004). Examples are private unarmed security guards in many states (Emsellem 2005), jobs involving children and other vulnerable populations (Holzer, Raphael, and Stoll 2004), and trucking jobs involving hazardous materials (Kurlychek, Brame, and Bushway 2006). Although the fraction of jobs that explicitly bar convicted felons is small, such restrictions clearly limit the opportunity set faced by former inmates.

Moreover, many inmates fail to accumulate non-institutionalized work experience while incarcerated. Although the typical inmate in the United States serves two years, the majority of inmates serve multiple prison terms on a single conviction and often serve time on multiple convictions. Thus, the prison experience of young offenders is likely to be characterized by cycling in and out of prison over a fairly lengthy period of time.[8] Harry Holzer, Steven Raphael, and Michael Stoll (2004, 2006) show that employers of low- and semiskilled workers are quite reluctant to hire ex-offenders, and they are increasingly using formal screening mechanisms (checking criminal history records) and informal mechanisms (discriminating against suspected ex-offenders) in their hiring decisions. Devah Pager (2003) and Pager and Bruce Western (2005) show that job applicants with prior prison time, especially black males, are considerably less likely to receive callbacks from a first interview. As a result, both employment and wages are strongly affected by incarceration (Holzer, Offner, and Sorensen 2005; Western 2002).

The connections between incarceration and other markers of the transition to adulthood are likely to be mediated in part by these economic prospects. Being unable to procure steady and well-paying employment certainly inhibits economic independence and may lead former inmates to rely more heavily on family and friends. Moreover, having diminished employment prospects is likely to diminish the marriage prospects of former inmates. To be sure, incarceration may influence these transitions through other avenues. To the extent that serving time engenders antisocial attitudes, inhibits emotional development, and fosters violent tendencies, former inmates are likely to have difficulty negotiating non-institutionalized society (above and beyond the difficulty they may have experienced prior to becoming an ex-felon). Such traits may not only estrange former inmates from their families but also diminish their ability to function independently. In addition, these emotional traits clearly do not enhance the attractiveness of ex-offenders as potential mates.

There is ample evidence in the NLSY-79 that young men who eventually serve time perform poorly on several conventional measures of adulthood. These basic differences are displayed in figures 11.3 to 11.6. The figures compare average outcomes for young men from the NLSY as they age from eighteen to thirty-two. One group was never interviewed in prison or jail, and the other was. I looked at four outcomes: whether the young man still resides with his parents, whether he has ever been married, average annual weeks worked, and the average log hourly wage.[9]

Figure 11.3 shows that although the fraction of young men residing with their parents is initially lower for those who eventually serve time, this proportion increases during their early and late twenties relative to the fraction of youth who have not served time and live with their parents. This disparity rises to a high of ten percentage points by age twenty-nine and then declines.

Figure 11.3   Proportion of NLSY-79 Men Age Eighteen to Thirty-two Living with Their Parents, by Whether They Have Ever Been Interviewed in Jail or Prison

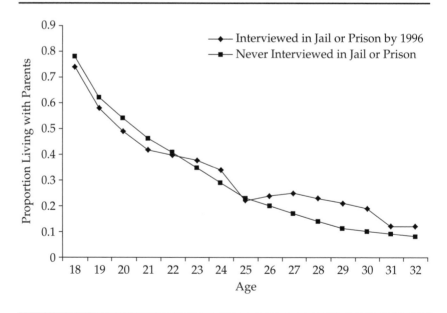

Source: Author's tabulations of data from the National Longitudinal Survey of Youth 1979.

Figure 11.4   Proportion of NLSY-79 Men Age Eighteen to Thirty-two Who Have Never Been Married, by Whether They Have Ever Been Interviewed in Jail or Prison

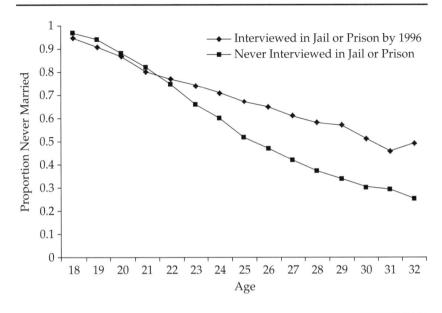

Source: Author's tabulations of data from the National Longitudinal Survey of Youth 1979.

Figure 11.4 shows trends in marriage. Again, men who serve time and those who do not have similar histories early on, yet large differences emerge and widen quickly. By age thirty-two, men who have served time are twenty-four percentage points more likely to have never married than men who have not served time.

For the two measures of labor market performance, those who eventually serve time perform poorly throughout the time span, with notable disparities from the very beginning. Figure 11.5 shows that the disparity in average weeks worked widens from eleven weeks at age eighteen to nearly twenty weeks by age thirty-two. The initial disparity in hourly wages is considerably smaller yet widens considerably with time: from 0.05 at age eighteen to 0.51 by age thirty-two. Whether these relatively inferior outcomes are a direct function of having served time is an open question to which I now turn.

The Direct Role of Prison in the Transition to Adulthood

The figures above clearly document that ex-inmates perform poorly on each of the displayed outcomes. However, the differences may be driven

Figure 11.5   Average Annual Weeks Worked Among NLSY-79 Men Age Eighteen to Thirty-two, by Whether They Have Ever Been Interviewed in Jail or Prison

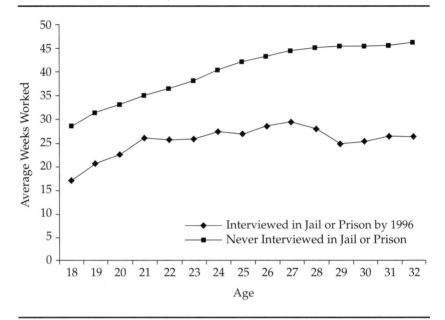

Source: Author's tabulations of data from the National Longitudinal Survey of Youth 1979.

by factors other than incarceration. For example, prolonged involvement in criminal activity will increase both the likelihood of going to prison as well as the likelihood of failing to meet these conventional markers of adulthood. Moreover, the widening of these differences may not correspond with the timing of the first incarceration of those who eventually go to prison. In other words, the time trends in the figure may simply reflect a widening of these differences that has nothing to do with going to prison.[10]

I therefore created a strategy for obtaining more precise estimates of the effect of a prison record on the four markers of adulthood. Following closely the strategy employed by Western (2002), I exploit the panel aspects of the NLSY-79 to assess whether the timing of the incarceration spells corresponds with a departure in the men's average outcomes compared with those who do not serve time. In particular, I assess whether going to prison corresponds in time with a worsening in the average performance on each of these outcomes relative to those men who have not been to prison. See the appendix for method and details.

Figure 11.6   Average Log Hourly Wages Among NLSY-79 Men Age Eighteen to Thirty-two, by Whether They Have Ever Been Interviewed in Jail or Prison

Source: Author's tabulations of data from the National Longitudinal Survey of Youth 1979.

With this method, I am able to capture the person's "fixed effects," adjusting for all personal characteristics that are immutable. I also am able to adjust any common year-to-year changes in conditions that affect the outcomes of interest. In other words, the results show the relative pre-post incarceration change in the outcomes after netting out the effect of being currently incarcerated, the common year effects, and observable time-varying personal characteristics. Thus, the results show whether any relative erosion of the transition markers of living with parents, marriage, wages, and earnings is directly related to the first incarceration of ex-offenders.

I estimate the effects for two groups. The first identifies the effect of having ever been to prison by comparing the pre-post incarceration change in outcomes for those who have and have not been to prison. The second, and more stringent, test restricts the sample, following Western (2002), to youth who are at a high risk of offending. In this case, the high-risk group is the group of those youth who eventually serve time. With this restricted sample, I compare the outcomes for those who served time earlier with those who serve time later in life.

Since many survey respondents in the NLSY have missing observations for specific individual years, I present parallel results throughout that restrict the sample to youth for whom there are complete observations for each year between ages eighteen and thirty-one; I also present results using an unrestricted, yet unbalanced panel. A detailed discussion of the data source and the sample restrictions imposed is presented in the appendix.

Effects of Incarceration on Living Independently

Table 11.3 presents the effects of incarceration on the probability of living with parents. The first specification includes an indicator for ever having been to prison, being employed, being currently incarcerated, dummy variables for educational attainment and for race-ethnicity (black or Hispanic), a third-order age polynomial fully interacted with the race-ethnicity indicators, controls for region of residence and residence in a rural, urban, or suburban neighborhood, and a full set of year fixed effects. The second specification adds a complete set of person-specific fixed effects. Models 1 and 2 use all male observations in the NLSY with complete data, necessarily resulting in an unbalanced panel. Model 3 reestimates the fixed-effect specification, restricting the sample to men with complete information in each sample year. Finally, the fourth model restricts the sample to all male youth who eventually served prison time by 1996. Given the small sample used to estimate this final model, I do not present estimates for the eventually incarcerated sample restricted to a balanced panel.

The first three models suggest that having served time—but not currently serving time—increases the probability of residing with one's parents. Model 1, which omits individual fixed effects, shows that men who have served time are roughly six percentage points more likely to reside with their parents compared to men who have not, after controlling for the other covariates in the model. Interestingly, adding person fixed effects more than doubles the size of this estimate to thirteen percentage points. The sensitivity of this estimate to the inclusion of person fixed effects suggests that there are unobserved personal traits that are more prevalent among male youth who serve time and that these traits lower the likelihood of living with parents. For example, such youth may be more likely to come from disharmonious families (driven by either parental or youth behavior) or from families with limited resources. Restricting the sample to a balanced panel, the fixed-effects model yields a comparable estimate of sixteen percentage points.

Among the restricted sample of those who eventually serve time, there is little evidence that having ever served time has any impact on living with parents. Although this result may be driven in part by measurement error in the incarceration variable,[11] this more restrictive sam-

Table 11.3   Linear Probability Models of the Likelihood of Residing with One's Parents as a Function of Having Ever Been Interviewed in Jail or Prison

	(1)	(2)	(3)	(4)
Ever been to prison	0.059	0.130	0.161	−0.009
	(0.010)	(0.015)	(0.020)	(0.019)
Employed	−0.010	0.011	0.027	−0.061
	(0.004)	(0.004)	(0.006)	(0.012)
Currently incarcerated	−0.426	−0.472	−0.505	−0.468
	(0.015)	(0.014)	(0.021)	(0.016)
Less than high school	0.122	−0.088	−0.083	−0.149
	(0.006)	(0.013)	(0.018)	(0.104)
High school graduate	0.082	−0.169	−0.168	−0.097
	(0.005)	(0.010)	(0.013)	(0.101)
Some college	0.035	−0.134	−0.134	−0.067
	(0.006)	(0.007)	(0.010)	(0.095)
Person fixed effects	No	Yes	Yes	Yes
Balanced panel	No	No	Yes	No
Sample restricted to former inmates	No	No	No	Yes
Number of observations	64,220	64,220	33,813	5,961

Source: Models estimated using data samples drawn from the National Longitudinal Survey of Youth 1979.
Notes: Standard errors are in parentheses. Along with the explanatory variables listed, each model includes dummy variables for black and Hispanic, a third-order polynomial in age and interactions between the age variables and the race dummies, controls for region of residence in the United States, controls for whether the person resides in a rural, urban, or suburban area, and a full set of year fixed effects.

ple estimates the incarceration trends by comparing the paths of those incarcerated early with the paths of the youth who are perhaps most like themselves (in that they eventually serve time as well). For this reason, I view the results from this final specification as the most rigorous, and thus preferred, test for an incarceration effect.

Effects on Marriage

Table 11.4 presents a set of comparable linear probability models assessing the effects of having served time on marriage. The model specifications are identical to those in table 11.3 with one exception. Here I add an explanatory variable indicating whether the person has ever had a child, on the presumption that having a child with someone may have an independent effect on the likelihood of being currently or previously married.[12]

The results indicate that a prison record increases the likelihood of never having been married. For the first three specifications, those young men who have been incarcerated are roughly fourteen percentage points

Table 11.4   Linear Probability Models of the Likelihood of Having Never Been Married as a Function of Having Ever Been Interviewed in Jail or Prison

	(1)	(2)	(3)	(4)
Ever been to prison	0.147	0.138	0.140	0.062
	(0.008)	(0.011)	(0.015)	(0.012)
Ever had children	-0.469	-0.297	-0.308	-0.192
	(0.003)	(0.004)	(0.005)	(0.012)
Employed	-0.051	0.000	-0.002	-0.024
	(0.003)	(0.003)	(0.004)	(0.008)
Currently incarcerated	0.040	0.007	0.011	0.012
	(0.013)	(0.011)	(0.015)	(0.010)
Less than high school	0.001	0.004	-0.029	0.011
	(0.006)	(0.010)	(0.013)	(0.069)
High school graduate	-0.008	0.034	0.014	0.055
	(0.005)	(0.008)	(0.010)	(0.067)
Some college	0.014	0.046	0.023	-0.038
	(0.005)	(0.006)	(0.008)	(0.064)
Person fixed effects	No	Yes	Yes	Yes
Balanced panel	No	No	Yes	No
Sample restricted to former inmates	No	No	No	Yes
Number of observations	64,211	64,211	33,811	5,959

Source: Models estimated using data samples from the National Longitudinal Survey of Youth 1979.
Notes: Standard errors are in parentheses. Along with the explanatory variables listed, each model includes dummy variables for black and Hispanic, a third-order polynomial in age and interactions between the age variables and the race dummies, controls for region of residence in the United States, controls for whether the person resides in a rural, urban, or suburban area, and a full set of year fixed effects.

more likely to have never been married relative to those with no prison history. This result is not affected by including individual fixed effects or by restricting the sample (to the balanced panel). Restricting the sample to those who have served time lessens the effect, from fourteen percentage points to six percentage points. Here, however, this effect is statistically significant at the 1 percent level of confidence—meaning that there is only a 1 percent chance that the effect was caused by chance.

Effects on Employment and Wages

Tables 11.5 and 11.6 present results for two labor markets outcomes: annual weeks worked and hourly wages. Regarding the weeks worked models in table 11.5, the specifications are comparable to those in tables 11.3 and 11.4, although the dummy variables indicating being employed or ever having had children are dropped. I find a consistent negative effect of having served time on annual weeks worked. The simple ordinary

Table 11.5   Regression Models of the Annual Number of Weeks Worked as a
Function of Having Ever Been Interviewed in Jail or Prison

	(1)	(2)	(3)	(4)
Ever been to prison	−13.813	−9.470	−10.642	−6.265
	(0.405)	(0.556)	(0.764)	(0.844)
Enrolled in school	−6.725	−5.255	−5.305	−4.928
	(0.215)	(0.215)	(0.291)	(0.988)
Currently incarcerated	−9.814	−4.559	−3.783	−5.536
	(0.606)	(0.549)	(0.776)	(0.675)
Less than high school	−3.775	−3.358	−3.451	−4.098
	(0.259)	(0.564)	(0.736)	(4.597)
High school graduate	−1.115	−3.725	−3.524	−3.611
	(0.233)	(0.431)	(0.555)	(4.482)
Some college	−0.914	−4.029	−3.763	−1.808
	(0.253)	(0.329)	(0.440)	(4.233)
Person fixed effects	No	Yes	Yes	Yes
Balanced panel	No	No	Yes	No
Sample restricted to former inmates	No	No	No	Yes
Number of observations	64,221	64,221	33,814	5,961

Source: Models estimated using data samples drawn from the National Longitudinal Survey of Youth 1979.
Notes: Standard errors are in parentheses. Along with the explanatory variables listed, each model includes dummy variables for black and Hispanic, a third-order polynomial in age and interactions between the age variables and the race dummies, controls for region of residence in the United States, controls for whether the person resides in a rural, urban, or suburban area, and a full set of year fixed effects.

least squares (OLS) specification in model 1 indicates that those who have been to prison work fourteen fewer weeks per year than those who have not. Adding individual fixed effects to this model reduces this estimate to between 9.4 and 10.6 weeks, indicating that personal characteristics account for some of the effect. For the fixed-effects model using the sample of men who eventually go to prison, a prior incarceration spell reduces annual weeks worked by roughly six weeks per year. All of these point estimates are statistically significant at the 1 percent level. Note further that these effects are net of any effect of being in prison when interviewed on the previous year's weeks worked.

Finally, table 11.6 presents results on wages. By construction, table 11.6 is estimated using only those observations where the individual is employed at some point during the year and where an hourly wage is reported. The results for males indicate large negative effects of having served time on hourly wages in the first three specifications (ranging from 17 to 23 percent). These results are nearly identical to those presented in Western (2002), although the model specifications differ somewhat. There is no measurable effect in the final specification, in which the

Table 11.6   Regression Models of the Hourly Log Earnings of the Employed as a Function of Having Ever Been Interviewed in Jail or Prison

	(1)	(2)	(3)	(4)
Ever been to prison	−0.217	−0.148	−0.161	−0.026
	(0.012)	(0.021)	(0.028)	(0.029)
Less than high school	−0.373	−0.422	−0.419	−0.010
	(0.008)	(0.021)	(0.026)	(0.177)
High school graduate	−0.244	−0.420	−0.412	−0.053
	(0.007)	(0.016)	(0.019)	(0.172)
Some college	−0.223	−0.372	−0.356	−0.036
	(0.008)	(0.011)	(0.014)	(0.156)
Person fixed effects	No	Yes	Yes	Yes
Balanced panel	No	No	Yes	No
Sample restricted to former inmates	No	No	No	Yes
Number of observations	51,874	51,874	27,482	3,904

Source: Models estimated using data samples drawn from the National Longitudinal Survey of Youth 1979.
Notes: Standard errors are in parentheses. Along with the explanatory variables listed, each model includes dummy variables for black and Hispanic, a third-order polynomial in age and interactions between the age variables and the race dummies, controls for region of residence in the United States, controls for whether the person resides in a rural, urban, or suburban area, and a full set of year fixed effects.

sample is restricted to those who have served time. This contrasts with Western's findings, although his restricted sample is somewhat more inclusive than the one that I employ here.[13]

Does Timing of First Incarceration Matter?

The results thus far suggest that those who serve time perform poorly on the four transition markers, and that the timing of initial incarceration often corresponds to a permanent deterioration in this relative performance. Going beyond these pooled results, we might surmise that the impact of becoming an ex-offender varies by when one first goes to prison. For example, the period of early adulthood (say, between ages eighteen and twenty-five) may be a particularly crucial time period when ties to the labor market and a credit history are established, emotional relationships mature, and independence from parents and other relatives is established. Given the amount of development occurring at this time, we might suspect that a prison spell during this crucial time has particularly severe consequences.

Alternatively, potential employers or spouses may interpret an early prison spell as a youthful indiscretion unlikely to be repeated. In contrast, a first prison spell served after the age of twenty-five, when many of one's contemporaries have successfully negotiated many traditional markers of adulthood, may be interpreted as signaling some permanent personal deficiencies.

I have explored whether the model results differ when separate models are estimated for older and younger adults. In particular, I have estimated separate models for males between ages eighteen and twenty-five and for those between ages twenty-six and thirty-two. Although there is some evidence of a larger and more robust effect of becoming an ex-offender early in life on the likelihood of living with one's parents and on marriage prospects, these results are generally not statistically distinguishable across subsamples.[14]

Conclusion: Arrested Development

The findings clearly demonstrate that male youth who serve time in prison perform poorly on most conventional markers of the transition to adulthood. They are less likely to be married and more likely to reside with their parents, work less per year, and earn less when they do work. In addition, previous work on recidivism (Raphael and Weiman 2005) and life-course criminal activity (Sampson and Laub 2005) finds that many of these youth persist in criminal activity well into early adulthood. Regardless of whether prison exerts a causal influence on these outcomes, the data reveal a population of mostly young minority men who fail to advance in a timely manner toward mature and productive adult roles. Moreover, given that current lifetime incarceration probabilities are at historic highs, the size of the vulnerable population is much larger today than in the past and comprises sizable proportions of certain subgroups of U.S. males.

Beyond these descriptive patterns, which basically demonstrate associations, I also find evidence that the effects of serving time on several of the outcomes are likely to be causal. The positive estimated effects of prior prison time on the likelihood of never being married and employment stability survive quite stringent empirical tests. There is also some mixed evidence that serving time increases the likelihood that young adults will continue to reside with their parents and that serving time also diminishes hourly earnings, though these results are not as robust. To be sure, the fixed-effects models estimated here can never establish with certainty the presence of a causal effect of prior prison spells on these outcomes. Nonetheless, the strong partial correlation between serving time and the transition outcomes using the thin, within-person slices of variation in the data suggest strong empirical relationshi˷s that merit further research attention and perhaps attention from policym˷kers interested in the costs (both explicit and collateral) and benefits of incarceration.

Although one potential implication of this research is that reducing incarceration rates would alleviate some of the disparities documented here, such arguments have historically had little influence on sentencing and parole policies. However, the research does suggest a potentially important role for workforce development activities and basic educational programs in prisons. Current participation in prison education programs is quite low, especially considering the low levels of educational attainment among inmates (Raphael and Stoll 2004). Moreover, participation in substance abuse programs and reentry programs designed for soon-to-be-released inmates is far from universal, despite nearly universal need within the prison population (Petersilia 2003). Barring drastic changes in sentencing and parole policies, the reentry efforts of state corrections departments will be increasingly important in facilitating the transition of former offenders into society and into more productive adult lives. More solid evaluation research on which efforts work and which do not is clearly needed.

Appendix: Identifying the Effect of Having Served Time on Adulthood Transitions

Empirical Strategy and Description of the Data

Define the variable $Ever_{it}$ as a dummy variable equal to one if person i in year t has ever been to prison or jail and the variable $Prison_{it}$ as a dummy variable indicating that person i is incarcerated in year t. My estimates of the effect of being an ex-offender on the four transition outcomes derive from various estimates of the equation

$$Outcome_{it} = \alpha_i + \beta_t + \delta Ever_{it} + \lambda Prison_{it} + \Gamma'X_{it} + \varepsilon_{it}, \qquad (11A.1)$$

where $Outcome_{it}$ stands for one of the four transition outcomes (living with parents, never married, annual weeks worked, or the log of hourly wages), α_i captures person-specific fixed effects that adjust for all personal characteristics that are immutable with an impact on the outcome that is constant through time, β_t indicates a complete set of year fixed effects that adjust for any common year-to-year changes in conditions that affect the outcome of interest, X_{it} is a column vector of observable time-varying determinants of the outcome, Γ' is a conforming row vector of coefficient parameters to be estimated, δ and λ are additional parameters, and ε_{it} is a mean-zero error term.

The estimates of the effect of having ever been to prison on outcomes as estimated in equation 11A.1 should be interpreted conceptually in the following manner. The parameter δ represents the relative pre-post incarceration change in the outcome of interest after netting out the effect of being currently incarcerated, the common year effects estimated with all observations (those who serve time and those who do not), and the ef-

fects of observable time-varying covariates. Thus, the fixed-effects specification requires that any relative erosion of the outcome for ex-offenders
correspond in time with their first incarceration in order to register any
measurable effect of being an ex-inmate on the transition variables.

I estimate equation 11A.1 for each of the transition outcomes using alternative sample specifications. I first estimate the equation using all observations in the panel dataset. This inclusive sample identifies the effect
of ever having been to prison by comparing the pre-post incarceration
change in outcomes for those who have been to prison to the time path
of the outcome in question for all youth who have not been to prison.

A more stringent test for an effect of having served time would restrict
the sample to youth who are at a high risk of offending. Following Western (2002), I pursue a similar strategy and restrict the sample to those
youth who eventually serve time. Using this restricted sample, the effect
δ is identified by comparing the outcome paths for those who serve time
earlier to those who serve time later.

Table 11A.1 presents tabulations of the proportion of NLSY-79 male
respondents who had been interviewed in prison or jail by the 1996 interview. The table shows the proportion who had ever been incarcerated
by race-ethnicity and by level of education by the end of the panel. Not
surprisingly, the table shows the highest prevalence of a past incarceration among the least educated and among minorities.

Data and Restrictions

The data for this project come from the NLSY-79, a panel dataset com-
mencing in 1979, with annual follow-ups through 1994 and biannual follow-ups thereafter. Youth in the NLSY-79 were age fourteen to twenty-
two at the start of the panel. The initial sampling frame involved three
sampling strata: a main, nationally representative sample of youth
within the starting age range (age fourteen to twenty-two), a subsample
of youth from low-socioeconomic-status and minority households, and a

Table 11A.1 Proportion of NLSY-79 Male Respondents Who Have Ever Been
Interviewed in Jail or Prison by 1996, by Race-Ethnicity and
Educational Attainment in 1996

	Less Than High School	High School Graduate	Some College	College Graduate
Black	0.33	0.20	0.11	0.01
Hispanic	0.18	0.10	0.06	0.01
Not black or Hispanic	0.12	0.05	0.04	0.00

Source: Tabulated from the NLSY-79 using all interview waves from 1979 to 1996.
Notes: The sample excludes the military subsamples and employs the 1996 sample weights.

military subsample that was not followed beyond the initial years of the panel.

I restrict the analysis to the first two strata and employ the provided sample weights throughout. I analyze the annual waves between 1979 and 1994 as well as the first biannual follow-up in 1996. To focus on the effect of adult incarceration, I restrict the sample to observations where the surveyed youth are between eighteen and thirty-one years of age. Given the initial age range of the panel, this age restriction necessarily creates an unbalanced panel, since youth who were over eighteen in 1979 will have missing observations by design. Moreover, there are many individuals who were not interviewed in all years. To assess whether the estimation results are sensitive to this aspect of the analysis, I present parallel results throughout that restrict the sample to youth for whom there are complete observations for each year between ages eighteen and thirty-one, as well as results using an unrestricted, yet unbalanced panel.

At each interview, the NLSY-79 interviewer asks about the respondent's current residence. Among the possible answers to this question are residence in prison or jail at the time of the interview. I use this variable to construct the indicator of current incarceration in any given year and to construct the variable indicating the youth has been incarcerated at some time in the past.

To be sure, this measure of incarceration is imperfect and may be biased downward by the periodicity of measurement and biased upward by the inclusion of jail in the definition. Regarding the first source of bias, an individual is sentenced to state or federal prison having been convicted of a felony that carries a prison sentence of at least one year. Thus, assuming that individuals sentenced to at least a year serve at least a year, annual interviews with a marker for being interviewed in prison or jail should capture all first-time incarcerations. However, many inmates serve second or higher terms in prison on a given court commitment, usually for violating the conditions of their parole, and time served on these subsequent parole violations is often less than a year (Raphael 2005). Moreover, those youth sentenced to a year or more who are paroled early (for good behavior, for example) may also be missed. Thus, the annual interview is likely to miss some prison terms served by NLSY-79 youth.

On the other hand, the possibility of being interviewed in jail will overstate prior prison incarceration rates. Offenders are held in jail for minor offenses while awaiting adjudication of a charge or while serving a sentence of less than a year. To the extent that the NLSY-79 is interviewing respondents in jail who are being temporarily held for minor infractions, my measure of prior incarceration will be biased upward.

The proportion of youth incarcerated by 1996 in the NLSY-79 is somewhat higher than what we would expect from the lifetime risk of incarceration figures tabulated by the BJS for this particular age cohort. For example, by 1996, when respondents were between thirty and thirty-eight years of age, roughly 6 percent of males and 1 percent of females had been interviewed in prison. Both figures are slightly higher than the proportions of all men and women who were either currently incarcerated or had ever been incarcerated in the United States in 2001. By race and ethnicity, roughly 10 percent of male Hispanic respondents, 18 percent of male black respondents, and 4 percent of male white respondents had been interviewed in prison or jail by 1996. Again, these numbers are just slightly higher than the proportion ever incarcerated in 2001.

Table 11A.1 presents more detailed tabulations of the proportion of NLSY-79 male respondents who were interviewed in prison or jail by the 1996 interview. The table shows the proportion ever incarcerated by race-ethnicity and by level of educational attainment by the end of the panel. Not surprisingly, the table shows the highest prevalence of a past incarceration among the least educated and among minorities. While these figures are, again, slightly higher than what we might expect for this particular age cohort, the figures are clearly in the ballpark of the estimates presented by the BJS.

I thank Sheldon Danziger, Cecilia Rouse, and the participants in the January 2006 conference on "The Economics of the Transition to Adulthood" for their valuable input.

Notes

1. For example, Megan Kurlychek, Robert Brame, and Shawn Bushway (2006) note that felons are disqualified from unarmed private security jobs in twenty-four states.

2. I calculate these figures with data from the 5 percent public use microdata samples (PUMS) from the decennial Census of Population and Housing, which enumerates both the institutionalized and non-institutionalized population. The PUMS for each census includes a flag for the institutionalized as well as microlevel information on age, education, race, and all other information available for non-institutionalized long-form respondents. Within the institutionalized population, we can separately identify individuals residing in nonmilitary institutions. This category includes inmates of federal and state prisons, local jail inmates, residents of inpatient mental hospitals, and residents of other non-aged institutions. I use residence in a nonmilitary institution as the principal indicator of incarceration. In prior research (Raphael 2005), I show that incarceration population estimates from the PUMS are comparable to those by the Bureau of Justice Statistics. See Kristin Butcher and Anne Morrison Piehl (1998) and Rucker Johnson

and Steven Raphael (2005) for other research using the PUMS to identify the incarcerated.

3. The likelihood of entering prison is estimated from annual surveys of recent prison admissions, while mortality rates are based on mortality rates for the entire population adjusted upwards by a fixed factor to account for observed average differences in mortality rates between ex-offenders and the general population.

4. This is because earlier cohorts faced lower risks of incarceration during the high-criminal-activity portion of their life.

5. Each record contains information on an internal California Department of Corrections (CDC) ID number that can be used to uniquely identify inmates. Thus, the administrative records can be purged of inmates who serve multiple prison spells. See Steven Raphael and David Weiman (2005) for a complete description of this administrative dataset.

6. The prisoner survey estimates of the joint age-education-race density are needed because the California administrative records do not contain information on educational attainment.

7. This does not mean that more than 100 percent of black men in this cell have served time in the past ten years. There are a number of factors that are likely to bias upwards the count of unduplicated prisoners relative to the 2000 population. First, I calculated prisoner counts by age in 2000 without taking into account either the likely mortality of many of the inmates serving time during the 1990s or the likelihood that many of these inmates may have moved to another state after being released. In addition, a prisoner may be assigned additional internal California Department of Corrections prisoner identification numbers for subsequent prison terms, thus artificially inflating the number of unduplicated spells. Non-unique prison ID codes, however, are unlikely to be a substantial source of bias given that tabulation on the basis of prisoner Social Security number yields quite similar counts to the tabulations using CDC identification codes.

8. In a previous analysis of administrative data from California (Raphael 2005), I analyzed the total amount of time served and the amount of time that had elapsed between the first admission to prison and the final release observed over a ten-year period for inmates age eighteen to twenty-five who entered prison in 1990. The median inmate in this category served approximately three years over a five-year period. At the seventy-fifth percentile, inmates served approximately five years over a nine-year period.

9. By taking the natural log of wages, the difference between averages at any given point in time can be interpreted as approximately a percentage difference.

10. Although the identification problem explored here pertains to isolating the true causal effect of incarceration on the transition outcomes, the potential endogeneity of having served time is indirectly related to the debate between Terrie Moffit (1993, 1994) and Robert Sampson and John Laub (1993, 1997, 2003, 2005) regarding the existence of life-course persistent offenders. A somewhat crude summary of Moffit's hypothesis is that criminal offenders fit into a discrete set of types, with the most serious offenders (roughly corresponding with those who eventually serve time in prison) being char-

acterized as life-course persistent offenders who exhibit little evidence of declining activity with time. Sampson and Laub contest this characterization, finding little evidence for a group of life-course persistent offenders in a long panel of offenders and individuals at high risk of offending as youth. Moreover, these authors find evidence that certain life events, such as getting married, having children, or being steadily employed, correspond with desistence in adulthood via a "knifing-off" of the past from the present. The relevance of this debate to the question raised here concerns whether those who serve time are fundamentally different people who would perform poorly on the outcome measures irrespective of a spell in prison. Moffit's typology approach to criminal offenders would suggest so. The emphasis on life-course transitions and the cumulative effects of disadvantage emphasized by Sampson and Laub would suggest otherwise.

11.   In analyses of panel data, random measurement error in a key explanatory variable tends to bias the panel data estimate of the variables effect toward zero (for a discussion of attenuation bias to the estimate of union wage effects, see Card 1996; Raphael 2000). Given that the variable I am using to measure prison incarceration in the NLSY is far from perfect, my measure of prior incarceration is certainly measured with error.

12.   Of course, having been married is likely to have an impact on whether one has ever had a child, and having had a child is likely to be correlated with other unobservable determinants of marriage. I have estimated these models with and without this independent variable, and the results are nearly identical.

13.   In particular, Western (2002) includes in his high-risk subsample all individuals with any acknowledged involvement in criminal activity as well as those who eventually serve time, while here I restrict the sample to those who are eventually interviewed in prison.

14.   These results are available upon request.

References

Bonczar, Thomas P. 2003. *Prevalence of Imprisonment in the U.S. Population, 1974–2001*. Special report NCJ 197976. Washington: Bureau of Justice Statistics.

Butcher, Kristin F., and Anne Morrison Piehl. 1998. "Recent Immigrants: Unexpected Implications for Crime and Incarceration." *Industrial and Labor Relations Review* 51(4): 654–79.

Card, David. 1996. "The Effect of Unions on the Structure of Wages: A Longitudinal Analysis," *Econometrica* 64(4): 957–79.

Emsellem, Maurice. 2005. "The 'Smart on Crime' Agenda: Increase Public Safety by Reducing Barriers to Employment for People with Criminal Records." Paper presented to the Congressional Black Caucus Foundation thirty-fifth annual legislative conference, September 24, 2005, Washington, D.C.

Holzer, Harry, Paul Offner, and Elaine Sorensen. 2005. "Declining Employment Among Young, Black, Less-Educated Men." *Journal of Policy Analysis and Management* 24(2): 329–50.

Holzer, Harry J., Steven Raphael, and Michael A. Stoll. 2004. "The Effect of an

Applicant's Criminal History on Employer Hiring Decisions and Screening Practices: Evidence from Los Angeles." National Poverty Center working paper 04-15. Ann Arbor, Mich.: University of Michigan.

———. 2006. "Perceived Criminality, Racial Background Checks, and the Racial Hiring Practices of Employers." *Journal of Law and Economics* 49(2): 451–80.

Johnson, Rucker, and Steven Raphael. 2005. "The Effect of Male Incarceration Dynamics on Male Infection Rates Among African-American Women and Men." Unpublished paper. University of California, Berkeley.

Kurlychek, Megan C., Robert Brame, and Shawn Bushway. 2006. "Scarlet Letters and Recidivism: Does an Old Criminal Record Predict Future Offending?" *Criminology and Public Policy* 5(3): 483–504.

Lochner, Lance, and Enrico Moretti. 2004. "The Effect of Education on Crime: Evidence from Prison Inmates, Arrests, and Self-Reports." *American Economic Review* 94(1): 155–89.

Moffit, Terrie E. 1993. "Adolescence-Limited and Life-Course Persistent Antisocial Behavior: A Developmental Taxonomy." *Psychological Review* 100(4): 674–701.

———. 1994. "Natural History of Delinquency." In *Cross-National Longitudinal Research on Human Development and Criminal Behavior*, edited by Elmar G. M. Wietekamp and Hans-Jurgen Kerner. Amsterdam: Kluwer Academic.

Pager, Devah. 2003. "The Mark of a Criminal Record." *American Journal of Sociology* 108(5): 937–75.

Pager, Devah, and Bruce Western. 2005. *Race at Work: Realities of Race and Criminal Record in the New York City Job Market*. New York: New York City Commission on Human Rights.

Petersilia, Joan. 2003. *When Prisoners Come Home: Parole and Prisoner Reentry*. Oxford: Oxford University Press.

Pettit, Becky, and Bruce Western. 2004. "Mass Imprisonment and the Life Course: Race and Class Inequality in U.S. Incarceration." *American Sociological Review* 69(2): 151–69.

Raphael, Steven. 2000. "Estimating the Union Earnings Effect Using a Sample of Displaced Workers." *Industrial and Labor Relations Review* 53(3): 503–21.

———. 2005. "The Socioeconomic Status of Black Males: The Increasing Importance of Incarceration." In *Poverty, the Distribution of Income, and Public Policy*, edited by Alan Auerbach, David Card, and John Quigley. New York: Russell Sage Foundation.

Raphael, Steven, and Michael A. Stoll. 2004. "The Effect of Prison Releases on Regional Crime Rates." In *The Brookings-Wharton Papers on Urban Economic Affairs*, Volume 5, edited by William G. Gale and Janet Rothenberg Pack. Washington: Brookings Institution.

Raphael, Steven, and David Weiman. 2005. "The Impact of Local Labor Market Conditions on the Likelihood That Parolees Are Returned to Custody." Unpublished paper. University of California, Berkeley.

Sampson, Robert J., and John H. Laub. 1993. *Crime in the Making: Pathways and Turning Points Through Life*. Cambridge, Mass.: Harvard University Press.

———. 1997. "Life-Course Theory of Cumulative Disadvantage and the Stability of Delinquency." In *Developmental Theories of Crime and Delinquency*, edited by Terrence P. Thornberry. Trenton, N.J.: Transaction.

————. 2003. "Life-Course Desisters? Trajectories of Crime Among Delinquent Boys Followed to Age Seventy." *Criminology* 41(3): 555-92.

————. 2005. "A Life-Course View of the Development of Crime." In *Developmental Criminology and Its Discontents: Trajectories of Crime from Childhood to Old Age*, edited by Robert J. Sampson and John H. Laub, *Annals of the American Academy of Political and Social Science* 602(1): 12–45.

Settersten, Richard A., Jr., Frank F. Furstenberg Jr., and Rubén G. Rumbaut, editors. 2005. *On the Frontier of Adulthood: Theory, Research, and Public Policy.* Chicago, Ill.: University of Chicago Press.

Western, Bruce. 2002. "The Impact of Incarceration on Wage Mobility and Inequality." *American Sociological Review* 67(4): 526–46.

Index

economic conditions and the transition to adulthood, cross-national trends in, 47–50; education and the transition to adulthood, cross-national trends in, 49–50; employment patterns in, 32–35; household headship rates in, 29–32; household income adequacy in, 41–47; immigration, cross-national effects of, 48–49; worsening economic conditions for young adults, trends in, 10. *See also* Europe

Institute of Medicine, 105n1

Italy: delayed departure from parental home, benefits perceived from, 208, 224; illegal housing in, 228n4.)

Jaeger, David, 58, 130n4

Jencks, Christopher, 269

job stability: churning (short-term jobs), 73–75; data on job duration, 78–81; education and mean job tenure, 63–65; gender and mean job tenure, 60–63; health insurance coverage and, 84–85 (*see also* health insurance coverage); immigration and mean job tenure, 66–69; long-term employment, measures of, 69–73; measuring changes in, 59–60; research on U.S., 57–59; tenure, evolution of mean job, 60–69; tenure by sex, age, and birth cohort, **61**; trends in U.S., 10–11, 56–57, 75–78

Jovanovic, Boyan, 82n12

Juhn, Chinhui, 166n7

Kane, Thomas, 119, 132n21, 134n33, 261–62, 270, 275n4

Katz, Lawrence, 166n7

Kerry, John, 132n18

Kim, Dongwook, 171

Kurlychek, Megan, 301n1

labor markets: data and procedure for studying living arrangements and outcomes in, 142–4, 158–9; employment and living arrangements, descriptive statistics of, 144–47; em-

ployment and living arrangements, results of analyses of, 154–6, 183; in Europe, living arrangements and, 211–9; living arrangements and experiences in, 141–2, 157; variable construction for studying living arrangements and outcomes in, 159–65. *See also* earnings; employment

Laub, John, 302–3n10

Lee, Chul-In, 267, 270

Lemieux, Thomas, 142, 167n15

Lewin, Alisa, 142

Li, Jui-Chung Allen, 4

life satisfaction, impact of delayed departure from parental homes on, 217–23

Lifetime Learning Tax Credit, 121, 132n23, 133n25

living arrangements: changes from 1970 to 2000, by age, 175–6; child care costs and, 173–5, 179, 186, 193–4; factors potentially influencing decisions about, 141–2; housing costs and (*see* housing costs); incarceration, record of and, 288, 292–3; labor market experiences and (*see* labor markets); linear probability models predicting, 147–56, 162–5; noneconomic variables and, 155, 157; transportation expenses and, 173–5, 179, 183, 186, 193; trends in, 5–6, 14–17; of young adults in 1984 and 2002, **147**; of young adults, descriptive statistics on, 146–7; of young adults in Europe (*see* Europe). *See also* marriage; parental nests

Lochner, Lance, 284

Long, Bridget, 121, 132n25

Lovenheim, Michael, 110, 131n12

Ludwig, Jens, 269

Luxembourg Income Study (LIS), 28

Manski, Charles, 275n4

marriage: college enrollment and, 115; incarceration, record of and likelihood of, 289, 293–4; linear probabil